Living Faith
An Introduction to Theology
Second Edition

Eileen P. Flynn
Gloria Blanchfield Thomas

SHEED & WARD

Lanham, Chicago, New York, Oxford

As an apostolate of the Priests of the Sacred Heart, a Catholic religious order, the mission of Sheed & Ward is to publish books of contemporary impact and enduring merit in Catholic Christian thought and action. The books published, however, reflect the opinion of their authors and are not meant to represent the official position of the Priests of the Sacred Heart.

Printed in the United States of America

ISBN 1-55612-217-9

Published by Sheed & Ward
An Imprint of the Rowman & Littlefield Publishers, Inc.
4720 Boston Way
Lanham, MD 20706

98-37741
CIP

PO Box 317
Oxford
OX2 9RU, UK

Contents

To our husbands and children.

Introduction

Living Faith: An Introduction to Theology fills the need for a survey of fundamental theological themes. This book does not presume that its readers are familiar with all the people, events and terms which have been woven into the fabric of Catholic theology. It seeks, therefore, to provide information for students of theology while taking care not to overwhelm or oppress them. *Living Faith* will be valuable for both classroom and small group use because it offers a relevant presentation of theology within a context which recognizes that faith is more than content to be learned: It is a life to lived.

Each chapter of *Living Faith* contains a glossary explaining unfamiliar words and concepts and identifying persons who may be unknown to the reader. Arrangement of the contents of this book into twelve chapters makes it adaptable to both academic and small group settings. Discussion questions serve a twofold purpose: they enable readers to test their comprehension of concepts and contents, and they provide points of departure for sharing reactions and viewpoints.

Living Faith: An Introduction to Theology was written by two busy women who are committed to their families, their academic careers, and active involvement in Church and community. Their book is a response to the requests of those with whom they have shared faith in classrooms, living rooms and church halls. With the help and support of Robert Heyer, Editor-in-Chief of Sheed & Ward, it became a reality.

Chapters 2, 5, 6, 10, 11 and 12 were written by Eileen P. Flynn. Dr. Flynn's background in moral theology, scripture and ecclesiology prompted her to address such topics as faith, the bible, the Catholic Church, Catholic social teaching, sexual ethics and the meaning death holds for Christian believers.

Chapters 1, 3, 4, 7, 8 and 9 were written by Gloria Blanchfield Thomas. Dr. Thomas' theological work and teaching experience enabled her to approach the topics of God and God's revelation, Christ, the sacraments, liturgy, prayer and contemporary perspectives in theology.

If *Living Faith: An Introduction to Theology* assists its readers in attaining theological literacy and/or theological updating, along with an understanding of how life is enriched by faith, it will achieve its purpose.

Eileen P. Flynn, Ph. D.
Department of Theology
Saint Peter's College
Jersey City, New Jersey 07306

Gloria Blanchfield Thomas, Ph.D.
Department of Religious Studies
Marymount College
Tarrytown, New York 10962

1

The Mystery of God

The notion of God is fundamental to the study of any religious tradition. Humankind has worshiped divinity from its earliest roots. The mystery of God's existence and humanity's response to that mystery undergirds all religion. The actual possibility of human beings communicating with a divine being is part of that mystery. Who is God? What is God? Where is God? And are these very questions crucial, or even important, to human life? People of faith believe that God does exist and that relationship with God does, in fact, give meaning to their lives.

The Existence of God

People believe in God's existence for a variety of reasons. Many cannot articulate their reasons with complete clarity, but their faith is nonetheless unshakeable. Many people have grown up in families where faith in God and religious practice has been part of their lifestyle. Others are attracted to belief in God's existence through good relationships with people who believe and worship. Believers whose lives and values are a positive witness to an active relationship with God often have great impact on half-hearted or non-believers. The marvels of the universe and the amazing wonders of nature bring some people to belief in a Creator, a caring power beyond themselves who is the designer and source of it all.

Primitive humanity, in touch with the cycles of the cosmos and the richness of the earth, itself, personified the powers of nature and bowed down before them. Ancient Sumerian and Babylonian people worshiped the Sky Father and the Earth Mother, and annually offered sacrifice, appeasing these gods and begging fertility and generous harvest. In ancient Egypt, nearly three thousand years before the birth of Jesus of Nazareth, the King was considered divine. Later, worship shifted from divine royalty to the Sun, and the King was looked upon as the Sun-God's Son.

Both ancient Greece and ancient Rome were religious cultures. Ideals of wisdom and love, and sources of power and fertility, were the many gods of polytheism.* (cf., Glossary) Although mystery religions were part of the Hellenistic culture and household gods were an important part of the Roman world, the central religious act of Greece and Rome was that of sacrifice.* These ritual offerings were performed by a priesthood in temples where the images of the gods were kept. Although the understanding of divinity was often distorted and the perception of God sometimes warped, religion has always been part of the human landscape.[1]

Where did the notion of God come from? If worship of divinity has always been part of human experience, it is certainly not possible to assert that philosophers, or theologians, or church leaders, invented the theory of God's existence. Some skeptical thinkers point to God as a kind of childhood memory, the obsolete hope of an ignorant, oppressed human race. Despite our history, it is difficult to prove that the idea of God has a common ground of reference for all people in all places. Is God merely part of our deepest desire to be fulfilled? Is God an untouchable mystery, strangely attractive, but beyond the reach of humanity? Primitive religions spoke of God in myth, an anthropomorphic* God bearing the perfect human image through the highest perfection of all human qualities.

Is God a person? Does God have a personality? In ordinary expression, when someone says, "God bless you," what image of cosmic divinity comes to mind? Is God a kindly, fatherly Santa Claus-type figure, or an impersonal power, a source principle of cosmic creativity? Do you ask an impersonal power to bless a sneezing child? People of faith believe in a personal, caring God, yet struggle with God's elusiveness and often apparent absence. Most people have experienced times of extreme challenge or heart-breaking suffering. At these painful times, when human effort seems exhausted, sometimes a new hope, or an unexpected surge of strength makes a difference, makes it possible to overcome, forgive, or be healed. Such courage or strength emerges from the very depths of one's being. It is the kind of courage which a young mother speaks to her children after the tragic death of her husband. It is the intense courage of a soldier who risks his life for a wounded buddy. It is the complete trust of an elderly lady facing death with a calm peace that amazes her children and grandchildren.

Paul Tillich, a twentieth-century theologian, whose own perspective of God and religion was changed after the suffering in Nazi Germany during World War II, describes God in this way:

> The name of this infinitive and inexhaustible depth and ground of all being is *God*. That depth is what the word *God* means. And if that word has not much meaning for you, translate it, and speak of the depths of your life, of the source of your being, of your ultimate concern, of what you take seriously without any reservation. Perhaps, in order to do so, you must forget everything traditional that you have learned about God, perhaps even the word itself. For if you know that God means depth, you know much about Him. You cannot then call yourself an atheist or unbeliever.[2]

An understanding of God as the source of all that exists appeals to many people. Yet, others simply find no basis for such faith.

Arguments for God's Existence

Through the centuries, great thinkers have offered proofs of God's existence. Such proofs are very helpful, yet remain always dependent upon an individual's interpretation of one's personal life experience. Thomas Aquinas used his experience of the world to develop his proofs of the existence of God. Thomas was a Dominican theologian of the thirteenth century. He is universally acclaimed as the preeminent spokesperson of the Catholic tradition of reason and divine revelation. Thomas' greatest work, *Summa Theologica,* which was incomplete at his death, deals with the whole of Catholic thought. This great teacher of the medieval church has been honored with the titles Angelic Doctor and Doctor of the Church. His five proofs, which depend on natural reason, have been foundational in Catholic theology. Thomas states his five points clearly.

1. There exists a *Prime Mover* in the universe, apart from whom nothing else could possibly have movement.

2. There is a *First Cause* apart from whom no other cause in the world could have an effect.

3. There is a *Necessary Being* who cannot be said *not* to
   be, and apart from whom no other being would be real.

4. There is a *Greatest Good* apart from whose existence
   it would be impossible to speak of anything being
   'good' or 'less good.'

5. There is an *Intelligent One* who designs and directs
   all things, and apart from whom the meaningful
   structure and ordered process of the universe would
   not be possible.[3]

Modern theologians point to the weaknesses in Thomas' medieval cosmology* upon which his Five Ways are constructed.
Nonetheless these arguments remain foundational for Catholic
theology. For Thomas creation is an act requiring infinite power
in the creating agent. A created being is not capable of creating,
for created beings change and change by its very nature precludes the possibility that existence can be produced through it.
Although finite agents can cause something to become this or
that, only an infinite being can cause something to come into
existence. Only such a being can create. Thomas calls this *Primary Mover,* this *First Cause,* this *Necessary Being,* this *Greatest
Good,* this *Intelligent Being*—God.

Karl Rahner, the brilliant German Catholic theologian of the
twentieth century, demonstrates God's existence in a different
way. His explanation answers the objections some people offer
to Thomas Aquinas' Five Ways of Causality. Those who claim to
know the existence of an Infinite* Cause have difficulty explaining why finite* effects or movements demand the existence of an
infinite or ultimate cause. Rahner would admit that from finite
and dependent effects we can be sure only of finite and dependent causes. However, Rahner poses another question. How do
we learn that the objects of our own experience are finite?
Sense experience does not provide that knowledge. Rahner explains that we do know our experience is finite, for as soon as
we know any reality at all, our intellect pushes beyond it and
refers it to an ultimate, or necessary, reality. Simply stated,
everything we get to know, we know that it is. Yet, nothing we
experience *simply is.* Everything is something. It is this or
that. Rahner explains that the human intellect keeps looking
for something, for a reality that is not limited or specified. Our
intellect seeks the reality that simply is. Such a reality is the
fullness of being. It is God. So Rahner concludes that God is
the ultimate, limitless horizon against which we measure all

that we know. Thomas Aquinas, the great Catholic theologian of the Middle Ages, spoke of God as the efficient cause of our universe. In the twentieth century, another great Catholic theologian, Karl Rahner, spoke of God as the final cause of humanity's thinking and feeling.[4]

In *A Rumor of Angels: Modern Society and the Rediscovery of the Supernatural,* Peter L. Berger, modern sociologist, approaches the existence of God from another perspective. He suggests a type of empirical* evidence from within the human situation that contributes to an understanding of the supernatural. Berger points to prototypical human gestures found within "natural" reality, but which themselves point beyond that reality. These reiterated acts and experiences Berger calls *Signals of Transcendence.* To him they appear to express essential aspects of human life.[5]

The first Signal of Transcendence Berger points to is the human propensity for order, an *argument from order.* The inclination for order is rooted in a basic belief that, ultimately, reality is ordered, that somewhere all is in order, as it should be. Psychologists tell us that a child cannot mature without a faith in ultimate order, without the trust that everything will be all right. This reiteration of a common human faith in a final ordering was experienced in the visions of a medieval mystic, Julian of Norwich. God's revelations to the anchoress Julian stressed the idea that "all would be well, all manner of thing will be well."[6] For Julian and for modern sociologist, Berger, the argument from ordering implies a transcendent order, a supernatural ordered existence.

Berger's second Signal of Transcendence is called the *argument from play.* Play is usually a joyful activity; it is a special time, a separate enclave in ordinary chronological time. Berger believes that in joyful play, human beings move temporarily out of chronology into eternity. There is a suspension of the time of the serious world. A musical concert can suspend ordinary time; its listeners are completely into the music, forgetting all else. A game can so engross people that for its duration the outside world has ceased to exist. Play is an affirmation of the ultimate triumph of a time without pain and without suffering. This experience can be found in ordinary reality, but Berger believes it points beyond that ordinary reality to transcendence. Children easily experience this joyful play; adults at times also know this transcendent joy and are lifted beyond themselves.

The third Signal of Transcendence for Berger is the *argument from hope*. Human existence always stretches toward the future. We live in hope. Human hope gives people courage in the face of devastation and tragedy. The common experience of hope in all human experience points to a defiance of ultimate defeat, a defiance of death. Hope looks toward the future. Viktor Frankl's account of his life in a concentration camp in Nazi Germany is a story of hope.[7] Stripped of all dignity, separated from their loved ones, facing death each day, the prisoners of Auschwitz lived in hope. The universality of the human experience of hope points to a supernatural reality where all hope is vindicated.

The fourth Signal of Transcendence Berger calls the *argument from damnation*. This argument points to deeds that simply outrage all human beings. Such deeds cry out to heaven, violating a fundamental dignity of all humanity. They are horrendous deeds, like the murder or torture of the totally innocent, of children. These deeds demand condemnation; their doers put themselves outside the human community. These deeds also separate their perpetrators from the moral order that transcends the human community. Berger believes such deeds point to an ultimate condemnation. Hope and damnation are both set in a religious context, in a belief in an eternal God; they are two aspects of the same encompassing vindication, two sides of the same coin. The argument from damnation springs from the human experience of moral outrage, crying out for final justice. From Berger's perspective, based on empirical evidence, hell seems to be a necessity. This argument might be difficult to balance with a faith perception of a completely loving, forgiving God.

The fifth and final Signal of Transcendence offered by sociologist Berger is the *argument from humor*. Humor is dependent upon the comic situation. Comedy requires two separate, or independent, events that can be interpreted in two entirely different ways at the same time. Comedy points to discrepancy and reflects the imprisonment of the human spirit in the world. Our ability to truly laugh at this imprisonment implies that the imprisonment of the human spirit is not final. It will be overcome. Humor understands that human power is always precarious; the mightiest fall. When people laugh, they understand that the "absolutes" of the world are really quite relative. Humor also can point to final truth. In many situations, humor can see that although the victim is to be pitied, the person of power is the one actually suffering illusion. The King has no clothes. And the clown has real wisdom. Laughter at such illusion points to ultimate truth.

Peter Berger's research offers an empirical study beginning with common life experiences. The reiteration and commonality of such experiences points to the ultimate transcending of their human limitations. Berger's Signals of Transcendence lift us beyond ourselves to God, the Creator, and fulfillment of all experiences.

God Is Dead

During the 1960s, a theological movement concerned with the influence, or lack of influence, of God on human existence offered the world a startling slogan—*God is dead.* At the end of the nineteenth century, Ludwig Feuerbach and Friedrick Nietzsche, German philosophers, declared that the transcendent God of all eternity was dead. What we call divine, or supernatural, they said, is just another way of describing the human and the natural. Feuerbach regarded God as a human projection of our own nature. Nietzsche offered a notion of man as superman, which later influenced the emergence of Nazism in Germany. The theories of Feuerbach and Nietzsche were foundational in the development of the death-of-God movement.[8]

The *God is dead* slogan, and the movement behind it, caused an enormous stir in theological circles and in the minds and hearts of all believers. *Time* Magazine featured the slogan, as a question, on the cover of its April 8, 1966 issue. The *Is God Dead?* question startled and confronted American readers. The debate was launched on every level of American life. When the righteous anger cooled, and the theological dust cleared, believing Americans were forced to ask themselves if God was, indeed, dead in their own lives. Was the old image of God, sitting on his golden throne in heaven, the one that was dead? Was the God who seemed to forget his chosen people in Nazi extermination furnaces dead? And who really cared? Had the advance of science killed the Biblical Creator God of the universe? Had modern culture, with its marvelous human accomplishments, simply overcome our need for God?

The death-of-God movement, principally led by theologians Thomas Altizer, William Hamilton and Paul van Buren, forced all believers to question the existence of a personal God. In our modern, technological world, why has God become so very hard to believe in, so easy to dismiss as some type of childish fantasy? God, the wonder-worker of the cosmos, whose presence and power explained the world's mysteries, has lost much of his credibility.

In the fifth century, the great theologian of North Africa and Bishop of Hippo, St. Augustine, wrote his famous *City of God*. This work assured Christians of the fifth century that those following God's will would create upon earth the image of the heavenly city of perfect peace. In 1958, Baptist theologian Harvey Cox wrote his famous work, *The Secular City*. In his book, Cox explained one important aspect of secularization* as a process that does not believe religion has the answer to every problem. The word secular comes from the Latin word for world, *saeculum*. Secularization places a great responsibility on humanity, itself, for the solving of the world's problems. This perspective is actually quite biblical. In Genesis, the first book of the Old Testament, God asks Adam and Eve to name the animals and have dominion over all of creation.

Modern science has been the strongest agent in the secularizing process. Copernicus discovered that the sun simply did not travel around the earth. Isaac Newton's reflection on gravity and motion offered more scientific explanations of the mystery of the universe. Charles Darwin's evidence of evolution disturbed the literal acceptance of the bible's creation story. In our own time, science has provided both miraculous cures and destructive weapons beyond the imagination of scientists of just a few decades ago. Computers have changed entirely the world's information and communications systems. Modern theologians now agree that the existence of a personal God, one who cares about the human family, simply cannot be proven by reason alone. The death-of-God movement contributed much to a new approach to the God question. Many theologians have moved away from religious presuppositions about God, shifting their attention from God to humanity, from revelation to the world. The new starting point is based in anthropology*. It starts with men and women and seeks to define a God who is part of their lives, one who touches human emotions and human minds. This approach centers on human existence and the responsibility of men and women in Creation. The death-of-God slogan points clearly to an uneasiness with the traditional ways of speaking about God. It has forced believers to focus on God's apparent absence in the world.

Karl Barth, a great Protestant theologian of this century, resisted any theological approach which began with human experience. He saw danger in an anthropological approach, clearly maintaining that God is "wholly other" and can only be known by God's own self-revelation. Jesuit Theologian, Karl Rahner, tells us God speaks to us not on ancient stone tablets, but in whispers in our hearts. For Rahner God may be experienced as an "anonymous presence." It is clear that no proof of God's existence or slogans announcing God's lack of existence can solve the eternal mystery. The question of God, and our relationship to God, remains alive and very much with us.

God Language

Science requires a particular language to express its data. A precise, objective language is usually demanded. However, today modern science sometimes uses models to express the mysteries of our cosmos. Human words simply cannot fully portray the marvels of the earth, let alone the universe.

Speaking of God and God's relationship with humanity calls for a special language too. What kind of words can describe God? What does the word "God" mean? When people hear the word "God" spoken, some type of human model, or image, comes to mind. For most believers, God is a cosmic figure, beyond humanity, but possessing human features and characteristics. Does God have a real personality which expresses itself in preferences and priorities? Does God have a gender? Or is, as Albert Einstein concluded, belief in a personal God merely a primitive superstition? Einstein considered himself religious, for he remained fully in awe of the mystery of the universe. The great physicist never lost his reverence for life itself, yet he could not accept a personal God. However, most people who believe and worship are not content with an impersonal cosmic-source God.

A God who does not bear the characteristics which give dignity to human life is not trusted or loved by human beings. Attributes of freedom, creativity, power and intelligence are assumed to be part of divinity. These qualities are predicated to God to an ultimate degree. It would be very difficult for believers to feel trust or consolation from a God who is less than human. Nonetheless, using the word "God" as the biggest, best, most loving and powerful human personality is surely inadequate. It is just as inadequate to characterize God as non- personal, devoid of personality, as we experience it in a human dimension.

The question of God's gender has been considered in recent times. Theologians and spiritual writers alike have spoken of the feminine aspects of God as just as present as the masculine characteristics of God. Actually, God is neither male or female. Yet, it seems strange to speak of God as neuter, without gender. Theologian Hans-Georg Gadamer's expression of the neuter of divinity, however, provides an interesting consideration.

> Notice the neuter: "the divine." I think the neuter is one of the most mysterious things in human language wherever it is preserved. German and Greek have the excellence of preserving the neuter. The neuter occurs very often in poetry. What is the neuter? To use the neuter—for example, "the beautiful"; in German *das schoene*; in Greek *to kalon*—expresses something of ungraspable presence. It is no longer "this" or "that," male or female, here or there; it is like filling empty space . . . The neuter represents in a way the plentitude of presence, the omnipresence of something. Hence the divine is indeed an expression for such omnipresence.[9]

Human language is never completely adequate in speaking of God. At best, theology is an attempt at "God-talk." It is a human articulation of divinity, viewed from the human perspective. Our words are spoken out of the limitations of our own human experience. It is the only arena we have in which to know God, and it is, as humans, that we struggle to articulate this knowledge and experience.

St. Augustine said that God is truth—the basis, or ground, of all truth. And, surely, the scriptures clearly state God is love— the One who embraces all love, the source of love, perfect love. God-language is always incomplete, for human articulation cannot fully express divine mystery. God-language is the language of analogy. Metaphors are used to speak of God. When we say, "Our Father," we are actually speaking a metaphor. The metaphor of fatherhood is certainly appropriate; Jesus, himself, used this metaphor. But God is not a father in the same way that each one of us has a biological father. Yet, it clearly speaks the image of a caring, protecting, loving, strong parent. The metaphor of God, as father, has become so common in the Christian tradition that we sometimes forget it is a metaphor.

Alfred Whitehead, a contemporary American philosopher, speaks of God as a lure, beckoning reality to greater and better things. Whitehead uses analogical language describing God as the "poet of the world, with tender patience leading it by his vision of truth, beauty, and goodness."[10] Rosemary Haughton, contemporary Catholic theologian, describes a God of passion in her book, *The Passionate God*. The analogies used by Haughton offer a God who loves deeply, passionately, all people and all of the world. God's love, Haughton tells us, pursues us, almost unreasonably. She speaks of God as a passionate lover. In his classic poem, Francis Thompson images God as the *Hound of Heaven*. It is the story of the divine pursuit of a man turned from God, looking elsewhere for peace. The English poet, Francis Thompson (d. 1907), expresses his own flight from God and God's constant and deliberate pursuit of him. Perhaps the poet's words sound strange, but they surely speak the reality of his own experience in his struggle to believe.

I fled Him, down the nights and down the days;
I fled Him down the arches of the years;
I fled Him down the labyrinthine ways
Of my own mind . . .

But with unhurrying chase
And unperturbed pace
Deliberate speed, majestic instancy,
The beat—and a Voice beat
More instant than the Feet—
All things betray thee, who betrayest Me.

Yet, another image which perhaps sounds a bit bizarre is that of psychologist/theologian, Sam Keen. Keen's book, *To A Dancing God,* describes a God who is found in spontaneity and joy, as often as in decision-making and times of suffering. Keen tells us that God simply cannot be pinned down, neatly boxed in human speech or logic. God is always more. "As always, the sacred shatters all the categories we necessarily use to understand the sacred. So the dance continues."[11]

No single image, or metaphor, can fully describe God. Certain aspects of God are emphasized by the use of particular analogies. The characterizations of God, as King, our Maker, Just

Judge, Healer, or even Lord of the Dance, are all helpful metaphors. They are human attempts through analogy to describe
divinity. Different as they are, each speaks of a God who does
relate to human creatures and creation.

Images of God in the Old Testament

The Old Testament is the first part of the Bible, which contains the books of the Hebrew Scriptures. It records the story of
God's relationship with the Jewish people before the birth of
Jesus of Nazareth. Although some history is included, the Old
Testament is not a history of the Jewish people. Its concern is
the relationship of God with the Israelite nation. This relationship is one of promise, a covenant between God and God's people. The Old Testament is the story of God's pursuit of the Israelites, a pursuit against all odds of unfaithfulness and denuncia-
tion. The language of the Old Testament is a rich language of
symbol and myth. The Old Testament is filled with great stories
that recount God's actions toward the Hebrew nation. The stories of God's actions and interventions describe God himself.
Myths are stories that grapple with the greatest truths known
to humankind. Myths do not offer concrete, factual, scientific
truths; myths proclaim absolute truth about ultimate reality,
about God. Myths proclaim the greatest of truth in concrete
fashion, in story and symbol.

The first book of the Old Testament, Genesis, tells the Creation story. Modern science precludes a literal understanding of
the Creation myth. Yet, the image of a loving, caring Creator is
forever timely. The ultimate love and concern of the Creator
God structures the whole reality of the authors of the book of
Genesis. After creating the entire world and all its living creatures, the author tells us God climaxes his creative activity with
the making of humanity.

> Then God said: "Let us make humanity in our image,
> after our likeness. Let them have dominion over the
> fish of the sea, the birds of the air, and the cattle, and
> over all the wild animals and all the creatures that
> crawl on the ground.
>
> God created man in his image; in the divine image he
> created him; male and female he created them. (Gene-
> sis 1:26-27)

Many of the psalms also image God as a Creator. The psalmists offer praise to a God who has created all. The image of God is anthropomorphic. God has hands and a face. In speaking of the earth's creatures, the psalmist proclaims:

> They all look to you to give them food in
> due time.
> When you give it to them, they gather it.
> When you open your hand they are filled with
> good things.
> If you hide your face, they are dismayed;
> if you take away their breath, they perish
> and return to their dust.
> When you send forth your spirit,
> they are created,
> and you renew the face of the earth. (Psalm 104:27-30)

In the Old Testament, God is not thought of only as a great human being, though human words proclaim his word and human deeds perform his will. The author of the first book of Kings is very aware of the transcendence of God.

> Can it indeed be that God dwells upon people on
> earth? If the heavens and the highest heavens cannot
> contain you, how much less this temple which I have
> built? (1 Kings 8:27)

In the book of Exodus, God is identified in two ways. The divine power that sends Moses back to Egypt to set the people free is carefully described as the One, same God who guided Moses' ancestors. "I am the God of your father, the God of Abraham, the God of Isaac, the God of Jacob" (Exodus 3:8). And in the very same chapter, continuing the story of Moses, the author describes the transcendent, eternal God as Yahweh.

> But said Moses to God, "When I go to the Israelites
> and say to them, "The God of your fathers has sent
> me to you, if they ask me, What is his name?' what
> am I to tell them?" God replied, "I am who am." (Exodus 3:13)

The name Yahweh (I am who am) is somewhat difficult to translate. It is a form of the Hebrew verb *hawãh*. Although *hawãh* means to be, the name implies personal divine reality, proclaimed and experienced. Most translations offer *I Am Who*

Am or *He Who Is.* Other scholars propose a translation, "He brings into being whatever comes into being," designating God as Creator. In the book of Deuteronomy God is described as Liberator, freeing the people Israel from Egyptian oppression.

> When the Egyptians maltreated and oppressed us, imposing hard labor upon us, we cried to the Lord the God of our fathers, and he heard our cry and saw our affliction, our toil and our oppression. He brought us out of Egypt with his strong hand and outstretched arm, with terrifying power, with signs and wonders; and bringing us into this country, he gave us this land flowing with milk and honey. (Deuteronomy 26:6-10)

The prophet, Jeremiah, uses several images of God to describe his understanding of divinity and its relationship to humanity. He speaks of God as a potter molding the people of Israel in his hands.

> Indeed like clay in the hand of the potter, so are you in my hand, house of Israel. (Jeremiah 18:6)

Also he speaks for God, saying, "For I am a father to Israel" (Jeremiah 31:9), and again "he guards them as a shepherd his flock" (Jeremiah 31:10). In another chapter, Jeremiah expresses God's covenant, or promise, to the Hebrew people. Again Jeremiah's image is anthropomorphic. The prophet proclaims that the Lord has promised to write upon our hearts.

> I will place my law within them, and write it upon their hearts; I will be their God and they shall be my people. (Jeremiah 31:33)

Another great prophet from the Old Testament, Isaiah, describes God as one who offers tender love and protection.

> Can a mother forget her infant,
> be without tenderness for the child of her womb?
> Even should she forget
> I will never forget you.
> See, upon the palms of my hand
> I have written your name. (Isaiah 49:15-16)

And in another chapter, Isaiah compares God to a loving mother. This passage stresses the tender nurturing attributes of God. Such qualities are most often assigned to the feminine gender.

As nurslings you shall be carried in her arms,
and fondled in her lap;
as a mother comforts her son,
so I will comfort you. (Isaiah 66:12-13)

The God of the Old Testament is not only a Father of protection and a Mother of tenderness. The Israelite nation often characterizes God as One of judgement and even revenge. An early Israelite understanding of divinity clung to the idea that God would bring suffering and doom upon all those who opposed the Chosen People. Often psalmists would call upon God to act in this warrior role.

God of vengeance, Lord,
God of vengeance, show yourself.
Rise up, judge of the earth,
render their deserts to the proud. (Psalm 94:1-2)

Many images of a great King of Glory, a warrior hero victorious in battle and of an avenging judge, appear in the Old Testament. Yet, gradually an understanding of a compassionate Lord, One desirous of justice and love, emerges in the Old Testament. This God is One of forgiveness, Who asks not sacrifice, or holocaust, but loving hearts.

For it is love that I desire, not sacrifice, And knowledge of God rather than holocausts. (Hosea 6:6)

And in the book of the prophet, Micah, one of the final books of the Old Testament, God is described as the peace-loving God of forgiveness.

Who is there like you, the God who removes guilt
and pardons sin for the remnant of his inheritance;
Who does not persist in anger forever, but delights
rather in clemency, And will again have compassion
on us, treading underfoot our guilt? (Micah 7:18-19)

The imagery of the Old Testament is rich and varied. God is the transcendent power of eternity, as well as a loving tender protector, and a God of justice and healing. Through myth, symbol and anthropomorphic poetry, the revelation of the Old Testament offers believers a God Who is intimately involved with the people of Israel.

Images of God in the New Testament

The New Testament is the part of the Bible written after the birth of Jesus of Nazareth. It records the life and message of Jesus and the activity of the followers of Jesus after his death and resurrection. The missionary efforts of the apostles, and the early years of the Christian communities, are narrated in the New Testament. The authors of the New Testament were familiar with the Hebrew scriptures. They had grown up understanding God through the imagery presented in these scriptures. Much of the same imagery exists in the New Testament, but the Christ event has made a difference. As the followers of Jesus came to understand the divine mission of their leader, their understanding of the eternal God found new dimensions.

It was with much astonishment that the disciples heard Jesus call God *Abba. Abba* is a familiar, loving name—a term of endearment, one that a child would use for his male parent. It can be translated as Dad or Papa. To the Hebrew mind, *Abba* was a tremendous leap from the name of transcendent mystery, *Yahweh* (I am Who am). Jesus also used the term Father, *Our Father,* when he taught his disciples how to pray. In St. Matthew's Gospel, "Jesus spoke thus: Father, Lord of heaven and earth, to you I offer praise" (Matthew 11:25). Jesus also offers his listeners an image of God as Mother, longing to protect her children.

> O Jerusalem, Jerusalem, murderess of prophets and stoner of those who were sent to you! How often have I yearned to gather your children, as a mother bird gathers her young under her wings, but you refused me. (Matthew 23:37-38)

In St. Mark's Gospel, Jesus speaks of God's reign, and in so doing, offers an image of God.

> Let the children come to me and do not hinder them. It is to such as these that the Kingdom of God belongs. I assure you that whoever does not accept the reign of God like a little child shall not take part in it. (Mark 10:14-15)

In the fourth gospel, that of St. John, Jesus tells us, "The Father and I are one," and "whoever has seen me has seen the Father." He speaks also of the sending of the Paraclete, the Spirit of Truth, the Holy Spirit. This gospel offers the three images—Father, Son, and Spirit—of the Triune God. In a more earthy image, Jesus describes himself and God in this way.

> I am the true vine
> and my Father is the vinegrower.
> He prunes away
> every barren branch,
> but the fruitful ones
> he trims clean
> to increase their yield. (John 15:1-2)

One of the most familiar God images of the gospels is found in St. Luke, in the story of the Prodigal Son. In this parable, the wayward, sinful son is welcomed back with open arms by the generous father. No punishment is exacted. Instead, the generous father kills the fatted calf and throws the best of parties in celebration of his son's return. Jesus offers this image to tell his listeners what God is like.

The God Who Jesus calls *Abba* is a God of Love. In the first letter of St. John, we read:

> The person without love has known nothing of God, for God is love. . . . No one has ever seen God; yet if we love one another God dwells in us and his love is brought to perfection in us. (1 John 4:8,12)

The revelation of the New Testament is fundamental to the Christian understanding of God. The God revealed in Jesus Christ is the God whom the Old Testament prophets told us has written on our hearts. The God of Jesus is a God desiring relationship with and among God's people. The two great commandments of that God Jesus proclaims clearly to the Pharisees and to all believers.

> You shall love the Lord your God
> with your whole heart,
> with your whole soul
> and with all your mind.

This is the greatest and first commandment. The second is like it:

> You shall love your neighbor as yourself. (Matthew 22:37-38)

Developing One's Own Image of God

Most people are born into a religious tradition which has its particular stories of faith and images of deity. Within that tradition, each one of us also has our life experience and our own family environment. Martin A. Lang, Ph.D., in his book, *Acquiring Our Image of God,* explains the process of combining these two experiences to solidify our own values and meaning in life.

> Two sets of stories meld into each other. The personal story is a composite drawn from the landmark and impressive incidents in one's life. The communal story is a composite drawn from the landmark and impressive incidents in the life of the community to which we belong. The special dominance within our personal story seeks out the preferred images and values within the communal story, helping to form the life meaning system.[12]

In the communal stories of Christians and Jews, ultimacy rests with God. God, therefore, is the most important reality in their faith stories. Within this process of combining the experience of one's personal life and one's communal life, an image of God is formed. This image develops as the individual begins to understand and experience relationships to the important people in his/her life. The child also selects from the stories offered by family and Church, favorite images, favorite stories. Lang believes the bonding of a child with the favored parent also greatly influences the formation of one's God image. A young boy who is loved by a gentle father and experiences a bonding with that parent will image God in just that way. The God-image of a child closely bonded to a loving mother will have attributes of tenderness and nurture.

The communal stories of the Judaeo-Christian tradition offer far more masculine images of God than feminine ones. The major image of Father cannot be escaped by any child born into this heritage. Male dominance has been overpowering. Feminists are correct in challenging our religious stories. The image of God, as Father, dominates our scriptures. The masculine pronouns are deeply imbedded into the language. Nonetheless, the personal bonding of one's own relationships and the unique circumstances of one's personal life do contribute to the image that comes to mind when an individual thinks "God." Every believer must come to understand his/her own God image and how this image gives meaning and value to one's life. It is our own image of God that comforts or frightens us when we cry out for help in situations that seem beyond our human strength or endurance.

The Will of God

In the Lord's Prayer, all Christians pray, "thy will be done." It is the common prayer of believers. But what is the will of God? Are human beings capable of knowing God's will, or of being assured that they are doing God's will? It is often very difficult to accept the tragedies of life as God's will. Does God will that a young man driving home from work should be suddenly struck down by a drunken driver? Does God will that a baby girl suffocate through smoke inhalation, as her frantic mother attempts to rescue her from their burning home? And what of floods and volcanos, and drought and famine? Is God testing the endurance of people? Rabbi Harold Kushner, in his recent book, *When Bad Things Happen To Good People,* completely rejects the idea that God wills or causes tragedies. Much of Kushner's time as a rabbi is spent offering comfort to members of his congregation in the tragedies of their lives. When doctors told Kushner and his wife that their own baby son had progeria (the disease of rapid aging) and would die in his early teens, Kushner came directly into confrontation with the question of God's will. Kushner, and many other theologians and people of faith, came to believe that God cannot prevent the tragedies of life. It is not within God's power to alter the inevitable laws of creation. These laws treat everyone alike. Rain soaks the dry earth and homeless people shivering on park benches. And human beings are free agents, free to love and be responsible and free to do evil and wreak havoc. Kushner holds fast to the Judaeo-Christian idea of a loving, comforting God, One Who is saddened by tragedy just as we are.

People often try to find meaning, even in horrendous misfortune, by assigning it to God's will. "God has His reasons," they say. This provides a type of comfort, a coping mechanism. But underneath the seeming acceptance of God's will, most people scream silently, "Why me?" Some believe that God is testing them or punishing them for past sins. A God of love does not torture people. God is not pleased when they suffer through hunger and disease. The God Who has created humanity and the whole world with an amazing abundance of potential surely does not want such potential wasted. Rabbi Kushner sums up this understanding of a God whose real power is limitless love:

> God does not cause our misfortunes. Some are caused by bad luck, some are caused by bad people, and some are simply an inevitable consequence of our being human and being mortal, living in a world of inflexible natural laws. The painful things that happen to us are not punishment for our misbehavior, nor are they in any way part of some grand design on God's part. Because the tragedy is not God's will, we need not feel hurt or betrayed by God when tragedy strikes. We can turn to Him for help in overcoming it, precisely because we can tell ourselves that God is as outraged by it as we are. I would say that God may not prevent the calamity, but He gives us the strength and the perseverance to overcome it.[13]

Fully understanding the will of God is not possible within our human limitations. Our own life experience and the image of God, which structures our reality, however, guide us as we confront this mystery. The notion of an omnipotent God, all powerful, is not easily reconciled with a God who seems to permit human suffering beyond endurance. Process theologians speak of God as Fellow Sufferer. The omnipotence of God, they say, is the all-powerfulness of love. God's power is love, constantly poured upon all people. Julian of Norwich, medieval mystic, says God is the One Who bends always to where the hurt is in a person. The mystery of the real power of love, which often is humanly judged as powerlessness, is part of the very mystery of God. A God who would intervene in some situations, stop some oncoming cars and crashing airplanes and leave others to take their natural course, is not a God of power, surely not a God of love, but a capricious magician, picking and choosing by a whim.

The Triune God

In the Catholic tradition, we bless ourselves and each other, in the name of the Father and of the Son, and of the Holy Spirit, Amen." When we say, "Amen," "I believe," or "so be it," to this blessing, we are affirming our faith in the mystery of the Triune God, the Blessed Trinity—One God of three divine persons.

Our Catholic faith stands upon the shoulders of the Jewish religion. Our roots are in Judaism; and it was Judaism that first proclaimed belief in One God. "I, the Lord am your God, who brought you out of the land of Egypt, the place of slavery. You shall not have other gods beside me" (Exodus 20:1-3). Monotheism* was cherished by the Israelite nation. Against all pagan cultures, the prophets proclaimed, "Our God is One." God's revelation to Abraham and his descendents rejected all types of polytheism*. Although their images of God were many, the faith of the Hebrew people insisted that God is One. Into this tradition was Jesus born. And from this tradition, the early Christian communities emerged. These new faith communities existed within the Roman Empire and were surrounded by its pagan culture. The struggle to understand Jesus, as the Anointed of God, God's Son and the Messiah, was not easy for the Hebrew mind. The early fathers of the church struggled to preserve the cherished doctrine of the Oneness of God, while explaining the Christian revelation of the Trinity.

In St. Mark's Gospel, Jesus, Himself, quotes the Old Testament Book of Deuteronomy. "Hear, O Israel! The Lord our God is Lord alone." This scripture passage expresses the foundation of monotheism. Upon it is based biblical faith. Jesus is proclaiming from within His Jewish heritage that there exists one true God. Yet after His resurrection from the dead, Jesus commissions His disciples in these words.

> Full authority has been given to me
> both in heaven and on earth;
> go, therefore, and make disciples
> of all the nations.
> Baptize them in the name
> of the Father,
> and of the Son,
> and of the Holy Spirit.
> Teach them to carry out everything
> I have commanded you.
> And know that I am with you always,
> until the end of the world. (Matthew 28:18-20)

The one God of all eternity has been revealed as a trinity. Christianity cherishes monotheism as did its Hebrew roots, but speaks of the One God in a threefold or trinitarian way.

In the first centuries of Christianity, the fathers of the church offered the people explanations of the mystery of the Trinity. Their faith in the Christ-event assured them that God had been manifested in Jesus of Nazareth. Christ, the Lord, was the Word of God. St. John's gospel begins this way:

> In the beginning was the Word;
> the Word was in God's presence,
> and the Word was God . . .

> The Word became flesh
> and made his dwelling among us,
> and we have seen his glory;
> the glory of an only Son coming
> from the Father,
> filled with enduring love. (John 1:1,14)

Explanations of a mystery are not the same as explanations of a mathematical problem. Such explanations approach the mystery from a faith stance, believing beyond rational understanding. Such explanations offer reasonable ways to view the mystery. They are carefully formulated to preserve that which revelation has presented. In the Trinity, all such doctrinal explanations hold in tension the ultimate Oneness of God and the threefold essence of the Godhead; that is, One God in three divine persons. The word *person* presents some difficulty for the modern believer. It is from the Latin *persona*. The word *person* in Roman usage of the second and third century did not possess any sense of a separate center of consciousness, or personality, as does the modern word *person*. Its Roman meaning as a theatrical mask was closer to role or function. An understanding of a Godhead with three persons having individual personalities would not be monotheism, but tritheism. However, the ancient understanding of the three persons of the Trinity did not understand person as merely temporary role or function. Today, a better term than person might be mode or aspect. Yet, these modern terms also present a problem. Modes, or aspects, are impersonal, lacking in the quality necessary to portray a loving, personal God. Somewhere between the idea of a concrete, individual being (person) and an abstract quality (mode) lies the mystery of the Trinity. Karl Barth, the great modern Protestant theologian, and Karl Rahner, the great modern Roman Catholic theologian, have both suggested that the three persons of God be interpreted as "three ways of being God." The three persons of God are the three ways in which we know God; they are also the three ways God *is*. For God has revealed Him/Herself as God is. Once again human language is simply inadequate.

St. Augustine, of the fifth century, whose theological work included the book *De Trinitas, On The Trinity,* offered explanations of this mystery through analogy. Augustine saw traces of the Trinity in much of life. He used the analogy of the human spirit:

1. the consciousness of the mind,
2. the words or insight that emerges from it and
3. the love that comes forth.

These three dimensions are within one person. He also offered an analogy of human love.

1. he who loves,
2. that which is loved and
3. the power of love.

Augustine also saw the human mind in three dimensions.

1. memory,
2. understanding and
3. will.

Augustine deeply believed in a Trinitarian God; he understood the threefold mystery as foundational to much of human life. Tertullian, the father of Latin theology, who wrote nearly two centuries before Augustine, also used analogy to approach the Trinity. He compared the Trinity in Unity to a root, its shoot, and the fruit—three in one—and also to the sun, its sunbeam and the illumination point. Tertullian also used the Latin term *substantia,* meaning a piece of property. Thus the Trinity was defended as one *substantia,* one piece of property owned by three.

All analogies, as all human language, fall short. The great Creed of our faith from the Council of Nicaea preserves the unity and threefold distinction of God. The mystery remains; philosophy and theology ponder it; analogical language attempts to express it; and faith holds fast, believing that the eternal God, Father-Creator, is eternally the same substance as the Son and eternally active as inspiring Spirit of the world.

God in Human Experience

As children, we learned that God is everywhere. But what does that really mean? Is God somewhere out there, up there, over or under our world? Is God above us, looking down at creation, or below us, supporting us as our rock and our foundation? In the nineteenth century, Cardinal John Henry Newman, a Catholic convert from the Anglican Church of England, asserted that "God is everywhere as absolutely and entirely as if He were nowhere else."

Some religious people stress the transcendent God, One who is above the ordinary, beyond the concrete and tangible. The otherness of God is their emphasis. The extreme of a transcendent approach to God is deism.* A deist believes God has created the world, but maintains no further relationship with it. The God of deism is a clock-maker God, who carefully puts the world together, arranging its many intricate parts, but when it is complete, remains forever aloof from it. Religious people on the other side, stress the immanence of God, God's presence in creation and all creatures. Their emphasis is on the God within. The extreme of an immanent approach is pantheism,* where God's relationship with creation becomes one of total identity. In Christianity, God is revealed as both transcendent and immanent. The eternal God is fleshed out in Jesus of Nazareth, the Incarnation, the Word made flesh. The Christian God is both the God of all eternity and the God who has walked among us.

People of Christian faith believe God is the ultimate reality. They structure their lives in accordance with that reality. Human beings have a responsibility to choose their reality, to believe or not to believe. Men and women through the centuries have given witness to their belief in a God of love—One who cares deeply about the world and all its people. Proof of the existence of God is tenuous. Proof of the existence of the personal, loving God of Christianity is impossible. Yet, people of faith do believe. Millions have believed through the centuries.

No one can ignore forever the God question. And no one can make one believe or not believe. The choice belongs to each one of us. It is our response to life itself. And upon this very response, we structure our reality and find the meaning of life.

Endnotes

1. Richard McBrien, *Catholicism* (Minneapolis: Winston Press, 1981), p. 257.

2. Paul Tillich, *The Shaking of the Foundations* (New York: Charles Scribner's Sons, 1948), p. 57.

3. Thomas Aquinas, *Summa Theologica,* Part I, Question 2, Art. 3.

4. Karl Rahner, *Do You Believe in God?* (Paramus, NJ: Newman Press, 1969), pp. 66-72.

5. Peter L. Berger, *A Rumor of Angels* (Garden City, NY: Doubleday and Company, Inc., 1969) pp. 52-53.

6. Edmund Colledge, O.S.A., and James Walsh, S.J., eds., *Julian of Norwich: Showings* (New York: Paulist Press, 1978), p. 231.

7. Viktor Frankl, *Man's Search for Meaning* (New York: Simon and Schuster, 1959).

8. McBrien, *op. cit.,* pp. 314-317.

9. Hans-Georg Gadamer, "Articulating Transcendence," in *The Beginning and The Beyond,* ed. Fred Lawrence (Chico, CA: Scholars Press, 1984), p. 5.

10. Alfred North Whitehead, *Religion in the Making* (New York: Meridian Books, World Publishing Co., 1960), p. 16.

11. Sam Keen, *To a Dancing God* (New York: Harper and Row, 1970), p. 5.

12. Martin A. Lang, *Acquiring Our Image of God* (New York: Paulist Press, 1983), pp. 39-40.

13. Harold Kushner, *When Bad Things Happen to Good People* (New York: Schocken Books, Inc., 1981), pp. 134, 141.

Glossary

Anthropology: The study of humankind through which human beings study their own nature and culture.

Anthropomorphism: The conception, or imaging, of God under a human form or with human characteristics.

Cosmology: The branch of metaphysics dealing with the universe as one orderly system.

Deism: Belief in a Supreme Being, Creator God, who takes no active part nor has any concern with the world or its people after its divine creation.

Empirical: Depending on observation and experience for data and understanding

Finite: Having limitations, limited, bounded; applied to humanity.

Infinite: Without limits, or boundaries; applied to time, space and divinity.

Monotheism: The belief in one God.

Pantheism: The belief that every creature in creation is not only a manifestation of God, but identical with God.

Polytheism: The belief in many gods.

Sacrifice: The act of offering anything to God or to the gods; to consecrate or present to some divinity; to offer to divinity by slaughter, or burning, of victims.

Secularization: The conversion from interest in the religious, or sacred, to interest in the present world and things of the world.

Discussion Questions

1. What are Thomas Aquinas' arguments for God's existence? Are they meaningful to you? Why? Why not?

2. What is the *God-Is-Dead* movement? Has this movement influenced your faith, or understanding, of God?

3. What is God-language? What are the limitations of God-language?

4. How do you understand God's will? In Creation? In daily life? In good fortune and tragedy?

5. Offer examples of images used to describe the Trinity.

6. What is your image of God? Has your image changed since childhood? Does your image help you relate to God?

Additional Reading

John F. Haught, *What Is God?* (New York: Paulist Press, 1986).

Harold S. Kushner, *When Bad Things Happen to Good People* (New York: Schocken Books, Inc., 1981).

Martin A. Lang, *Acquiring Our Image of God* (New York: Paulist Press, 1983).

John Shea, *Stories of God* (Chicago: Thomas More Press, 1978).

2

Faith, The Decision to Believe

Faith is a significant aspect of life. As people mature they become aware of how important it is to believe in themselves and others. The vast majority of people also choose to have faith in God. What is religious faith? Is it wise or foolish to put one's faith in God? Why is it that we distinguish between "faith" and "the Catholic faith"? These questions are not easy to answer. Since religious faith is both subjective and objective, it is difficult to explain. However, while religious faith cannot be adequately defined, it is still possible to examine its unique characteristics. For those who are engaged in the study of theology, such an examination is of crucial importance because theology is faith seeking understanding.

Faith, A Human Reality

What does it mean to believe in oneself? We answer this question differently at different times in our lives. The toddler lets go of the table and discovers the thrill of walking. A child who is not a natural athlete learns in elementary school that he or she can play a significant, if not predominant, role on an intramural team. The teenager caught in the rut of academic underachievement learns how to turn it around and perform well in the scholastic arena. The college student manages to adapt to life away from home, to make new friends, and to handle the responsibility which goes with independence. Newly married men and women determine that patience, hard work and sensitivity can turn their promised commitment into a life of blessed fulfillment. People of all ages who succeed at working through grief, disappointment, physical and spiritual suffering testify to the inward strength which they discover in the process. They come to believe in themselves. Knowing that we are good and that through our efforts we can attain many goals leads to a sense of self-esteem. Self-esteem is the absolute prerequisite for psychological health and normal development. If we are to flourish, we must believe in ourselves.

We do not live in isolation. Even very reclusive people need occasionally to rely on others. There are different levels of reliance. We depend far more on our parents, siblings and friends than we do on government clerks, astrophysicists or telephone operators. It is important to be able to believe that parents teach their children important values and that people who cut hair, for example, have the best interests of their customers at heart. If we found ourselves incapable of believing in the essential reliability and trust-worthiness of others, we would be incapable of normal interaction and impaired at every level of interpersonal functioning.

People today live in a world distinguished by very sophisticated technology. Physicians can treat ailments which heretofore were untreatable, pilots can fly passengers to destinations previously considered unreachable, and teachers can communicate knowledge about a wide range of subjects which were not even part of the curriculum a generation ago. One must be able to trust the physician, the pilot and the teacher if one is to live twentieth century life in a full and satisfying way.

It makes sense to believe in oneself and in others. Sacred scripture presents us with compelling justification to strengthen us in our faith. In the book of Genesis, after recounting the first story of creation, the author wrote: "God looked at everything he had made, and he found it very good" (Genesis 1:31). Belief in the essential goodness of oneself, others and all creation provides the foundation for a sense of self-esteem and the ability to trust others. While people who have faith encounter personal and interpersonal problems, they possess the resources to work through difficulties and to interact meaningfully with others.

In the context of the study of theology it is imperative to determine whether or not it makes sense to place one's faith and trust in God.

Does Religious Faith Make Sense?

The question, "Does religious faith make sense?" can be answered by saying "yes" or "no," or with a shrug of the shoulders. This last response is likely to come from those who consider the question irrelevant. Let us consider the rationale which leads to each answer, beginning with those who think that it does not make sense to believe in God.

Atheists and agnostics deny or doubt the existence of the object of religious faith. They say that there is no God (atheists), or that it is impossible to know whether God does or does not exist (agnostics). Atheists argue that the universe is self-programmed and self-contained, and not the result of a conscious act of creation by an all-powerful supreme being. Nonbelievers often point to the enormous amount of human suffering and conclude that an all-knowing and good God would not allow such pain and misery to afflict humankind. Following such influential thinkers as Freud and Marx, nonbelievers frequently tend to discredit the motivation of people of faith. They assert that the faith of believers rests on shaky foundations.

Karl Marx' Critique of Religious Faith

Karl Marx, a German social philosopher who lived from 1818 to 1883, was the chief theorist of socialism and communism. Marx, an atheist, was influenced by his contemporary, Ludwig Andreas Feuerbach, who understood religious feelings to be merely a product of human yearning and not connected to a transcendent being.

Karl Marx is famous for his analysis of the class struggle and his description of how religion functions to preserve the class system. The Marxist philosophical method is known as dialectical materialism.* This theory holds that economic determinants are of primary importance in ordering the major events and political arrangements in history. As Marx studied history he became more and more convinced that what was going on during each epoch was the struggle between classes. The economically productive class always turned out to be the ruling class. When one ruling class lost its economic dominance, it was destined to be replaced by the next productive class. Thus, the feudal nobility of the late middle ages was replaced by the bourgeois class. The bourgeois class was preeminent during the Industrial Age, the time when Marx formulated his theory.

Marx considered the economic exploitation of the proletariat by the bourgeoisie as the predominant reality of his time. The bourgeois, or capitalist, class enjoyed power and a fine standard of living, while the members of the proletariat, or working class, struggled under oppressive conditions to eke out a miserable livelihood. During the years following the Industrial Revolution working people labored long hours under unsafe conditions and the workers included pregnant women and children. Marx was struck by the passivity of the members of the proletariat, and he felt compelled to explain what caused this phenomenon. Why were so many people so willing to toil so hard and weep so much while being denied a fair share of the profits? What could possibly motivate the members of the proletariat to work and work and work in order to enrich the bourgeoisie?

Karl Marx decided that the wealth of the bourgeoisie and the poverty of the proletariat following the Industrial Revolution was attributable to the influence of religion. Religious leaders, according to Marx, preached fatalism* and subservience to the members of the working class, thus keeping them dispirited and passive. Marx thought that organized religions were a tool of the bourgeoisie whose purpose was to perpetuate bourgeois dominance. Describing religion as the "opium of the people," Marx contended that the usefulness of religion would disappear once a new socioeconomic order was instituted.

It should be noted that what Marx primarily attacked were what he perceived to be the negative social and economic effects of religion. Karl Marx did not examine the many positive aspects of faith which are subjectively experienced by believers. Instead, he concentrated on one cause and one effect which he indicated were due to the influence of religion. Marx contended that religious leaders preached the maintenance of the status quo, enjoining believers to bear their burdens serenely, and instructing them to hope for a substantial reward in the hereafter. This preaching was taken to heart by believers who were willing to endure dreadful working conditions and low wages while providing inordinate profits for capitalists. Marx reductionistically* concluded that if there were no classes there would be no exploitation of one group by another, and there would be no need for religion. For Karl Marx, religion served a deceptive socioeconomic purpose. Marx never entertained the possibility that religious faith might be evidence of a dynamic relationship between a person and God. And Marx never recognized that prophetic religion* could function to promote justice for the oppressed.

Atheists who are convinced of the correctness of Marxist theory are apt to argue that belief in God is absurd because there is no God. Further, they are likely to maintain that people who claim to believe in God do so because they are misled by the teaching and promises of religious leaders.

Freud's Assessment of Religious Faith

Another thinker who contributed substantial arguments to the atheist case was Sigmund Freud. Freud, the founder of psychoanalysis, was an Austrian physician who lived from 1856 to 1939. He developed a theory about how the unconscious* functions and provided an explanation for the influence of unconscious forces on human behavior. Undeniably a brilliant psychiatrist, Freud moved beyond the area of his competence when he analyzed the phenomenon of religious belief. To the gods Freud assigned a threefold task:

> The Gods retain their threefold task: they must exorcise the terrors of nature, they must reconcile men to the cruelty of fate, particularly as it is shown in death, and they must compensate them for the sufferings and privatizations which a civilized life in common has imposed on them.[1]

Freud theorized that immature people want to have a god or gods to protect them. Adults remember how their powerful fathers took care of them when they were little children, and, subconsciously, they wish that another father figure were there to dissipate the terror present in many traumatic situations. They are inclined to transform their wish for a protective father into an illusive object of faith. God, therefore, according to Freud, is an illusion. Freud disparaged the need to believe in God, describing it as a mark of immaturity. He thought that emotionally stable adults were capable of coping with the difficulties of life by themselves. Freud equated religious faith with an illusion which is fabricated in order to alleviate the anxiety which people experience. If people were mature and capable of taking charge of their lives, they would have no need of religion and would not fashion the concept of a father God.

Atheists dispute the objective reality of God's existence but they recognize that religious faith is a powerful force in the lives of believers. They deny, however, any validity to the claim which believers make that God exists. They see the childish needs of believers as the reason for religious faith, and do not entertain the possibility that religious believers might enjoy a living relationship with God.

Atheists of the Marxist or Freudian stamp make some good points. If religions preach fatalism and/or function in collusion with the rich and powerful, then they deserve to be exposed and discredited. To the extent that religious faith engenders a false dependency, it should be shown to be incompatible with human dignity. The purpose of religion is not to enshrine the status quo. Religious faith is not meant to retard personal, emotional and intellectual development. Religious leaders and people of faith have reason to be grateful for the challenge to keep faith from deteriorating into a detrimental reality. The important question to resolve, however, is whether or not, in the final analysis, the case of the atheist is a convincing one.

The Agnostic Worldview

In contradistinction to atheists there is a second category of nonbelievers, agnostics. Agnostics reason that God may exist or God may not exist, and that there is no definitive way to resolve the issue. Since the existence of God cannot be irrefutably established, agnostics adopt a worldview which excludes a place for God. Accordingly, agnostics live their lives as if God does not exist. They do not pray, or worship, or see the universe as God's handiwork. Neither do agnostics acknowledge that a supreme being has dominion over them. They tend to be thoughtful people who will commit themselves only to what they can know with absolute certitude and who consider the risk entailed in religious faith an unacceptable gamble.

The Indifferent

Both the atheist and the agnostic spend time and exert effort in considering the question of God's existence. But this is not true of the majority of unbelievers. They fall under the heading of "indifferent." Life is more complicated and hectic today than it ever was before, and many people find themselves preoccupied, busy and overwhelmed by the tasks of living. Consequently, they simply do not bother to examine the issue of whether or not to believe in God. Young people are apt to count on the fact that they will have the rest of their lives to consider questions relating to God's existence. Since young adulthood is envisioned as a time for a variety of pursuits (intellectual, social, career-oriented, among others), there may be a temptation to put faith-related issues aside. Unfortunately, people who think that religious faith should only be a concern of sedate, older folks miss the point that faith is just as important for young people as for their parents and grandparents. Young adults need to recognize how difficult it is to face life without knowing the answers to the ultimate questions.* They want to know if death is the end of their existence or if they are immortal. They want to know if their deepest desires will ever be fulfilled and if the God who created the cosmos has any concern about them. They feel a need for a value system which makes sense and which offers an alternative to the rat race. As they discover their uniqueness and giftedness they want to become acquainted with the source of the good which they reflect. When they feel sinful, depressed or afraid they experience a need to reach beyond themselves to the God of mercy who will heal them. And when they think about love and sex and marriage they want to know how God intends human intimacy to be lived out.

The Alienated

In addition to atheists, agnostics and persons who are indifferent to religious concerns, there are also legions of former members of organized religions. These people usually continue to have faith in God, but they have lost their confidence in their particular religion and have become alienated. Alienation is a painful phenomenon characterized by estrangement from a community of faith. The reason alienation is painful is because individuals are separated from groups to which they once belonged, and they suffer from the misunderstanding and isolation which accompany their separation. Each instance of alienation has its own unique aspects, and there is no simple way to resolve the phenomenon of alienation. According to triumphalistic reasoning,* for example, the Church is not at fault in instances of alienation. On the other hand, an extreme cynicism would absolve the alienated person of any culpability, and point the finger of blame solely at an institutional church. Since both of these responses lack balance, neither takes adequate account of what is involved in alienation from organized religion. While it is possible to believe in God without belonging to a community of faith, alienated persons, by their own testimony, recount how difficult it is to sustain belief in God without the support, encouragement and challenge of other believers. And many churches, alarmed by ever-dwindling congregations, are seeking to understand and remedy the causes of alienation.

Dissatisfaction with Some Expressions of Faith

Persons who are considering whether or not to believe in God may be deterred by what they see as the excesses of some so-called "religious" people. In recent years some fundamentalists and members of religious cults have given a negative impression of faith and religion. In generalizing about any phenomenon there is always a danger of inaccuracy. With this in mind, it is still essential that we identify the dissatisfaction with faith as it is practiced by fundamentalists and cultists.

Fundamentalists tend to interpret the bible literally, to espouse the political philosophy of the far right, and to be intolerant of the opinions of those who disagree with them. Some cultists appear to surrender their personal autonomy to the leaders of the cult; they follow blindly and, in extreme cases, appear to have been brainwashed. On November 18, 1978, at a jungle settlement in Jonestown, Guyana, nine hundred men, women and children committed suicide or were murdered following orders from their leader, the Rev. Jim Jones. Cultists will never go further in manifesting tragic and bizarre allegiance than they did on this occasion.

It is not surprising that persons who have yet to work through the soul-searching preliminary to religious faith are wary of excess. It is important to recognize, however, that the religious faith manifest by a member of a fundamentalist church or a cult is not the only possible kind of faith. As this chapter unfolds it will become apparent that such faith differs markedly from a liberating faith in the living God. It is to an understanding of such a faith that we should now turn our attention.

What Is Religious Faith?

Religious faith is one's choice to believe in God and to live life in relationship to God. If, as in Christian belief, God is understood to be triune, then religious faith is accompanied by powerful insights into the meaning of life. God, our Mother and Father who cannot be without tenderness for the child of her womb (Isaiah 49:15) and who provides our daily bread (Matt. 6:11), is understood to be source of life, creator of all that is, keeper of promises. Jesus is known to be one in being with God, the unique revelation of God's personality and characteristics. Jesus is also teacher par excellence of the attitudes and actions which should characterize the life of a believer. To live the kind of life Jesus lived—honest, open, unselfish, loving, forgiving, generous, nonjudgmental—seems to be an impossible task. And it probably would be an impossibility if God's Holy Spirit were not with believers to energize and enable them, transforming hearts of stone into loving hearts of flesh. (Ezekiel 36:26) Ezekiel revealed the promise of God to transform their hearts to the Jewish people who were scattered and subject under the Babylonians. Before the Hebrew people could unite under the rule of the Lord, they needed God's assistance to be rid of their sins and focused on God's sovereignty. People of faith believe that they require God's help in order to respond to God and neighbor with the love and trust which faith requires.

Since faith is intangible and is unique in each believer's heart, it is difficult to fashion a precise definition of what faith is. Faith can be the dominant force in one person's life. To another it can be a barely flickering ember. Some people mistake superstition for faith, and others confuse faith with the abdication of all personal responsibility. Faith is not a simple phenomenon, but this does not mean that faith is a reality whose particular characteristics cannot be known.

Faith Is a Gift

People who believe in God know that their faith is a gift. God is the giver of the gift of faith. God gives the gift of faith to the believer who is free to accept or reject it. The wise person appreciates the value of the gift of faith and seeks to nourish it so that it can grow and develop.

A parable* is recounted in the gospel of Mark in which Jesus teaches his followers that God expects people to respond to the gifts which are given to them (Mark 9:11-27). The story is about a man of noble birth who gives ten of his servants ten units of currency each. After giving the gifts the nobleman told the servants, "Invest this until I get back." The gospel tells us that some of the servants were wise and diligent in their investment of the currency, realizing various profits. One, however, hid the money and the sum never grew. That slothful, unimaginative servant angered the nobleman who had expected that his gift would be better tended. Likewise the Lord God who gives the gift of faith expects that recipients will appreciate what has been entrusted to them and will nourish its growth.

Two questions arise in connection with the fact that faith is a gift. Persons who are born into a faith and raised within the immediate context of a believing family and the larger context of a faith community may think of faith as a given or as something which they have always possessed. They might wonder when it was that God offered them faith and that they accepted God's gift.

A second question relating to faith as a gift is: Does God offer the gift of faith to some and not to others? Does God offer the insight and relationship which accompany faith to some privileged people, while denying to others the possibility of believing?

In answer to the first question, parents, grandparents, siblings, teachers, priests, pastoral ministers and others undoubtedly provide environments which are conducive to nurturing faith.

By good example and sincere witness believers positively influence others in regard to the depth and strength of their faith. No person, however, can transmit faith to another. No mother can force her son to believe, no teacher can program a student to become a believer. At one time or another each individual has to decide for himself or herself whether or not to believe in God, whether or not to accept the gift which God offers. Because becoming a believer entails the acceptance of the personal gift of faith, faith follows upon a mature and conscious decision.

In responding to the question, "To whom does God offer the gift of faith, to some or to all?" we are faced with a puzzling situation. Faith is such a vital part of life, and we are so inclined to think of God as fair, that we tend to reason that God, our divine Parent, offers to each and every person the same opportunity to believe. As we have seen, however, substantial reasons keep atheists from believing in God, allegiance to rationality keeps agnostics from religious faith, the pace and demands of the present moment distract the indifferent, and many are turned off by the fanaticism of religious extremists. Given the number of nonbelievers, it becomes difficult to understand how God could be enlightening their hearts with the understanding which is a prerequisite for faith.

Karl Rahner, S.J. (1904-1984), a German Jesuit priest, is counted among the foremost theologians of the twentieth century. During his lifetime Rahner examined the major theological concerns seeking to uncover understanding of such phenomena as widespread unbelief. In respect to the issue of persons who do not believe in God, Rahner suggested an enlightening analysis. There is no question that persons who do not want to be religious believers have a right not to believe. In respect to whether or not God somehow offered faith to unbelievers which they chose to reject, Rahner was confronting a question of speculative theology. Rahner's task was to determine whether or not God offers each person a spiritual insight which would enable the person to know that there is a God and to respond to this insight by choosing to believe or not to believe. Or, are there some people with whom God chooses not to communicate in any way? Rahner's conclusion was that God communicates with each and every person, but some human persons are incapable of penetrating the truth that a loving parent, the almighty creator of all, is speaking to them. While these people are incapable of grasping the fact of God's personal identity, they do, nevertheless, understand that goodness is appealing and that they should live their lives with integrity. In responding to the attractiveness of goodness Rahner sees these people as responding to God, and he calls them "anonymous Christians."

The term "anonymous Christian" may sound condescending to a Muslim, a Buddhist or a Jew because they do not put their faith in Jesus Christ. The concept, however, is not meant to demean nonchristian religious traditions but rather to indicate the Catholic belief that salvation and grace come to humanity through the mediation of Jesus Christ.[2]

Most people are accustomed to clear-cut distinctions such as Christian and nonchristian, saved and condemned. And these are precisely the conclusions which they draw. However, these distinctions are simplistic and they do not do justice to either God's universal salvific will or the mystery of human nature. The brilliant analysis of Karl Rahner in disclosing the category "anonymous Christian" takes account of both these realities. Human persons, by their very nature are ordered toward God, and are open to God's self-communication. Since this is the case, why is it that so many people are unaware of this aspect of their nature? Most likely because they lack instruction or because they have been unable to comprehend the religious information which they have received. People who do not culpably turn their backs on God and Christ's Church are not guilty of a fault. If they live virtuous lives and crave actualization, and if the rightness of becoming Christian never occurs to them, then they participate unknowingly in Christ's grace and his Church, and should be considered anonymous Christians.

Faith May Be Obscure

Faith is often obscure. In the gospel of Mark there is an account of a conversation between Jesus and a man who came to ask for Jesus' help in curing his son who was possessed by devils. The discussion proceeded along these lines: The father said, "If out of the kindness of your heart you can do anything to help us, please do!" Jesus replied, "If you *can*? Everything is possible to a person who trusts." The father recognized his lack of faith when he responded, "I do believe! Help my lack of trust." (Mark 9:17-29).   `

The obscurity of religious faith is located in the psychological reality of the human person, and not in the object of faith, God, who often seems remote from us. The inconstancy of human emotions seems to be more the rule than the exception. There are days when we feel integrated and we think we know ourselves and God. And there are other times when we feel depressed, confused and disconnected, and we seemingly lack the ability to evaluate our convictions and commitments. This is the reality of the human condition and it accounts for why we sometimes experience our personal faith in God as obscure.

A second reason why an individual's faith might seem obscure is that people today are not inclined to speak about or demonstrate their beliefs. Religious faith is seldom in evidence in the marketplace or in the recreational complexes where we spend so much of our time. Even in their homes people spend little time reflecting on their faith. When faith-related concerns are at the very back of our minds it is not surprising that this precious gift seems vague and obscure.

Faith Is Marked by Certitude

After this description of the obscurity of religious faith, it might appear curious to state that certitude is also a characteristic of religious faith. This, nevertheless, is the case. It is just as likely that persons would be willing to lay down their lives for their faith as to wonder about whether or not they believe. The missionary sisters and priests who, as young persons, decide to commit their lives totally to Jesus are so certain of God's existence and his call to them that they are willing to spend an entire lifetime in foreign lands teaching others about the gospel. From the beginnings of Christianity even to the present some people have been forced to make a cruel choice: deny their beliefs, or be executed. Martyrs are so certain of their beliefs, so convinced of God's existence and their relationship to God, that they do not even consider denying their faith. The certainty of the martyr's faith is so strong that it is the reason for the martyr's willingness to die.

Saint Thérèse of Lisieux (1873-1897) died when she was a young woman of twenty-four. Thérèse was remarkable for the depth of faith which she had in God, and for her total commitment to loving others. When she was sixteen years old Thérèse became a Carmelite nun. When she was twenty-two she became gravely ill with tuberculosis, and she suffered terribly for over a year before she died, Weak and in pain, Thérèse had to contend with more than the physical debilitation caused by her illness. She also had to endure temptations against her strong faith in God. Abbé Combes, a biographer of Saint Thérèse, wrote of Thérèse's faith, her temptation, and her resolution in dealing with temptation.

> (Saint Thérèse's) faith in eternal life had always been
> so vivid and so real that it was for her the central
> truth around which everything revolved. Now a mock-
> ing voice kept saying to her: "There is no heaven; you
> are destined to annihilation."[3]

Combes tells us that Thérèse coped with her temptation by forcing herself to believe that God would keep his promise and give her eternal life. In her heart of hearts she was certain that God existed and that God loved her, and she would not permit herself to capitulate to torturous doubts.[4]

Faith Entails Risk

Faith always entails risk. The God in whom believers place their trust has never been seen or touched. They could be mistaken, thinking that God exists when, possibly, there is no God. If this were the case, then believers have been deluded, have worshiped a phantom. This is the risk a believer takes. During seasons of doubt the believer is very conscious of the risk. Paradoxically, it is because faith is so resilient, so deeply rooted, so certain, that people of faith are able to take the risk of believing.

Some people who are not sure whether or not to believe in God decide to hedge their bets. They join a church, contribute to collections and say a prayer now and again. They observe the limits of morality (more or less). Their motivation is simply to meet the minimum requirements of religious faith. *If* there is a God and *if* there is a hereafter, they resolve to do enough to qualify for entrance into heaven. They reason that they have nothing to lose and possibly a great deal to gain. Such a calculation, however, is a far cry from true religious faith. It does not include the whole-hearted commitment to a deep and loving relationship with God characteristic of the faith of a true believer.

Faith Must Be Deeply Rooted

In order for believers to withstand the attraction of false gods, faith must be deeply rooted. What false gods tempt and lure people today? The list of false gods is extensive, including the obsessive pursuit of such things as money, status, power and pleasure. The attitude which usually accompanies pursuit of these things is a "me first" one, devoid of sincere concern about anyone other than oneself.

To be a person of faith means to act in accordance with God's commands and to reject the temptations of false Gods. Believers appropriate the values and priorities found in the gospel. An excellent summary of how faith should translate into attitude and action is recounted in the discourse on the Great Commandment:

> One of the scribes came up, and when he heard them arguing he realized how skillfully Jesus answered them. He decided to ask him, "Which is the first of all the commandments?" Jesus replied: "This is the first:
> 'Hear, O Israel! The Lord our God is Lord alone!
> Therefore, you shall love the Lord your God
>   with all your heart,
>   with all your soul,
>   with all your mind,
>   and with all your strength.'
> This is the second,
> 'You shall love your neighbor as yourself.'
> There is no other commandment greater than these."
> (Mark 12:28-31)

The roots of faith must be deep if believers are to be reverent, unselfish, compassionate and caring. In other words, only a strong faith in God and a belief in God's constant assistance* can enable a Christian to live according to the Great Commandment.

Theological Attempts to Explain the Essence of Faith

The Old Testament contains the sacred writings of the Hebrew people. Compiled over a period of more than five hundred years, these writings provide a rich understanding of the nature of faith. Some of the insights recorded in the Old Testament will be helpful to us as we attempt to flesh out a picture of religious faith.

Abraham

At the beginning of the history of Israel, God is depicted as addressing Abraham and instructing him to undertake a journey to a new land where he will play a major role in God's plan of salvation. In response to God's injunction, "Go out from your land and your clan and your father's house to a land that I will show you," (Gen. 12:1) Abraham exhibited remarkable trust in God, venturing into the unknown. In addition, Abraham believed God's promise that he would become the father of a great nation. We read in Genesis:

> He took him outside and said, "Look up at the sky
> and count the stars if you can. Just so," he added,
> "shall your descendants be." (Gen. 15:5)

Abraham made himself secure by believing in God's promise. And, for Abraham, faith did not go unrewarded. Because he believed so completely God removed the burden of sterility from Abraham and his wife Sarah and blessed them in their old age with a son, Isaac.

Moses

Moses, too, provides an example of faith. A Hebrew by birth, Moses was reared apart from his people. Adopted as an infant by a princess of the Pharaoh's family, and raised in the Pharaoh's household, as an adult Moses became aware that he was a Jew, not an Egyptian. Moses' loyalty to his own people was exhibited when he killed an Egyptian who was cruelly treating the

Hebrew slaves. His first direct encounter with the God of the Hebrews occurred at the burning bush as God told Moses about his plan to save Israel. God also disclosed to Moses his personal name during that encounter. The relational aspect of religious faith is very evident in the dialogue recorded in the Book of Exodus:

> "When I go to the Israelites and say to them, 'The God of your Fathers has sent me to you,' and they say to me, 'What is his name?' what shall I answer them?" And God said to Moses, "I am who I am; and thus you will say to the Israelites, I AM has sent me to you." And God spoke again to Moses, "Say this to the Israelites: Yahweh, the God of your fathers, the God of Abraham, the God of Isaac and the God of Jacob, has sent me to you. This is my name forever; this is my title generation after generation." (Exodus 3:13-15)

The God who spoke to Moses was a God who was with his people. God was not only with the Hebrew people; God was also for them. Through a series of interventions God freed the Hebrews from their bondage in Egypt. On Mount Sinai, while the Israelites were on their journey to their new homeland, God gave the ten commandments* to Moses. Along with giving the commandments God is said to have made a promise of how he would respond to those sons and daughters who faithfully observed his regulations: I, the Lord, will bestow "mercy down to the thousandth generation on the children of those who love me and keep my commandments" (Exodus 20:6).

Moses is a complex figure who is portrayed in different lights by various Old Testament authors. Moses' faith and his openness to being God's messenger have combined to make him an outstanding personage in Judaeo-Christian history.

Isaiah

The message of Isaiah, who was considered by many to be the greatest of the prophets*, was that Israel and Judah* should trust exclusively in God. They should not expect success from playing human games like power politics. Because the kings to whom he spoke did not heed the words of Isaiah, Isaiah looked to a new king in Israel's future who would bring the full measure of God's blessings to the people. This new king was Jesus.

And Isaiah's warning to the Israelites that they ought to walk in holiness and uprightness before God underscores the active commitment which is at the heart of religious faith.

Jeremiah

Jeremiah was a prophet who instructed Israel for a period of approximately forty-five years. They were turbulent years in the history of Israel and included the event of the fall of Jerusalem in 586 B.C. Jeremiah was an extraordinarily gifted speaker who preached incessantly against the two major evils of his day, idolatry and injustice. Jeremiah's message was essentially one of obedience to the divine will expressed in the covenant God had made with Israel. For Jeremiah, faithfulness or fidelity is what God required of the people. Knowing the frailty of the human condition, Jeremiah was an eloquent spokesperson for God's willingness to forgive and restore an errant Israel. However, Israel's refusal to heed Jeremiah's warnings made Jeremiah depressed about the situation. A collective faithlessness precipitated the collapse of Judah.*

The New Testament and Religious Faith

In the New Testament the meaning of faith is closely linked to the concept of *metanoia*. *Metanoia* means conversion, the kind of converting or changing which entails a radical redirection of one's heart. Jesus expected his followers to become people of faith, i.e., people who would decide with their minds and hearts to be committed to him. The act of converting to Jesus, of becoming a person of faith, involves developing a new set of priorities according to which the love of God and service of others become one's primary concerns.

In the synoptic gospels* Jesus is recorded as teaching many lessons about faith. These lessons are instructive for us as we seek to understand the meaning of faith.

Since the faith of believers is their most precious possession, Jesus warned his followers against ever doing anything that would undermine the faith of a simple believer. The words attributed to Jesus are both powerful and uncompromising: "It would be better if anyone who leads astray one of these simple believers were to be plunged in the sea with a great millstone fastened around his neck" (Mark 9:42). By this warning Jesus was trying to teach his followers that people should be supported and affirmed in their faith. Believers need the assistance of a faith community so that they can flourish in their faith. This is true for all believers, but the need for support is especially true for those who are just beginning their faith journey.

Jesus taught us that faith is powerful and that it enables us to be and to become the persons we want to be. He said: "I give you my word, if you are ready to believe, whatever you ask for in prayer, it shall be done for you" (Mark 11:24). While we should guard against naive interpretations of this passage we need to realize the reality of God's provident care. A personal God is deeply committed to those who have faith, and is ready to respond to the needs of believers.

Church Councils* and Teaching on Faith

In its Decree on Justification which was formulated in 1546 and 1549, the theologians and bishops of the Council of Trent commented on the process of coming to faith. They said that justification (becoming a person of faith) is initiated by God and accomplished through the grace of Jesus. They also held that the Catholic faith* involves assent to those revealed truths which are taught by the Church.

In 1870 the first Vatican Council presented its synthesis on faith. Some of the points made in the document on faith, (*Dei Filius,* Son of God) concern the fact that God's veracity insures the vapidity of faith, and that there could be no faith without the enlightenment of the Holy Spirit. Vatican I spoke of the believer's "free obedience" in coming to faith because it sought to emphasize the person's active role in faith.

In the 1950s and 1960s, pre-Vatican II theology distanced itself from analyses of faith as an abstract reality. An appreciation of faith as an abstract reality. An appreciation of faith as a dynamic dimension of human experience, with emphasis on the personal aspects of the phenomenon of faith, was emerging. The scriptures were consulted to great advantage in discovering the nature of faith. Vatican II (1962-1965) affirmed what the Church had consistently held in respect to faith, and also refined the traditional understanding of faith. The Council fathers taught that the subjective insights and choice which result in belief for some and nonbelief for others must be respected because of the dignity of each individual conscience. They also held that noncatholic Christians are united to Christ and justified by their faith. The fact that they are not members of a Church which hierarchically traces its history through the centuries back to the apostles does not demean their faith. "All those justified by faith through baptism are incorporated into Christ"[5] and their faith is worthy of our sincere reverence.

Action for Justice: A Constituent Dimension of Faith

During the past generation there have been many theological attempts to connect the intellectual and volitional aspects of faith to concrete commitments to work for justice. This movement is a reaction to the tendency to define faith in largely abstract and ethereal terms. These efforts, however, do not represent something which is totally new. As early as the epistle of Saint James Christians were challenged to connect their faith to lives lived in response to the needs of others:

> What good is it to profess faith without practicing it? Such faith has no power to save one, has it? If brothers or sisters have nothing to wear and no food for the day, and you say to them, "Good-bye and good luck! Keep warm and well fed," but do not meet their bodily needs, what good is that? So it is with the faith that does nothing in practice. It is thoroughly lifeless. (James 2:14-17)

Avery Dulles, S.J., a contemporary American theologian, explained that definitions of faith are incomplete if they do not include the notion that the person of faith ought to be committed to work to bring about the kingdom of God.[6] While the kingdom of God can only be partially and imperfectly realized in this world, nevertheless, actions on behalf of justice would make this world the kind of place Jesus wants it to be. The evils apparent in our time need to be exposed, and action ought to be taken to insure that human rights are protected. Materialism, sexism, racism, greed, and many other dehumanizing forces keep individuals and groups from realizing their dignity. The faith of believers should spur a commitment to participate in the enormous task of working for justice. It was of just such a commitment that the Catholic bishops spoke at their synod (meeting) in 1971:

> The mission of preaching the Gospel dictates at the present time that we should dedicate ourselves to the liberation of man even in his present existence in this

world. For unless the Christian message of love and justice shows its effectiveness through action in the cause of justice in the world, it will only with difficulty gain credibility with the men of our times.[7]

Religious Faith and the Fundamental Option

The choice to believe or not to believe in God is of paramount importance in each human life. Believers usually wonder about whether they believe, when they began to believe, and why it is that they believe.

Although faith can be understood as obscure and elusive, people usually have little trouble identifying themselves as believers or nonbelievers. They can generally indicate a time after childhood or adolescence when they chose to adopt the judgments and values of believers. They can also cite what it was that attracted them to Jesus' message and God's sovereignty. One of the most basic and certain choices of their lives is the fundamental option to believe in God. In making this choice they establish their most significant relationship and set the standards by which they will live their lives.

In choosing to believe, Christians decide whom they will follow (Jesus), how they will live (by love), and what they will value (generosity and service to others). The fundamental option, or basic choice to believe in God, begins as a fragile decision but grows into a strong and vibrant conviction which gives meaning and structure to the whole of life.

The decision to believe inaugurates a process during which an individual's faith develops according to a predictable pattern. James W. Fowler's seminal work, Stages of Faith (San Francisco: Harper & Row, 1981), details the universal stages people go through as they develop belief systems. The reader may want to consult Fowler's work in order to learn about the developmental aspects of growth in faith.

Jesus Is the Light of the World; Jesus' Word Gives Life

The yearning of the human heart is for light and the integrity of human fulfillment. Religious faith, we learn in the gospel of John, is the vehicle by which we can attain what our hearts crave.

John recounts the powerful and awesome proclamation in which Jesus identified himself as light: "I have come to the world as its light, to keep anyone who believes in me from remaining in the dark" (John 12:46). It is by Jesus' grace that believers, faith brings life which is unending. "Whoever believes in the Son has life eternal" (John 3:36). Confusion, turmoil and death occasion great sadness and terror within the human heart, but believers manage to move beyond this pain and find peace and hope in Jesus' promises.

Every human person knows what it is to be broken, divided and frustrated. We long for wholeness and completion, for a state of being in which our psychological and moral weaknesses no longer cause us suffering. The good news of the gospel of John is that Jesus will fulfill those who believe in him. After all, he told us, "I myself am the bread of life. No one who comes to me shall ever be hungry, no one who believes in me shall ever thirst" (John 6:35). Our human completion, the satisfying of our deepest hungers and thirsts, is to be accomplished through faith.

People of Faith

We can learn about faith from people of faith. The twentieth century has had no shortage of people who have believed in God and manifested their faith in lives of great accomplishment. We are enriched by knowing their stories.

Dorothy Day

Dorothy Day (1897-1980) was perhaps the most influential lay person in the history of American Catholicism. As a young woman she was very unconventional; she set her own agenda and lived her own life. On December 28, 1927, after months of wrestling with questions of God and religion, Dorothy was baptized a Catholic. Prior to her baptism, Dorothy had separated from the man she had lived with, the father of her only child, a daughter, and was supporting herself as a freelance writer. After her conversion, Dorothy Day responded in a radical way to the challenge of Jesus. She lived a life of voluntary poverty, began the Catholic Worker movement* to serve the indigent, and spoke out tirelessly as a pacifist. What was the secret of Dorothy Day's faith, a faith that was eloquently expressed in a life of service to the poor? Dorothy saw love as the demand God made of those who believed:

> Love makes all things easy. When one loves, there is at that time a correlation between the spiritual and the material. Even the flesh is energized, the human spirit is made strong. All sacrifice, all suffering is easy for the sake of love. [Love] will solve all problems, family, national, international.[8]

Dorothy Day's faith was single-minded; it consisted in knowing that she obeyed God when she loved her neighbor.

Thomas Merton

Religious faith was the core of Thomas Merton's life (1915-1968). But Merton's faith was neither simple nor static; it changed and grew, bent and stretched as he himself did over the course of a lifetime.

A prolific writer, mystic, Trappist monk, social activist, and a man open to the wisdom of both Eastern and Western religions, Thomas Merton's faith is one of the most intriguing religious subjects of the latter decades of the twentieth century. In a letter to a Muslim friend Merton recounted the connection between his faith and his prayer, leaving us a description of how he understood the essence of his relationship with the transcendent God:

> Strictly speaking I have a very simple way of prayer. It is centered entirely on attention to the presence of God and to His will and His love. That is to say that is centered on faith by which alone can we know the presence of God. One might say this gives my mediation the character described by the prophet as "being before God as if you saw Him." Yet it does not demand imagining anything or conceiving a precise image of God, for to my mind this would be a kind of idolatry. On the contrary, it is a matter of adoring Him as invisible and infinitely beyond our comprehension and realizing Him as all . . . There is in my heart this great thirst to recognize totally the nothingness of all that is not God.[9]

For Thomas Merton, God was the center of life, the giver and sustainer of life. All forms of selfishness, sin, hatred and violence were evaluated by Merton as nothing because they were not of God and they kept people from knowing and loving God. To be a person of faith meant to fix one's gaze on God, worshipful and peaceful in the knowledge that God accepts and loves us as a Divine Parent. Merton's insight is that of the mystic*, and there is at least some little trace of mystical contemplation in the faith of each believer.

Jean Donovan

Jean Donovan (1953-1980) was a young woman who loved parties; she was an adept storyteller who was fun to be around. Jean graduated from Case-Western Reserve University with an MBA and went off to work in the business world. She also joined a faith-sharing community and began trying to answer the ultimate questions which kept popping into her mind.

A friend described Jean's faith and searching by saying, "Jean was trying to figure out where she fit with God. She wasn't religious in the tiresome sense, but she was committed. She felt she needed to do something because she had been given so much. She owed it . . . to God, to other people."[10] Jean Donovan answered the call she heard within her heart. She decided to serve for two years as a lay minister in El Salvador. Jean kept the mission books, transported refugees to shelters and conducted sacrament preparation classes. Although she was not involved in El Salvador's politics, there was fear that she and the other missionaries might be organizing the local people to revolt against government leaders. As a result of this fear, combined with a dreadful tolerance for inhumane violence, in 1980 Jean Donovan and three other women missionaries were abducted, brutalized, murdered and buried in a common grave.

In the aftermath of Jean's death, her family, friends and strangers from all over the world wanted to know what it was that prompted an attractive, gregarious, accomplished young woman to leave her affluent surroundings and place herself in danger in order to help poor people find God and overcome their devastating poverty. The answer is stark in its simplicity. Jean Donovan believed in God. She believed that God wanted her to do the work of a lay missionary. Her faith brought Jean to El Salvador, and her commitment to do God's work kept her there. Though her days were cut tragically short, those who believe

God's promises trust that jean now enjoys the complete fulfillment and blessedness which only God can impart.

Conclusion

If people do not believe in themselves and others they are destined to lead painful, isolated lives. If people do not believe in God they will never know of God's greatness or God's compassion. People who are related to God in a blessed, vibrant way possess the gift of faith. This gift is something which they only partially understand, but it is also something which they treasure more than anything else. Those who have faith and live by faith transcend much of the confusion which mars the contemporary world. They know the place God ought to occupy in their hearts and the way they ought to order their lives.

In this chapter we considered the case against faith made by atheists, agnostics and the indifferent. What are nonbelievers missing? By reviewing the characteristics of religious faith and consulting the scriptures for their instruction regarding faith we learned how deeply valuable is the faith of believers. We also noted that action on behalf of justice is a constituent element of faith, and saw how people of faith such as Dorothy Day, Thomas Merton and Jean Donovan put their faith into action.

Endnotes

1. Sigmund Freud, *The Future of an Illusion,* James Strachey, trans. and ed. (New York: W.W. Norton & Co., Inc., 1961), p. 18.

2. For further elucidation of Rahner's thought on the "anonymous Christian" the reader should consult the work of Rahner scholars such as Gerald McCool, S.J., ed., *A Rahner Reader* (New York: Seabury, 1975), p. 211 and Anita Röper, *The Anonymous Christian* (New York: Sheed & Ward, 1966), in its entirety.

3. Abbé André Combes, *St. Thérèse and Suffering,* trans. Msgr. Philip E. Hallett (New York: P. J. Kenedy & Sons, 1951), p. 104.

4. Ibid.

5. Decree on Ecumenism, 3.

6. Avery Dulles, S.J., "The Meaning of Faith Considered in Relationship to Justice," in John C. Haughey, ed., *The Faith That Does Justice* (New York: Paulist Press, 1977), pp. 10-46.

7. Text in J. Gremillion, ed., *The Gospel of Peace and Justice* (Maryknoll, New York: Orbis, 1976), p. 521.

8. William D. Miller, *Dorothy Day* (San Francisco: Harper & Row, 1982), p. 326.

9. Michael Mott, *The Seven Mountains of Thomas Merton.* (Boston: Houghton Mifflin Company, 1986), p. 433.

10. Pat Rowantree, "From Fun-loving Life to Jungle Death," *The Floridian,* November 29, 1981, p. 9.

Glossary

The Catholic faith: Belief in the doctrines taught by the Roman Catholic Church.

Catholic Worker Movement: A movement started by Dorothy Day to assist the poor by housing them at Catholic Worker houses. Those who staff the houses live simple lives of prayer and service. The *Catholic Worker* was published in conjuction with the movement. Its writings stressed pacifism and adherence to the gospel.

Church councils: Worldwide meetings of church officials and theologians to deliberate on matters of Church discipline and/or doctrine. The last two ecumenical (worldwide) councils were held at the Vatican in Rome in 1870 and 1962-1965 (Vatican Council I and Vatican Council II).

The collapse of Judah: in 586 before the army of Nebuchadnezzar.

Dialectical materialism: Everything is material and change occurs through the struggle of opposites. Through the working of definite laws, the conflict of opposing forces leads to growth, change and development. For Marx, this meant that the revolution of the working class was the precondition for the establishment of a communist society in which there would be no class distinctions.

Faith as Commitment: Stresses the relational and volitional aspects of faith: to be in union with God and do God's will.

Fatalism: An attitude according to which a person believes that economic, political and social conditions have been preordained and are to be patiently accepted by everyone.

God's constant assistance, i.e., grace: God shares life with believers, enabling them to keep their faith. This divine assistance is called grace.

Israel and Judah: Two kingdoms into which the Hebrew people were organized. Israel was the northern kingdom, Judah, the southern kingdom.

Mystic: One who enjoys prayer of union with God, experiencing God's presence in a very intense way.

Parables: Stories told by Jesus to illustrate a point. For example, the story of the Good Samaritan shows us that we should be neighbor to everyone (Luke 10:30-37).

Prophetic religion: The religious message preached by churches which criticize the paganism, harshness and indifference of societies and instruct people that God is offended when people are unjust or idolatrous.

Reductionist: The tendency to take a complex problem or situation and explain its existence based on only one apparent cause.

Synoptic gospels: Since the gospels of Matthew, Mark and Luke proceed along similar lines, presenting a complementary picture of Christ and his teaching, they are called synoptic.

The Ten Commandments: The rules of life given by God to Moses. They are enumerated in Exodus 20:2-17.

Triumphalistic reasoning: A way of understanding the Catholic Church which would accord to the Church a special and unchallengeable competence in the search for truth; a way of looking at the Catholic Church which would place it above, and better than, all other churches with a tendency to ignore or dismiss these other churches.

Ultimate questions: Issues which everyone confronts at one time or another: They include, "Is there a God?" "What is the purpose of life?" "Who am I?" "Is love stronger than hatred?" "Why is there evil in the world?"

The unconscious: or subconscious was described by Freud as a submerged but vast portion of the mind. Containing the repressed residue of unacceptable experiences, the unconscious can unknowingly motivate many human actions.

Discussion Questions

1. Relate an incident or series of incidents which caused you to believe in yourself. What connection do you see between faith in oneself, other, and faith in God?

2. Describe how you would respond to the attacks on religious faith which were formulated by Karl Marx and Sigmund Freud. In the final analysis, does the Marxian or Freudian atheist put forward a convincing case?

3. Describe the characteristics of religious faith and give an example of each characteristic based on your experience and/or observation.

4. State one lesson about faith which can be learned from each of the following: Abraham, Moses, Isaiah and Jeremiah.

5. What does *metanoia* mean? What concrete effects do people experience as a result of *metanoia*?

6. What kind of assistance or support do people require so that they can continue and grow in their faith? How can faith communities help individuals to deepen their faith?

7. Describe the manifestations of a "me-first" attitude. Why do religious believers reject a "me-first" attitude?

8. Does belief in God have credibility if it is not tied to action on behalf of justice? In what kinds of action should believers engage? In what specific actions did Dorothy Day, Thomas Merton and Jean Donovan engage?

Additional Reading

Gregory Baum, *Faith and Doctrine: A Contemporary View* (New York: Newman Press, 1969).

Hans Küng, *Does God Exist? An Answer for Today* (New York: Doubleday, 1980).

Karl Rahner, *Foundations of Christian Faith* (New York: Seabury Press, 1978).

3

Jesus the Christ

Who is Jesus? The question has resounded through the centuries. Who is Jesus, the Christ? Jesus, himself, asked his apostles, "Who do people say that I am?" And more pointedly, "Who do you say I am?" (Mark 8:27-29). Answering this most basic question of Christianity is not easy. Theologians and historians, alike, have studied the life and message of Jesus from many perspectives. Who is Jesus? What did Jesus do? What did Jesus say? Jesus of Nazareth is an historical reality. Jesus lived at a time in history. And Christians throughout the world believe this same Jesus is God's own Son, Lord of history, the summit of God's revelation, the Alpha and Omega of Creation.

The Historical Jesus

The gospels of the New Testament (Matthew, Mark, Luke and John) are not histories. They are testimonies of the faith of the early church communities. These authors were not primarily interested in facts about the Jesus of history, but were concerned with the Christ who had become the center of their lives. The life and message of Jesus is offered to us through the living faith of his followers. They recalled the Jesus whose Spirit was now alive in their church communities. All historians write history with the mind of their own age. There is no pure history. People perceive events through the filters of their own life experience. The so-called hermeneutic circle* is inescapable. The self cannot be entirely objective; the account of Jesus' life, as all of history, is necessarily interpretative.

The four gospels are interpretations, written by people of faith. The evangelist, Mark, who probably wrote between 65-70 A.D., is interested in portraying the hidden Messiah, Christ the Liberator. Mark does not emphasize the parables and words of Jesus; his stress is on the miracles and exorcising actions of Jesus. Mark's Jesus is a man of action, victorious over death

54

and the devil. His role, although he refuses to publicly acknowledge his Messiahship, is liberating the earth from the forces of evil and bringing a divine peace. "I assure you, among these standing here, there are some who will not taste death until they see the reign of God established in power" (Mark 9:1).

Matthew's gospel was written after the destruction of Jerusalem in 70 A.D., probably around 85 A.D. The author was preaching to Jewish Christians and Greeks of Syria. His emphasis is on Jesus, the long-awaited Messiah of the Israelite nation, the New Moses. Matthew quotes the Old Testament prophecies to prove that Jesus is truly the Savior of Israel, offering a new gospel, yet fulfilling the old law of the Hebrew Nation. "Do not think that I have come to abolish the law and the prophets. I have come not to abolish them but to fulfill them" (Matthew 5:17).

Luke is the evangelist to the Greeks and Gentiles.* The author of Luke's gospel, who wrote around 85-90 A.D., is concerned with the compassionate Jesus, liberator of the sick, the poor, sinners, all those marginalized socially or religiously. Luke offers Jesus as a model for all whose lives will be transformed. Jesus is revealed as perfect man and as Son of God deeply concerned for humanity. He is serene and confident of the coming of the Kingdom of God. "Do not live in fear, little flock. It has pleased your Father to give you the Kingdom" (Luke 12:32).

John's gospel, more than the three Synoptics,* is theological in its approach. The last gospel, written between 90-100 A.D., speaks of Jesus, the Logos,* eternal Word of God, Son of God, who lived among human beings. The image of Jesus that emerges from the gospel of John is a transcendent Jesus; one of the emphases is on his divinity. The facts of Jesus' life are important to the author for their theological significance. Written nearly seventy years after the death of Jesus, John's Jesus has already been experienced as the Christ of faith. "I am the way and the truth and the life" (John 14:6).

St. Paul, although a contemporary of Jesus, did not know the historical Jesus. In his letters, Paul proclaims the Risen Jesus, Savior of all history. In the communities established by Paul and his missionary friends, Jesus is Lord, Head of the mystical body, Center of the universe, the Wisdom of God. The cross and resurrection of Jesus have brought salvation to all who believe. "God it is who has given you life in Christ Jesus. He has made him our wisdom and also our justice, our sanctification, and our redemption" (1 Corinthians 1:30).

The evangelists were people of faith, and their testimony emerged from their early church communities. Nonchristian witnesses also exist. Roman historians, Pliny, Suetonius and Tacitus, mention the man Jesus, as does the Jewish historian, Flavius Josephus. These sources merely prove the historical reality of Jesus of Nazareth. It is the biblical writing that provides the sources of depth. These exist because faith in Jesus continued after his death. Believers felt a need to write down their testimonies of faith for their own communities and all those who followed. Contemporary faith in Jesus Christ is built firmly upon the faith of these early witnesses. Faith in Christ springs from encounters with the faith of other Christians.

At the time of the Reformation, Protestant Reformers were concerned with returning to the New Testament, the Word of God in the gospels. Following the Reformation, with its great emphasis on the authority of scripture over the authority of the church, much research into the life of Jesus was begun. In this new research, biblical scholars intended to withdraw the traditional authority from the church and place biblical authority above all else. Many histories of the life of Jesus emerged in the following centuries.

In Germany theologians of the nineteenth century, led by Frederick Schleiermacher, attempted an indepth research of the Jesus of history. Schleiermacher's thrust was to present the human Jesus in such a way that "we perceive it as the expression or effect of the divine which was within him."[1] The search for the historical Jesus led ultimately back to the question of interpretation. In the beginning of the twentieth century, biblical theologian Albert Schweitzer, later to become famous scientist-doctor of Africa, summed up the movement in his *History of Research Into the Life of Jesus*. He believed that the life of the historical Jesus, presented by various authors at different times in history, were actually reflections of each author's particular ideas from a personal perspective. "And so each subsequent epoch in theology found its own ideas in Jesus, and could find no other way of bringing him to life. Not only epoches found themselves in him. Each individual recreated him in the image of his own personality."[2]

The Christ of Faith

The constructing of an accurate history of the life of Jesus remains a theological dilemma. Yet in modern times, scripture scholarship now credits the original gospel writers with preserving much more of the historical Jesus than their nineteenth century counterparts were willing to accept. The early church communities certainly may have been selective in their remembering, but they did remember. The apostolic communities to which the evangelists belonged were mirrors reflecting Jesus. Surely the particular community, with its particular goal in writing, superimposed some of its own community image on the offered image of Jesus. Nonetheless, a Jesus emerges who inspires faith. This man, Jesus, had a special mode of being; his authority transcended that of any ordinary rabbi. Even the most historically exacting research would admit that this Jesus comported himself as no ordinary person. Nor was he just another prophet or miracle worker; he was recognized as one who spoke for God. The faith communities that wrote about him described Jesus as Lord, Messiah, Savior, Son of Man, the Christ, Anointed One and, ultimately, Son of God. These titles were given to Jesus following the resurrection, as the believers struggled to understand his full significance. The resurrection gave a new focus, an entirely new dimension to the words and actions of Jesus. Gradually, the believers came to grasp the meaning of the Christ event.

The Jesus of the gospel stories cannot be understood without understanding his relationship to God. Jesus himself was a person of deep faith. He spoke often of his Father, calling God *Abba,* a term of endearment, Dad or Papa. The Kingdom he preached was not limited to a nation or territory; the Kingdom which Jesus began was God's Kingdom. The faith of Jesus was fundamental to his mission. Leonardo Boff, liberation theologian of Latin America, believes a posture of faith is necessary to understand the historical Jesus.

> Can the historical Jesus himself be understood outside of the dimension of faith, if he himself, Jesus of Nazareth, understood his entire life as a life of faith? Is it not precisely faith itself that gives the proper atmosphere and perspective that enables us to understand the historical Jesus? It was not without reason that the primitive community identified the

fleshly historical Jesus with the Christ risen in glory.
History always comes to us in unison with faith. . . .[3]

To acknowledge Jesus as the Christ is to proclaim in faith
that Jesus is the Messiah, the Anointed One of God, whom the
Jewish nation awaited. When in the scriptures Jesus asks his
disciples, "Who do you say that I am?" it is Peter who answers,
"You are the Christ" (Mark 8:29). And in St. John's gospel, near
the conclusion, the author says clearly that the gospel has been
written "to help you believe that Jesus is the Messiah, the Son
of God, so that through this faith you may have life in his name"
(John 20:31). The Jewish people lived in covenant with God.
God liberated them from the slavery of Egypt (Exodus event)
and had promised a leader, a Savior who would establish the
Kingdom of God upon earth. It is from this history and these
expectations that the followers of Jesus slowly grasped the implications of the life, death and resurrection of Jesus, the universal significance of the Christ event. Although Christians
speak now of Jesus Christ as a full name, the early followers
understood *Jesus* as the historical side of the Christ event from
the person of Jesus of Nazareth. They understood *Christ,* the
name literally means "anointed one," as the theological significance of the Christ event. Christ is the presence of God among
us, the promised Savior who is God's own Son. The Jesus of
history was recognized as the Christ of faith by the early Christian communities. The reality of God was made present in Jesus. Divinity was fleshed out in the human Jesus. Incarnation
literally means to become flesh.

Incarnation

The dogma of the Incarnation is very simply the coming together of God and humanity in Jesus. Jesus' humanity is the
unique response to divinity, a place where God's self-communication is fully received. Humanity longs for God, longs to transcend its own existence, longs to encounter God. The more open
a human being is to life, to other people and to God, the more
filled with God a person becomes. Jesus of Nazareth emptied
himself of his own desires and his own will. Jesus desired only
the will of God. He lived completely for others and for God. In
the very class-conscious system of the Jewish-Roman world, Jesus discriminated against no one. He reached out to the poor
and oppressed. He ate with sinners. Those cast aside by society

were embraced in his all-encompassing love. Since Jesus remains totally open to God, he understands himself from God's perspective. The depth of this intimate relationship enabled him to say, "I and the Father are one" (John 10:30). In the Incarnation, Christians believe that in Jesus Christ full divinity and full humanity existed in total unity. For this reason, we say Jesus is truly God and truly human. The man, Jesus of Nazareth, is not God's vehicle or receptacle, the man-Jesus is God—God who lived in the world and is part of its history. Scripture tells us, "The word was made flesh, and lived among us" (John 1:14).

Jesus of Nazareth was human like all of us. And humanity does have within its own human nature a capacity for the infinite. Human nature has been created bearing this possibility. We can empty ourselves of our own personal concerns and prejudices and fill ourselves with the concerns of others and with God. Jesus filled himself so completely with others and with God that he was able to identify with the Infinite. The Incarnation points to the ultimate destiny of all humans. In the second century, St. Irenaeus, father of the earliest church, told us that God became human so humanity could become divine. In our lives, we do experience a relationship with God, but this relationship is incomplete. Sin, alienation and selfishness limit our capacity to be filled with God. Yet, the capacity remains. Incarnation is the foundation of Christian hope for all humanity and all creation.

Infancy Narratives

Although each of the four gospels concludes with the passion, death and resurrection of Jesus, each begins differently. Mark's gospel, the earliest, begins as John the Baptist, precursor* of Jesus, is calling for repentance, "Prepare the way of the Lord" (Mark 1:2). Jesus is baptized by John, and immediately the Spirit of God, in the form of a dove, comes upon Jesus, and a voice from heaven proclaims, "You are my beloved Son" (Mark 1:10-11). Matthew's gospel offers another beginning. This evangelist, concerned that the Jewish community would recognize Jesus as the Messiah, begins with a genealogy from Abraham through the family of David to Joseph, husband of Mary. Jewish genealogy did not mention the woman's family, yet Matthew wants to be specific about Jesus being born of the Virgin Mary and the Holy Spirit. The evangelist does not actually explain how Jesus, who had no human father, could be in this lineage, but instead tells the story of Mary's conception through the Holy Spirit. Joseph, however, names the child, thus asserting his legal guardianship. The author is most interested in showing that Jesus is the fulfillment of the Old Testament prophecies. "The virgin shall be with child, and bear a son, and his name shall be Immanuel" (Isaiah 7:14). The author of Matthew's gospel was also aware of the Jewish tradition concerning the appearance of stars at the birth of God's great ones. Stars appeared in the sky at the births of the Jewish patriarchs, Abraham, Isaac, Jacob and Moses. The star of Bethlehem followed this tradition.

The traditional Christmas story is found in St. Luke's gospel. Luke's infancy narrative, written long after the significance of Jesus, the Christ, Son of God, has been established, is not offered from an historical perspective but from a theological one. He tells the marvelous account of Jesus' birth in Bethlehem, fulfilling the prophecy of Micah, "But you, Bethlehem, too small to be among the clans of Judah, from you shall come forth for me one who is to be ruler in Israel" (Micah 5:1). Luke is pointing immediately to the messianic significance of Jesus' birth in Bethlehem. The angels who proclaim his birth point to the approbation of God, while the welcoming shepherds are part of the poor who will be especially dear to Jesus in his lifetime. The virginal birth emphasizes the divine nature of Jesus' conception and birth. The evangelist stresses that this child is from God; God alone is his father. The last gospel, like the others, has its own distinctive beginning. This evangelist's focus is on the divinity of Jesus, and so he begins with a hymn to the eternal Word of God made flesh in Jesus. The beginning of Jesus' life is important to the evangelists, for they have experienced the great impact of the end of his life and his resurrection to new life. The gospel writers were not interested in bare, historical facts. The accounts of Jesus' birth are not simply stories. They were not intended as mere factual narrations, but as proclamations of the birth of the Messiah. The details surrounding the story point to a specialness, an extraordinary birth, a divine event. Their truth is a deeper truth; it is the witness of believers who joyfully tell of the nativity of God's own Son.

Christology

Christology* is the study of the relationship between Jesus of Nazareth and the eternal Son of God, the union of God and humanity, divine and human nature in the one person of Jesus

Christ. It is the perfect humanity of Jesus mediating divinity which enables us to approach divine mystery. We are aware of his divinity through the kind of human being he was. As a person of authority, Jesus used the expression, "But I say to you." He did not rely on authority from the outside. Jesus rejected the law if the law oppressed people, always placing love above laws, but not encouraging lawlessness or irresponsibility. The demands of love are stronger than the demands of the law. Jesus often frees people from the bondage of society's oppressive conventions. Jesus redefines authority as service, demanding a new lifestyle from his followers.

> You know how those who exercise authority among the Gentiles lord it over them; their great ones make their importance felt. It cannot be like that with you. Anyone among you who aspires to greatness must serve the rest, and whoever wants to rank first among you must serve the needs of all (Matthew 20:25-27).

Jesus rejected religious laws as a type of guarantee of God's favor. He was not concerned with externals. Jesus was concerned with attitudes of the heart. He required that his followers be a new type of people, fully human, open to God and others, and to life itself. Jesus offered new hope to the world. Accepting human life and loving all people, Jesus broke through the world's evil; the Kingdom of God began in Jesus. Leonardo Boff, in *Jesus Christ Liberator*, explains Jesus' attitude toward people.

> By thus overcoming the profound alienations that had encrusted humanity and its history, Jesus gave people back to themselves. In the important questions of life no thing can substitute for the human person: neither law, nor traditions, nor religion. People must decide from within, before God and before others.[4]

Through the perfect humanity of Jesus, divinity is revealed. God truly enters history; God's self-expression occurs in human events and is spoken in human language. Through the centuries, and even now in our time, religions of all cultures strive toward meeting God. Yet, at the very same time, religions often emphasize the great chasm that exists between God and God's people. Although longing for encounter, people experience distance and estrangement. Christianity experiences this divine-human encounter in Jesus Christ. Jesus assures all people that

God is not far from us, but among us. The life Jesus calls us to is a life of divine-human relationship. Karl Rahner, great Catholic theologian of the twentieth century, grounds his theology in a Christology that represents this unique fulfillment of anthropology.* Rahner believes that all human beings who fully accept and embrace their human lives implicitly accept and encounter Jesus Christ, even if they are unaware of Jesus and Christian faith. From this understanding Rahner develops his theory of the anonymous Christian.*[5]

Christology has been approached from two basic perspectives. High Christology, or Christology "from above," is offered in St. John's gospel and the letters of St. Paul. Its stress is upon the divinity and transcendence of the Risen Jesus. Low Christology, or Christology "from below," is offered in the synoptic gospels. Its stress is upon the humanity of Jesus, God among us. As we have seen Jesus, the Christ, is fully God and fully human. Catholic doctrine always holds in tension the two natures of Christ.

In Christology "from below," we see the human Jesus experiencing life as we do. "Against all tendencies to deify Jesus, it must constantly be stressed even today that he was wholly and entirely man with all the consequences of this (capacity for suffering, fear, loneliness, insecurity, temptation, doubts, possibility of error). Not merely man, but true man."[6] He was understood initially as a teacher-prophet of first century Palestine. This human Jesus gradually grasps his own identity and messianic role. His death on the cross resulting from conflicts with Jewish and Roman authorities, is understood as an expression of complete human integrity and total love. Christology "from below" emphasizes the resurrection and the unity between the Jesus before the resurrection and the Jesus following the resurrection. In low Christology, salvation for others comes through personal commitment to Jesus and Jesus' lifestyle. Emphasis is given to the ongoing presence of Jesus and the Kingdom of God among us.

In Christology "from above," we see a Jesus fully aware from his birth of his identity as God's Son and of his role as Messiah, One sent from God. The emphasis is on the Incarnation, the pre-existent Word of God, second person of the Trinity, becoming human at a point in history. The understanding of Jesus' death on the cross is an act of perfect sacrifice, "laying down his life for our sins." This act saves us, restoring our relationship with

God after humanity's fall from grace. Jesus redeems us, and salvation is ours through baptism and living the will of God as discerned by the authority of the church. High Christology points to the tremendous gulf between God and us, which was bridged by Jesus. Low Christology stresses the unity of God and us, which Jesus made possible. It was during medieval times that Christology became "so high" that a balance was needed. The search for the historical Jesus, following the Reformation, provided that balance. In modern times, with its great valuing of personal experience, we look to the human Jesus to understand the divine.

Christological Heresies and Councils

The church of the first centuries struggled with its articulation of Jesus' identity. Monotheism* was a central and deeply cherished belief of the Jewish people. "Our God is One." Understanding Jesus as God, or even God's Son, presented immense difficulties to the Hebrew mind. The early fathers of the church were faced with innumerable heresies which denied the full humanity or full divinity of Jesus. These heresies were the effort of well-meaning thinkers in the church to specify exactly the mode of the Incarnation. Christological issues shook the very foundations of Christianity. The New Testament clearly understands that the man Jesus was confirmed by God through resurrection. He was the long-awaited Messiah, the Suffering Servant, spoken of by the prophet Isaiah. God had been present to his people through Jesus of Nazareth, and God's Kingdom was at hand. The primitive church celebrated the Christ event and lived guided by His Spirit. It was contact with other cultures that began to raise questions. Gentiles and Greeks began to ask, "In what sense was Jesus the Son of God?" As the church moved into an open-ended universalist situation, such questions had to be considered.

The Jews and the Hellenistic* world shared the understanding of the Logos. *Logos* means word or reason. It was understood as the all-pervading principle of rationality of the universe. For the Jewish people, this idea was actually the basis of religion; this rational principle was God's active presence in the world, in history. Greek philosophy also accepted an overarching principle of truth and rationality in the universe. The author of John's gospel was familiar with Hebrew and Hellenistic thought. Jesus was presented as the Logos made human, the

"Word made Flesh." Thus, Jesus was understood as the key to all of history and the universe. Jesus, the Christ of faith, was given universal appeal. The divine principle walked among us. In carrying this understanding to an extreme, heresies emerged. Docetism,* a Gentile heresy, developed before the end of the New Testament period. Docetists could not separate themselves from the Greek philosophic notion of a transcendent God, far above the world. Greek philosophy placed the spiritual and the intellectual far above the realm of the physical. For Aristotle it was human reason that pointed to divinity. The Greek God could not be involved with creation, could not have feelings or a body. They concluded Jesus only appeared to have a body. He did not actually suffer and die. St. Jerome angrily criticized the Docetists. "The blood of Christ was still fresh in Judea when his body was said to be a phantom."

Gnosticism* and Arianism* were heresies that nearly extinguished the Christian conception of God. The Gnostics believed that salvation is based on the communication of some special divine knowledge, totally above the prison of the physical, material world. Jesus, therefore, did not have a physical body, but was a mystical figure who offered the knowledge that saves. Docetists and Gnostics denied the humanity of Jesus. St. Ignatius of Antioch (110 A.D.) defended staunchly Jesus' humanity, understanding that if Jesus "were not part of humanity, he cannot be the Savior of humanity." In the very beginning of the third century, St. Irenaeus wrote a long treatise against false Gnostics, stressing the full humanity and divinity of the Savior. It was Arius, a priest of Alexandria in the early fourth century, who led a heresy that nearly rent Christianity apart. Arius clung to the Hellenistic understanding of God as unknowable, unchangeable and unreachable. The incarnation of such a being was impossible. Christ, for Arius, was a subordinate, a created deity, a type of demi-god, a mediator between the unknowable Godhead and the created world. This controversy had the whole world taking sides. The Emperor Constantine eventually called the first Ecumenical Council that met at Nicaea in 325. Not without bitter disputes, the Council fathers condemned Arius and Arianism, drawing up the Nicene Creed.

> We believe in one God, Father, all sovereign, maker of all things seen and unseen, and in one Lord Jesus Christ, the Son of God, begotten from the Father as only begotten, that is from the substance of the Fa-

ther, God from God, light from light, true God from true God, begotten not made, one in being with the Father, through whom all things came into existence, the things in heaven and the things on the earth, who because of us men and our salvation came down and was incarnated, made man, suffered and arose on the third day, ascended into heaven, comes to judge the living and the dead; and in one Holy Spirit.

After the Council of Nicaea, two theological schools, one in Antioch, Syria, and the other in Alexandria, Egypt, took opposite perspectives on the Christological problem. The Alexandrian school emphasized the divinity of Christ and the unity between the Word of God and the flesh of Jesus. The extreme position of the Alexandrian school was taken up by a saintly scholar, Bishop Apollinarius. Apollinarius explained that the divine Logos taking flesh in Jesus replaced the human spirit, the human mind. This attempt at explaining the unity of God and humanity was unacceptable, for the Apollinarian union was between God and only the body part of humanity. The Church rejected Apollinarius' theory, always insisting that Jesus, the Christ, was fully human. The perspective of the School of Antioch stressed Jesus' humanity. Again, extreme positions were explored. Nestorius, a monk at a monastery near Antioch and later Bishop of Constantinople, so emphasized the humanity of Jesus that he denied that Mary was the Mother of God. This position was very unpopular among the people devoted to Mary. At the Council of Ephesus (431), the Church condemned the view of Nestorius, asserting that Mary was not only the Mother of Christ, but the Mother of God. The great Christological Council of Chalcedon (451) worked out a synthesis between the Alexandrian and Antiochene schools. The council's formula, "One Lord, Jesus Christ, one and the same Son, perfect in his divinity and humanity," satisfied the Alexandrians. "Truly God, truly man of a rational soul and a body of one nature with the Father, consubstantial...like us in all but sin," satisfied the School of Antioch. Several heresies did continue, but for the most part, the compromise of Chalcedon settled these questions in the West. The language of Chalcedon presents difficulties to modern theologians; yet, its great work remains foundational to traditional Christological theology even today.

The Message and Ministry of Jesus

What did Jesus say? What did he speak about to the crowds that followed him? What did he do? Jesus proclaimed the gospel, the good news that God, our Creator, accepts us, believes in us and loves us, and desires to be deeply involved in our lives. Jesus touched peoples' lives. He healed them of their hurts and sickness, and Jesus forgave their sins. Jesus was understood by the people around him as a prophet. Jesus calls himself a prophet, when speaking in the synagogue at Nazareth. "No prophet gains acceptance in his own country" (Luke 4:24). Often those about him called him a prophet. The Jewish people understood the authority of a prophet, a messenger from God. Jesus' authority offered a new dimension to the ordinary authority of a prophet. His use of the "Amen" was one indication. In *The Reality of Jesus,* Dermot A. Lane explains this point.

> The normal practice for a Jew was to conclude his prayer to God with the expression 'Amen' in the hope that God would act on it, whereas Jesus prefaces his words with an 'Amen', thereby indicating a prior rapport with God.[7]

The listeners of Jesus surely picked up this indication of a special relationship with God. Even more startling were Jesus' compassion and words of forgiveness to sinners. Jews believed those who committed sin were to be shunned, for they had broken the covenant with God. The Jews were more than amazed when this prophet, Jesus, went out to sinners and spoke forgiveness to them. His words and actions offered healing for the broken relationship between God and the outcasts. One of the highest priorities of Jesus was forgiveness and healing. Jesus believed in people; he stood for second chances. He wanted no one to remain frozen in their sinfulness. Jesus went out to all those who needed healing. When the scribes complained to his disciples about Jesus eating with sinners, he described himself as a physician.

> People who are healthy do not need a doctor; sick people do. I have come to call sinners, not the self-righteous (Mark 2:17).

Jesus promised salvation to all. He excluded no one. Yet, his demands were strong. He spoke of a new lifestyle. Externals of the law, even religious law, were not to be cherished above intrinsic goodness. His law was the great commandment: Love of God and neighbor. This message was difficult for the religious Jew, whose religious laws had the authoritative impact of their God, Yahweh. To them, disregarding the law of the sabbath was real blasphemy.* Jesus was acting like God and calling Yahweh his Father (John 5:18). Good and conscientious Jews were unable to accept such a prophet who put himself above the law. In our day, the Church must continually check its own authority, careful not to put itself above the law of love. Catholic Christians, of good conscience, listen to the Church's authority, seeking the help of its tradition, yet are called beyond to respond to Jesus and his radical ethic of interior love.

The Kingdom of God

Jesus proclaimed the Kingdom of God. This expression is mentioned 122 times in the Gospels; 90 times in the words of Jesus. Jesus understands himself as the beginning of the Kingdom. The Kingdom of God is not territorial or national; it is the reign of God. The Kingdom is present when people treat one another with love, when they view others from God's perspective, when God's love is the accepted rule. Jesus is the Kingdom, for his perspective is God's. Origen, ancient father of the church, says that Jesus was the *autobasileia,* the Kingdom in person. In Jesus, the reign of God was truly at hand.

Jesus continually spoke to his friends about God's Kingdom. The Kingdom, already present in Jesus, would usher in a new order. People of the Kingdom would respond to each other in a new way. St. Paul understood God's Kingdom in Christ. In his letter to the people of Galatia, he describes the followers of Jesus, people of God's Kingdom.

> Each one of you is a son of God because of your faith in Christ Jesus. All of you who have been baptized into Christ have clothed yourselves with him. There does not exist among you Jew or Greek, slave or freeman, male or female. All are one in Christ Jesus. (Galatians 3:27-28)

Jesus amazed his listeners in many ways. He made no distinctions among people. All were accepted and loved. In his day, women were completely oppressed. Jewish men did not even speak to women, even their own wives, in public. Yet, Jesus treated women as equals. Among his disciples were women.

The egalitarian relationship that Jesus had with women is significant in his ministry and in the concept of the new life of the Kingdom of God. (Jesus' relationship with women will be more fully developed in Chapter 9, which includes feminist theology. Included also will be Jesus' relationship to Mary, his mother, and Mary's relationship to the Church.)

The Jewish understanding of the Kingdom of God developed through the ages. Jews believed the new order would be a time of prosperity and peace. Life would return to the harmony of paradise. The prophet, Isaiah, of the Old Testament, described this new era by contrasting images of wild and tame animals. In God's Kingdom, all would live in harmony.

> Then the wolf shall be a guest of the lamb. And the leopard shall lie down with the kid. The calf and the young lion shall browse together, with a little child to guide them. The cow and the bear shall be neighbors, together their young shall rest; the lion shall eat hay like the ox (Isaiah 11:6-7).

The Jewish people expected a messiah who would begin this new age, this new lifestyle. During Jesus' time the Jewish people were suffering under Roman rule. Their expectations of a new order had narrowed and were now focused upon a triumph over the Romans. Jesus' listeners were eager for victory from oppression. They longed for a leader who would crush their enemies. In addition to these hopes of nationalistic triumph was an apocalyptic* hope for a "new heaven and a new earth." The Jewish mind pictured their nation's final triumph at the end of time. John the Baptist, prophet and forerunner of Jesus, proclaimed the immediacy of the reign of God. "Reform your lives! The reign of God is at hand!" (Matthew 3:2).

Jesus preached a different kingdom. His understanding did not include military victory. It did not include the suppression of any people, but a new order where all would live as equals. Leonardo Boff explains it this way.

> The preaching of Jesus about the kingdom of God concerns not only persons demanding conversion of them. It also affects the world of persons in terms of a liberation from legalism, from conventions without foundation, from authoritarianism and the forces and powers that subject people.[8]

Jesus was, however, also part of the apocalyptic framework. He speaks of the Kingdom in two ways. For Jesus, the Kingdom is not simply near, as John the Baptist proclaimed; the Kingdom is dawning. It is here. To proclaim the Kingdom, Jesus used the familiar words of Isaiah, the prophet, describing the vindication of the Jewish people and the coming of God's reign (Isaiah 35:5-6). "The blind recover their sight, cripples walk, lepers are cured, the deaf hear, dead mean are raised to life, and the poor have the good news preached to them" (Matthew 11:5).

Jesus also speaks of a future dimension of the Kingdom. "I assure you that whoever does not accept the reign of God like a little child *shall* not take part in it" (Luke 10:15). The Beatitudes, included in Matthew's and Luke's gospels, are the core of Jesus' teaching about the call for radical conversion, the new lifestyle of the reign of God. The Beatitudes announce spiritual blessings and fulfillment for the poor and suffering. The Beatitudes speak a future fulfillment; they speak of a time when the reign of God will exist in totality.

> Happy are those who know they are spiritually poor; the Kingdom of heaven belongs to them!
> Happy are those who mourn; God will comfort them!
> Happy are those who are humble; they will receive what God has promised!
> Happy are those whose greatest desire is to do what God requires; God will satisfy them fully!
> Happy are those who are merciful to others; God will be merciful to them!
> Happy are the pure in heart; they will see God!
> Happy are those who work for peace; God will call them his children!
> Happy are those who are persecuted because they do what God requires; the Kingdom of heaven belongs to them!

The Beatitudes are the heart of Jesus' teaching. They assure the lowly ones of Israel (*Anawim*) of a future of happiness and contentment. In the words of Jesus, there is a definite tension between the present in-break of God's Kingdom and the future fulfillment of the Kingdom. This tension of "now" and "not yet" is not one of inconsistency. Jesus is saying that the present is not devoid of salvation. Instead, the present is most precious; the present and future aspects of God's Kingdom are bound together. In Jesus, hope for the future demands faith in the present.[9]

Parables

Jesus speaks of the Kingdom indirectly in parables. He offers stories and vivid images to his listeners to awaken their minds and hearts to the Kingdom. Parables are short narratives that use ordinary situations and ordinary people as comparisons to spiritual concepts. Parables are a marvelous teaching tool. They offer information, look for response, yet do not force meaning upon the listener. Parables draw the listeners into the story, enabling them to test its impact on their own life situation. Parables remain open-ended, food for continued thought. C.H. Dodd, biblical scholar, offers the classic definition.

> At its simplest, the parable is a metaphor or simile, drawn from nature or common life, arresting the hearer by its vividness or strangeness, and leaving the mind in sufficient doubt about its precise application to tease it into active thought.[10]

Jesus offers many parables of the Kingdom. He compares it to a mustard seed, smallest of all seeds, but one that grows into the largest of plants (Matthew 13:31-33). He tells his listeners God's Kingdom is like a field where wheat and weeds grow together until harvest (Matthew 13:24-30). Jesus speaks of yeast kneaded by a woman into a large measure of flour until the whole mass begins to rise (Luke 13:20). The Kingdom is like a buried treasure found in a field or the pearl of great price for which one sells every other possession (Matthew 13:4-46).

The world remembers many of Jesus' great teachings through his parables. Jesus preached love of neighbor several times, yet the parable of the Good Samaritan makes the greatest impact. The Jews hated the Samaritans. Political and religious conflicts had existed between these people for seven centuries. The Samaritans had separated themselves from the religious influence of Jerusalem, building their own temple on Mt. Gerizim. The antagonism between Samaritans and Jews was very deep. Yet, it is a Samaritan whom Jesus makes the hero of his parable. This Samaritan treats the wounded man with tenderness and compassion after a priest and Levite, respected members of the Jewish community, have passed by. The Jews listening to Jesus were startled and, perhaps, annoyed by the vignette; yet, the definition of a good neighbor was inescapable (Luke 10:25-37). After his cure of the ten lepers, Jesus also points favorably to the behavior of a Samaritan. Leprosy was a dreaded skin disease, very contagious and, in those times, incurable. Lepers were completely separated from and shunned by society. One cannot help thinking in our times of AIDS sufferers. Jesus has great pity on all lepers. In this account, he cures all ten lepers, instructing them to go show themselves to the priest. The one who returns to thank Jesus, "praising God in a loud voice," was a foreigner, a Samaritan. Jesus relates his gratitude to faith, which is a sign of the Kingdom. "Your faith has been your salvation" (Luke 17:11-17).

Jesus' priority of forgiveness and divine mercy is the focus of several parables. The man who leaves his ninety-nine sheep to search for one that is lost and rejoices, hoisting the lost sheep upon his shoulders, is an image of the forgiveness God offers all people and desires them to offer each other. The woman who finds the lost coin calls in her neighbors for a celebration. Jesus notes the great joy that God experiences over even one repentant sinner (Luke 15:1-10). The prodigal son parable, sometimes called the generous father, describes God's eager forgiveness even after deep hurt. The Jewish listeners were poignantly aware of the depth of sin that a young man would commit, if he turned against his family and demanded his inheritance before the death of his father. The family's shame would be overwhelming. Jesus understood the feelings of his listeners. He was part of the Jewish tradition. Again, he points out that externals are not the essence; the young man's change of heart, his repentance, is the key. The father of the returned son forgives and embraces him immediately. He stands on no ceremony; he holds no grudges. He throws a party. This jubilant party-thrower is an image of our God who, Jesus has told us, rejoices in our repentance.

Miracles

The miracles of Jesus are sometimes a stumbling block for the modern mind. Yet, the miracles are part of our earliest tradition. St. Mark, the first evangelist, develops his gospel around miracle stories. Scripture scholars tell us that many of the nature miracle stories are projections back into the earthly life of Jesus, from a post-Resurrection/Easter perspective. The stories of the raising of Jairus' daughter, the son of the widow of Naim and Lazarus, point to the Risen Jesus clearly as the Lord over life and death. Yet, all exegetes* concur that Jesus does actually perform miracles. The terms used in the gospel are *dunameis* (acts of power) and *semeia* (signs). These events are signs causing great wonder. The Jewish mind was familiar with the great miracles of the Hebrew scriptures. The Old Testament does not view nature as reality but as God's creation. Therefore, the signs performed by Jesus turned the minds and hearts of his followers to God, the author of all creation, all reality. Modern thinkers must consider scientific causes and principles. Nonetheless, the ultimate nature of the entire system of causality in creation cannot simply be answered by science. The ultimate meaning of all existence draws into active play philosophical and theological considerations.

In the gospels, Jesus' miracles are signs that the Kingdom of God has arrived. They can be understood against the whole backdrop of belief in a new age, in a new world, where sin, sickness and decay would be overcome. The prophecies of the Old Testament expected those wondrous signs. "The blind see; the lame walk." These miracles show the presence of God's power in Jesus. "But if it is by the finger of God that I cast out devils, then the reign of God is upon you" (Luke 11:20). The Kingdom of God preached by Jesus is a Kingdom of empowerment. The world is cherished and exalted; the world's great power of love is released by the "in-break" of the Kingdom. "The intensity of creation's independence grows in direct and not inverse ratio to the intensity of God's action."[11] Many of Jesus' miracles point to Jesus' authority which always raises love above legalism. The author of Mark tells us the Pharisees began their plot with the Herodians to destroy Jesus after witnessing his cure of a man with a shriveled hand on the Sabbath (Mark 3:1-6). In the midst of these challenges, Jesus insists that "The sabbath was made for man, not man for the sabbath" (Matthew 2:27). Jesus also performed signs of wonder accompanying the forgiveness of sins. When challenged with charges of blasphemy ("Who can forgive sins except God alone?"), Jesus healed a paralytic. " 'That you may know that the Son of Man has authority on earth to forgive sins,' (he said to the paralyzed man), 'I command you: Stand up! Pick up your mat and go home' " (Mark 2:1-12). The miracle stories point to faith, faith in the arrival of the Kingdom through Jesus, faith in God's overwhelming care for all people and all creation.

The real object of this belief is not various extraordinary phenomena, but God. What Jesus' miracles are ultimately saying is that in Jesus God was carrying out his plan, and that God acted in him for the salvation of humankind and the world.[12]

The Paschal Mystery

The Pasch, or Passover, is the Hebrew celebration of Israel's deliverance from Egypt. The original tradition indicates that the word itself comes from *pasah,* "to passover," as the Lord passed over the houses marked with the blood of a lamb. The tradition of Exodus in the Old Testament tells us these houses of the Jewish people were spared from the plagues which God sent to Egypt. Later the "passing over" was connected with the people's own exodus, as God led them out of Egypt to the promised land. In Jewish thought, this memorial celebration recalled God's redemptive act, intervening to save his people. For Christians, the paschal celebration commemorates the death and Resurrection of Jesus, the Savior. When St. Paul speaks of Christ as our Savior, he says, "Our paschal lamb has been sacrificed" (1 Corinthians 5:7). In the liturgical worship of the church, we pray, "Lamb of God, who takes away the sins of the world, have mercy on us." As the Jewish Passover recalls their nation's covenant with God, the Christian Easter feast celebrates the new and eternal covenant all people have in Christ.

The popularity of Jesus among the people, especially the poor and outcasts, caused much concern among the Jewish authorities. His words often stung the rich and people of power and privilege. He was labeled a trouble-maker (John 7:11). Jesus was relentless in his fight against meaningless externals and legalities. He was interested in hearts (Luke 16:15). Jesus angered the Pharisees and scribes, experts on the Jewish law, by attacking religious fanaticism and hypocrisy. He insisted that only what emerges from within a person, and nothing else, makes one impure (Mark 7:1-23). Eventually, his enemies banded together in their plots against him. Aware of their plans, Jesus, nonetheless, proceeded to Jerusalem to celebrate the Jewish Passover feast with his friends. Despite whisperings of the chief priests' plot to kill Jesus, crowds of his followers welcomed him, proclaiming him King of Israel as he entered Jerusalem. They hailed him, waving palm branches as he passed. "Hosanna!

Blessed is he who comes in the name of the Lord! Blessed is the King of Israel" (John 12:12).

Each of the gospels relates the story of the Last Supper. The Passover meal Jesus ate with his friends becomes central to faith in Jesus and to the coming of the Kingdom. Jesus believed that his fate would be sealed in Jerusalem. Jesus understands himself as God's eschatological* representative. His life and message had centered upon the coming of God's Kingdom, new life in a new age. His call for radical conversion demands a complete breaking off with the present age. A focus of St. Luke's gospel is an anticipation of the coming of the Kingdom. His words focus upon its eschatological significance. Jesus understood himself as of God, One bringing about the total coming of the Kingdom.

> When the hour arrived, he took his place at table, and the apostles with him. He said to them: I have greatly desired to eat this Passover with you before I suffer. I tell you I will not eat again until it is fullfilled in the Kingdom of God (Luke 22:14-16).

Jesus certainly was aware of the Jewish apocalyptic belief that, before the final breakthrough of God's reign, the forces of good and evil would do battle. In view of the failure of his own ministry, the opposition of the authorities and the plots of his enemies, Jesus surely must have considered the possibility of great suffering or violent death. Yet Jesus remains faithful, bearing his fears. He prays in the Garden of Gethsemane before his betrayal. "Abba (O Father), you have the power to do all things. Take this cup away from me. But let it be as you would have it, not as I" (Mark 14:36).

From this eschatological perspective, Jesus' death on the cross is not just the consequence of his courageous integrity and radical preaching, but the final summit of his whole message. Within the conditions of the times, total loyalty to the Kingdom of God resulted in a powerlessness, a desolation and, ultimately, in death. In unwavering faith, Jesus died leaving the way of the Kingdom's coming to his Father. Through the disappointment of betrayal, the loneliness of a mockery trial and the intense suffering of crucifixion, Jesus had remained faithful to God. He did not compromise with the pre-established religious laws and structures. He died as he lived, consumed by the Will of God. Crucifixion, carried out by the Roman authorities, convinced many that God had abandoned Jesus. Death by crucifixion was a clear sign of shame and failure.

The early Church did not fully comprehend the meaning of Jesus' death until after the resurrection. Dietrich Bonhoeffer, reflecting from a Nazi prison camp during World War II, sums up the meaning of Jesus' death and its continued challenge to all believers.

> Jesus does not call us to a new religion. Jesus calls us to life. What sort of life? To participate in the weakness of God in the world.[13]

Resurrection

There were no actual witnesses to Jesus' resurrection. The New Testament provides no description of the event. What is known more clearly is what happened to the apostles. After the death of Jesus, the apostles scattered in fear. It was Joseph of Arimathea, "an upright and holy member of the Sanhedrin, who had not been associated with their plan of action, who laid Jesus' body in a tomb hewn out of rock" (Luke 23:50-53). Yet within a few days, these same fearful apostles were proclaiming Jesus as Lord. The four gospels and St. Paul's letters speak of the risen Jesus. The women—Mary Magdalene, Mary, the mother of James, and Salome—arrived early on the day following the Sabbath to anoint Jesus with perfumed oil. They found the empty tomb. An angel told them Jesus had risen. While the women were carrying the good news back to the disciples, Jesus himself, appeared to them (Matthew 28:1-10). Interestingly enough, the testimony of the women is particularly strong. If the evangelists had decided to falsify the story of Jesus' resurrection, they certainly would not have chosen women as witnesses. Women were second class citizens in the Jewish community. Just like children, they were not even allowed to testify in legal situations. The disciples themselves refused to believe Mary Magdalene's testimony. The gospels also record Jesus' appearance to two disciples on the road to Emmaus, to the eleven apostles, and to Peter and the other disciples at the sea of Tiberias. St. Paul speaks of his appearance to "five hundred brothers at once," and "Last of all he was seen by me" (1 Corinthians 15:6-8). The appearances of the risen Jesus do cause some problems. Was Jesus now only a spirit? "While they were still speaking about all this, he himself stood in their midst.

'Peace to you,' he said. In their panic and fright they thought they were seeing a ghost" (Luke 24:36-37). Jesus understood their fear. He asked them to touch him and even give him something to eat. Jesus had been transfigured, yet, he was recognizable. He was not pure spirit. There was a difference in Jesus, yet there was a definite continuity between the pre-resurrection and the post-resurrection Jesus. The resurrection is not the resuscitation of a corpse; it is a radical transformation. Jesus' resurrection was an actual, concrete beginning of the new life of God's Kingdom. All Jesus said and did was confirmed by God through the reality of resurrection.

Death has been overcome. Life is not hopeless, even in the face of oppression, meaningless suffering and even death. The core of Christian faith rests on Jesus' resurrection. St. Paul tells us that "all will be brought to life in Christ" (1 Corinthians 20:22). Jesus realizes fully his humanness, and God gives him new life—life no longer threatened by alienation or death. This new life is Kingdom life. The faith of Jesus' followers in his resurrection was an empowering faith. The men and women who believed in him gradually came to understand the significance of his words, of his forgiving, healing acts and of his death. They began to accept the violent death of Jesus as redemptive. The potential of humanity was once again affirmed, for Jesus had accepted the cross out of love and desire for the emergence of God's Kingdom. Various interpretations were offered by the early church in their grappling with the crucifixion. They recalled the suffering servant prophecies of Isaiah. "Through his suffering my servant shall justify many, and their guilt he shall bear" (Isaiah 53:11). In the epistle to the Romans, St. Paul speaks of Jesus' death as sacrificial expiation for the world's sins (Romans 3:25). In the second letter to the Corinthians, St. Paul explains that "for our sakes God made him who did not know sin, to be sin, so that in him we might become the very holiness of God" (2 Corinthians 5:21). Jesus' disciples were empowered by Christ to form communities of love, sharing their possessions and serving one another. They proclaimed their faith in Jesus as Lord, beyond the Jewish community to all people. Gradually, they understood that Jesus' life and death and Resurrection had universal significance. The very destiny of humankind was involved in this new reality. The summary explanation Leonardo Boff, liberation theologian, offers on the meaning of Jesus' death and resurrection reflects the oppression and suffering still prevalent in the world.

> . . . we ought to say that Christ's death was a consequence of the atmosphere of ill-will, hatred, and selfishness in which the Jews and all humanity lived and still live today. Jesus did not allow himself to be determined by this situation, but loved us to the end. He took on himself this perverted condition; he was in solidarity with us. He died alone so that no one else in the world would die alone; he is with each person so that all might partake of the life that manifested itself in the resurrection; eternal life in communion with God, with others, and with the cosmos.[14]

Images of Jesus for Today

Even in this brief discussion of Jesus and his universal significance, many different aspects of Jesus, the Christ, have emerged. Many images are offered in scripture. Messiah means anointed. In the Hebrew tradition, it was the designation of a King, a Son of David, one who would bring about the definitive salvation of his people at the end of time. Gradually, people came to understand Jesus as Messiah and King, though his mission and his Kingdom are startlingly different from anything previously experienced. The title, Son of God—most often found in John's gospel—points to the sonship of Jesus, where the words of Jesus stress his union with his Father. In St. John's gospel, Jesus also calls himself the Good Shepherd. The title, Son of Man, originates in the Old Testament. It denotes the tradition of the eschatological figure believed to be created before the creation of the world. Until judgment day, this Son of Man was to be hidden with God in heaven. His manifestation would signal the end of the world. Also from the Old Testament, especially in the book of the prophet Isaiah, we read of the Suffering Servant image. This servant is to receive glory and salvation for others through profound humiliation. Jesus is also called rabbi, a Hebrew teacher of the law and the scripture, a prophet, one who speaks for God and in the sacrificial context of the Passover, Lamb of God. In the letters of St. Paul, as part of the author's developed theology, Jesus is called the New Adam and the High Priest, as one who atones for the sin of the first man and a cultic figure who offers his own life in sacrifice to

God. In the Acts of the Apostles, Christ is imaged as the corner-stone of the Church which has been raised from the foundation of the prophets and apostles.

In modern times, believers have developed new images or models of Jesus. No image could ever capture the totality of Jesus. Yet images serve us well in relating to Jesus in our own lives. Although the Council of Chalcedon (451) held in tension the humanity and divinity of Christ, the image of Jesus Christ as the eternally begotten Son of God, second person of the Blessed Trinity, became the predominant model to express his significance. This model placed Jesus in the divine framework of the Trinity. From this perspective, the Incarnation and his birth into human history were viewed. The meaning of his min-istry and his passion, death, resurrection and exaltation were grounded in his pre-existent divine sonship. This image re-mained the paradigm* for fifteen hundred years, articulating a Christology "from above" to answer all questions concerning Je-sus. In this model, problems of human weakness and sin can be easily handled.

> If the theology of Jesus is taken from above, then all questions of sin and temptation must be considered as the possibility of sin on the part of the Second Person of the Blessed Trinity and the possibility of tempting the Logos. All such considerations come immediately to naught.[15]

As Second Person of the Trinity, Jesus' divinity is emphasized; his humanity, though never denied, is somehow soft-pedaled. Roman Catholics remained faithful to this model for centuries. It served well the teaching of the church, as founded upon di-vine revelation, and provided security for the faith of its mem-bership. Nonetheless, in our own day, the paradigm has begun to shift. The shift of major paradigms points to a dramatic change in religious understanding. The biblical search for the historical Jesus influenced this shift. It was the return of the Catholic Church to its roots in holy scripture that brought ques-tions to this model. Very little can be found in scripture to sup-port the Second Person of the Trinity. The New Testament does speak of God as Father, Son and Spirit, yet the understanding of God, as Trinity, is not fully developed in New Testament times. This model, although capable of offering ultimate theological an-swers, does not offer people an understanding of Jesus, as one like us, who really understands human feelings and frustrations because he shared them. The Vatican II Council offered a theological approach grounded in human experience which opened the doors to new models. With this broadening of understanding of Christology, new perspectives in the Catholic Church did appear and new images of Jesus renewed the ancient faith of Catholic people.

Following the Second Vatican Council, several models of Jesus emerged in theological circles and in the faith of the people. The model, Man for others, was introduced by Anglican Bishop, J.A.T. Robinson, in his book, *Honest to God*. Robinson developed his work from the theology of Bonhoeffer and the great Protestant liberal theologian, Paul Tillich. Bishop Robinson wanted to emphasize the humanity of Christ so that believers would be challenged to model their lives after him. It was Jesus who totally emptied himself out of love for others and, in so doing, perfected his own humanity and was one with God.

> It is the life of the 'man for others,' the love whereby we are brought completely into one with the Ground of our being, manifesting itself in the unreconciled relationships of our existence. It was manifested supremely on the Cross, but it is met wherever the Christ is shown forth and recognized . . . the Christian community exists, not to promote a new religion, but simply to be the embodiment of this new being as love.[16]

Faith in Jesus is faith in a life of kingdom-building, a life of serving, reconciling the world to God. This image appeals to women and men who dedicate their lives to the care of the sick and the poor. They live united to Jesus, the Servant.

The charismatic-pentecostal movements of the 1960s gave birth to another image of Jesus. This image of Jesus, as my Savior, was never absent from Catholic tradition. Yet, in the last few decades, it has become far more accepted. Believers who relate to Jesus as their personal Savior are interested in spirituality and their souls' salvation. The power of Jesus to forgive sins, heal one's soul and one's body is a major concern to them. Fr. O'Grady describes this model, focusing on dependence on personal commitment.

> The call for a commitment in faith to Jesus, as personal savior, emphasizes the role of individual faith as the foundation of Christianity. We cannot go through

the motions of being committed to faith without the
personal relationship to the Lord.[17]

This model offers believers great personal comfort. It is an
ecumenical model. The lines of religious denominations are easily crossed through love of the Savior. Television evangelists,
perhaps, are the extreme examples of this model.

Another model offered in modern times is Jesus, as the human face of God. Jesus offered all people a new understanding
of God. The Father he spoke of was not the vengeful God of the
Old Testament, but a God of love and intimacy—*Abba*. This
model preserves the historicity of Jesus and yet offers him in his
totality as the manifestation of the living God. Believers are
encouraged to truly know God through Jesus. The chasm between divinity and humanity falls away when we consider Jesus
as the human face of God. This image is very scriptural. In St.
John's gospel (14:9), Jesus tells his followers that "Whoever has
seen me has seen the Father." This model brings Christology
into the lives of ordinary believers who can easily relate to Jesus, as the human face of God.[18]

The approach of liberation theology, which has come from the
third world countries—especially Latin America, describes Jesus
as a Liberator. This model—Jesus the Liberator—is related to
the Lord's preaching on the Kingdom of God. Its deepest roots
are in the Old Testament, God liberating the Israelite nation
from the oppression of the Egyptians. This model has found life
in many small-group communities of the southern hemisphere.
It springs from the faith of impoverished, oppressed people who
long to be free. This image challenges the present-day Church
and its self-understanding. Christ, the Liberator, is the model of
the Church of the poor. (A further treatment of this model and
its foundation in liberation theology will be offered in Chapter
9.)

Jesus has made more impact on civilization than any other
figure of history. Christian believers know him as alive in today's world. His is remembered whenever people relate to one
another as people of God's Kingdom. For it was Jesus who
made the Kingdom actual; and it is God who will bring it to
fulfillment. The message of Jesus is a message of hope. In and
through Jesus, we know that humanity has been redeemed and
all of creation is loved by God. No matter what, life is not

meaningless. Jesus has made its meaning divine. "I have come to give you life, that you might live it to the full" (John 10:10).

Endnotes

1. F. Schleiermacher, *Das Leben Jesu,* Section 1, Volume 1 (Berlin, Germany: 1864), p. 35.

2. A. Schweitzer, *Geschichte de Leben-Jesu-Forschung,* Second Edition (Tubingen, Germany: 1913), p. 4.

3. Leonardo Boff, *Jesus Christ Liberator* (Maryknoll, NY: Orbis Books, 1978), p. 19.

4. Boff, op. cit., p. 78.

5. Walter Kasper, *Jesus, The Christ* (New York: Paulist Press, 1976), pp. 49-50.

6. Hans Kung, *On Being a Christian* (Garden City, NY: Doubleday and Company, Inc., 1976), p. 449.

7. Dermot A. Lane, *The Reality of Jesus* (New York: Paulist Press, 1975), p. 36.

8. Boff, op. cit., p. 72.

9. Eta Linneman, *Parables of Jesus* (Holy Trinity Church, London: SPCK, 1966), p. 38.

10. C.H. Dodd, *The Parables of the Kingdom* (New York: Scribner and Company, 1961), p. 16.

11. Kasper, op. cit., p. 95.

12. Ibid., p. 98. Note: I am primarily indebted to Walter Kasper's discussion of miracles for the material in the section on miracles. See *Jesus, The Christ,* pp. 89-99.

13. Dietrich Bonhoeffer, *Letters and Papers from Prison* (New York: Macmillan, 1953), pp. 347-348.

14. Boff, op. cit., p. 133.

15. John F. O'Grady, *Models of Jesus* (Garden City, New York: Doubleday and Company, Inc., 1981), p. 43.

16. J.A.T. Robinson, *Honest to God* (Philadelphia PA: Westminster Press, 1963), p. 82.

17. O'Grady, op. cit., p. 148.

18. Ibid., pp. 112-114.

Glossary

Anonymous Christian: Karl Rahner's theory which states that all human beings who live according to authentic human values, even if they are unaware, are experiencing life in Christ.

Anthropology: The study of humans and their culture. From a theological perspective, the study of humanity as related to God.

Apocalyptic: Pertaining to a thinking which emphasizes predictions, visions and signs of a future beyond history, to be accomplished by divine power.

Arianism: A heresy condemned by the Council of Nicaea (325), which believed that the Son of God was the highest of all creatures, but subordinate to God.

Blasphemy: The act of insulting or showing a lack of reverence for God.

Christology: The theological study of Jesus Christ, fully human and fully divine.

Docetism: A heresy that believed that Jesus Christ did not really have a human body.

Eschatological: Pertaining to a theological perspective which views all reality in the light of the future coming of the Kingdom of God.

Exegetes: Scholars involved in scriptural interpretation.

Gentiles: People who are not Jewish.

Gnosticism: The earliest Christian heresy which believed Christ provided a mystical, saving knowledge. This complex heresy also denied the goodness of all physical matter and all creation.

Hellenistic: Philosophically or theologically influenced by Greek culture, whose emphasis was on the realm of the intellect and ideas, rather than concrete and changeable experience.

Hermeneutical Circle: Hermeneutics is the science of interpretation, especially scriptural texts; in interpreting any text of life experience, the culture and the present situation of the interpreter cannot be separated from the object to be interpreted.

Logos: The eternal Word of God, made flesh in Jesus of Nazareth through the Incarnation.

Monotheism: The belief in one God.

Paradigm: An exemplary or major model or example.

Precursor: Forerunner, one who comes before another, preparing the way. John the Baptizer is the precursor of Jesus the Christ.

Synoptics: The first three gospels—Mark, Matthew and Luke. These are somewhat similar in structure and content and can be read side by side.

Discussion Questions

1. What is Christology? Are you more comfortable with a Christology "from above" or a Christology "from below?" Why?

2. What is the Kingdom of God? How did Jesus describe the Kingdom? Why is the Kingdom described in a tension of "now" and "not yet?"

3. What is a parable? Why did Jesus teach in parables? Locate some of the parables in the gospels. Read them carefully.

4. What is the paschal mystery? Why is it the foundation of the Christian faith?

5. Describe fully four images of Jesus. What images are appropriate to Christology "from above? from below? What is your image of Jesus, the Christ? How do you answer the ancient question, "Who do you say that I am?"

6. In his book, *What Are They Saying About The Resurrection?* Gerald O'Collins offers several models of resurrection. Read these models in Chapter one of this book. Describe the models.

7. Hans Kung develops a Christology "from below." In *On Being a Christian* read the section entitled, "The Distinction." What are Kung's Christological insights? What contribution is offered in the subsection, "Jesus the Jew"?

Additional Reading

Boff, Leonardo, *Jesus Christ Liberator* (Orbis Books, Maryknoll, NY: 1986).

Kung, Hans, *On Being a Christian* (Garden City, New York: Doubleday and Company, Inc., 1976).

Lane, Dermot A., *The Reality of Jesus* (Paulist Press, New York: 1975).

O'Collins, Gerald, *What Are They Saying About Jesus?* (Paulist Press, New York: 1977).

Shea, John, *The Challenge of Jesus* (Thomas More Press, Chicago: 1975).

4

Revelation and Grace

Grace* and revelation* are bottom-line categories in Christian theology. Actually, God's grace and revelation precede theology. Theology's task is to reflect upon humanity's relationship with God. This is possible through God's initiative of self-revelation and loving presence, which we call grace. Through God's gifts of revelation and grace, people come to know God and respond in faith. Human beings have, within their very nature, a drive to get beyond themselves, to get beyond ordinary life experience. This drive is part of our make-up. Everyone experiences some wonder about good and evil, life and its meaning. Often we hear the age-old question, "Is that all there is?" Will our longings ever be satisfied? Will our guilts be healed? Will our lives be meaningful to ourselves, to others, to God? An exploration of revelation and grace touches the whole of human experience in all its relationships and in its ultimate meaning.

God's Self-Communication

Through the centuries, religious thinkers have struggled with the very idea of communication between divinity and humanity. Can the eternal God communicate to humans? Can humans really understand God? People of faith believe that God speaks to his/her people. They interpret their life experience as filled with the action of God. Christian Catholics perceive God's presence in people, in events and in all of creation. God's loving hand and divine energy guide our relationships and our decisions. We believe God's self-revelation is an on-going, dynamic process in our lives. And we also believe that God has offered us special revelation through the prophets and the Covenant* of the Old Testament and in Jesus Christ and the apostolic teaching of the New Testament. Roman Catholics cherish the Judaeo-Christian tradition, God's self-communication experienced and recorded in the words of the Sacred scriptures and in the living faith tradition of our Church. Yet we believe God's self-communication is offered to all people, for God reaches out to draw all creatures and all of creation back to him/herself.

Revelation is not simply God's self-communication. Sometimes religious people picture God totally apart from creation, from our world, speaking from a high throne in a mighty voice. Thus, we might think he/she spoke to Abraham, Moses, Noah, Isaiah and all the prophets of antiquity. But revelation cannot happen simply through God's self-communication. It is not one-sided. The powerful voice of God must be heard and accepted by people. God's self-communication becomes revelation when it is heard and believed by people whose lives are transformed by its acceptance. Revelation happens in this encounter when God's self-communication meets human openness and longing for God. The believing response is part of revelation. Nothing is revealed, if someone doesn't absorb it. Just as in human dialogue, deep communication occurs when people truly understand each other and are changed by what is communicated. Nothing is revealed by even the greatest of orators, if the audience is absent, deaf or unconcerned. Revelation is not outside of human reality. It is within it. God reveals him/herself through human experience in history. Although revelation is of divine initiative, we humans are an essential part.

Prophetic Tradition

Every religious tradition is rooted in relationship with God. Catholicism, and all of Christianity, rests firmly on the shoulders of the Hebrew religious tradition. The revelation of the God of Israel is a significant part of Christian revelation. The Old Testament is a record of God's free intervention into history, the history of the Israelite nation. In Genesis, the first book of the bible, God's call to Abraham, father of the Israelite nation, is presented as an encounter of God and Abraham, with the eternal God speaking, offering direction and promise (Genesis 12:1-9). Abram, whose name God changes to Abraham, follows God's direction in faith, as does Abram's wife, Sarai, whose name God changes to Sarah. In biblical tradition, those special hearers of God's word often have their names changed. Names were most significant to the Israelite people. A change of name was indicative of a real change in the person, a transformation in faith. In the Old Testament, God often manifests him/herself to the leaders of Israel. The particular nature of these manifestations is not clear. Although the text often says, "And God spoke . . .", these manifestations could have been interior experiences or dependent upon some exterior sense experience. What is clear is that the Israelite people believed that the eternal God had intervened in their lives and set up a covenant with them. The term which is repeated in the Hebrew scripture is the "Word of Yahweh." Whatever the revelatory experience entailed, the hearing of God's word was at the core. This "Word of Yahweh" spoken in the Old Testament develops a personal relationship between God and his/her people. The revelation of the Old Testament is definitely inter-personal. The Israelites were confronted with God's Word—a word needing a response. The "Word of Yahweh" demanded faith and action. Refusing the Word of God is refusing to be in relationship with God and with other people of faith. Refusal of the Word is sin. Acceptance of the Word brings salvation*. In the Old Testament, revelation was understood in terms of the covenant with God. God had revealed him/herself and was acting in the history of the Israelite nation. To refuse faith in this revealing God, to refuse to trust that God would always care for the people of the covenant, was the great sin of idolatry.

The prophets of the Old Testament were speakers of God's Word. Often the prophets are very reluctant to speak for Yahweh. They make excuses, beg off of their mission. The prophet, Jeremiah, pleads, "Ah, Lord, God! I know not how to speak; I am too young" (Jeremiah 1:6). But the Lord, God, takes no excuses.

> Say not, 'I am too young.' To whomever I send you, you shall go; whatever I command you, you shall speak. Have no fear before them, because I am with you to deliver you, says the Lord. Then the Lord extended his hand and touched my mouth saying, See, I place my words in your mouth (Jeremiah 1:7-10).

The words of the prophets are part of God's revelation. These words spoken by God were absorbed by the prophets; their lives, and the lives of all who listened to them, were transformed. Revelation in the Old Testament occurs in the events of history where God's power and faithfulness are experienced. The tenderness and merciful love of God is revealed, gradually unfolding the divine plan of salvation. The great prophet, Isaiah, understands a loving God. "As nurslings, you shall be carried in her arms, and fondled in her lap; as a mother comforts her son, so will I comfort you" (Isaiah 66:13). Isaiah looks forward to the coming of the Lord's servant who will "bring forth justice to the nations" (Isaiah 42:1).

In the New Testament, the idea of revelation is centered upon Jesus Christ. In Jesus, God's intervention into history is a total intervention. The author of the Epistle* to the Hebrews begins this book of the New Testament with a statement of God's self-revelation in Christ.

> In times past, God spoke in fragmentary and varied ways to our fathers through the prophets; in this, the final age, he has spoken to us through his Son. (Hebrews 1:1-2).

In Jesus, the Old Testament "Word of Yahweh" became flesh and lived in history. Jesus was a prophet, one so filled with the Spirit of God that the believers came to identify him as God's own Son. The teaching of Jesus has the authority of the eternal God. Throughout his ministry, Jesus asks faith from all who hear him. The plan of God, freely offered in love through Jesus, is a plan of salvation for all people. It is through a faith response that people come to recognize this plan and are willing to live in its mystery.

Revelation found its summit, its highest point, in Jesus. Every human spirit longs for God; according to one's openness, the Spirit of God is manifest in one's life. Jesus was totally open to God, and the fullness of God was completely revealed to Him. Revelation occurs in God's approach to us in word and deed. In Jesus, word and deed are completely joined. In the Old Testament, the prophets were the interpreters of the events and deeds of history. The Spirit of God speaking intensely in their lives enabled them to explain life's experiences from God's perspective. God was revealed in the person of Jesus of Nazareth, the greatest of the prophets—God's Son.

Revelation and the Church

The response of faith has always been part of the church's teaching on revelation. In the early church, the believers converted to a new way of life, gathered together remembering Jesus. Accepting Jesus, as Lord and Savior, was the core of membership in these primitive Christian communities. The early Christians, guided by the Holy Spirit, continued to pass on God's revelation as they proclaimed faith in Jesus as the Christ raised from the dead by God and as they lived the Good News.

In the patristic* times, the fathers of the church do battle with philosophers who degrade revelation to an intellectual knowledge, not dependent upon God's self-disclosure. Tertullian is willing to admit that there are natural ways of knowing God, yet he describes these ways as imperfect. Only through faith in Christ and the teaching of the apostles can God's truth be known. The fathers are strongly attached to the apostolic teaching, solid in their belief that the written words of scripture, and the spoken words of tradition, are deposited in the church—passed down from the original apostolic churches. The continuity of apostolic teaching is very important to the fathers. St. Cyprian, out-spoken church leader and bishop of Carthage in the third century, stresses the role of the church in preserving and passing down the apostolic tradition. For Cyprian, the apostolic tradition deposited in scripture is revelation. He believes scripture is found in the church and, therefore, counsels complete faithfulness to the church. "A man cannot have God for his Father, if he does not have the Church for his Mother" (*On Church Unity*, 6).

St. Augustine, Bishop of Hippo in the fifth century, adds another dimension to the understanding of revelation. Against the intellectual pride of the philosophers, Augustine stresses our total dependence upon God. If the Spirit of God is not working within us, it is impossible to recognize or accept the truth of the gospel message. For Augustine, faith or understanding was impossible without the gift of God's grace. Grace is personal, internal revelation which must accompany the external revelation of truth. This grace is an illumination* and an inspiration within a person, attracting her to belief. Very simply, it is God speaking within a person, which enables one to have faith.

St. Thomas Aquinas, in the Middle Ages, offers additional insights to the understanding of revelation. In his classical work, *Theology of Revelation*, René Latourelle stresses the coherence of St. Thomas' teaching:

> According to his constant thinking, all knowledge is accomplished only in judgment. Revelation, being knowledge to the highest degree, implies, like every other knowledge, an acceptance of the material and a light which permits the enunciation of judgment . . .
> Two things are required in faith; on the one hand, an object to believe the truths which are proposed; and on the other hand, assent to these truths

> . . . Everything comes from God: both revelation and
> the faith which is its response.[1]

Theologians of the later middle ages offered little beyond the
thinking of Thomas Aquinas. At the Council of Trent in 1546,
following the Protestant Reformation, defining the sources of
revelation is a central task. This teaching was clearly directed
against the Reformers' strong stance declaring that the Word of
God is found in sacred scripture *alone*—there available for all to
understand and interpret with the guidance of the Holy Spirit.
Against the Protestant understanding of *Sola Scriptura**, the
Council declared:

> The gospel, which is the source of all saving truth and
> rules of conduct, is contained in the written and un-
> written traditions which have come down to us, hav-
> ing been received by the Apostles from the mouth of
> Christ himself, or from the Apostles by the dictation
> of the Holy Spirit, and have been transmitted as it
> were from hand to hand . . . and preserved in continu-
> ous succession in the Catholic Church (Decree on Sa-
> cred Books and on Traditions to be Received, Session
> IV 1546).[2]

For centuries, Roman Catholics defined the two sources of
revelation as scripture and tradition. Vatican I (1869-1870) reaffirmed the teaching of Trent. The council fathers of Vatican I
were deeply concerned with the rising influence of the Modernists* and the Rationalists.* The Modernist movement de-emphasized the supernatural origin and content of revelation. Modernists identified revelation simply with the human process of
coming to know God—a process they characterized as universal
in nature and present in the everyday experiences of life. The
Rationalists down-played all spirituality, disbelieving everything
that could not be proven by reason. Vatican I stated that God
can be known by the natural light of reason, but there are mysteries of faith that are above reason. These mysteries come to
us through revelation. The Incarnation and the Trinity would
be examples of such truths. Vatican I clearly drew lines between the supernatural and the natural, and the mystery of
revelation was placed on the supernatural level. In modern
times, the Second Vatican Council, under the guidance of Pope
John XXIII and Pope Paul IV, took a different approach.

Dei Verbum

Years after the Vatican II Council, we tend to forget the drama and debate the council years (1962-1965) brought to the Catholic Church and the Christian world community. The development of the Constitution on Revelation was most significant. Latourelle points to the profundity of the document's introduction and its importance to the entire work of the Council. ". . . the tone of this first paragraph is amply justified by the fact that the Constitution, *Dei Verbum,* is logically presented as the first great document produced by Vatican II."[3]

> Therefore, following in the footsteps of the Council of Trent and Vatican I, this present Council wishes to set forth authentic doctrine on divine revelation and how it is handed on, so that by hearing the message of salvation the whole world may believe, by believing it may hope, and by hoping it may love (Introduction, paragraph 2, *Dei Verbum*).

These words, recalling the words of St. Augustine, are pastoral*. They show concern for all people. This introduction also offers an ecumenical* tone, open to dialogue. The first schema for a document on revelation, submitted during the first session, *De Fontibus Revelationis,* took an approach similar to the Councils of Trent and Vatican I. Its conservative tone stressed revelation as a body of divine truths called the deposit-of-faith.* These stated the documents are contained partly in scripture and partly in tradition. The role of the *Magisterium,* * as the authoritative teaching body of the church, was also stressed. Many of the council fathers had major reservations concerning this schema. After a week of haggling, Pope John XXIII intervened and set up a special theological commission. The Pope urged the commission to develop an open-ended, ecumenical and pastoral document. He was not pleased with their intellectual, rigid approach to the first schema. The whole spirit of Pope John's approach to the Council was one of openness. The original commission had been chaired by the conservative churchman, Cardinal Alfredo Ottaviani, head of the Holy Office. Along with Cardinal Meyer, a Scripture scholar and co-chairperson with Ottaviani, the Pope added people concerned with ecumenical considerations. John XXIII was interested in opening the windows of the Roman Catholic Church to the world.

The second schema, *Dei Verbum* (Word of God), accepted after four revisions, was a major shift in church thinking. From a classical model where revelation was viewed from an objective, static perspective, this schema was presented from an historical point of view. It situates the mystery of revelation in history. Revelation is offered not simply as the divine communication of particular truths, but "is realized by deeds and words having an inner unity: the deeds wrought by God in the history of salvation manifest and confirm the teaching and realities signified by the words, while the words proclaim the deeds and clarify the mystery contained in them" (*Dei Verbum*, 7:2,3). The emphasis of revelation, as God's approach to us in words and deeds, offers a far more dynamic style. The deposit of faith is no longer portrayed as a closed, static entity. Growth in understanding and development of insights is part of the unfolding of God's revelation. The document does reflect back to Trent and Vatican I, presenting the church as the authentic interpreter of the Word of God, but adds that the magisterium is "not above the Word of God but serves it, teaching only what has been handed on, listening to it devoutly, guarding it scrupulously and explaining it faithfully in accord with a divine commission and with the help of the Holy Spirit" (*Dei Verbum*, 10). This emphasis on the place of the bible in the church moved the Catholic tradition closer to Protestant Christianity. Although the Dogmatic Constitution on Divine Revelation, *Dei Verbum*, did not withdraw any of the statements of previous councils, its historical, biblical approach offered a broader dimension to the mystery of revelation. Scripture and tradition are seen as the environment of God's revelation. Modern theologians, following Vatican II, make a distinction denoting scripture not as revelation itself, but as a mirror of revelation.

Revelation: Objective or Subjective?

The classical stance concerning revelation fundamental to church councils before Vatican II was objective in approach. The divine truths were primary. The term "deposit of faith" spoke clearly the completeness and static quality of the body of divine truths. The intellectual, cognitive understanding of these truths was also central to the church's method of catechesis.* In contemporary times, the approach of historical consciousness gives much more weight to subjective experience. The church has always taught that God's self-disclosure was not revelation unless it was received in faith. Nonetheless, the central focus was on the divine truths themselves. In the present day, the model used to explain revelation is not unconcerned with the truth, but it is equally concerned with God's dynamic presence in the encounter of faith. Our modern age spends much energy and time on communication and relationships. Impersonal technology and enormous commercial enterprise have created a greater need in us for deep understanding and communication in our own relationships. Thousands of small encounter-type groups exist all over the country, aiding people in their special needs or problems to share with those of similar concerns. When two people relate, there is both an objective aspect (that which is understood between them) and a subjective aspect (the willingness to relate, to share lives). The process of communication includes not only the understanding and acceptance of what is communicated, but the acceptance of those communicating. American theologian, Gabriel Moran, whose ideas on revelation are concerned with the ongoing process of revelation (especially in its concrete, present expressions), makes experience the ultimate norm.[4] Within human experience, there are moments of a revelatory nature, where people perceive a presence beyond the ordinary reality, a divine presence—God. For Moran, these types of experiences are available to all people. Moran, therefore, concludes that the primary meaning of revelation is within the present, a social and practical reality. This reality is not available only to Christians, but to all humankind.[5]

Revelation is a difficult concept to pin down. It is so easy to look at it from a Catholic Christian point of view, that is, as God's marvelous gift of self-disclosure through the ancient Israelite prophets and in the fullness of time through the person of Jesus Christ. Yet, there are some questions about the receiving of God's revelation. These questions enabled the fathers of Vatican II to leave the document open-ended. More thought, more study and deeper acceptance of God's revelation may provide more enlightenment. Avery Dulles, another American theologian and a Jesuit, has done much work on revelation. His great gift is his ability to synthesize the differing opinions of many theologians In a lecture, *The Meaning of Revelation*, presented after the conclusion of Vatican II, Dulles offered this summary:

> Hence we may conclude that according to Catholic
> teachings all men, at least at some time in their lives,
> in ways known to God, receive sufficient revelatory

enlightenment to be able to respond with an act of salutary faith. The Council does not try to work out a theory of when or how this enlightenment occurs. But what the Council deliberately refrained from doing by authoritative decree, theologians are implicitly invited to do by unofficial inquiry. Attempting to penetrate the how and the why, theology may construct theories which bring out the full meaning, intelligibility and credibility of the official doctrine.

Revelation: Particular or Universal?

Revelation comes to all people in the very depths of their being. It comes in words and in silence. It comes in personal relationships and in communal events. Believing that God continually offers him/herself to all, that this divine call can convert our hearts, alter our consciousness, change our horizons and enable us humans to experience our own experiences in a new way, we must conclude that by God's grace, revelation is universal. But what of our religious tradition? Do Catholics or any other religious groups possess a privileged revelation? The church does pass on God's total self-revelation in Jesus Christ by our living faith. People come to faith from witnessing the faith of others. Those of us who believe that the message spoken in the life, death and resurrection of Jesus gives present meaning to our own experience have responded to the Spirit of God within us. And through this response of faith, we are able to share faith with others. Truth does not have real existence as a separate entity; it exists only in the minds and hearts of those who believe it. Revelation comes to us in an incarnate way—through other people, through nature, through events of history. Since humans are social people, the locus of revelation is the human community. The Christian revelation founded a community, and this community—the Church—continues the revelatory process. Catholic Christians believe the Christ event is the highest manifestation of God's self-revelation. Nonetheless, we do not believe it is God's exclusive self-revelation, for we believe firmly in the universal salvific will of God—that is "God wills all people to be saved" (1 Timothy 2:4).

We must conclude that there is a general revelation to all people, for God desires to save all people, and our experience tells us that all people long for God in some way. Yet we are rooted in our Judaeo-Christian tradition, and we hold firmly

that Jesus, the Christ, God's personal Word, is a unique definitive expression of divine revelation. There exists a universal
divine call to all people; this call demands response to be actually revelatory. It demands a "Yes" to the meaning of one's own
existence—a "Yes" to life and to its ultimate meaning—God.
This response occurs within the framework of the universal self-
disclosure of a God of love. The special revelation in Jesus
Christ also demands response, a depth response of faith in
Christ, which brings a new consciousness, a new commitment to
oneself, to all other people, to life, itself, and to God. This response is Christian faith and commitment to the gospel. The
creeds and dogmas of our church express the content and constant patterns of revelation. Yet revelation is not closed or finished in these written expressions. Avery Dulles assures us that
revelation is on-going, and we continue to be part of it.

> Revelation does not exist apart from the self-manifes-
> tation of God within the consciousness of those who
> are called to believe. To the extent that God contin-
> ues to communicate himself in love to those whom he
> calls to union, he must be said to continue to reveal
> himself.[6]

The Grace to Respond

What makes a person believe? What is the specific factor
that enables someone to trust another, to love another? Two
people can hear the same plea for help. One will be moved to
total commitment, while another remains aloof to the situation.
In a situation of crisis or emergency, one person may trust the
advice or help of a stranger, or take a courageous risk, while
another person recoils in fear, closes up, afraid to trust or risk.
What makes the difference? Surely childhood, cultural background and the hurts or successes of life's experience contribute
to a person's response. Yet is there another factor? Sam Keen,
founding editor of the periodical, *Psychology Today,* theologian
and psychologist, offers some insight. "I am interested primarily
in those experiences in which the individual is dissolved and has
the sense that he is being moved by a power beyond himself."[7]
Keen speaks of situations where there is a yielding of the illusion of control, a willingness to trust the other, a kind of dissolv-
ing within us when our defenses are down and a new energy
emerges.[8]

. In our Catholic Church tradition, grace and revelation are often described together. God's self-disclosure becomes real to people in graced moments. These moments are moments of trust when our defenses are down, and we believe, perhaps for the first time, perhaps with new depth or commitment to action or change in lifestyle. Most people have known in their own lives "graced" moments, special experiences of goodness. These moments were not merited, not deserved. They happened gratuitously. They were gifts that enabled one to make a response of great love, heroic sacrifice or faith-filled courage. It is grace that brings to life such moments.

The true story of a married couple offers such an example. Ted and Marci were a happy couple. Life was good. Then Ted was stricken with terminal cancer. Marci left her job and spent her days with Ted, caring for him and being present to him through his long and difficult illness. One of Ted's final wishes was to be present at the ordination of a friend, a Franciscan priest. Ted didn't get his wish. He was too sick to attend the ordination, but the newly-ordained priest visited Ted and Marci between the celebration of his first Mass and the reception following. Very shortly after, he celebrated Ted's funeral Mass. A few weeks later, Marci called her priest-friend, telling him that she, too, had been diagnosed with terminal cancer. In the conversation, the priest asked Marci when she had received this painful diagnosis. Marci explained that she had learned about her condition just a few months after Ted had been diagnosed! "I knew Ted needed me to get through his ordeal. After fifty-four years of marriage I knew I'd be able to care for him."

Where does such strength come from? What is the key to this type of sacrifice? Grace is the term we use to express this reality. Grace describes the reality of God's love emerging in human experience. Just as revelation does not happen outside of human history, grace is not a supernatural commodity sprinkled upon certain situations. It is God's love, the constant divine urging toward goodness meeting an open, willing human heart. Grace has no existence of its own. Our prayers begging God for grace might sound like requests for a spiritual charge, but grace does not exist by itself. Grace exists in experiences where the gift of God's presence is accepted.

St. Paul and Grace

In the New Testament it is St. Paul who offers a theology of grace. The term "grace" is mentioned hundreds of times in his letters. The basic meaning Paul offers for grace is simply the gift of God in Jesus Christ. God has always graced humankind. The relationship between the eternal God and all of creation is one of grace. Yet in Jesus, this relationship was revealed in abundance. God's loving desire to be united to all humans was accomplished in Jesus. St. Paul emphasizes grace as the gift of the Father, gratuitously given out of merciful love. Paul learned initially of God's grace in a most personal experience. Paul was not a believer. Quite the opposite; Paul hated the followers of Christ and persecuted them. While on his way to Damascus to pursue and arrest Christians, Paul had a conversion experience. This event is told in the Acts of the Apostles, the book following the four Gospels in the New Testament.

> As he traveled along and was approaching Damascus, a light from the sky suddenly flashed about him. He fell to the ground and at the same time heard a voice saying, 'Saul, Saul, why do you persecute me?' 'Who are you, Sir?' he asked. The voice answered, 'I am Jesus, the one you are persecuting.' (Acts of the Apostles 9:3-5)

Paul had worked to destroy the Christian community. He had kept the Jewish law, living the traditions of his ancestry. Yet Paul became the great Christian missionary to the Gentiles. He preached to the believers of Rome that their relationship with God was no longer under the Old Law, but now a relationship of grace (Romans 6:14, 15). Writing to the Christians of Corinth, Paul stresses their new relationship of love.

> Clearly you are a letter of Christ . . . a letter written not with ink, but by the Spirit of the living God, not on tablets of stone, but on tablets of flesh in the heart.

> This great confidence in God is ours, through Christ. It is not that we are entitled of ourselves to take credit for anything. Our sole credit is from God (2 Corinthians 3:3-5).

Paul understood grace as undeserved, unexpected gift. His own experience of complete surprise, followed by deep conversion, was described as grace. For Paul, it was a very concrete experience. Following his surprise on the road to Damascus, Paul was temporarily blinded. A follower of Jesus, Ananias, was sent by the Lord to lay hands upon Paul. Immediately, the scripture tells us, Paul recovered his sight and was filled with the Holy Spirit. After this experience of grace, Paul spent his entire life spreading the Good News of Jesus.

Through the acceptance of grace, Paul became a new person. He was now called Paul, instead of Saul. He knew that God had graciously saved him. The keeping of the Old Law could not bring people into union with God. We are united to God through grace, the acceptance of God's love in our hearts. Our nature was created with this potential, but it is God's gift of grace that enables us to turn from the letter of the law to the spirit. As St. Paul tells us, "The letter of the law kills, but the Spirit gives life" (2 Corinthians 3:6).

Throughout his preaching St. Paul repeats again and again the utter giftedness of God's love to us. This love enables us to believe in Jesus. It empowers us to preach about his life and message. And it gives us strength to serve one another. Paul is very clear that all we possess is from God, "this treasure we possess in earthen vessels, to make it clear that its surpassing power comes from God, and not from us" (2 Corinthians 4:7). Paul's life is not an easy one. Far more than he persecuted others, is he, himself, persecuted; nonetheless, he remains faithful. "Paul, an apostle of Christ Jesus, by the will of God" (Colossians 1:1).

Created and Uncreated Grace

Grace is a mystery, for it speaks of God's relationship with all people, with the world. The term attempts to describe the foundational and dynamic quality by which God continually reaches out in love to us and we seek to live united to God. Just like love, grace cannot be seen. Its existence within history, however, can certainly be evidenced. As God is love, so God is grace. Yet, it is clear to us that God and God's love within people are not identical. Theologians have speculated upon these notions for centuries. To get a better grasp of the mystery, grace was categorized and distinctions were made. Peter Fransen offers these definitions.

> In theology, *uncreated grace* stands for God giving
> Himself to man in love. In contradistinction to this,

created grace signifies the result God's self-communication produces on man. Evidently that result cannot be God Himself; therefore, it is something other than God, something created, a gift from God.[9]

These distinctions led to other questions. Did created grace add something to the nature of human beings? Is being "in the state of grace" a condition that is above human nature? These considerations led to many theological problems. Is grace totally dependent upon God's free-giving? Or do we "get more grace" if we accept more fully, or receive less if we turn away? It is simply not appropriate to speak of grace in a quantitative fashion. Doing this reifies grace, and we are back to a "piling up of a spiritual commodity." The problem is the preserving of the balance between the two poles involved: God and humanity. An additional problem is finding the language to express this balance.

In the history of the Christian tradition and its theological reflection, the balance between God and us has been tipped in different directions. In the Greek Christian tradition, the emphasis is on God and the deification* of humanity. Grace through Jesus Christ is the way human beings come to share the divine life. In the West, in the Latin Christian tradition, the sinfulness of the human condition and its estrangement from God is stressed, and grace through Jesus Christ is the way human beings come to salvation. The fifth century suffered the heresy of Pelagianism.* St. Augustine, to whom the Church has given the title "doctor of grace," did theological battle with the monk Pelagius who preached that salvation can be merited by human effort without grace. Augustine, although most mindful and convinced of the severity of human sinfulness, also understood the depths of God's gracious love. The mystery of this love he explained as an indwelling of God. God, Augustine preached, is closer and more intimate to us than we are to our own inner selves. Scripture uses the images of father/child and mother/child to express this mystery. St. Paul calls us God's children because we are led by the Spirit. For this reason, we can call out to God as *Abba* (Romans 8:14-16).

The relationship between uncreated grace and created grace is difficult to explain. Scholastic* theology of the Middle Ages added distinctions to the discussion on grace. Grace, theologians of medieval times explained, is a virtue or an action. But before this virtue can be realized, an additional quality is needed in the soul. Aware that this quality was grace, and not a substance, the Scholastics described grace as an added quality, presupposing human nature, which enabled human beings to produce virtue. This distinction did not offer complete clarity. This additional quality, created grace, was understood as the necessary disposition for uncreated grace—that is, the Spirit of God dwelling within a human being. The terminology is difficult, and we are left with an image of "something added to ordinary human nature" without which God cannot be present.

Martin Luther, father of the Protestant Reformation, attacked the medieval doctrine of grace. Luther was an Augustinian monk. His theological education was grounded in the thought of St. Augustine; Luther rejected the whole idea of created grace. He did not grapple with the relationship between created grace (the quality within a soul, enabling one to produce virtue) and uncreated grace (God and God's love). He eliminated created grace entirely, strongly asserting that we are justified (find eternal salvation) only through the grace spoken of in scripture—that is, grace as God's love for us. Luther held fast to this belief of *sola gratia*.* His agony with the medieval church contributed to Luther's stance on grace. The authority of the church was a major focus of his attack. Corruption did exist in the church and, indeed, in those holding authority in the church. Reform was needed. Luther rejected church hierarchical authority, accepting only the Word of God in scripture. From this position, *sola Scriptura,* Luther understood that justification* is not something that humans are able to merit by any type of good works. Justification, he believed, is ours totally from our faith in Jesus Christ, in whose merits we participate. Although Luther and the other reformers who followed him did not reject the guidance of the Holy Spirit within us, nonetheless, their focus was on our imperfection, our sinfulness which only God's merciful love (grace) in Jesus Christ could overcome. Luther recovered the notion of individual trust and faith in God—our need to rely completely on God's love for us. His understanding of grace was built on a foundation of personal relationship between God and human beings. This was an improvement upon the sterile speculations of the scholastic theologians.

The Council of Trent took issue with Luther's position on grace, declaring that scripture does place value on our good works. Nonetheless, the council's statements made clear "that our good works can be of value in the eyes of God only insofar as they have been done in loving union with Christ."[10] Following the council, both Protestant and Catholic positions became rigid. In this defensive posture, created grace was once again stressed by Roman Catholics. As the centuries passed, the popular mind understood grace as some type of spiritual commodity, one that could be owned and even stored up as purchase-proof for a ticket into heaven. It was in this mind-set that the grace of our sacraments took on an almost magical connotation.

Catholic theology struggled with the problem of grace through the centuries. The one extreme, Pelagianism, emphasized human nature, as such, and its ability to merit union with God. This position down-played the transcendental dimension of salvation, God's free gift of salvation. The other extreme emerged from Protestantism which focused mainly, though not exclusively, on our absolute dependence upon God. This position down-played human freedom and our human ability to respond to God in willingness and love. In the nineteenth century, philosophical thought emphasized life and experience over nature and being. Theologians looked again at mysticism* and the spiritual, interior life. Grace was then described as the life of the Trinity—Father, Son and Spirit—dwelling in the inner depth of human beings. The twentieth century, with its emphasis on personalism,* brought a modern approach to the theology of grace. Karl Rahner's idea of the supernatural existential* focused upon the universal capacity of human nature for God. From this perspective, humans are always in contact with God and God's grace unless they close in upon themselves through serious sinfulness. God created human beings with this supernatural existential. That is, we are created with a desire for God, a desire that cannot be fulfilled completely in any other way. In his treatment of grace, Latin American theologian Leonardo Boff explains it this way.

> It was God himself who structured human beings in such a way that they are permanently open to hearing the voice of God as it comes to them through things, their own conscience, other human mediations, and God himself. The natural desire to love God is not merely human exigency. . . . It is the call which God places within human beings. They hear that call and cry out for God. The cry of human beings is merely an echo of God's voice calling them.[11]

Centuries before, St. Augustine, Doctor of Grace, said "Our hearts are restless until they rest in thee."

Grace, Transcendent and Immanent

In medieval times, people viewed reality in dualistic terms, believing in two distinct worlds. The world of history, where human beings experienced life, was the natural world. The eternal world was God's home—hopefully the future home of humanity. This world was considered supernatural. Contemporary theology, receiving impetus from the Vatican II Council, focused upon the interpenetration of the natural and the supernatural. The only way God can be present to humanity is within the world, the present reality. Our present existence in history is not isolated or apart from God. We are graced from the moment of our birth, for God created our nature in such a way to enable us to receive God's own presence and God's own self-communication. Human nature is destined for God from all eternity, for God has made it so. The distinctions between the natural end of humanity and the supernatural end of humanity often lead to confusion. In the *Pastoral Constitution of the Church,* Council fathers avoid these terms, speaking often of the one vocation of humanity. (Cf. *Pastoral Constitution of the Church,* Sections 10, 11, 57, 59, 61, 63, 91.) Following this contemporary theological understanding, we perceive human beings as creatures of relationship. We relate to ourselves, to other people, to ideas, to our dreams, to our daily environment, to nature and to the creator of all—God. We are matter and spirit; these two entities are not standing side by side; they exist as one. My spirit is my whole self. Every human being lives as a human spirit, and every human spirit remains unfulfilled in history. For every human spirit, as we have explained, longs for total fulfillment, which is transcendence—union with God. And it is God, graciously working within the depths of the human spirit, the immanent God, the God within, who urges a person to act graciously in all relationships.

Grace comes from beyond us and grace comes from within us, for our God is transcendent and immanent. As love requites love, grace requites grace. People who experience their loveableness and giftedness are loving and gracious to others. If a person feels really loved and trusted, he/she is able to love and trust others. Grace is working in such a person. All human relationships are affected by grace, for God is never apart from us. Yet human beings can close themselves to God's love, for we remain free. Love and graciousness can only exist in free relationships. God does not force human beings to accept love; God does not force human beings to accept the Spirit's urging from within. Grace is the encounter of a loving, gracious God offering him/herself to a human being who willingly responds to God's initiative, opening and giving him or herself to God.

> Grace establishes one single world where opposites meet: God and humans, Creator and creatures . . . Grace implies the alteration of both God and humans. It establishes an encounter, a dialogue, and a flow of mutual love. Both are vulnerable because grace operates in the framework of freedom, where there can be a flowering of the unexpected or degeneration on the part of human beings.

> Grace is not just God, not just the human being. It is the encounter of the two, each giving of self and opening up to one another.[12]

Grace, Mediated and Universal

In our age, the world's people are very conscious of our interrelationships on the planet. World events have repercussions far beyond their borders. National and geographical boundaries no longer protect us from the world's agonies. Over-population, disease and poverty cannot be localized. Wars between border nations quickly escalate into world crises. The resources of the world, controlled by far too few, bind us together through our common needs. Communication beams events of disaster, as well as good news, throughout the world in seconds. Even music and fashions circle the globe in record time. Never have the world's people been so aware of the daily trauma and successes of their brothers and sisters on the earth. Never before has the world's conscience been made so aware of the problems and needs of those in poverty. The countries of the third world confront the privileged people of the first world. International organizations seek solutions for the world's suffering. Through all the tensions and national conflicts, the concept of the human family is slowly emerging. Human solidarity is growing into a recognized reality. John Paul II, in several of his encyclical* letters, speaks of the Christian foundation for the solidarity of the human family. He understands the solidarity of humankind as both a recognized reality and a task to be accomplished.

Underneath the political and socio-economic struggles of the human family, there is a unity. Deep within even the most independent individual exists a desire for relationship, for understanding, for union. Popular expressions point to this feeling of oneness. "People are all alike." "There's nothing new under the sun." This oneness can be recognized in the smiling communication between strangers who speak different languages. It can also be recognized in the shared grief of strangers in an unexpected disaster. There is something that binds all of us together. Deep within us, though often buried under pain, fear and the crippling effects of lovelessness, there is something within us that knows the answer to the question. "Am I my brother's (or sister's) keeper?" *Yes* . . . For we are all part of one humankind.

> Human solidarity is above all a spiritual reality: Together with all other people, we stand before God as a family, a community of persons.[13]

Grace is more than God's gift to an individual person. Grace, we have said, exists in the relationship between persons. Grace cannot be studied in isolation—for all grace is mediated*—that is, it exists in concrete, human experience. It exists in the way people treat one another. Sin, too, can exist in the way people treat one another. Grace can be experienced in people's attitudes toward themselves and toward others. Grace can be felt by those who are forgiven by others or by those who are willing to forgive those who have hurt them. The warmth and healing we feel when we are forgiven are part of the forgiveness and healing that God offers us continually. They are graced encounters.

Those within the Christian tradition believe that Christ's Incarnation united Christ to all people, to the entire human family. The union of humanity and God in Jesus is the perfect model of the union that God offers to all people. People willing to respond openly to God's love live in this union of grace. Christians, gifted with faith, are particularly aware of this union. But it is available to the entire human family. Christian lifestyle is rooted in a special friendship with Christ. Essentially, it is an awareness of Jesus as Lord and Savior. It is a relationship of faith and intimacy with Christ and the Christian community.

The Catholic Church has always taught that all people are under God's loving care, even those who do not respond to this love. However, in its missionary work, it did not always act upon this idea of God's universal family. "For all its sympathetic understanding, the Church always found difficulty in coming to grips with divine grace in those who did not profess explicit faith in God or Christ."[14] Today, theologians and missionaries, alike, speak of evangelization* of non-Christians as helping people to recognize the God within themselves. Christians believe that Christ is present to all people even when unrecognized. Missionaries or evangelists do not bring God to people; God is already there. God's presence, the energy of God's dynamic love, is within all people. Yet, many people have not experienced God's care in their relationships with other people, nor have they seen God's face in the loving smile of a friend. These people do not know God; yet God knows and loves them. They are not shut out of God's family. They are graced for all human existence is graced. The universality of God's grace is indeed a mystery. When we look around at the world's problems and pain, it is often extremely difficult to believe that God's grace is stronger than evil. Yet scripture assures us that through Christ, grace is more abundant than sin. (There is a fuller treatment of evil in the appendix which follows chapter 12.)

God chose to relate to the world and all its people through the Incarnation—that is, through complete union with humanity. We do not experience God directly; we experience God in the stuff of life, in the flesh and words of people, in music, in ritual, in sunshine and in the laughter of children. All creation mediates the divine. The world mediates grace. "...the law of the Incarnation tells us that the experience of grace is never pure grace; it is also the world. And our experience of the world is never mere world; it is also grace."[15] As Christians, particularly aware of the Incarnation, we must be particularly aware of our responsibility to mediate God's presence. Grace exists within life, within history. Experiencing grace is allowing the Holy Spirit to overtake us, to guide our lives. An experience of grace does not lessen our human personality. We remain ourselves; we are even more ourselves, more fully human, able to use our own abilities and creativity to work in history.

The Communion of Saints

The Church has a wonderful expression which points to the universality of grace and the responsibility of all believers in this world and in eternity to care for one another—the communion of saints.* It is a linking of all Christians living and dead. Universal grace and the special friendship of those who believe in Jesus Christ and follow Him enable such a bonding to be a spiritual reality, a true communion. Grace is God's loving energy offered unceasingly. And grace is also the loving energy people offer to one another. The communion of saints assures us that God's care and our own care for one another truly extend beyond the grave. Christians are resurrection people, aware that Jesus, the Christ, broke through the sin of the world and conquered death. Jesus, fully God and fully human, experienced perfect human nature, totally graced by God. His life and death witnessed perfect love. All of Jesus' relationships were gracious, for Jesus freely offered Himself to God, to other people and to the world. His life of total concern for others is the perfect model for all Christians. It is the foundation for the communion of saints.

Those of us who follow Jesus and struggle to live loving, gracious and just relationships with one another can be inspired by the women and men who are part of the communion of saints. Through the centuries and into the modern age, many people have been recognized as people who responded fully to God's grace, people whose lives were transformed as they, indeed, transformed the lives and environment of people around them. Such people are aware of their participation in the resurrection of Jesus. They are aware that Jesus' resurrection is an actual fulfillment of those seeds of indestructibility that exist in the Spirit and heart of every human being. They are aware of the richness and depth of grace. In the Roman Catholic tradition, such people are called saints. Saints are holy people, yet made from the very same human stuff as the rest of us. They are not more graced. Saints have experienced grace in the encounter with God, others and the world with greater intensity. With freedom and generosity of spirit, they opened themselves to God and, thus, lived their humanity to its fullness. They are the prophets of our age, speaking out for justice as they respond to God's call. Through grace, they are made whole. Fully human, they are holy; their lives reveal the love of God.

The Catholic tradition offers us a marvelous variety of saints. Who could forget St. Thomas More, a man for all seasons? Thomas More, Lord Chancellor of England, the highest political position in the British Empire, courageously walked in faith to the Tower of London rather than approve the lifestyle of King Henry the Eighth. Or the great Spanish mystic, Teresa of Avila, a woman of leadership in a man's world of the Middle Ages, who struggled to reform the Carmelite Order. Very human to the end of her life, she is quoted as saying *"Oh, my Lord! How true it is that whoever works for you is paid in troubles. No wonder you have so few friends!"* Perhaps the best known Christian saint since the apostles, St. Francis of Assisi transformed Western civilization by his example. Transformed himself by the love and grace of Christ, the rich, carefree jet-setter of the twelfth century, Francesco di Pietro di Bernardone became the saint of total sacrifice and self-imposed poverty. Francis' graced existence freed him to follow the gospel so radically that succeeding generations once again began to take the Gospel seriously. Grace requites grace. Francis' graced life also freed him to respond with deep sensitivity to nature and all of life. Environmentalists of our modern world have made St. Francis of Assisi their patron.

Other saints of the Catholic tradition are remembered for their strength and courage against tremendous obstacles. Joan of Arc was a young woman of great strength and courage, who lived five hundred years ago. Her life story seems strange, almost bizarre today. Yet Joan opened herself to God, courageously following what she sincerely believed to be God's call. Fearlessly, she led an army into battle to deliver her beloved France from the control of the English. Steadfast in her belief that she heard the voices of angels and saints directing her, Joan of Arc eventually suffered death, burned at the stake.

Kateri Tekakwitha, a young Iroquois Indian girl, sickly and almost blind, spoke out against the senseless torture of captured Indians of the Mohican tribes. Attracted by the Jesuit missionary priests, Tekakwitha voiced her desire to become a Christian. Mocked and mistreated by her family, she secretly left her village and the only people she knew and joined a Christian community two hundred and fifty miles away. Baptized Kateri, the young Indian lived only three more years. Close to death, Kateri told a friend, "I will love you in heaven, I will pray for you, I will help you."

The lives of saints from other ages cannot always be judged by the standards of our modern age. Though legend may be added to some of their life stories, we can recognize within the lives of these saints a response to God and a response to the needs of others. Their example provides a real witness to gospel values. They revealed to the people of their time the love of Christ, mediating for all time the continued presence of God in history.

Yet saints are not merely a phenomenon of past history. Each generation hears the call of God and responds to that call. In our present age, those who respond with great intensity emerge as the saints of our time. Through grace, Christ continues to be revealed.

Who are these present-day saints? There are many sainted people that the world will never know. People open to life, making decisions of justice and peace for all, exist all over the world. Such people are recognized by those whose lives they have transformed. Saints are found in ordinary environments; they are ordinary people, living extraordinary lives. They are members of the Christian Church, and they are people outside of our religious tradition. God reveals him/herself to all people. The Spirit of God works where it will. Grace is universal. God's initiative of love urges all of humanity to respond in love. Jesus, the Christ, has responded perfectly to God's call. And all people of all generations share in this mystery of grace, the incarnate union between God and humanity. The following women and men are a few models for our generation. These people are not one of a kind. Nor did they handle the problems that confronted them in similar fashion. They are not puppets of God. Responsive to God's call, with the full intensity of their own personalities, they live (or lived) fully human lives. These saints of modern times have lived graced lives. Guided by the Holy Spirit, they reveal Christ's love, mediating the continued presence of God among us.

Mother Teresa

Agnes Bojaxhiu, a Yugoslavian born in 1910, traveled to India as a high school geography teacher. The stark misery and deprivation of the poor of Calcutta brought Agnes immediately to work in the city streets. Today, Mother Teresa and her sisters of the Missionaries of Charity work among the poor and dying in thirty-one countries. This woman, known to many as the "saint of the gutters," offers loving care to people whose human dignity has been forgotten by others. Mother Teresa, recognized by the world community for her vision and her work, was awarded the Nobel Peace Prize in 1979. Mother Teresa believes that "being unwanted is the worst disease any human being can ever have."

Tom Dooley

The poor and sick people of Southeast Asia had special names for Tom Dooley. In Laos, they called him *Thanh Mo America,* "respectful man of medicine from America." In Vietnam, he was known as *Bac Sy My,* "good American doctor." Tom Dooley grew up in St. Louis, Missouri, graduated from Notre Dame University and St. Louis University School of Medicine. As a naval medical officer in the early 1950s, Dr. Dooley experienced first hand the needs of the native people in Viet Nam, Cambodia and Laos. Tom's ship picked up thousands of homeless refugees. As a doctor and a human being, Tom Dooley was deeply moved by the suffering of the frightened boat people. After his military career, Dr. Dooley, responding to a deep call within him, returned to serve the needs of the poor in remote villages of Southeast Asia. Most of the people had never seen a doctor or a Christian. Tom shared with these people his medical skills and his faith. He set up hospitals, training native volunteers. He returned to America to raise funds across the nation, writing books and giving talks. When Tom Dooley realized he had cancer, he worked harder than ever, training the Laotian people to carry on his work. A very young man, Tom Dooley died of cancer in 1982. President Kennedy credited Tom Dooley's ideas and ideals with the formation of the Peace Corps.

Maximilian Kolbe

Former Polish Army Sergeant Franciszek Gajowniczek, eighty-two years old, attended the canonization* of St. Maximilian Kolbe at St. Peter's Basilica. Gajowniczek was fully convinced that Maximilian was, indeed, a saint. In 1941, the commander of Auschwitz, furious over the successful escape of one prisoner, ordered that ten prisoners be locked in a bunker and starved to death. Sergeant Gajowniczek was chosen. Franciscan Friar, Fr. Kolbe, then forty-seven years old, offered his life in the place of Gajowniczek. This gesture of total self-sacrifice places Maximilian Kolbe among the saints of our time.

Mother Seton

Elizabeth Ann Bayley could never have predicted the direction of her life when she married William Seton, son of a prosperous and prominent family in American banking and shipping. In the happy years following her fashionable wedding at New York's Trinity Episcopal Church, the Setons had five children. When the Seton business failed, William's health was affected. Attempting recuperation on a trip to Italy, William died of yellow fever. Broken-hearted, Elizabeth was comforted by the Filicchi family with whom they were staying. It was here that Elizabeth became interested in the Catholic faith. Returning to New York, she supported her family by teaching. Her conversion to Catholicism brought the ostracism of her staunchly Protestant family and friends. Elizabeth's hardship turned her life in a new direction. With the help of a friend, Father Louis Dubois, she opened a Catholic school in Baltimore. Next, Mrs. Seton founded a religious community, the Sisters of Charity. Elizabeth's life was now a life of service. Her courage and perseverance was a model for the many women who followed her. Elizabeth Seton began a movement which was to build Catholic schools and hospitals throughout the United States. In 1975, Elizabeth Ann Seton was the first native-born American to be officially designated as a saint by the Church.

Oscar Romero

> We know that every effort to better society, especially when injustice and sin are so ingrained, is an effort that God blesses, that God wants, that God demands of us . . . whoever out of love for Christ gives himself to the service of others will live, like the grain of wheat that dies, but only apparently dies. If it did not die, it would remain alone . . . Only in undoing itself does it produce the harvest.[16]

Oscar Romero, Archbishop of San Salvador in El Salvador, was shot to death on March 24, 1980, before the end of the Mass at which he spoke those words in his last homily. Against El Salvador's tyrannical government and even some of his fellow churchmen, Archbishop Romero spoke out for the oppressed of his nation. He was a "voice for the voiceless." A month before he died, the Archbishop was informed that his name was on a list of those to be eliminated by government forces. His prophetic words of response live on in the hearts of the poor *campesinos* of Central America: "But let it be known that no one can any longer kill the voice of justice." Oscar Romero's response to grace brought martyrdom. His witness to Christ and the gospel lives on in the lives of his people.

Dorothy Day

Until her death in 1980, Dorothy Day was a very independent woman. Dorothy responded freely to life, open to the Spirit of God within her. She remained very much her own person, hemmed in by neither the church nor the government. Although her personal loyalty to the church she loved never waivered, her conscience was responsive to Christ and his gospel. She was passionately concerned about people, especially the poor. Dorothy spent most of her days working in the slums of New York City. In 1933, with the help of her visionary friend, Peter Maurin, she published a newspaper, *The Catholic Worker*. This penny newspaper confronted the issues of poverty, war and racism. It printed the social justice encyclicals* of the church. *The Catholic Worker* is still published in New York City. Dorothy Day was adamant about injustice. She was totally opposed to war. Dorothy was jailed several times while protesting various wars and injustices. She served the jobless and the homeless during the Depression, founding hospitality houses to provide needed care and shelter. Dorothy Day was arrested for the last time in 1973, when she was seventy-five years old. She had been demonstrating against the plight of the migrant farm workers in California. In her undaunted style, Dorothy said, "This jail is a paradise compared to others I have known." In one issue of the *The Catholic Worker* she wrote, "How to love— that is the question." Dorothy Day's life provided an answer.

Saints for All Humankind

The modern saints described above were members of the Catholic Church. Non-Catholics have also been real models of holiness for Catholics and all those searching for life's ultimate meaning. Martin Luther King comes to mind, as well as the great-souled, Mahatma Gandhi, whom King so deeply admired. Dietrich Bonhoeffer, German pastor executed by the Nazis in 1945, a saint of the Protestant tradition certainly ranks high among Christian martyrs. Women of tremendous strength and deep faith who suffered during the Jewish holocaust must also be remembered when we speak of sanctity: Etty Hillesum, Corrie ten Boom, Simone Weil and Edith Stein. Faith gave these women the courage to endure Nazi persecution and to reach out to others suffering with them. From our Catholic tradition the four women murdered in El Salvador, Sr. Ita Ford, Sr. Maura Clark, Sr. Dorothy Kazel, and Ms. Jean Donovan, are recent examples of holiness and martyrdom. Saints are among us. Women and men continue to live fully their humanity responding with complete openness to the universal call of God's grace.

Endnotes

1. René Latourelle, S.J., *Theology of Revelation* (Staten Island, NY: Abba House, 1966), p. 172.

2. Richard McBrien, *Catholicism* (Minneapolis: Winston Press, 1981), p. 214.

3. Latourelle, op. cit., p. 456.

4. Gabriel Moran, *Design for Religion* (New York: Herder and Herder, 1970), pp. 44-45.

5. Gabriel Moran, *The Present Reality* (New York: Seabury Press, 1972), pp. 299, 311.

6. Avery Dulles, *Models of Revelation* (Garden City, NY: Doubleday and Company, Inc., 1983), p. 79.

7. Jim Fowler and Sam Keen, *Life Maps* (Waco, TX: World Books, 1978), p. 104.

8. Ibid., pp. 105-107.

9. Peter Fransen, *The New Life of Grace,* (New York: Seabury Press, 1973), p. 87.

10. Ibid., p. 94.

11. Leonardo Boff, *Liberating Grace* (Maryknoll, New York: Orbis Books, 1979), p. 44.

12. Ibid., pp. 4, 15, 17.

13. Richard G. Cote, *Universal Grace: Myth or Reality* (Maryknoll, NY: Orbis Books, 1977), p. 22.

14. Ibid., p. 79.

15. Boff, op. cit., p. 50.

16. Jane P. Keegan, ed., *Third World Peoples: A Gospel Perspective* (Maryknoll, NY: Maryknoll Fathers and Brothers, 1987), p. 19.

Glossary

Canonization: The Church process of officially designating someone as a saint. This process begins after the death of the person.

Catechesis: The process of introducing young people and adult converts to gospel values and the major tenets of the Christian faith.

Communion of saints: All Christian believers, living and dead.

Covenant: The contract or promise between God and the Hebrew nation in the Old Testament and between God and all of humanity established in Jesus Christ in the New Testament.

Deification: The act of deifying, making one god-like.

Deposit of faith: The body of truths; the content of the Christian faith given by Christ and the apostles and preserved by the church ever since.

Ecumenical: Pertaining to the religious attitude that is attentive and open to the reflections of other Church traditions.

Encyclical: A letter written by the Pope and offered to the entire Church and the whole world.

Epistle: A letter in the New Testament; the letters written by St. Paul and the other early Christian missionaries to Christian communities.

Evangelization: Proclaiming the Gospel of Jesus Christ to others.

Grace: The presence of God. Grace is mediated in people, relationships and events in history.

Illumination: The act of enlightening, providing awareness.

Justification: The event by which God, through Jesus Christ, makes us just (holy). The final effect of justification is eternal salvation.

Magisterium: The teaching authority of the Church; theologians contribute, but the office of the Pope and the bishops are the official magisterium.

Mediation: This theological principle states that God's presence comes to us in history, through people, events, nature, things.

Modernists: Members of an early twentieth century movement that denied the permanence of doctrine and de-emphasized the supernatural.

Mysticism: A human's personal experience of God.

Pastoral: Pertaining to the actual life of the Church, especially on the parish level.

Patristic: Pertaining to the fathers of the Church, the writers of the Church between the second and eighth centuries. The patristic period had a great impact on the doctrines of the Church.

Pelagianism: A heresy led by the monk, Pelagius, in the fifth century, stating that human beings could merit salvation on their own without grace.

Personalism: A philosophical or theological view which stresses the importance of the individual person in moral decision-making.

Rationalists: Adherents of a philosophical view that nothing can be true, if it cannot be proved by human reason.

Revelation: God's self-disclosure; the encounter between God's self-communication and human openness and acceptance.

Salvation: The permanent union of people with God and one another; the goal of all creation.

Scholastic: Pertaining to a general school of medieval theology whose approach was intellectual, abstract and doctrinal.

Sola gratia: By grace alone; the Protestant principle stating that we are saved by God's grace alone, not by our efforts at all.

Sola scriptura: By scripture alone; the Protestant principle stating that the Word of God is revealed to us in the tradition and faith of the church.

Supernatural existential: Theologian Karl Rahner's term for the universal and radical capacity for God within every human being.

Discussion Questions

1. Explain revelation in terms of the Judaeo-Christian tradition. How are present-day Christians recipients of that revelation?

2. Distinguish between the objective and subjective aspects of revelation. What is special or particular revelation? What is universal revelation?

3. Define uncreated grace and created grace. Reflect on examples of created grace in your life and the lives of your family and friends.

4. Discuss the universality of grace. How do the ancient theologian, St. Augustine, and the modern theologian, Karl Rahner, contribute to this discussion?

5. Research the life of one of the saints of the Catholic Church tradition. How was the Gospel revealed in the life of the saint? How was grace mediated in the experience of the saint? What is the particular contribution of this saint? Why is this person considered a saint? What was revealed to you through this research?

6. Research the life of one saint from the Protestant or Jewish tradition. How was holiness expressed in the life of this saint? How does this contemporary figure compare with the saints of the Catholic tradition?

Additional Reading

Leonardo Boff, *Liberating Grace* (Maryknoll, NY: Orbis Books, 1984).

Lawrence S. Cunningham, *Our Catholic Heritage* (New York: Crossroads, 1983).

Avery Dulles, *Models of Revelation* (Garden City, NY: Doubleday and Company, Inc. 1983).

Gabriel Moran, *Theology of Revelation* (New York: Seabury Press, 1966).

5

Scripture, the Word of God

The bible is an international best seller. Each year thirty million copies are sold. As of 1988 the bible had been translated into 1,884 languages and dialects, and was available to people in every corner of the world. Why is the bible the world's largest selling book? Why do people of every race, culture and socio-economic class read the bible?

The bible is a fascinating assortment of writings which vary in content, form and message and which were collected over a period of more than one thousand years. It is also a rich and multifaceted resource which contains an abundance of insight into the meaning of life. For Jews and Christians, the scriptures (or the bible) are far more than just literature. The scriptures are revered and valued because they contain God's revelation to women and men of every generation. The scriptures are the Word of God.

If, as Jews and Christians believe, God is pure spirit, it follows that God is not embodied and does not have a voice box or a mouth. How then did the words which are recorded in the scriptures come to be regarded as God's own words, inspired revelation? A simplistic response to this question might suggest that God put biblical authors into trances and had them speak divine thoughts while they were in trance-like states. This was not the case. A nuanced understanding of the nature of revelation is contained in the "Dogmatic Constitution on Divine Revelation" of Vatican II:

> In composing the sacred books, God chose men and while employed by Him they made use of their powers and abilities, so that with Him acting in them and through them, they, as true authors, consigned to writing everything and only those things which He wanted.

> Therefore, since everything asserted by the inspired authors or sacred writers must be held as asserted by the Holy Spirit, it follows that the books of Scripture must be acknowledged as teaching firmly, faithfully, and without errors that truth which God wanted put into the sacred writings for the sake of our salvation.[1]

There are seventy-three books in the bible, some of which were written by one author, some by more than one author, and others which were put together by editors who worked with various oral and written traditions. Since none of the original manuscripts of the books of the bible remain today, in many cases it is difficult to be certain about who the authors were. If the original manuscripts were stored in archives, scholars could check to see who signed them or, if unsigned, if there were some other characteristics by which to identify them. Not having the originals is not the only problem in determining authorship. The ancient people who wrote and edited various books and parts of books understood authorship differently from the way we do today. It was not uncommon for a secretary or follower(s) to put someone's teaching into written form and attribute the text to the person whose teaching it was. Hence, the twentieth century desire for precise identification of each particular biblical author cannot be satisfied; research concerning questions of authorship, however, represents one of the most fascinating aspects of contemporary scripture scholarship.

The belief of the Catholic Church is that the people who were chosen by God to write, contribute to, or edit the books which comprise the bible were inspired to record the truths necessary for the attainment of blessedness or salvation. This does not mean that the authors and editors of scripture had at hand different literary tools or vocabularies from those available to their contemporaries. Neither does it imply that in every word of scripture God is telling us something. In fact, the bible includes a great deal of secular information which was of interest to the ancient peoples to whom the books of the bible were originally addressed. In addition, the bible contains many accounts of people's reactions to God's invitations and deeds, revelations of *their* faith, not God's will. In what, then, does God's revelation consist? Certainly in God's mighty acts, God's faithful presence to believers, God's invitations to enter into a relationship of faith (covenant), and God's self-disclosure in the person of Jesus. It would be incorrect to think of revelation as a line here, a paragraph there, or even an entire book. Instead, it is truer to the spirit of the bible to think of revelation as the dialogue which God has initiated with humanity. Many elements of this dialogue are contained in scripture, but its vitality and urgency are also known in the insights of contemporary faith communities.

An Overview of the Bible

The bible is divided into two major divisions. The scriptures which Jesus studied and preached about are made up of forty-six books and are known as the Jewish Bible, or, more commonly, the Old Testament. The New Testament is a collection of twenty-seven books which record accounts of Jesus' life, death and resurrection, and the faith of his early followers. The Old and New Testaments together comprise the bible to which Christians turn for instruction and inspiration.

The Torah

The Torah (Law) is made up of the first five books of the bible: Genesis, Exodus, Leviticus, Numbers and Deuteronomy. These books contain a primitive history of humankind presented in mythological terms. (A myth is a story which is told to explain a phenomenon concerning which people instinctively seek meaning.) They also contain God's choice of the Hebrews to be his people and God's establishment of a covenant with Abraham and through Abraham with his descendents. (Cf., Gen. 12:7, 13:15, 15:5, 17:4-7, and 18:18.) In addition, the religious legislation which God's people considered themselves bound to observe is found in the Torah, as are the Ten Commandments, a basic ethical code according to which Jews and Christians make moral judgments to this day. (Ex. 20:1-17)

Several scripture stories which are very familiar to most Christians are found in the Torah. These include accounts of Adam and Eve (Gen. 2:4b—3:24), Cain and Abel (Gen. 4), Noah and the flood (Gen. 6-9), the foolhardy attempt to build the tower of Babel (Gen. 11:1-9), Joseph and his brothers (Gen. 37-50), Moses and the struggle for freedom (Ex. 1-4), the miracle at the Red Sea (Ex. 13-15), and the years during which the Hebrew people wandered and complained in the desert. (Ex. 14-17 and Num. 11-21). The Sinai* event, in which Yahweh (God) set up his covenant* with Moses (the leader of the Jewish people who led them out of slavery in Egypt and continued as their leader during their years of wandering in the desert) is depicted in Exodus 19:1-6. One of the high points of the Torah, the establishing of the covenant with Moses, signaled the extension of the promises God had made to Abraham to all the Israelites.

The Historical Books

The following make up the historical books of the bible: Joshua, Judges, Ruth, 1 and 2 Samuel, 1 and 2 Kings, 1 and 2 Chronicles, Ezra, Nehemiah, Tobit, Judith, Baruch, Esther, Lamentations and 1 and 2 Maccabees.

As the category implies, the historical books of the bible give a general history of the Hebrew people. The authorship of these books is attributed to a person identified as the Deuteronomist whose goal was to formulate a theological commentary upon Israel's history. The standard by which the Deuteronomist judged God's people and their leaders was that of exclusive devotion to Yahweh along with total rejection of pagan forms of worship.

The historical books begin with an account of the conquest and settlement of the promised land (Canaan) by the Hebrews. (Cf., the book of Joshua.) The development of the kingdom of Israel as an ancient world power under Kings David and Solomon is recorded in 2 Samuel and 1 Kings. The special promise made by God to David has traditionally been understood as genealogically linking the promised messiah (whom Christians believe is Jesus) to Davidic ancestry. (Cf., 2 Sam. 7:12-16.)

The first and second books of Kings recount how Israel was marred by division after Solomon's death. The division resulted in the arrangement of God's people into two geographical-political kingdoms. The theological reason for the misfortunate division was the infidelity of God's people to the covenant. The northern kingdom was made up of ten tribes, and became known as Israel. The southern kingdom was named for the tribe which resided there, i.e., Judah. The temple, the center of Jewish worship, was located in Judah. This temple of Jerusalem contained a small portable shrine which had been built by the Israelites after they left enslavement in Egypt and before they settled in Canaan; it was known as the ark of the covenant. The stone tablets on which the Ten Commandments were written were kept in the ark.

Because the Hebrew people of the two kingdoms did not repent of their infidelity, but instead grew further and further from God and God's ways, the two kingdoms eventually fell to pagan captors. The humiliation of the Jewish people culminated with their being subject to captivity by the Babylonians (2 Kg. 24). After an approximately 50-year long period of captivity, the Israelites were allowed to return to Jerusalem and attempt to rebuild the city and its temple to their former glory. (Cf., the books of Ezra and Nehemiah for a description of the process of restoration.)

The Prophetic Books

The prophetic books record the prophesies of sixteen prophets who shared the mission of reminding the Hebrew people of the requirements of the covenant and of God's steadfast love and fidelity. The prophetic books are: Isaiah, Jeremiah, Ezekiel, Daniel, Joel, Amos, Hosea, Obadiah, Jonah, Micah, Nahum, Habakkuk, Zephaniah, Haggai, Zechariah and Malachi.

The prophets were men of God who were unique among people of ancient times and who continue to inspire people today. They were extraordinary preachers who dramatically exhorted, inspired and admonished God's people. It is said of the prophets that their mission was to afflict the comfortable and comfort the afflicted. Accordingly, when God's people grew lazy, self-indulgent, and careless about religious observances, they heard scoldings from prophets such as Amos:

> Hear this word, O men of Israel, that the Lord pronounces over you, over the whole family that I brought up from the land of Egypt:
> You alone have I favored, more than all the families of the earth;
> Therefore I will punish you for all your crimes. (Am. 3:1-2)

During their exile in Babylon the Jewish people felt disheartened and anxious about the future of their nation. Prophets spoke reassuring words to them about Yahweh's uncompromising fidelity. A representative prophetic utterance is that of Ezekiel in which he uses captivating and vivid imagery to describe how the Lord would assist Israel by delivering her from exile and restoring her to nationhood:

> The hand of the Lord came upon me and he led me out in the spirit of the Lord and set me in the center of the plain, which was now filled with bones. He

made me walk among them in every direction so that
I saw how many they were on the surface of the plain.
How dry they were! He asked me: Son of man, can
these bones come to life? "Lord God," I answered,
"you alone know that." Then he said to me: Prophesy
over these bones, and say to them: Dry bones, hear
the word of the Lord! Thus says the Lord God to
these bones: See! I will bring spirit into you, that
you may come to life. I will put sinews upon you,
make flesh grow over you, cover you with skin, and
put spirit in you so that you may come to life and
know that I am the Lord. (Ez. 37:1-6)

We learn of God's sovereignty and of God's values and requirements from reading the prophets. The prophets used their
unique imaginations and sensitivities to explain what God
wanted of the Chosen People. They were so close to God that
they shared the conviction articulated by Amos: "Indeed, the
Lord God does nothing without revealing his plan to his servants, the prophets." (Amos 3:7)

Poetry and Wisdom Literature

The poetry and wisdom literature found in the bible consist of
the following books: Job, Psalms, Proverbs, Ecclesiastes, Song
of Songs, Ecclesiasticus and Wisdom of Solomon. These books
contain a rich and varied collection of poetry, prayer, liturgy and
even include love songs.

The psalms are 150 poetic prayers arranged in a single book.
They provide us with insight into Israel's spirituality because
they record how God's people expressed praise, thanksgiving
and lamentation (regret) when they gathered for worship. The
psalms continue to be part of Christian worship today; a psalm,
or part of a psalm, is recited each time Catholics gather to celebrate the Eucharist.

Most wisdom literature dates from after the fall of Jerusalem
in 586 BC. Wisdom literature reflects the attempt of God's people to discern in what a truly good life consists and to determine
what people ought to do in order to live upright lives. According
to Lawrence Boadt, the wisdom books share these common characteristics:

> (1) a minimum of interest in the great acts of
> divine salvation proclaimed by the Torah and

the prophets;

(2) little interest in Israel as a nation or in its history;

(3) a questioning attitude about the problems of life: why there is suffering, inequality and death, and why the wicked prosper;

(4) a search for how to master life and understand how humans should behave before God;

(5) a great interest in the universal human experiences that affect all people and not just believers in Yahweh;

(6) a joy in the contemplation of creation and God as creator.[2]

An ancient Greek translation of the bible, known as the Septuagint (LXX),* was accepted by the early Church as the complete collection of sacred writings of the Hebrew people. The Catholic Church, throughout its history, has stood by the authenticity and inspiration of the forty-six books of the Septuagint. During the Sixteenth Century, at the time of the Protestant Reformation, the reformers contested the validity of seven books accepted by the Catholic Church, (Judith, Tobit, Baruch, 1 and 2 Maccabees, Ecclesiasticus and Wisdom of Solomon), and set their own canon (official list) at thirty-nine books.

The New Testament

The books of the New Testament are usually arranged as follows: the four gospels, the letters of Paul, the so-called "Catholic" letters, and other writings (Acts, Hebrews and Revelation).

The Four Gospels

The first three gospels, those of Matthew, Mark and Luke, are called the synoptic gospels. The adjective synoptic is used because when these gospels are arranged side by side, strong parallels in message and content become apparent. The synoptic gospels record the recollections of believers who committed themselves to the risen Jesus. Each has a particular audience in mind. The Gospel of Matthew was written about 85 A.D. primarily for believing Jews to instruct them about how Jesus fulfilled the messianic prophecies (Old Testament promises of a redeemer). Mark, the oldest and shortest of the gospels composed about 70 A.D., probably was written for gentile Christians in Rome. The Gospel of Luke, dating from approximately 90 A.D., is lengthier and more detailed than that of Mark, and it, too, was addressed to a gentile audience.

The Gospel of John, also written between 90 and 100 A.D., is different from the synoptics. Its purpose was to show that Jesus is God's eternal son, and it reflects early attempts to develop a theology about the meaning of Jesus' exaltation and divinity.

Pheme Perkins tells us that the various New Testament authors worked out their own ways of proclaiming the gospel.

> These different visions cannot and need not be made into one amorphous lump. Doing so would be like mixing together all the paints on your palette to get some muddy color rather than enjoying the wide spectrum of colors. In order to understand the concepts and symbols used in the New Testament, we must find out everything we can about its world.[3]

The Epistles

Fourteen epistles are attributed to Saint Paul. These are letters which were addressed to early Christian communities or to individuals; they are usually dated between 51-57 A.D. Paul was a Jew who converted to Christianity and who worked to educate Greek Christians about the faith he shared with them. His epistles contain brilliant analyses of how belief in Jesus should find expression in personal and communal living.

First and second Timothy and Titus, the so-called "Pastoral Epistles," were written in Paul's name by one of his second generation followers. These letters date from about 110 A.D. The consensus among scripture scholars is that these epistles which bear Paul's name could not have been his own work.

The so-called "Catholic" letters are seven epistles: one by James (c. 60 A.D.), two by Peter, three by John, and one by Jude, all of which are dated between 100-110 A.D. These letters are called catholic because they were sent to the universal church of that time, rather than to individual churches, as Paul had done. The writers of these letters offered guidance and encouragement to early Christian communities, some of which experienced harassment and persecution.

The Other Writings

The other writings found in the New Testament are Acts, Hebrews and Revelation. The Acts of the Apostles is a supplement to the Gospel of Luke in which Luke described the origin and spread of Christian communities during the last decades of the first century. Luke gave us an account of the adaptability of the early Church. This Church underwent a transition from being a primarily Jewish community in Jerusalem to a catholic, i.e., universal Church in which the action of the Holy Spirit, enabling men and women of Greco-Roman culture to respond to God's invitation, was apparent. The Acts of the Apostles was probably written in the late nineties A.D.

The epistle to the Hebrews is a theological treatise which intermingles doctrinal teaching and moral exhortation. Scholars are uncertain about its authorship but they think it was written around 90 A.D. Readers are predictably impressed by the literary quality of Hebrews, as well as by sophisticated theological concepts, such as the priesthood of Christ, which it presents.

The book of Revelation, the last entry in the New Testament, is an example of apocalyptic literature which dates from about 90 A.D. The writer of Revelation makes use of images and symbols to suggest the cosmic dimensions of the struggle between good and evil and to emphasize that God, the Lord of history, will ultimately be victorious over evil. The enduring lesson of Revelation is that Christians rightly hope in the Lord.

Significant Dates from Biblical Times

Just as there are many unresolved questions about authorship of the various books of the bible, it is not possible to assign precise dates to most of the Old Testament books. By consulting the following chart, however, we become aware of the different cultural-political events in the lives of the Hebrew people and the early Christians. Such a cursory overview is informative because much of the salvation history recounted in the scriptures was written in response to concrete events experienced by the Hebrew people and the early Christians.

Important Dates of Biblical Times

B.C.   1800   The age of the patriarchs, the Hebrew leaders Abraham, Isaac, Jacob and Joseph

         1400   Hebrews enslaved in Egypt

1300	Hebrew exodus from Egypt and wandering in the desert
1200	Settlement of Canaan begun under Joshua
1100	Canaan ruled by Judges in a tribal federation
1000	Monarchy of David and then of Solomon, the high point of Israel's power and prestige as a nation
900	Divided monarchies of Israel and Judah at odds with each other as well as the small states surrounding them
722	Fall of Israel (northern kingdom) to the Assyrians
586	Fall of Judah (southern kingdom) and the beginning of the Babylonian exile
539	Restoration of Jerusalem; beginning of modern Judaism
332	Greek domination of the Hebrew people under Alexander the Great
175	Maccabean revolt; achievement of limited freedom for Judah
63	Roman rule of Judah
A.D. c. 1	Birth of Christ
c. 27-29	Activity of John the Baptist
c. 29-33	Ministry of Jesus
c. 33	Crucifixion of Jesus
c. 35	Conversion of Paul
70	Fall of Jerusalem to the Romans
132-135	War with the Romans

Finding the Meanings of Scripture

Were the first two humans a man named Adam and a woman named Eve? How many animals did Noah transport on the ark? When Jesus said that it would be harder for a rich person to enter heaven than for a camel to pass through the eye of a needle (Matt. 19:24), did he have in mind a fine embroidery needle, a large darning needle, or some other kind of needle? When he said that his followers should not worry about what to eat, drink or wear (Matt. 6:31), did Jesus intend to counsel people against saving for a rainy day? When Paul alluded to the perversity of homosexual genital acts (Romans 1:26), did his comments imply condemnation of committed, faithful, permanent homosexual relationships? Should the elaborate prophesies about future famines, catastrophes, wars and the end of the world which are routinely made by TV preachers who take the bible literally be believed? Questions such as these prod us to review the way in which we approach the scriptures as well as the process in which we ought to engage in order to discover the meanings of biblical texts.

The Catholic Church rejects a fundamentalist reading of the bible. The reasons for the Church's non-fundamentalistic stance will be explored later in this chapter. The main purpose of this section is to examine the process by which individuals and communities can come to an understanding of the meanings of the scriptures.

The historical-critical method for understanding the bible is endorsed by the Catholic Church as well as by many other churches. The process of historical criticism is made up of two components: literary criticism and historical analysis.[4] Before determining in what literary criticism and historical analysis consist, let us look at who does the work of interpreting the bible and why.

Exegeisthai is a Greek verb which means to be a leader, to expound or interpret. An exegete is a person who leads another person or a community to understanding. In regard to the bible, an exegete interprets ancient texts, seeking to disclose their meaning both within their original context and in today's very different world. Exegesis is the term used for the process in which an exegete engages. It is important to remember that exegetes (or scripture scholars) do not have magic insight or privileged knowledge; what they have is a method by which to attain answers. The reason why biblical exegesis is such an important science and art is because the scriptures are an account of God's revelation and, as such, are of incalculable importance to God's people.

Literary Criticism

The process of literary criticism requires answering a number of questions in the hope of finding a nuanced understanding of a given text. The scholarly task of literary criticism consists in a seven-step process.

1. *Textual problems.* Are there any words in the text which are uncertain because of transmission or antiquity? The small italic footnotes in the bible indicate textual problems. It is important to be aware of what possible alternative senses of meaning might be conveyed by a word or phrase.

2. *Context.* What precedes and follows the passage? How is the passage related to the context? Has the context, for example, given new meaning to a tradition which originally had a different setting and function?

3. *Form criticism.* In what literary form is the passage written? If it is prose, is it a narrative, story, legend, liturgical or legal text? If poetry, is it a song, oracle, prayer or hymn? Can a particular form be identified as a miracle story, call narrative, covenant lawsuit, catechesis (teaching device), primeval myth, etc.? How does the author use the form? Is it in keeping with the original function (if that can be known), or does the author use it for a different purpose? Why was this particular literary form used? Could other examples of this form in the bible shed light on the passage under consideration?

4. *Structure.* What structural patterns can be detected? Is there parallelism, or inclusion (an echo of the beginning at the end)? Is there a movement evident in the text? How do the parts relate to each other?

5. *Source criticism.* Is there evidence of more than one source in the passage? Are there glaring inconsistencies of style or fact within it? Are there discrepancies which cannot be explained? Is more than one viewpoint evident? If more than one source or author is probably involved, other scripture scholars should be consulted to determine who they think the authors are. It is necessary to determine the source or sources responsible for each biblical passage as well as the date and setting in which the passage was formulated.

6. *Redaction criticism.* If there is evidence of an editor's hand in the passage, how does the work of the editor relate to the more original level of tradition? How has the editor blended various sources into a unified piece of work? What is the editor's point of view? How has the editor reinterpreted the tradition? What questions was the editor trying to answer?

7. *Key words and motifs.* What are the most significant words used in the passage? There may be theologically significant words; it is necessary to find out what they meant for the

authors who used them—what they mean today is beside the point. When key words have been identified, a concordance* is used to discover the range of meanings of the word or words within biblical literature. Knowing if an author is using a word in a traditional or a new way, and recognizing the nuances the word takes on in the text will provide clues as to the intended meaning of a passage.

Historical Analysis

Literary criticism goes hand-in-hand with historical analysis. Historical analysis is carried out in two steps.

1. *Historical content.* Does the passage contain material of historical importance (for example, anachronisms or editorial comments which can be dated)? What extra-biblical data provide information which helps reconstruct the historical and cultural context of the passage?

2. *Date and setting.* When was the passage written? What historical situation is reflected? What were the issues and questions of the time?

When we consider this overview of literary criticism and historical analysis, it is obvious that the work of the exegete is complicated and demanding. An exegete needs to be proficient in the languages in which the bible was written. The original languages of the Old Testament are Hebrew, Aramaic and Greek; the New Testament was composed in Greek. It is important for exegetes to be aware of the secular literature of biblical times as well as pagan religious practices and beliefs. Familiarity with archaeological discoveries enables exegetes to point to concrete examples of customs and practices mentioned in the bible.

The trained eye of an exegete picks up on such things as the four sources which a redactor (editor) called upon in compiling the book of Genesis. Scripture scholarship reveals that these sources are J, P, E and D. The Jahwist tradition refers to God as Jahweh, spelled *Jahweh* in German, hence the abbreviation J; common English usage is of Yahweh. The P tradition is the priestly source, so called because of references to traditions associated with worship and the temple. In the Elohist or E tradition, God is referred to as Elohim. The fourth source D or Deuteronomist, is named for the tradition and style found in the book of Deuteronomy. Exegetes describe how a redactor (who may have been the Priestly author) put two stories of creation back to back in the first two books of Genesis, and inform us that both these stories adapt myths of the ancient Near East to teach theological lessons.

In the New Testament we find two different accounts of Jesus' birth, Matt. 1:18-2:12 and Luke 2:1-19. Exegetes explain that the reason for the different stories is that different audiences were being addressed and different points were being made. When we read the gospels, exegetes recommend that we remember that the stories of the life of Jesus which have come down to us are composed of three stages of tradition. The first stage consists in Jesus' own words and actions; the second stage consists in the apostles' preaching about the meaning of the life, death and resurrection of Jesus, as well as about Jesus' message; and the third stage, which culminated in the evangelists' (gospel writers) actually putting their narratives into writing.

Theological Analysis

Before we can discern the meaning the scriptures have for us today it is imperative that we comprehend what meaning the author or editor meant to convey in the place and at the time the passage was written. After this has been accomplished, we can address the matter of the theological meaning of the passage, both in its original context and for believers today. As with literary criticism and historical analysis, theological analysis proceeds in a succession of steps.

1. Identify the concerns of the author. What were the questions of his community for which a given passage provides answers? The uncovering of key words and motifs often leads to the discovery of the theological purpose of a passage.

2. What view of God is expressed in the passage, and how are God and God's people understood to interact?

3. To whom is the passage directed? Who are the opponents of the author, and what is their point of view? Are there reasons for concluding that one or another point of view is orthodox (a true religious belief)?

4. How might the passage originally have functioned in the community of faith? What questions did it address? In the Old Testament, if the passage shows evidence of extensive editing, it probably functioned differently for different generations of Israelites.

5. What were the hermeneutical* principles of the author(s) and editor(s) of the passage? That is, if an ancient tradition was reinterpreted, what were the reasons for the modification? What theological message was being conveyed?

6. Most scriptural passages had several different "meanings" by the time they were put into final form. Exegetes seek to point out the full range of theological meanings.

By reading and studying the bible believers learn that God has been present to people of faith throughout all of salvation history. The scientific investigation of scripture provides support for the faith of Christians and Jews. It also leads to the belief that God is still present to those individuals and communities which are marked by the sign of faith.

An Example of an Old Testament Exegesis

You will probably want to read Gen. 1:1-2:4a, The Priestly Creation Account, before considering the brief sample exegesis which follows.

Textual Problems: "Then God said: 'Let us make man in our image, after our likeness'" (Gen. 1:26).

Since the Hebrews believe in one God, why are plural pronouns which are translated "us" and "our" used? Exegete Pauline A. Viviano tells us that there is no entirely satisfactory explanation for this usage.[5]

Context: The Priestly creation account is placed at the beginning of Genesis, the book of beginnings. The reason for its being placed first may be its literary distinctiveness, the extent of its popularity, or simply an editorial decision.

Form: Gen. 1:1-2:4a is a narrative (story) written in a hymn-like style which makes use of rhythmic repetition. This passage existed as a story which was told and retold for centuries before it was recorded in written form. The use of repetition made its memorization possible; it was handed down from generation to generation.

Structure: Parallelism is evident in the text; the acts of creation of the last three days are correlated with those of the first three days:

First day: Light	Fourth day: Heavenly lights
Second day: Sky	Fifth day: Birds and fish
Third day: Earth and vegetation	Sixth day: Animals and humans

There is movement in the text to the most significant event: God's creation of humanity. The amount of detail used in describing the creation of man and woman, as well as the fact that the universe is the dwelling place for humanity, illustrate the author's desire to highlight the creation of humans.

Source criticism: There is a consensus among scripture scholars that Gen. 1:1-2:4a is the work of a single person or group known as the Priestly author. The unity evident in the text points to a single author with a particular viewpoint who fashioned ancient material into a cohesive narrative.

Redaction criticism: The Priestly author is thought by many scripture scholars to be the redactor who edited the entire book of Genesis. If this is the case, it may explain why his account of creation was placed before the second account contained in Gen. 2:4b-2:24. In editing the oral and written accounts of God's orderly creation of the universe over a period of six days, the redactor or Priestly author probably used his judgment in committing to writing what he considered to be the most memorable formulations of the various verses.

Key words and motifs: Gen. 1:16 reads: "God made the two great lights, the greater one to govern the day, and the lesser one to govern the night...." In the pagan world the sun and moon were deities which were worshiped. Because the Priestly author professed the radically monotheistic faith of Israel (uncompromising belief in one God), he avoided references to celestial bodies which pagans worshiped. In addition, he simultaneously taught the lesson that the greater and lesser lights are two of God's creations, not superhuman powers to be feared or worshiped.

Historical content: An extra-biblical source which provides useful information is the *Enuma Elish,* the Babylonian creation myth which dates from about 1700 B.C. Israel's use of the imagery of this pagan myth reveals how the prescientific Eastern worldview affected the Hebrew imagination.

Date and setting: The Priestly author put Gen. 1:1-2:4a into final form during the Babylonian exile, probably around 550

B.C. The issues and questions of that time had to do with understanding how the relationship between God and the Hebrew people was affected by their loss of political sovereignty.

Theological analysis: A concern of the author of Gen. 1:1-2:4a might have been to remind the Hebrew people in exile of their mission from God to exercise stewardship over creation (Gen. 1:28-29). By recording that humankind was created in God's image (Gen. 1:27) the Priestly author conveyed what God wanted believers to be—his representatives on earth. In the ancient world the term which is translated "image" referred to a statue of a king which was sent to distant corners of a kingdom where a king could not go to visit. The "image" served as a representative of the king in that region. By extension God's people, the Hebrews, were destined to be God's living representatives. This reminder of God's plan for his people, as well as the goodness and providence of God evident throughout the text, probably served to bolster morale during the difficult experience of exile.

Those who believed the *Enuma Elish* were pagan polytheists who worshiped many gods. Some of these gods were good and others were not. The myth recounts an episode of warfare among the gods and says that humans were created from the blood of one of the defeated gods. The Priestly author's theology is in sharp contrast to the *Enuma Elish*. He is a radical monotheist who holds that God is one, all good, and created humans through the power of his word.

As oral tradition, in its final written form, and in possible earlier written versions, the account of creation in six days and the seventh day of Sabbath rest functioned to instruct the Hebrew people in God's transcendence and their dignity. During the days when David and Solomon reigned and the nation enjoyed prosperity, the oral recounting of the creation story may have reinforced the Hebrew conviction of their special destiny. Centuries later, during the Babylonian exile, the retelling of the Priestly account of creation challenged the Hebrew people to remember their God-given dignity and to trust in God's promises.

Consulting Scripture Scholars to Determine the Meaning of a Passage

As we have seen, biblical exegesis is a time-consuming process which requires a considerable amount of scholarly research. When one is unable to engage in the complex task of exegesis, it is still possible to discover the meaning of a scriptural text by consulting scripture scholars and benefitting from their research. As an example, let us consider a saying attributed to Jesus: "I repeat what I said: it is easier for a camel to pass through a needle's eye than for a rich man to enter the kingdom of God" (Matt. 19:24).

Scripture scholar John P. Meier tells us that Jesus employs hyperbole when he uses the imagery of a camel passing through the eye of a needle. By hyperbole is meant an exaggeration which is used for effect; it is not meant to be taken literally. The passage is found within the overall context of Matt. 19:16-26 which records the story of the rich young man and Jesus' teaching about who can be saved. Jesus' intention is apparent within this context; he wants to correct his disciple's misconception that riches were a sign of God's favor and that rich people would be granted eternal salvation. According to Meier, Jesus' point is:

> Salvation *is* impossible, if it must be achieved by human beings, no matter how rich. The good news is that salvation is the free gift of the omnipotent God . . .[6]

Another scripture scholar, Daniel J. Harrington, S.J., presents an analysis which is very similar to Meier's:

> Not only is it difficult for the rich to enter God's kingdom (v. 23); it is practically impossible as the saying about the "needle's eye" in verse 24 makes clear. The disciples' amazement in verse 25 stems from their assumption that wealth is a sign of divine favor. In verse 26 Jesus teaches that no one can enter the kingdom because of his or her own possessions; the kingdom is God's gift.[7]

The Bible in Liturgy and Private Prayer

Readings from the Old and New Testaments as well as a selection from one of the four gospels are part of the liturgy of the Word, the first part of the Catholic eucharistic celebration. A homily or sermon is given by a deacon or priest after the gospel has been read. In the homily the meaning of the biblical passages is explained and devotional and practical applications are suggested. If the Beatitudes (Matt. 5:1-12) are read, for example, the homilist may challenge his listeners to critically evaluate the consumerism, militarism, and narcissism prevalent in contemporary society, and may explore the types of attitudes which are consistent with Jesus' values.

Today more and more Catholics are turning to the bible for spiritual nourishment and to find the prodding they need to pursue their discipleship. Vatican Council II encouraged lay people to undertake a devout and prayerful reading of the scriptures:

> . . . they should gladly put themselves in touch with the sacred text itself, whether it be through the liturgy, rich in the divine word, or through devotional reading, or through instructions suitable for the purpose and other aids which, in our time, are commendably available everywhere, thanks to the approval and active support of the shepherds of the church. And let them remember that prayer should accompany the reading of sacred scripture, so that God and man may walk together; for "we speak to him when we pray; we hear him when we read the divine sayings."[8]

Catholic Teaching and the Bible

Many Jews were among the first Christians. As Jews they had a profound respect for the Word of God found in the Jewish scriptures. Naturally, they also revered the oral and written accounts of the words and deeds of Jesus because the new covenant* established by Jesus represented the fulfillment and completion of the faith into which they had been born. Gentile Christians, too, valued the history of salvation, the instruction and wealth of spirituality contained in the sacred writings which were available to them. Jesus, absent now in space and time, became present in a very real sense when his words were proclaimed and his deeds recalled.

Unfortunately, as Christianity grew and Christians were separated by centuries from Christ's life, death, resurrection and ascension, the bible became less and less a part of their life. The only bible available to a church community was chained to an altar in church. The overwhelming majority of Christians were illiterate, and, even if they had the time to spend hours by the book at the altar, they would not have been able to read its words. The possibility of slowly remedying this situation occurred following Gutenberg's invention of the printing press around 1436, but by then a more than one thousand year old legacy of unfamiliarity with the bible was a fact of Christian life. As it happened, the exchanges which occurred in conjunction with the Protestant Reformation in the sixteenth century resulted in the continuation of Catholic distance from the bible. Reformers such as Martin Luther overreacted to the non-scripturally based spirituality of Christians. The slogan *"sola scriptura!"* (Scripture alone!) is attributed to him. Regard for Christian doctrine which had been developed beyond, and apart from, the bible, fear of the possible pitfalls attendant to private interpretation of the bible, combined with an unwillingness to acknowledge that Luther had a legitimate point, resulted in counter-Reformation Roman Catholic policies which actually discouraged reading the bible.

During the Reformation the issue of which books were inspired and should be considered part of the bible was finally resolved by the Catholic Church. In other words, the canon was set. By the canon of scripture is meant the official list of inspired books of the bible. The Council of Trent, which was summoned in response to the Protestant Reformation, (Cf., the summary of the ages of the Church in Chapter 6), decided the canon of scripture in 1546. Since Trent the Roman Catholic Church has held that the Jewish bible contains 46 inspired books and that the Christian scriptures are made up of 27 inspired books. In so deciding the Council Fathers accepted the fifth century Latin Vulgate translation of Saint Jerome (d. 420) as the definitive bible of the Church.

In the aftermath of Trent the Catholic Church did not encourage its members to read the bible. Attendance at mass, reception of the sacraments, memorization of the catechism,* and the devotional use of prayer books made up the religious practice of Catholic people. Except for what they learned in occasional sermons about biblical themes, Catholics knew little of the bible. It was not until 1943, with the issuance of the encyclical *Divino Afflante Spiritu* by Pope Pius XII, that the situation began to change.

In *Divino Afflante Spiritu* Pius XII endorsed a scientific, scholarly approach to the study of scripture. The advisability of reading biblical texts in the languages in which they were originally written, and of procuring the oldest extant texts, was acknowledged. Pius recognized the obvious need of scripture scholars to refer to history, archaeology, ethnology, linguistics and other sciences so as to decipher the meaning of biblical texts. Pius' sophisticated appreciation of the nature of the bible led to the development of widespread interest in, and commitment to, scripture scholarship within the Church.

Vatican II's "Dogmatic Constitution on Divine Revelation" (*Dei Verbum,* 1965) emphasizes how scripture, tradition and the magisterium (teaching office) function together. The Catholic Christian should come to the scriptures with faith in Christ, faith in the Church which through its history has been guided by the Holy Spirit while simultaneously offering guidance to its members, and faith in the power of the Word of God recorded by the sacred authors. In marked contrast to Trent, Vatican II encouraged all Catholics—priests, religious and lay alike—to approach the scriptures devoutly and often, and to make bible reading a valued religious practice.

On March 26, 1987, a committee of U. S. Catholic bishops issued "A Pastoral Statement for Catholics on Biblical Fundamentalism." In it the bishops rejected a fundamentalist, or literal, reading of scripture. They said that fundamentalists tend

> "to interpret the Bible as being always without error, or as literally true . . . For some Biblical Fundamentalists, inerrancy extends even to scientific and historical matters. The Bible is presented without regard for its historical context and development."[9]

The bishops cautioned against a fundamentalist inclination to deny the necessity for the Church to guide the faithful in the interpreting of scripture. Some fundamentalists see little need for the existence of the Church. In response to such a way of thinking, the bishops wrote:

> It is important for every Catholic to realize that the Church produced the New Testament, not vice-versa. The Bible did not come down from heaven, whole and intact, given by the Holy Spirit. Just as the experience and faith of Israel developed its sacred books, so was the early Christian Church the matrix of the New Testament. The Catholic Church has authoritatively told us which books are inspired by the Holy Spirit

and are, therefore, canonical; the Bible, then, is the Church's book. The New Testament did not come before the Church, but from the Church.[10]

The Growing Importance of the Scriptures in the Life of the Church

In the years since Vatican II the scriptures have grown increasingly more important to Catholics. There is every reason to think that this trend will continue in the years ahead.

The Church is currently undergoing a radical process of self-evaluation. The world is smaller now than it ever was before, technology affects every facet of human life, the sphere of the secular has been separated from that of the sacred, and deeply held beliefs are routinely challenged. It is within such a context that the Church seeks to discover and remain faithful to its true identity. Scripture scholarship, especially that concerning Jesus' intentions and the dynamisms operative in New Testament faith communities, is of crucial importance to the Church as it attempts to adapt to the times while remaining true to the gospel.

Base communities in Latin America find continual, on-going inspiration in the scriptures. So, too, do *Renew* groups which, since 1977, have been formed in parishes all across the United States and in several foreign countries as well. *Renew* encourages Catholics to meet in small groups, listen to and discuss the Word of God, and take seriously the responsibility of applying the bible to everyday life.

Charismatic Catholics are convinced that Jesus is Lord by the power of the Spirit to the glory of the Father.[11] They experience a deep personal faith and feel themselves to be close to God and the other members of their communities. While some charismatics can be faulted for interpreting the scriptures in a fundamentalist way, the zeal of nonfundamentalist charismatics in reading the scriptures and taking them seriously is to be applauded. Pope John Paul II said that he sees the future of the Church lying in spiritual renewal movements and groups such as charismatic faith communities.[12]

Nowadays individual Catholics are turning more and more to the bible in order to draw close to God and learn about the meaning of life, death, good and evil. In their prayer lives Catholics are finding spiritual nourishment from meditating on the scriptures. They are employing such prayer forms as the psalms to express praise of God. They want to be rooted and built up in Jesus so that they can grow ever stronger in faith. (Cf., Col. 2:7.) And they recognize that one of the ways in which they can encounter Jesus is through seeking him in the living Word of scripture.

Conclusion

This chapter has been about the bible. It is important to be aware of the distinctions and information contained herein. However, it should be obvious that there can be no substitute for actually reading the bible. Reading the bible is not a project to be carried out over the course of a semester or during a summer vacation. It is the work of a lifetime, a book to which people of faith return again and again. Their testimony is that the scriptures contain a living Word which illuminates the darkness of the world and points the way to the light of Christ.

Endnotes

1. *Dei Verbum,* 11.

2. Lawrence Boadt, C.S.P., *Reading the Old Testament* (New York: Paulist Press, 1984), pp. 472-473.

3. Pheme Perkins, *Reading the New Testament* (New York: Paulist Press, 1978), p. 10.

4. My summary of literary criticism, historical analysis and theological analysis is adapted from photo-copied class notes distributed by Mary C. Callaway, Ph.D., of Fordham University in conjunction with the seminar on the Old Testament Dr. Callaway taught in 1980.

5. Pauline A. Viviano, *Genesis* (Collegeville, MN: The Liturgical Press, 1985), pp. 12-13.

6. John P. Meier, *Matthew* (Wilmington, DEL: Michael Glazier, Inc., 1986), p. 221.

7. Daniel J. Harrington, S.J., *The Gospel According to Matthew* (Collegeville, MN: The Liturgical Press, 1983), p. 79.

8. *Dei Verbum,* 25. Section quoted is from St. Ambrose, an early and respected theologian who died in 397 and is numbered among the Fathers of the Church.

9. Ad Hoc Committee on Biblical Fundamentalism, "A Pastoral Statement for Catholics on Biblical Fundamentalism" (Washington, DC: USCC, 1987), p. 2.

10. Ibid, pp. 5-6.

11. Bishops' Liaison Committee with the Catholic Charismatic Renewal, "A Pastoral Statement on the Catholic Charismatic Renewal" (Washington, DC: USCC, 1985), p. 7.

12. Ibid.

Glossary

Catechism: A handbook of religious information presented in a question and answer format.

Concordance: A reference tool for bible study which provides information regarding each and every usage of a given word in the bible. (The chapter and verse of each usage is cited.) By consulting a concordance one can determine the contexts in which biblical authors used particular words and can then speculate about how the usual meaning might be altered by a specific context.

Covenant: "The Hebrew word *berit,* which is used most often to express the idea of a covenant, originally meant a "shackle" or "chain," but it came to be any form of binding agreement. It expresses the solemn *contract* between Jacob and Laban in Genesis 31:44, or the *alliance* of friendship between David and Jonathan in 1 Samuel 18:3. It describes the *peace pact* made by Abraham with a whole tribe of Amorites in Genesis 14:13, and the *bond of marriage* in Proverbs 2:17 or Malachi 2:14. And it can be a solemn treaty between kings, as is the case with Solomon and Hiram of Tyre in 1 Kings 5, or with Ahab and Benhadad of Syria in 1 Kings 20:34. But most often it is used of the special alliance between Yahweh and Israel. . . . Yahweh was a *personal* God who demanded personal loyalty. The sides were by no means equal. Israel recognized that the covenant was a gift from Yahweh and an honor for them and not the other way around." (Boadt, pp. 174-175)

Hermeneutics: A term derived from the name of the Greek-messenger god Hermes, it is a process which seeks to determine the religious message in a scripture passage.

New covenant: By his willingly accepting death on the cross, Jesus established a "new covenant in his blood" (Luke 22:20). This new covenant extends the special relationship

God established with the Israelites to each and every person, regardless of race or national origin.

Septuagint (LXX): Translation into Greek of the Hebrew and Aramaic Old Testament between 250 B.C. and 100 B.C. Its name comes from the fact that legend ascribes the work to a group of 72 scholars and it is designated by the Roman numerals LXX.

Sinai: The name of the holy mountain on which Yahweh established the covenant with Moses.

Discussion Questions

1. How familiar with the bible are you? What would motivate you to study the bible? How do you think devotion to reading the bible impacts upon a person's faith?

2. For what reasons do Jews and Christians maintain that the scriptures are inspired? What does inspiration mean?

3. What are the major divisions of the Jewish bible? What kind of information is found in each division?

4. What are the gospels? What does "synoptic" mean? How much can you learn about Jesus by reading the gospels?

5. What is the difference between the epistles written by Saint Paul and the Catholic epistles? Read one epistle and summarize its content.

6. Describe the process in which exegetes engage, and state the purposes of exegesis. In answering this question refer to literary criticism, historical analysis and theological analysis.

7. Prior to 1943, how important was the bible in the life of the Catholic Church? How important are the scriptures today?

8. Catholics do not take the bible literally. Explain why this is true.

Additional Reading

The Jerusalem Bible and *The New American Bible*. (Both these recommended bibles are excellent translations and provide an abundance of notes which inform the reader of pertinent literary and historical analysis.)

Lawrence Boadt, C.S.P., *Reading the Old Testament* (New York: Paulist Press, 1984).

Pheme Perkins, *Reading the New Testament* (New York: Paulist Press, 1978).

Information regarding resources for Catholic bible study is available from:
The U. S. Center for the Catholic Biblical Apostolate
1312 Massachusetts Ave., N.W.
Washington, DC 20005

6

The Church: God's People on Pilgrimage

As with much of organized religion, the contemporary Catholic Church struggles to overcome mixed reviews. Many Catholics say that they are turned off by the Church. Their list of complaints tends to be somewhat repetitive: Liturgies are boring. Homilies are irrelevant. They feel talked down to, treated like children. There are too many moral prohibitions. The Church seems incapable of changing with the times; it is a very conservative, patriarchal and sexist institution. Rules and penalties abound, but vital dynamic communities are hard to find. More reasons are given for sleeping in on Sunday mornings than for getting up and going to church. The disaffected think it more honest to say that Church is not for them than to engage in a superficial form of association with the Church. They prefer not to have their names on the rolls.

It is not easy to respond to negative stereotypes of the Catholic Church. Merely dismissing complainers and complaints would be irresponsible because it would constitute disrespect for people and their opinions. By the same token, accepting an overly pessimistic assessment of the Church would be irresponsible because such an assessment does not correspond to objective reality. People today will come to accept the relevance and necessity of the Church only after they understand the fundamental premises of ecclesiology* and the range of human needs which are satisfied in the Church. The purpose of this chapter is to establish the fact that the Catholic Church is an institution with a divine origin and destiny, which exists in the world today in a variety of communities, and which holds out hope, help and promise to all people. The truth is that believers are enriched beyond measure by the love and support they receive in communities of faith.

142

What Is the Church?

What is the Church? While there is no simple answer to this question, there are several ways of approaching it. The Old Testament revealed a special relationship, called a covenant, which existed between God and the Hebrew people. The New Testament records the fact that Jesus established a new covenant in his blood (1 Cor. 11:25). This covenant relationship is meant to be for all people, without regard to sex, social status or national origin. Accordingly, we could say that the Church is a community of equals which holds Jesus to his promise of fidelity* and in which people seek to love one another in imitation of Jesus' example. Or, we could restate the biblical images of Church presented by Vatican Council II: the Church is a flock shepherded by God; the Church is a tract of land to be cultivated; the Church is an edifice made up of living stones with Christ as the cornerstone; the Church is the new Jerusalem*; the Church is the Spouse of the Spotless Lamb*.[1] Each of these attempts at a theological conceptualization of the nature of the Church is composed of two elements: the human and the divine. So, too, is the Church. And while it is possible to define the Church in sociological terms, as a group of people who consider themselves to be followers of Christ, any definition which omits the Holy Spirit's active, dynamic involvement with the community is essentially lacking. It misses the point that the Church has a divine element, leaving the Church open to dismissal because it is a flawed human institution.

Because the Catholic Church is a complex reality, and because people tend to see the Church from a variety of perspectives, it is possible to understand what the Church is according to several different models. Avery Dulles, S.J., an American theologian, assessed the many aspects of the Church in his book, *Models of the Church.*[2] Dulles proposed five major approaches for understanding the nature of the Church. While it is possible to identify the Church as one of the five types, it would be inadequate to do so because the reality of the Church is far richer than any one typology. As we review Dulles' models, this fact will become apparent.

(1) The Church as Institution: The Catholic Church is an institution with office holders, laws, procedures, unique features and considerable visibility. As a human society, institutional aspects are a given. However, if the institutional element of the Church

is treated as primary, and the Church is defined chiefly or solely in institutional terms, we are left with a distorted image of the Church. Clericalism, juridicism and triumphalism emerge. The pope, members of the hierarchy, and ordained clergy assume active roles, in contrast to the passivity of the laity. The freedom promised to Christ's followers becomes hard to find because there is so much emphasis on governance and obeying laws. In addition, it is likely that a triumphalistic attitude will prevail, with the Catholic Church considered perfect while the witness of other Christian churches is devalued.

Among the difficulties associated with thinking of the Church in solely institutional terms are the facts that there is little scriptural warrant for so-doing, there is a noticeable absence of provisions for assessing how the institution conforms to the directives of the Holy Spirit, and there are few opportunities for lay members to give input or actively participate.

It is easy for liberal Americans to understand the inadequacy of an overly institutionalized form of Catholicism, but it is also important for them to accept the caution that an institutional framework must undergird an international organization of 825 million members.

*(2) The Church as Mystical Communion:** In the New Testament the Church was understood as *koinonia,* i.e., a community of believers bound to one another by the reconciling grace of Christ, and guided by the Holy Spirit. A somewhat ideal summary of a Jerusalem community of believers is found in the Acts of the Apostles:

> They devoted themselves to the apostles' instruction and the communal life, to the breaking of bread and the prayers. A reverent fear overtook them all, for many wonders and signs were performed by the apostles. Those who believed shared all things in common; they would sell their property and goods, dividing everything on the basis of each one's need. They went to the temple area together every day, while in their homes they broke bread. With exultant and sincere hearts they took their meals in common, praising God and winning the approval of all the people. Day by day the Lord added to their number those who were being saved. (Acts 2:42-47)

There is no question that contemporary Catholics want to experience the mystical and communal aspects of Church. There is a hunger and thirst for spiritual fulfillment and an evident desire to develop habits of prayerfulness. People likewise want to belong to communities in which they share friendship with co-members; they want their needs to be taken seriously and their gifts called forth for the building of God's kingdom. They think that the Church should be known for its vitality and the broad-based participation of its membership.

Those who advocate emphasizing the mystical-communal aspects of the Church would err if they were to seek to eliminate the Church's institutional structure. Likewise, they would be mistaken if they tried to reduce the Church to the kind of fellowship embodied in clubs or other voluntary organizations. The Church, known metaphorically as Body of Christ, has a divine life-principle, the Holy Spirit, through whom "it can grow, repair itself, and adapt to changing needs."[3] A community of Christians must be aware of the Spirit's guidance, and obedient to that guidance, in order to be a church.

(3) The Church as Sacrament: During the past two generations some theologians (namely, Yves Congar, Henri de Lubac, Karl Rahner, and Edward Schillebeeckx), who sought to explain the nature of the Church in theological terms, voiced the opinion that the Church can best be understood as a sacrament. Their theory requires the application of sophisticated theological concepts to the divine and human reality which is the Church. Their conclusion is simply that the Church is a sacrament because it makes Christ present. In a concrete way members of the Church express their faith, hope and charity through witness, worship and service. Through what they believe and what they do they disclose that Christ is present in them by his grace, and Christ acts through them to bring healing and salvation to the world. On the theoretical plane, the Church as sacrament signifies in a mysterious way the power of Christ's grace to become actualized. At its simplest, people experience God, and are reminded of God's provident care, when they encounter Christians who perform the works of charity. The notion of Church as sacrament requires comprehension of Jesus' continuing involvement in salvation history:

> Christ, as the sacrament of God, contains the grace
> that he signifies. Conversely, he signifies and confers

the grace he contains. In him the invisible grace of
God takes on visible form. But the sacrament of redemption is not complete in Jesus as in a single individual. In order to become the kind of sign he must
be, he must appear as the sign of God's redemptive
love extended toward all mankind, and of the response of all mankind to that redemptive love.[4]

An obvious advantage of understanding the Church as sacrament is that both the institutional and communal aspects are
compatible with this model. In addition, it is readily admitted
that the symbolic expressions of grace presented by the Church
are never all that they could be, leaving room for greater effort
to make the Church a more effective sign of Christ's presence in
the world.

(4) The Church as Herald: Twentieth century Protestant theologians such as Karl Barth and Rudolf Bultmann understand the
Church as a particular gathering in which the word of God is
proclaimed and faithfully heard. The bible is seen as neither a
set of timeless ideas nor a record of salvation history; instead,
the proclamation of scripture becomes a concrete event in which
there is an encounter between God and a community of believers. Dulles, summarizing Barth's conception, writes:

> For the Church to be a place in which the word of God
> is truly heard, it is necessary that the word should
> never be imprisoned or bracketed by the Church. The
> word of God is not a substance immanent in the
> church, but rather an event that takes place as
> often as God addresses his people and is believed.
> The Church therefore is actually constituted by the
> word being proclaimed and faithfully heard. The
> Church is the congregation that is gathered together
> by the word—a word that ceaselessly summons it to
> repentance and reform.[5]

According to the herald model, Christians are bound to one
another by faith. The celebration of sacraments is secondary to
the preaching of the word. Salvation comes through acceptance
of the gospel. Institutional structures as well as historical continuity between contemporary churches and the first generations
of Christians are not considered characteristics essential for believing communities to possess.

The Church as herald has a strong biblical foundation, a clear sense of identity and mission, and a humble reverence for God's sovereignty. This model is deficient, however, because in it church becomes a series of disconnected happenings without existential reality apart from individual instances of proclamation and acceptance of the gospel. In addition, the absence of an authentic teaching office for interpreting the scriptures constitutes a significant liability. And the much greater emphasis on witness than on action is not consistent with the overall vision of the bible.

(5) The Church as Servant: The Church today is not subject to the world; neither is the world subject to the Church. Church and world are parallel structures and any interrelationship between the two is entered into on a voluntary basis. There is an evident tendency on the part of the world to deny the relevance of the Church. The Church, however, contends that it is related to the world, and sometimes even identifies its mission in terms of service to the world. As a servant the Church helps people with the problems of human life by healing, reconciling and binding up wounds. Inspired by the gospel, the Church as servant wants to assist people in practical ways to keep alive hope in the midst of so much darkness, and to lead people in laying the foundations for God's rule of peace and freedom in this world.

In deciding whether servanthood is an apt metaphor for the Church, one must determine whether service to the needy comprises the essence of the meaning of church. Is the Church primarily a benevolent organization, or do such notions of the Church as People of God, Body of Christ, Sacrament of Christ's grace and proclaimer of God's word suggest a more theologically valid model? There is no question that the Church as a corporate entity, as well as individual Christians, should be of service to all who are in need. Catholic social teaching has constantly emphasized this belief. (See Chapter 10.) However, from our review of models two, three and four, it is obvious that the Church is much more than a servant. In addition, according to Dulles, there is not much biblical basis for understanding the Church primarily in terms of a servant:

> . . . in the New Testament, where the notion of the Church is explicitly addressed, salvation is individualized and spiritualized. The emphasis is apocalyptic*

rather than prophetic.* The Church is seen as existing for the glory of God and of Christ, and for the salvation of its members in a life beyond the grave. It is not suggested that it is the Church's task to make the world a better place to live in.[6]

Our brief review of Dulles' five models of the Church reveals the many elements which the Church ideally should embody. There is a need to integrate the institutional, communal, sacramental, proclamative and servant aspects of the Church into an all-inclusive reality. The Church is not meant to be just one of the five models; by right, it ought to combine all of them in a balanced way. In order to achieve such a combination, it is obvious that the Catholic Church would have to yield some of its authoritarian structure in favor of a less hierarchically-dominated institutional model. Since it is difficult for church members to experience community in very large parishes, a plan would have to be put in place to move beyond the anonymity, impersonality and complacency characteristic of many Catholic congregations. Because the Church continues Christ's work in the world, it ought to strive continually to grow in holiness so that it can more truly signify Christ's presence. The Catholic Church, as well as the Catholic people, have not been sufficiently open to the wisdom and power of the scriptures; the need to be nourished and challenged by the Word of God should be emphasized. Finally, the Church is not true to Christ's wishes if it is content to protect the reputation of a detached ascetic sect. Using Isaiah's words, Jesus proclaimed his mission,

> "The spirit of the Lord is upon me; therefore he has anointed me. He has sent me to bring glad tidings to the poor, to proclaim liberty to captives, recovery of sight to the blind and release to prisoners." (Lk.4:18)

The Church needs to translate the conviction of Jesus into programs of practical outreach.

What Is the Work of the Church?

Colleges provide students with the setting and the courses for a higher education. Fast food restaurants provide barely edible nourishment for hungry folks of all ages. Video rental centers provide a vast assortment of movies which can be viewed in the comfort of one's home and meet one's need for diversion and entertainment. Churches, too, are there for people. While it is imperative to realize that the Church in a very real sense is the people, it is also accurate to think of the Church in its institutional, communal, sacramental, heraldic and servant modes as a corporate entity whose particular functions can be examined in an objective way. Therefore, the question, "What does the Roman Catholic Church do?" arises quite predictably.

The Church performs a variety of functions. To assure its continuance as a visible community and in order to provide a process through which nonmembers can join Catholic faith communities, the Church has established procedures for the admission of new members. The infant children of Catholic parents are baptized, thus insuring their membership in the Church. Adolescents and adults who choose to become Catholics go through a process known as the Rite of Christian Initiation for Adults before they are baptized. Both infant and adult baptism signal decisive faith commitments, and neither should be entered into without thorough preparation. Accordingly, preparatory programs are provided by the Church for parents and godparents of newborns, and the Church also commits herself to supporting parents as they go about the work of raising their children. The RCIA is an extensive program of preparation which is provided by parishes for people interested in converting to Catholicism. Participation in this program enables converts to come to an appreciation of the splendid gift which is faith.

From the very beginning of its existence the Church has understood its mission in terms of evangelization, i.e., the proclamation of the gospel. The commitment to evangelization comes from the commission which Jesus gave to his followers immediately before his ascent into heaven:

> "Go, therefore, and make disciples of all the nations. Baptize them in the name of the Father, and of the Son, and of the Holy Spirit. Teach them to carry out everything I have commanded you." (Matt.28:19-20)

Evangelization takes two forms; the first occurs when a believing community is asked to listen to the preaching of the Word of God with an attitude of humility, willingness and expectancy. Believers experience an ongoing need to humbly assess their discipleship and to repent of the sins which keep them from living according to the standards of the scriptures. Believers are also required to be willing to fully live out their discipleship. One of the saddest accounts in the gospel is that of the rich young man who was unwilling to sell his possessions, give the proceeds to the poor, and devote himself completely to discipleship. (Matt.19:21-22)

The second form which evangelization takes is that of missionary activity. Beginning with Saint Paul's missionary journeys to the gentiles (as the non-Jewish people in the first century AD were called), the Church has commissioned missionaries in each succeeding generation to bring the gospel to those who have not heard Jesus' message of peace and love. Since Vatican Council II there has emerged a growing sensitivity to respect the cultural traditions of peoples who are evangelized. Today missionaries encourage the people to whom they bring the gospel message to incorporate Christian beliefs and practices into their own cultures. Attempts to impose a foreign culture, as well as the tenets (beliefs) and practices of Christianity, are no longer part of missionary activity. The freedom of each person to choose to become a Christian, and the way of life endemic to each region, are respected by missionaries. Established Catholic communities support missionaries in distant lands through their prayers and financial contributions.

In celebrating the Eucharist the Church remembers the saving work of Christ as well as the bonds of unity which join his followers one to another. In the words of Vatican Council II,

> Taking part in the Eucharistic Sacrifice, which is the fount and apex of the whole Christian life, they offer the divine Victim to God, and offer themselves along with It. Thus, both by the act of oblation* and through holy Communion, all perform their proper part in this liturgical service, not, indeed, all in the same way but each in the way which is appropriate to himself. Strengthened anew at the holy table by the Body of Christ, they manifest in a practical way that unity of God's People which is suitably signified and wondrously brought about by this most awesome sacrament.[7]

By celebrating the other sacraments (See Chapter 7), and by its sponsorship of prayer services, healing services, and programs designed to meet the needs of members, the Church becomes a place where God can be worshiped and where healing, nourishment, forgiveness and human growth take place.

In addition to acting as Church by performing functions such as those we have just reviewed, the Roman Catholic Church also seeks to be faithful to four characteristics which allow her to identify herself as a true Church of Christ. These characteristics are that the Church is one, holy, catholic and apostolic. Prior to Vatican Council II it was customary to argue that the Catholic Church was the true church because of her uniformity of belief, language and practices (oneness). External and almost measurable quantities of piety, were cited as indicative of the Church's holiness. The fact that communities in every nation on earth professed Catholic beliefs confirmed the universality (or catholicity) of the Church. By asserting the existence of an unbroken chain linking Peter, who held the position of leadership among the twelve apostles, with the present pope, the Church claimed an incontestable connectedness to the first Christian community (apostolicity).

Since Vatican Council II the Church tends to interpret its marks in a different fashion. She sees herself as called to continual conversion and holiness so that she can more effectively preach God's Word and signify God's presence. The apostolicity of the Church is more likely to be understood in a dynamic way. Recalling the power and inspiration which the Holy Spirit imparted to the apostles after Christ's ascension into heaven, the Church seeks to be open to the Spirit so that she can do God's work today. The catholicity which should characterize the Church is the eagerness of faithful communities to reach out to everyone and bring the gospel to the ends of the earth.

The Gospel of John records Jesus' prayer for unity:

> That all may be one
> As you, Father, are in me, and I in you
> I pray that they may be one in us,
> that the world may believe that you sent me.
> (John 17:21)

The tragic reality is that Christians are not one; instead of a situation of unity, disunity abounds. A task which the Roman Catholic Church shares with other Christian denominations is to overcome the divisions which have ruptured the bonds of unity among Christians. Vatican Council II endorsed the work of ecumenism,* and serious study, dialogue and interfaith religious services have subsequently been encouraged. The sincerity of the Catholic commitment to ecumenism is evident from the

Church's admission that she shares in the causes of division. The Catholic Church approaches ecumenism with profound respect for other Christian denominations and with a new understanding of the way in which the Catholic Church is the Church of Christ. In the words of Vatican Council II:

> This Church, constituted and organized in the world as a society, subsists in the Catholic Church, which is governed by the successor of Peter and by the bishops in union with that successor, although many elements of sanctification and of truth can be found outside of her visible structure.[8]

The usage of the term "subsists in" is significant because it implies that the Catholic Church does not yet completely conform to what the Church of Christ ought to be, and because it allows that many aspects of Christ's Church are also realized by non-Roman Catholic communions.

Ministry in the Church

Faith in God provides the center or core of a believer's life, the perspective from which all the events and issues of a lifetime are approached. People who believe in the revelation of Jesus usually seek to live out their faith as members of a church. As church members they try to identify the specific kinds of services which they ought to perform. The various works performed by church members are called ministries. Ministry encompasses all the kinds of services which are designated by the Church to enable the fulfillment of her mission.

The explicit acknowledgment that there are many ministries in the Church dates back to the very early community at Corinth which was addressed by Saint Paul. Note Paul's belief in the role played by the Holy Spirit in the organization and direction of the community:

> There are different gifts but the same Spirit; there are different ministries but the same Lord; there are different works but the same God who accomplishes all of them in everyone. To each person the manifestation of the Spirit is given for the common good. To one the Spirit gives wisdom in discourse, to another the power to express knowledge. Through the Spirit one receives faith; by the same Spirit another is given the gift of healing, and still another miraculous pow-

ers. Prophecy is given to one; to another power to distinguish one spirit from another. One receives the gift of tongues, another that of interpreting the tongues.* But it is one and the same Spirit who produces all these gifts, distributing them to each as he wills. (1 Cor. 12:4-11)

How is it that Christians come to an understanding of themselves as suited to specific roles? How do the homilists,* teachers, persons devoted to the human services and charismatics* begin to know that these are the roles which they are meant to fill?

In order to decide which type of ministry should be engaged in, people ordinarily go through a process of discernment. This process entails using one's reason as well as one's intuitive judgment in order to discover the gifts and talents one has been given for the enrichment of the community. Discernment also results in the determination of the overall context in which individuals will minister. In the Catholic Church some people experience an attraction, or call, to priestly and religious vocations.* These women and men are impelled by the Spirit to devote themselves exclusively to ministry within the Church. They choose not to marry, embracing a celibate lifestyle so as to be free to give of themselves in service to the community. The majority of Catholic Christians discern that theirs is a vocation which does not require a commitment to celibacy. These people, married and single, are known as "the laity." Within the Church there are a variety of ministries available to lay Catholics.

Both single and married men have the option of serving the community as ordained deacons. Deacons assist bishops and priests in a variety of ways. They can officiate at baptisms and marriages, preach and conduct prayer services. The ancient office of deacon was reestablished in the Church as a result of the directives of Vatican Council II. Although the diaconate today is comprised exclusively of men, there is a significant amount of interest in the possibility of extending an invitation to women to consider joining this ministry.

What other ministries are open to the laity, male and female? The participation of the laity in liturgical celebrations is welcomed. Both men and women fill such roles as eucharistic minister, lector and leader of prayer services. The bishops of the United States, in the 1988 draft of their pastoral letter, "Partners in the Mystery of Redemption," proposed that both girls and boys be accepted as altar servers, and this suggestion was accepted in 1994. Ministries such as visiting the sick, extending support to individuals and families in times of crisis, being present to the bereaved as they grieve, and extending practical outreach to the poor and homeless are routinely embraced by lay Catholics. Lay Catholics are also beginning to fill administrative positions in Catholic churches, schools and other institutions. Catholic men and women are studying theology, spirituality and pastoral ministry in seminaries and graduate schools in order to prepare for academic and ministerial work within the Church.

Prior to Vatican Council II the tendency was to understand the interrelationship among ministers in the Church in a pyramidal way. Today, in view of the growing respect for women in society, and the renewed regard for the dignity of all humans of both sexes, there seems to be a real possibility that the stratification associated with the old system will disappear. When ministry is understood more in terms of putting one's gifts at the service of the community than of status, office and power, the communities in which people minister will be much closer to the New Testament ideal.

Ministry tends to become a sterile concept if it is defined in relationship to an institution instead of a person. The most happy and effective ministers know that they are doing God's work. One lay minister told a poignant story which illustrates this insight. He was a soldier in Europe during World War II and came with his battalion to a bombed out church. Among the ruins was a statue of Jesus with no hands. Etched in the base of the statue was the request of an unknown GI: "He has no hands but yours. Will you give him your hands?" The former soldier, now a husband, father and grandfather, came to think of himself as doing Jesus' work. He long ago lost count of the clothing drives he conducts, the hours he volunteers in a soup kitchen and the junior high religious education classes he teaches. He never fails to impress the people he meets because he is always cheerful. He considers his invitation to be Jesus' hands a very special gift.

The Church Throughout History

The formulation of doctrines, the particularization of devotional practices, various theories of institutional structure, and even the Christian community's sense of self-identification, have developed throughout history. They have also been affected by the events of history. A familiarity with the history of the Church is, therefore, a prerequisite for anyone who wants to understand the Church today. Serious study of church history requires a commitment to many years of scholarly investigation. Since this is not possible for most people, the following survey is presented for the purpose of identifying significant events and movements in the history of the Church.

In the beginning, was there a Church? *When* was the beginning? These, of course, are the first of the historical questions. To answer them adequately requires appreciation of the divine and human dynamic which was present in the Church from its inception. After Jesus ascended into heaven, his followers went to the Upper Room, the same place in which Jesus and his apostles had celebrated the Last Supper. There they passed ten days, recalling the events of Jesus' public ministry, supporting one another, and praying for guidance. On the tenth day they experienced a radical religious renewal and began to do the work to which they felt God was calling them. In the Acts of the Apostles we read a vivid account of Pentecost Sunday:

> When the day of Pentecost came it found them gathered in one place. Suddenly from up in the sky there came a noise like a strong, driving wind which was heard all through the house where they were seated. Tongues as of fire appeared, which parted and came to rest on each of them. All were filled with the Holy Spirit. They began to express themselves in foreign tongues and make bold proclamations as the Spirit prompted them. (Acts 2:1-4)

St. Luke goes on to relate how Jews who were visiting Jerusalem from many different nations understood the single dialect in which the men from Galilee spoke. They *understood,* but they could not believe their ears. ["What does this mean?" they asked one another, while a few remarked with a sneer, "They have had too much new wine!" (Acts 2:12-13)] When Peter spoke in clarification, however, explaining how the Apostles were transformed by the Holy Spirit, the events of Jesus' life, and the ways in which Jesus fulfilled the scriptures, many accepted Jesus' message and were baptized. (Acts 2:5-40)

Tradition cites Pentecost as the "Birthday of the Church." Ecclesiologists today affirm the fact that the Church existed in the community of the Apostles, other acquaintances of Jesus, and the first "converts." However, they remind us that, in the beginning, believers in Jesus considered themselves Jews, worshiped in synagogues, and were unaware of many of the categories and definitions which we have since come to associate with the Church. As a matter of fact, neither the term "Christian" nor the term "Church" was part of their vocabulary.

It was with the admission of gentiles into the community that believers in Jesus began to understand themselves as distinct from Judaism. This understanding of their identity as a separate community led to their calling themselves an *ekklesia,* the Greek word for church. The churches about which we read in the New Testament are congregations gathered in the name of Jesus Christ. Sometimes *ekklesia* is used in reference to a small house community; at other times the reference can be to the universal Church, or the Church in a specific locality. The church at Antioch was made up of former Jews and former pagans who referred to themselves as Christians. The way in which all the various Christian communities came into being was similar: the gospel was preached; the Holy Spirit opened the ears of those who listened; those who believed asked to be baptized; the community of baptized believers met to celebrate the Eucharist, support one another in faith, meet each other's needs, and pass on the good news which they had heard. There was no uniform order or structure in these early churches; what they had in common was the depth and vitality of their faith commitments.

As the early Church realized that it was meant to be a community inclusive of Jews and non-Jews, an inevitable separation of Jewish Christians from the temple in Jerusalem and the synagogues in other places occurred. The ideal of shared fellowship among Jews and pagans, slaves and free persons, men and women was articulated (Galatians 3:28), and a spirit of regard for the gifts which all could bring to the community was fostered.

In the first decades of Christianity there was a continual growth in numbers of Christians and numbers of Christian communities. Several offices came into being in response to the needs of these communities for leadership, liturgical ministry, and service to those in need. A bishop (*episcopus*) was chosen by the community to be its overseer, to preach, to teach, administer the sacraments, and serve as liaison with other churches. The care of church buildings was entrusted to people called porters; acolytes (altar servers) and lectors were chosen to assist the bishop in the eucharistic celebration. Deacons were appointed to care for the poor of the community. Further increase in membership led to the establishment of the office of presbyter or priest. When it became impossible for all the Christians in one area to be present at the eucharist celebrated by the bishop, presbyters were commissioned to lead individual communities in worship.

Up until the early fourth century Christian communities were ordinarily located in towns. Christianity provided a sharp contrast to the pagan religions which existed in the Roman empire, and, on many occasions during the first three hundred years, Christians endured persecutions. Those who died as a result of being persecuted for their faith were called martyrs, and were venerated by the community because of their holiness. The situation changed markedly when the emperor Constantine was converted in 312 A.D. Constantine revised Roman law so that it supported Christian values, and many privileges were granted to Church leaders. A new wave of Christian missionary activity resulted in the evangelization of rural areas, with ever-greater reliance on presbyters to preside at the eucharist for these outlying communities.

The growing Church, separated now by three centuries from the churches which were led by the apostles, had to face questions concerning beliefs and practices. William A. Scott, in *The Church Then and Now,* commented upon the manner in which such questions were addressed:

> The bishops of the area began to meet to deal with questions of faith, problems of discipline, and matters regarding liturgical worship. Their meetings, originally informal, gradually were formalized into synods that met regularly to decide matters affecting their churches and their decisions were accepted as normative by the communities they led. For questions affecting the entire Christian church, particularly matters of doctrine, the bishops came together in general

council* and their teaching was seen as an expression of authentic and apostolic authority.*[9]

From the fifth through the eleventh centuries Western Europe endured a succession of invasions by so-called barbarians. Early in these invasions the power and governance of the Roman Empire disintegrated. The bishop of Rome, successor to the chair occupied by Peter, the leader of the apostles, came to exercise significant influence in both religious and political capacities. The event which occurred on Christmas Day, 800, illustrates this point: Pope Leo III crowned the Frank, Charlemagne, emperor of the recently organized political entity known as the Holy Roman Empire. The pope and the emperor stood side-by-side as recognized authorities of church and state. Naturally, events such as this led to a far different understanding of the Church from that held centuries before by small communities of believers for whom persecution was a very real threat.

The supremacy of the Church and the independence of the papacy were not always in evidence during the Middle Ages. Occasionally the Church found herself under the domination of the emperor. Such was the case in the tenth century when Otto I, a German emperor, took it upon himself to determine who the bishop of Rome was to be. Within approximately one hundred years the Church wrested the power to name the pope from the emperor and placed it in the hands of the cardinals* in Rome. The history of the Church through the next four or five hundred years attests to both good and bad judgment on the parts of cardinals and popes, some of whom had the best interests of the Church at heart, and others of whom did not. That history includes a time at the beginning of the fourteenth century when a Frenchman was elected pope and moved the papacy from Rome to Avignon, France, where it remained for seventy-five years, and a time at the end of the fourteenth century when two men simultaneously claimed to be pope, one in Rome, the other in Avignon. This thirty-year crisis of leadership is referred to as the Great Western Schism.

The sixteenth century was a time of significant turmoil for the Church. Several factors conspired to cause what has come to be known as the Protestant Reformation. There was corruption and scandal associated with many priests and bishops. The papal office was impaired by political maneuverings and abuses of power. Superstition and an overemphasis on externals characterized the faith of many Christians. The growing spirit of nationalism fired an attitude of rebellion against men in authority who claimed the right to rule over an entire church or empire. The spokespersons of the Protestant Reformation were men such as Martin Luther, Ulrich Zwingli, and John Calvin. They protested against what they considered to be clerical abuses of power, and called for a return to the style of Christian community described in the scriptures. At the outset the reformers sought to change or modify the Roman Catholic Church to which they belonged. As it turned out, however, they founded their own Christian churches, separate and distinct from the Church of Rome. Tragically, the Church of Christ was splintered.

William A. Scott described the response made by the Roman Catholic Church to the Protestant Reformation:

> The Council of Trent was convened in 1545 to purify and reform the church in answer to the challenge of the reformers. Its accomplishments were impressive. In response to Protestantism, it spelled out in careful detail the elements of Christian belief. In matters of discipline, it corrected many of the abuses that had beset the church for centuries. But the organizational structure of the church was left intact. Roman Catholicism emerged from the council as a strongly centralized church with the pope exercising supreme teaching and ruling authority in a manner more absolute than at any point in its history.[10]

After Trent the Church saw herself as she had defined herself, as a changeless form. The form was ordinarily visualized as a pyramid: at the top of the pyramid stood the pope, under him the cardinals, then bishops, priests and vowed religious; the laity's place was at the bottom. As a result of this vision of the Church, there was an unmistakable tendency to relegate to the laity a very passive role. There was also an overreaction to Protestant reliance on and devotion to the scriptures, so that Church leadership continued to make the bible inaccessible to lay people. The catechism became a very important book for Catholics in that it, rather than the bible, was the vehicle for communicating Christian belief.

The Catholic focus on the papal office probably reached its zenith in 1870 at the first Vatican Council. This council, summoned by Pope Pius IX, defined papal infallibility and set forth the context in which a pope exercises infallibility. The doctrine of papal infallibility asserts that the Roman pontiff is infallible when, as direct successor to the apostle Peter, he speaks on matters of faith and morals, making clear his intention to use the prerogative of infallibility (*ex cathedra**). This prerogative has, in fact, very rarely been used, and there have been many calls for additional discussion of the concept.

From the 1830s until as recently as the years preceding the second Vatican Council the Catholic Church consistently articulated an anti-modernist attitude. Modernism was a movement within Catholicism which challenged the traditional teaching of the faith in eclusively classical terms,* and which emphasized the rational bases of dogma sometimes to the detriment of appreciating the mystery to which the dogma referred. For example, it is not possible to comprehend the mystery of the Blessed Trinity by memorizing a doctrinal formula. The essence of what it means for God to be triune will always be a mystery. In addition, modernists grasped the insight that there was more knowledge available to nineteenth and twentieth century scholars than had been available to those of the twelfth and thirteenth centuries. Modernists wanted to engage the secular world of learning and to incorporate knowledge from the physical and social sciences into the field of theology. Richard P. McBrien writes that the more sophisticated theological forms of modernism were correct about several important matters:

(1) The inner religious experience *is* an essential element of the life of the spirit and, in large measure, generates and supports the act of faith;

(2) dogmatic formulae are always inadequate to their object, which is God;

(3) revelation is first and foremost for the sake of salvation and the quality of human life rather than for the satisfaction of intellectual curiosity;

(4) revelation has only gradually unfolded in the life of the Church, and with many fits and starts; and

(5) the Bible, and indeed all the sources of Christian tradition must be studied according to the most scientifically critical methods at hand.[11]

In 1958 an elderly cardinal was elected to fill the position of interim pope. Angelo Roncalli took the name Pope John XXIII; people expected his papacy to be short, pious and uneventful. However, the five-year reign of John XXIII turned out to be the most decisive in modern history because of the pontiff's decision to convene Vatican Council II. Pope John XXIII did not fear the modern world, and he realized that there was a need to design a blueprint for a church which could replace the Church of Trent. Accordingly, he summoned cardinals, bishops and theologians from all over the world to come to Rome and consider all the pressing issues which faced the Church. Deliberations at Vatican II were carried out over a period of three years, and sixteen decrees (position papers) were adopted. In the words he used when he addressed the first session of the Council Pope John XXIII revealed a remarkably humble and open attitude: "Nowadays . . . the Spouse of Christ prefers to make use of the medicine of mercy rather than that of severity. She considers that she meets the needs of the present day by demonstrating the validity of her teaching rather than by condemnations." Pope John pointed to a new style of church as well as a new style of leadership. Carrying out the changes necessary to make the Church less of a clerically-dominated juridical structure and more of a Spirit-filled community of believers has turned out to be a difficult struggle. It is made that much more difficult by people whose loyalty is to the hierarchically ordered Church of Trent. Thus, the period of Church history at which we presently find ourselves is a time of significant tension. The tension exists because of an ideological conflict over what the Church is meant to be. The one thing which seems certain is that there will not be a quick or easy solution to the conflict.

Communities Which Identify Themselves as Church

From our survey of Avery Dulles' models of the Church, as well as from our familiarity with the similarities and differences with which people live out their faith, it becomes apparent that Catholic Christian communities will reflect a variety of concrete forms. What all of these communities have in common is the conviction which they express: "We are the Church." They believe that because of their faith in God and openness to the Holy Spirit they carry out the work of Jesus within the particular community to which they belong.

The vast majority of Catholics in the United States live out their faith in communities known as parishes. The parish is defined by the Code of Canon Law,* Canon 515, as "a definite community of the Christian faithful established on a stable basis within a particular church; the pastoral care of the parish is entrusted to a pastor as its own shepherd under the authority of the diocesan bishop." There are 19,500 parishes, 185 dioceses, and over 52 million Catholics in the United States today.[12]

Just about all Catholic parishes have a church building in which parishioners gather to celebrate the Eucharist (also referred to as attending mass or liturgy), and most have a priest who serves as pastor (the spiritual and, frequently, the administrative leader of the community). Some parishes are also served by associate pastors, who are usually priests, but may be deacons, religious sisters or brothers, or lay people. In the past, there was an unfortunate tendency in Catholicism for the laity to describe their identity as Catholic in terms of externals such as their belonging to a specific parish or attending mass in a particular church building. Since Vatican II there has been a growing awareness of the multifaceted richness of individual and communal faith. This awareness is evolving alongside the entity known as the parish and is leading to richer descriptions of Catholic identity.

Parishes come in a variety of sizes and shapes. Some long established city parishes encompass small geographical areas while serving thousands of families. (Parishioners in these parishes often experience difficulty in overcoming the anonymity and impersonality associated with large organizations. Various strategies for providing a sense of belonging need to be employed so that parishioners come to think of themselves as part of a believing family.) Many suburban and rural parishes established since the end of World War II have limited membership and seem like extended families, or are of manageable size, serving a few hundred families. U.S. parishes with affluent congregations can afford to provide many services, including Catholic elementary and secondary schools, and can afford to subsidize Catholic missionary activity. There are also many poor inner city and rural parishes which have difficulty meeting church payrolls and which rely on the assistance of wealthy congregations.

A major crisis facing the Church in the United States is the priest shortage.* The ratio of lay people to priests is growing, and, in view of a continuing decline in seminary enrollment, prospects for the years ahead are that there will be a steadily declining number of priests. Since we have come to think of Catholicism in terms of priestly leadership of parishes, the thought of future priestless parishes may seem alarming. Is such a phenomenon inevitable, and does it bode ill for Catholicism? Answering these questions will force us to examine some of the practices which have been institutionalized within the Catholic Church. Ordaining only males is the established tradition; requiring that they commit themselves to celibacy dates from the Middle Ages. Celibacy is a matter of ecclesiastical custom and law in the Roman Catholic Church; it is not a requirement attributable to God's will. Church law could conceivably be amended so that married men would be eligible for priesthood; it could also allow nonmarried ordained men the freedom to marry at any time after ordination. Such a change of policy might result in increased interest in priestly ministry. In addition, it is possible that the Catholic Church may one day extend to women the invitation to serve as priests. In spite of the fact that the Vatican precluded the possibility of ordaining women in its 1977 "Declaration on the Question of Admission of Women to the Ministerial Priesthood," the topic of women's ordination continues to be the subject of a great deal of popular and scholarly interest. Although Rome has spoken, the issue has not been closed. It stands to reason that if the Church allows women to minister as priests the number of priests will significantly increase. The ordination of women will come within a church which truly appreciates the dignity of women and women's innate equality. Of course, such an appreciation requires that the Church also come to a much deeper awareness of how she is a sacrament of God, the God who created both women and men in his/her own image.

In the years following Vatican II the leaders of the Church in Latin America recognized the need to put the spirit of the Council into practice. The bishops as well as the laity wanted to develop a context in which faith could be lived in a meaningful, dynamic way. In order to achieve this end, Catholic Christians began to form small communities which have come to be called base communities. These groups meet together to read the scriptures and allow the scriptures to speak to their lives. The presence of the Holy Spirit, guiding their process of discernment, is experienced by group members who witness to an ever-deepening growth in personal faith. The testimony of members of base communities about how God is present in human experience is influencing people throughout the world to become more aware of God's immanence. In Brazil, 100,000 base communities have come into existence in twenty years. This phenomenon has led commentators to speak of an "ecclesial genesis," that is, the birth of a new form of Church.

The form of church community at which college students usually gather while at school is provided by campus ministry. Priests, religious and lay staff members of campus ministry arrange eucharistic celebrations, penance and prayer services, retreats, and educational programs. Frequently, counseling and spiritual direction services are also provided. Students who attend religious services sponsored by campus ministry are encouraged to participate and become actively involved in church on campus. The disadvantage of experiencing church within the campus ministry setting is that the vast majority of members are in the same age group and tend to share the same history and perspective. The diversity evident in the typical parish in which people vary in age, occupation, goals, and even in understanding of the nature of the Church, is missing. However, the enthusiasm, commitment and sense of belonging which appear in the campus ministry context seem to offset its inherent drawbacks.

Some college graduates decide to pledge a year or two after graduation to living in a believing church community. Consider the lifestyle and commitment of one such community, the Jesuit Volunteer Corps, as described in a pamphlet on the JVC:

> JVC challenges each volunteer to live a simple and reflective lifestyle, an alternative to the consumerism of our society. A simpler lifestyle is an important step in eliminating the needless clutter that complicates life. The JVC stresses spiritual values over material possessions and invites the volunteer to integrate faith by working and living among the poor and oppressed. This allows the volunteers to experience, more directly, the lives of those they serve while raising their consciousness of the human needs that surround them.
>
> The JVC is committed to working for justice, through faith. Volunteers work together with others dedicated to serving physical and spiritual needs basic to human dignity. JVC encourages and nurtures the empowerment of the poor by supporting programs that allow people to help themselves. Through work and reflection on their experience, Jesuit Volunteers can

examine the causes of oppression and look for ways to bring about justice in our world.

The Reasons Why People Belong to the Church

People become members of the Church for a lot of reasons. Catholics who are sincerely committed to Christian discipleship are apt to cite a number of factors which contribute to their choosing to belong to the Church. These factors tend to be spiritual in nature. The kind of belonging to which we refer represents a real and significant affiliation, not just having one's name on a membership list so as to avoid difficulties when the time comes to arrange for a baptism, wedding or funeral.

Catholic Christians come to a mature acceptance of the Church after they hear Jesus say to them, "This is the time of fulfillment. The reign of God is at hand! Reform your lives and believe in the gospel!" (Mark 1:15). They experience in the depths of their hearts an understanding that people should live their lives according to God's plan, respecting the order of creation and the boundaries which properly limit human conduct. In addition, they feel an eagerness to repent of their sinfulness and to live according to the spirit of the gospel. By living as God's sons and daughters are meant to live, believers come to know the serenity and wellness promised by Christ.

It is fairly easy to articulate an act of faith after a religious experience which results in conversion. However, it is not so easy to sustain that belief through all the ups and downs of a lifetime. In fact, believers say that it is impossible to live the life of faith in isolation. They attest to a need for the support and encouragement of co-members of a community of faith. The spiritual, emotional and physical crises which beset each of us at one time or another often precipitate a reevaluation of our beliefs and attitudes. They may also require a strengthening of the bonds which unite us to Christ and his followers. The insights, affirmation, counseling, understanding and prayers which church members extend to those in difficult straits provide them with the needed help to get through life's more trying moments.

The Catholic Church is an international organization whose members share in common belief in Jesus. Jesus is the reason to belong to the Catholic Church. But who is Jesus? How is Jesus the paradigm (exemplar)? What do the words of Jesus

mean for people today? How can we know Jesus, avoid miscon-
struing the man and his message, come to the kind of spiritual
intimacy which we instinctively seek? It is in church that people remember Jesus, dialogue about the meaning of their discipleship, and are blessed with the direction of the Holy Spirit.
On the road to Emmaus the hearts of two of Jesus' disciples
burned within them as a disguised Jesus revealed the meaning
of the scriptures. (Luke 24:32) Any place where people gather
together in Jesus' name to pray, seek instruction and ponder the
meaning of scripture becomes a revelatory locus for them, a kind
of Emmaus. Throughout the history of the Church people have
considered themselves blessed because Catholicism provides the
milieu within which they could discover an ever-deepening
knowledge of Jesus and a trusting friendship with him.

On Holy Thursday, the night before he died, Jesus' apostles
gathered together in the Upper Room to celebrate an event
which happened centuries before, God's deliverance from exile of
the Hebrew people. It was at that Passover supper that Jesus
offered his very being to his friends and instructed them to come
together in the future to celebrate the mysteries of salvation.
An account of an early Christian community's celebration is contained in the writings of Saint Paul:

> I received from the Lord what I handed on to you,
> namely, that the Lord Jesus on the night in which he
> was betrayed took bread, and after he had given
> thanks broke it and said, "This is my body, which is
> for you. Do this in remembrance of me." In the same
> way, after the supper, he took the cup, saying, "This
> cup is the new covenant in my blood. Do this, when-
> ever you drink it, in remembrance of me." Every time
> then, you eat this bread and drink this cup, you pro-
> claim the death of the Lord until he comes! (1 Cor.
> 11:23-27)

Because Jesus rose from the dead on Easter Sunday, and because the Holy Spirit came to Jesus' followers on Pentecost Sunday, the first generations of believers gathered each Sunday to
celebrate the saving mystery of redemption. It is from their
ancient practice that the Catholic tradition of gathering the
community for Sunday mass originated. Catholics come together at mass to celebrate Jesus' love for them and their deliverance from bondage to sin. They also come with all their spiri-

tual hungers and thirsts to be nourished by the sustenance which Jesus continues to impart.

People do not belong to the Church solely because of what the Church can give them. They come to the Church with the conviction that they need to give something of themselves. As we have already seen, their self-gift can take the form of many different kinds of ministry. Among the really valuable aspects of the Church are the structures it provides for people who want to reach out in caring ways to those in need. Churches are becoming increasingly aware of the service they can provide by directing volunteers to useful endeavors, and by supporting volunteers and voluntary organizations in their work. The many requests Catholic people hear—from the soup kitchens, the food pantries, and the tutoring offices in inner city schools—challenge them to live up to the social commitment required by the gospel.

The Catholic Church is custodian of an almost two thousand year old tradition of teaching. Therefore, it is understandable why Catholics turn to their Church with questions of scriptural interpretation and concerns about moral issues. Catholics may also be troubled by the attitudes which are prevalent in contemporary society: the materialism, consumerism, narcissism, and even the biblical fundamentalism. It is difficult to understand how one can prevent these influences from weakening and distorting faith. The wisdom of the church's teaching office (magisterium) is a valuable resource as people attempt to be faithful to the vision of the gospel.

Conclusion

Even though the contemporary Catholic Church struggles to overcome mixed reviews, there are convincing reasons to commit oneself to church membership. Church members create the Church by their faith and involvement; they are aided in their growth to maturity by the wisdom and spirituality they discover in faith-filled communities; and they make Christ present to the world by the love and care they extend to all as they live out their identity as God's people on pilgrimage.

Endnotes

1. *Lumen Gentium,* 6

2. Avery Dulles, S.J., *Models of the Church* (New York: Doubleday, 1974).

3. Ibid., p. 46.

4. Ibid., p. 63.

5. Ibid., p. 72.

6. Ibid., pp. 94, 95.

7. *Lumen Gentium,* 11.

8. Ibid., 8.

9. William A. Scott and Frances M. Scott, *The Church Then and Now* (Kansas City: Sheed & Ward, 1985), pp. 9-10.

10. Ibid., p. 17.

11. Richard P. McBrien, *Catholicism* (Minneapolis: Winston Press, 1981), p. 645.

12. Joseph Gremillion and Jim Castelli, *The Emerging Parish: The Notre.Dame Study of Catholic Life Since Vatican II* (San Francisco: Harper and Row, 1987), p. IX.

Glossary

Apocalyptic: The revelation of a violent struggle in which evil is destroyed.

Authentic and apostolic authority: The Catholic Church claims that its authority is real and true (authentic) because the pope and bishops can trace their ancestry to the Twelve, the apostles, to whom Jesus entrusted the leadership of the community of those who believed in him, and because Church leadership is guided by the Holy Spirit.

Cardinals: Originally, persons who were appointed pastors of the great churches of Rome; since the eleventh century the members of the so-called "College of Cardinals" have elected the pope.

Charismatics: Persons who are especially devoted to the Holy Spirit and who manifest the gifts of the Spirit in their daily lives. Seven gifts of the Spirit are traditionally cited: wisdom, understanding, knowledge, counsel, piety, fortitude and fear of the Lord.

Classical terms: The way of thinking and speaking employed by the philosopher/theologian St. Thomas Aquinas and those who followed him. Classicism essentially holds that truth can be captured in propositions whose meaning remains unchanged and clear from one age to another.

Code of Canon Law: The official listing of laws binding within the Roman Catholic Church.

Ecclesiology: The study of the nature of the Church using theological categories, principles and insights.

Ecumenism: The movement which seeks to achieve unity among Christians.

Ex cathedra: Literally, "from the chair." The pope who sits in the chair of Peter, or who occupies the same office as Peter, the leader of the apostles, invokes the special grace which accompanies that office when he teaches infallibly. Thus, when making a solemn infallible declaration the pope is said to be speaking *ex cathedra*.

General Council: Twenty-one meetings have been held throughout the history of the Church to decide on matters of Church doctrine. The first general council was held at Niceae in 325; the most recent, at the Vatican in Rome from 1962-1965.

Homilists: Deacons and/or priests who preach at the eucharist; those who give the sermon.

Jesus' promise of fidelity: Before he ascended into heaven, Matthew reports that Jesus told his disciples that he would be with them and with all who believe in him: "Know that I am with you always, until the end of the world!" (Matt. 28:20).

Mystical communion: The experience of union with other believers which is achieved because all share common faith in God, the grace of Jesus, and the presence of the Holy Spirit.

New Jerusalem: Jerusalem was and is the Holy City of the Hebrew people. Vatican II likened the Church to a New Jerusalem because Christian ecclesiology teaches that the Church is God's dwelling place within the human community.

Oblation: An offering or sacrifice made to God.

Priest shortage: By 1990 it is estimated that the U.S. Catholic Church will be short 13,130 priests to render the level of priestly service available in 1975. Projections beyond 1990 indicate further increasing rates of decline in numbers of priests. (Dean Hoge, *Future of Catholic Leadership,* Sheed & Ward, 1987, p.35).

Prophetic: The office exercised by the Church when it holds God's standards up to an errant society. E.g., reminding self-centered, materialistic consumers that everyone has a moral obligation to provide for the needs of the poor and homeless.

Priestly and Religious vocations: God's grace enables some women and men to follow a call they hear in their hearts to serve the community as sisters, brothers and priests.

Spotless Lamb: John the Baptist called Jesus the Lamb of God (John 1:29). Jesus is a symbol of innocence who is sent by God and who freely consented to give himself totally out of love for God and all of humanity.

Tongues: A gift of the Holy Spirit also known as glossolalia. Those who have this gift can speak in one language and be understood by others who ordinarily speak and understand a different language.

Discussion Questions

1. In your opinion, is one religion as good as another? What, if any, objective criteria should be used in evaluating religions?

2. How do believers recognize God's presence in the Church? In answering this question refer to Avery Dulles' models.

3. Visit a Catholic parish and inquire about the procedures in place to admit new members, evangelize non-church goers in the community, extend help to the poor, and encourage lay participation in the celebration of the sacraments. Report on what you learn as a result of your visit.

4. Visit at least one Catholic and one non-Catholic church (or mosque or synagogue), and inquire about past and present efforts at interfaith dialogue. Report back concerning the matters which are under discussion at the local or diocesan level as well as any interfaith worship services which are regularly scheduled.

5. How would you go about deciding the form of ministry in the Church which would be appropriate for you? What ministries do you consider yourself capable of performing? How much time, money and talent would you be willing to commit to your parish or faith community?

6. Why is it important to have a sense of the history of the Church? Based on what you know of the tension within Catholicism, do you expect the Church of the 1990s to welcome or repress major changes?

7. Based on your reading of this chapter, present the reasons why believers should belong to the Catholic Church.

Additional Reading

Documents of Vatican II:
> *Lumen Gentium*
> *Gaudium et Spes*
> in Walter M. Abbott, ed., *The Documents of Vatican II* (New York: America Press, 1966).

Avery Dulles, S.J., *Models of the Church* (New York: Doubleday, 1974).

Joseph Gremillion and Jim Castelli, *The Emerging Parish: The Notre Dame Study of Parish Life Since Vatican II* (San Francisco: Harper & Row, 1987).

Richard P. McBrien, *Catholicism* (Minneapolis: Winston Press, 1981), chapters 17 through 20.

William A. Scott and Frances M. Scott, *The Church Then and Now* (Kansas City: Sheed & Ward, 1985).

7

Sacraments, Special Moments in the Life of Catholic People

Roman Catholics are a sacramental people. As part of our worship, the seven sacraments stand as assurance that God can be encountered through the ordinary stuff of life. The sacramental system marks Catholics as an incarnational people. Our God is not a far-off God, but One present, alive in all of creation. The sacraments ritualize the holiness of life itself. They provide special moments in our lives when we celebrate an occasion with God.

Jesus Is the Primary Sacrament

A sacrament is a visible, tangible sign of divine action in human life. A sacrament offers an opportunity to meet and experience the presence of the living God. At the very core of Catholic sacramental experience is Jesus Christ. The eternal God was incarnated, made flesh, in Jesus of Nazareth. Through Jesus, the presence of God was made known. Jesus is, therefore, our primary or basic sacrament. God was revealed in Jesus. In the New Testament, St. Paul writes in the letter to the Colossians: "Jesus Christ is the visible likeness of the invisible God" (Colossians 1:15). Jesus brings us in touch with the divine. In the prologue of St. John's gospel, we read the classical biblical statement, "And the Word was made flesh." Somehow the Wisdom of God is expressed in Jesus. The human personhood of Jesus is identified with God's Word, God's own Son. The life experiences of Jesus of Nazareth involve this divine identity for the values and priorities of Jesus are the values and priorities of God.

The divine understanding of the meaning of human life and human history is spoken by Jesus. His words are prophetic. But Jesus does more than speak divine meaning; Jesus lives divine meaning. Yet Jesus shared human life experiences with humans, with his friends, with his followers. He was part of human history. His life and death offered a new interpretation, new meaning to human existence. Many people offer new depth to the meaning of life. Poets, heroes, heroines, intensify life's meaning for all people. Scientists, philosophers and artists stretch our horizons and transform life's reality through their own insights and creativity. In his ordinary life experience, Jesus of Nazareth, filled with the Spirit of the eternal God, transformed ordinary life experience, gradually revealing its ultimate meaning. Our human experiences have been changed by poets and artists; our lives have been enriched, our horizons broadened. In a far more intense and ultimate manner, Jesus, the Word of God, has offered us new meaning. Jesus' understanding of what it truly means to be human is now part of history. Human existence has been reinterpreted by Jesus and human reality has been given new meaning for all future generations. Jesus not only spoke this new reality, he lived it; he was its very embodiment, its incarnation. Through Jesus, we know God's meaning; we know God's valuing of human existence. Jesus is, therefore, a sign of God's presence among us, a primordial* sacrament. Jesus is the sign of God's ultimate concern for humankind and all of creation. For this reason Jesus is God's sacrament.

Church as Secondary Sacrament

After the death, resurrection and ascension of Jesus, his followers clung together. They were confused and fearful. Jesus had instructed them to "Go teach all nations, baptizing them in the name of the Father, Son and Holy Spirit" (Matthew 28:19). Their mission became clear to them at Pentecost in the Upper Room, when they opened themselves to the Holy Spirit and received strength and courage. Pentecost is the birthday of the church. It is the day on which the disciples of Jesus became a community, a bonded people with a mission, a church. As Jesus had been the sign of God's presence in the world, the believers, joined in faith and fellowship, became a sign of God's presence. The mission of Jesus' disciples was the continuation of the mission of Jesus himself. As Jesus had given new meaning to human existence, his followers now proclaimed the good news of God's love and concern for all people and the ultimate meaning of human existence. The early Christian communities bound together in this faith and in this love, and guided by the Holy

Spirit proclaimed the coming of the Kingdom, a new age. They proclaimed the holiness of humanity and all creation. The Creator was not separated from human history. The church as a sign of this divine presence, is to be the place where God's love can be experienced and celebrated. The mission of the church is to be a sign pointing to the coming of God's Kingdom. As Jesus was the primary sacrament, the sign of God's presence and divine action in the world, now the church, continuing the mission of Jesus, must be that same sign. The church's role as a secondary sacrament is to be a place where faith in Jesus is found and his love is shared. The church must be a sign of Jesus' saving presence, as Jesus was a sign of the saving presence of God. The lifestyle of the church's membership must reflect the lifestyle of Jesus, his values; his priorities must be given witness. It is the message of Jesus, the Word of God, that must be heard. We are an incarnational church, a sacramental church, a sign of God's presence among all people. The church is, itself, a sacrament. Vatican II states in *Lumen Gentium,* the Constitution on the church in the Modern World, that the church is the universal sacrament of unity and salvation.

Definition of a Sacrament

Before the Second Vatican Council (1962-1965), Catholic people understood sacraments primarily as causers of grace. Priests and laity alike concerned themselves with the valid administration and the properly disposed reception of the sacraments. It was most important to put no obstacles in the way of sacramental reception. Obstacles, such as the state of mortal sin or a lack of faith, prevented the recipient from validly receiving a sacrament. St. Augustine, in the fifth century, defined a sacrament as a "visible sign of invisible grace." The emphasis, until the time of St. Thomas Aquinas in the twelfth century, was on sacraments as signs. Thomas himself had a deep understanding of sacraments. He taught in his *Summa Theologica* that sacraments are efficacious signs of grace, causing what they signify. Thomas saw as the purpose of the sacramental sign a way of recalling to the recipient the reality that was being signified. In his work *Catholicism,* Richard McBrien recounts what happened following St. Thomas.

> Although Thomas himself was exceedingly well-balanced in his understanding of the relationship be-

tween sign and cause, post medieval theology was not. The sign aspect of sacraments receded from the center of ecclesial* consciousness. The sacraments were perceived as instruments of grace, producing their spiritual effects by the very performance of the ritual according to the prescribed manner (*ex opere operato*,* 'from the works worked').[1]

Sacraments are signs. They are signs of Christ's presence and the very presence of the eternal God acting in the lives of people. Sacraments are signs of worship proclaiming the shared faith of the church. The Second Vatican Council describes the sacraments as signs which support, nurture, strengthen and express faith. Sacraments, however, are not only signs pointing to a new reality; the sacraments cause the new reality to be present. The sacraments are not magic acts, nor are the recipients passive receivers. Expressions like, "all Catholics have to get their sacraments," do a grave injustice to a full appreciation of sacraments. Sacraments are not spiritual injections or booster shots. Truly, sacraments are free gifts of God, God's willingness and loving desire to be active in our lives, but sacraments are also free acts of the recipients. Sacraments are encounters, meetings between God and us. Sacraments are not things; they are actions; they are experiences, events. The faith, openness and love we bring to the celebration of any sacrament is a most vital contribution. God does not force a sacrament on us, as a child is unwillingly given a penicillin shot. We experience a sacrament when the gift of God's presence meets an open, believing heart. The words, the rituals and the symbols are the matter and form of the sacraments. They bear divine life. They focus the divine presence in the particular manner of each sacrament.

The Sacramental Principle

The root of the word *religion* means "to be allied to," "tied into," "to care for." Religion is that which ties us to a power beyond ourselves, forming an alliance of caring with a power we cannot see, hear or touch. For centuries, long before the birth of Jesus, humanity responded to the eternal, but humanity, being what it is, needs concrete ways to get in touch with that which exists beyond us. As people of an incarnational God and an incarnational church, we use the tangible stuff of life to experience God. Simple gestures, like the exchanged vows of a marriage ceremony or the use of ordinary things like bread, oil and water, enable us humans to touch the divine. The sacramental principle is simply a belief that we can meet God through ritual events and symbols. The Catholic Church is a sacramental community which celebrates in concrete and symbolic ways the presence of Jesus, God incarnated among us. The sacramental principle affirms the holiness of all creation and all creatures.

Celebration of Sacraments

Long before the Sacrament of Eucharist was defined, Christians gathered together, remembering Jesus and sharing a meal of fellowship, one commemorative of the Last Supper. No one as yet had articulated in doctrinal form the meaning of this sacred meal. Yet the shared ritual was at the core of the existence of the early church. The significance of the eucharistic meal was understood by early Christians long before the ritual was conceptualized under the term "sacrament." Christians, like humanity in general, do things, live their symbols long before they name them or categorize such actions. Early Christians understood that these external rituals touched the intrinsic, the spiritual. The early Christians were celebrating mystery, the mystery of being united in faith, the mystery of being Church. We celebrate our oneness, our identification with Christ. Tad Guzie, sacramental theologian, offers a definition stressing the celebrative action. Fr. Guzie terms his definition a "workable" one.

> A sacrament is a festive action in which Christians assemble to celebrate their lived experience and to call to heart their common story. The action is a symbol of God's care for us in Christ. Enacting the symbol brings us closer to one another in the church and to the Lord who is there for us.[2]

Sacraments are not individual events. They are not actions of personal devotion. Surely one's own spirituality and personal work are enriched by sacramental celebrations, but the central concern is community building. The grace of the sacrament is understood in relation to the believers' participation in the Christian community, in the Body of Christ. Sacraments are expressions of church on its journey in Christ to God. In the Constitution on the Sacred Liturgy of Vatican Council II, the emphasis is on communal celebration. After the Council, revisions and adaptations of the rites were decreed in order to clarify their meaning and encourage the participation of all. This decree made possible the use of the vernacular language in liturgical and sacramental celebrations. As the rites were revised, the understanding of the sign of the Christian community, itself emerged.

Institution of the Sacraments

Jesus did not define sacraments. He did not even use the word. Although the early followers of Jesus celebrated their faith and actually lived the sacramental principle, the term *sacrament* was not part of their experience. The word *sacrament* is not found in the New Testament. Tertullian, a Latin Father of the Church (d. 225), was the first to use the word *sacrament*. In the Roman army the term *sacramentum* meant a sacred oath. Roman soldiers took this pledge of loyalty to the emperor. These soldiers, wherever they were serving, were signs of the emperor. Tertullian, a Roman lawyer before entering the service of the church, understood the soldier's oath, this *sacramentum*, to be similar to the baptismal pledges or promises made by new Christians. Just as the Roman soldiers had a long arduous period of training before taking their sacred pledge, the early Christians went through a long period of preparation before Baptism. Christians were loyal signs of Christ wherever they were in the world, just as the Roman soldiers were loyal representatives of the emperor. The word *sacramentum* was gradually applied to many special church rituals and to many symbols, such as statues, palms and crucifixes. Eventually, the church made a distinction between the seven special symbolic actions of the Christian community and other religious symbols. It is actually not possible to totally delineate what is strictly sacramental and what is not. Most Protestant Christians accept only two sacraments, Baptism and Eucharist. They believe only these ritual events were instituted or founded by Christ. The great German theologian Karl Rahner explained that the institution of the sacraments by Christ can be understood simply through the sacramental nature of the Church. The Church, essentially sacramental, offers God's salvation to all people through Jesus Christ. Although Rahner suggests that Eucharist, the Lord's Supper, is the only sacrament directly instituted by Christ, all seven offer the sacramental presence and the saving activity of God. The Council of Trent (1545-1563) following the Protestant Reformation, set the number of sacraments at seven. Under the attack of the Protestant Reformers who emphasized the Word of God available to all through the holy scripture, the Roman Catholic Church stressed the sacraments. Popularly speaking, the Catholic Church became a church of sacraments, and the Protestant Church became a church of the bible. It was not until contemporary times that ordinary Catholics began to read the bible. At the same time, Protestant interest in the rich tradition of symbol and ritual has greatly increased.

Sacraments of Initiation—Baptism, Confirmation, Eucharist

The Sacraments of Initiation are our community rituals for conversion and belonging. In the ancient church, people who were interested in becoming Christians were invited into a long process of initiation. Those who accepted the community's invitation began a journey of faith. This journey, lasting two or three years, was called the catechumenate,* and the candidates were catechumens. Supported by the Christians of the local community, the candidates entered into this process which led them toward full membership in the Christian community. The whole church was part of this faith journey. The believers would speak to the catechumens, sharing their faith, praying with them and for them, and instructing them in living the gospel values. The community understood well its responsibility toward those seeking membership. For the catechumens, it was a time of serious reflection. Joining the Christian church, breaking away from a life of pagan customs, was not taken lightly. The catechumens carefully discerned their new responsibilities in the life of the community. Such a commitment was not easily made, especially in the early centuries of persecution.

During the catechumenate years, special rituals were celebrated to mark the deepening stages of faith. The season of Lent was especially important. Catechumens used their final Lent as a type of forty-day retreat. It was a time of final discernment* in the preparation for conversion. Catechumens and church members prayed and fasted as they prepared for Easter. It was at the Easter Vigil, the night before the celebration of the Lord's Resurrection, that those catechumens who fully accepted the faith were baptized, confirmed and shared in the Eucharist. The already initiated members of the Christian community welcomed the new members and renewed their own baptismal commitment.

Christian initiation, as it existed in the early Church, was one sacramental experience. Later, initiation was divided into the three Sacraments of Baptism, Confirmation and Eucharist. In 313, with the conversion of the Emperor Constantine, Christianity became the accepted religion of the empire. Persecutions stopped and Christianity became fashionable. People now entered the catechumenate for opportunities in the empire. Many who entered for political or social reasons had no real intention of accepting Baptism. Gradually, the formation process became a formality. The involvement of the whole community lessened, then faded away completely. By the beginning of the fifth century, the catechumenate process was a ritual of the past. The three sacraments were celebrated separately. Gradually, adult Baptism declined and infant Baptism became the accepted norm. In 1972, the catechumenate (RCIA—Right of Christian Initiation for Adults) was revived. Nonetheless, these three sacraments are now celebrated at different times by most Catholics.

Baptism

Baptism is the basic sacrament. It is through Baptism that Catholics have a right to the other sacraments. Ecumenically it is certainly of great importance, for it is the sacrament we share with all our Christian sisters and brothers. Baptism is our ritual that celebrates our belonging to Christ and to the Christian community. Our whole Christian life is the living out of the faith we received at Baptism. Christians speak of being true to our baptismal commitment or to the call of our Baptism. Baptism enriches faith, yet it also presupposes faith. The baptismal promises are a public profession of faith. In the ritual of Baptism, this profession is summed up in the celebrant's words following the vows. "This is our faith. This is the faith of the Church. We are proud to profess it in Christ Jesus, our Lord."

Infant Baptism

Because of the necessity of faith for Baptism and all the other sacraments, the question of infant Baptism emerges. We have seen that in the early Church Baptism was part of the sacramental initiation offered to adults. How is it that our basic sacrament, central to desire for new life in Christ, is now routinely administered to infants? Does the necessary faith and the active commitment exist in a tiny baby in the arms of parent or godparent? Although not without theological problems, there is traditional precedent for infant baptism. One precedent can be found in the custom of the Hebrew nation, God's chosen people, the people of God's covenant.* In Israel, the sense of covenant found its strength within the community. God's covenant was not made with separate individuals, but with a whole people. God called a people to enter into a relationship with their God *and* with one another. Israel's practice of circumcising male children eight days after birth spoke strongly of the emphasis on covenant community. The baby (unfortunately only males were considered full-covenanted members) was admitted into the community long before he could give a conscious faith response to it. The people who followed Jesus were certainly aware of this practice. Jesus himself was brought by his parents to the temple for circumcision. As people of the New Covenant (believers bound together in faith), Christians of the early Church surely considered their offspring part of the Body of Christ. In the Acts of the Apostles, we read that Paul and Silas baptized a repentant jailer and "his whole household." When the jailer accepts salvation through Christ, he is able to mediate salvation to all of his household. Hippolytus, a Roman presbyter who wrote in the beginning of the third century, gives this description of Baptism in the *Apostolic Tradition.*

> When they come to the water, let the water be pure and flowing. And they shall put off their clothes. And they shall baptize the little children first. And if they can answer for themselves, let them answer. But if they cannot, let their parents answer or someone from their family.

The faith of the family and the whole Christian community spoke for the little ones. This profession was also a promise that the baptized children would be brought up in the faith of their family. Today parents and godparents make these promises for their children. Along with the gradual falling away of the catechumenate and the high infant mortality rate, the fifth century heresy of Pelagianism* strengthened the normative position of infant baptism.

Augustine stressed the reality of original sin, believing that infants needed cleansing before their adoption into God's family.

His great stress on original sin led fearful parents to desire Baptism as soon as possible after birth. The Sacrament of Baptism, as it was originally given, freed converted adults from all the sins of their past life and offered them a new life in Christ. By the fifth century, the stress was on original sin, believed by Augustine to be passed from parents to child at the time of conception.

The emphasis in the 1930s and 1940s on the church as the mystical body of Christ, coupled with Vatican II's stress of the community dimension in the liturgy and all sacraments, has gradually enabled Catholics to understand Baptism as a ritual of incorporation of an individual into the community of the church. Nonetheless, the hold-over from former times has not completely disappeared, and unfortunately some Catholics still regard Baptism as a magic act which rescues the baby from sin and makes entrance into heaven possible.

Baptismal Symbolism

The central symbol of Baptism is water, the source of life. Water is a natural symbol of life. In the Old Testament, the streams of flowing water symbolized life flowing from God to those who have faith. Christianity also uses this natural symbol, the "life-giving" water, to speak divine life. The Vatican Council II expresses the ancient tradition of the church. It is through Baptism that we are "reborn to a sharing of divine life" (Decree on Ecumenism, 22). The essential words of Baptism, "I baptize you in the name of the Father, and of the Son, and of the Holy Spirit," along with the pouring of water, symbolize God's sharing of his divine life. The liturgical symbolism springs from the natural relationship between life and water.

Water brings life, but it also can bring death. Very aware of the fearful destruction of water, along with its obvious refreshment, cleansing and life-giving qualities, the early Christians used full immersion in their baptismal rite. The local river was the scene of ancient Baptism. As the candidate was submerged, the symbolism of death and burial was experienced. After momentary submersion, the new Christian emerged from the water, overcoming the death of sin, victorious through Christ, sharing now through the power of God in Jesus' divine life. Through the power of the Holy Spirit and the faith of the community, the newly baptized experienced the passage through death and selfishness to new life. It is important to note that the Holy Spirit is received at Baptism. Too often Catholics associate the reception of God's own Spirit in our lives only with Confirmation. The early Church was very clear that those receiving Baptism received the Spirit. In his first letter to the Corinthians, St. Paul tells the new Christians, "You have been washed, consecrated, justified in the name of our Lord Jesus Christ and in the Spirit of our God" (1 Corinthians 6:11). This ritual passage of our Baptism is experienced many times in our daily lives. Over and over, Christians living their baptismal commitments die to sin and selfishness, and with Christ are able to rise again to new life.

The symbols of our present baptismal rite are those used centuries ago at the Easter Vigil. Many ancient Churches had baptismal pools, used instead of local streams. As the candidate emerged, he was dried off and anointed with perfumed oil. This anointing (the name Christ is the Greek word *Anointed One*), is the Christening, the receiving of the Spirit of Jesus Christ. A white robe, symbol of the Risen Jesus and the forgiveness of all sin, was then put on the newly baptized. Today, a special white robe is placed on the child at the baptismal fount. The candle held by a parent, or godparent, symbolizes the Light of Christ. The symbols used at our present Baptism are somewhat abbreviated. The impact of a fully submerged and reclothed adult, anointed and resplendent, holding a lighted candle for all the community to witness at the Solemn Easter Vigil, is not always present as a well-meaning priest pours water over a long line of infants. The great welcome of the ancient community which shared the long years of discernment and instruction with the candidate is not easily duplicated. Nonetheless, the newly-baptized is part of the Christian community. The faith of the Church has resounded in the promises of parents and godparents. The baptismal ritual, administered with a spirit of warmth and welcome, can strengthen the faith of the entire community, as one more person shares the life of Christ.

Confirmation

The Sacrament of Confirmation brings to mind the solemnity of the bishop's anointing and the strengthening of the Confirmation candidate through the reception of the Holy Spirit. Yet, we know that the Holy Spirit was received at Baptism. In the light of their history and origins, Baptism and Confirmation are essentially one sacrament. A later development in the history of the catechumenate offers us an understanding of Confirmation. Those anointed with oil by the priest were sometime later anointed by the bishop. The growing lack of availability of the local bishop caused this to change. Interestingly enough, history shows that this problem was solved in different ways in the East and West. The East decided to favor the ritual, keeping it together and delegating the priest to administer the entire ceremony. To retain the significance of the bishop as representing the universal Church, the oil used for the anointing was blessed by the bishop. The West handled the dilemma in quite the opposite way. History was not without influence. Barbarians had overrun Europe after the collapse of the Roman Empire in the fifth and sixth centuries. Bishops began taking up the leadership roles of deposed Roman administrators. The leadership of these bishops held civilization together in the West. Again the number of converts rose. The solution was a separation of the initiation rites. The local priest baptized and, when the bishop was in the area (sometimes a week, sometimes months or even years later), the second anointing and the laying on of hands occurred.

Many theologians believe a theology of Confirmation, as a separate sacrament, is not possible. The Second Vatican Council offers this perspective which is now part of the new rite of Confirmation:

> The rite of Confirmation is to be revised and the intimate connection which this sacrament has with the whole Christian initiation is to be more lucidly set forth; for this reason it will be fitting for candidates to renew their baptismal promises just before they are confirmed . . . (The Constitution on the Sacred Liturgy, 71)

The customs surrounding Confirmation have developed over the centuries. It is important to remember that all sacraments are part of the sacrament which is the Church. Confirmation is part of Christian initiation which is not a static, once and for all kind of event. Although Baptism surely makes one a member in the Church and Eucharist affirms full participation, Confirmation offers a special time in that dynamic process. Essentially Confirmation does not add any new and necessary element for being a Christian. Yet it is a time of celebration when a person can realize and appropriate her own status in the Spirit-filled

Christian community. Confirmation can be a powerful moment, a free decisive ratification of the baptismal event. Part of the Confirmation rite is the renewal of baptismal vows. The bishop's anointing and the ancient gesture of calling forth the strength of God's Holy Spirit upon the candidate symbolize a sacramental moment, a deeper reality in the unfolding process of Christian initiation. A new and deeper awareness of membership in a Spirit-filled community is the gift received as the bishop lays hands on the candidate and prays the ancient words, "Be sealed with the gift of the Holy Spirit." It is more than obvious that the full experiencing of this sacrament requires the support of a community truly alive in the Holy Spirit and actually guided by the Spirit's presence and power. It was within such a community that St. Paul tells us, "The fruit of the Spirit is love, joy, peace, patience, kindness, generosity, faithfulness, gentleness, self-control" (Galatians 5:22-23).

The age of Confirmation has caused many pastoral dilemmas. Those who believe the Spirit is first given at Confirmation eagerly demand the sacrament at an early age for their children. Pastoral and parish ministers, equally anxious to offer a more meaningful sacramental experience, desire to postpone its reception. The tradition of Confirmation, as the sacrament of maturity, demands a more mature young person. There is no easy answer. Remembering always that sacraments are not things to be given, but graced events to be experienced, we might well lean toward a time beyond the confusing years of puberty. The original order of initiation—Baptism, Confirmation, Eucharist—seems to be broken forever, at least for cradle Catholics. Good catechesis* offered in the heart of a Spirit-filled community can assure part of the needed readiness.

Symbols of Confirmation

An understanding of the symbol of laying on of hands, as a parental-type gesture communicating the strength of the Holy Spirit and the dynamic, living tradition of the Church, is basic to the reception of the sacrament. Although the symbol of oil does not have the tremendous impact it did in the early Church and in the Middle Ages, when those commissioned for service and leadership were anointed with oil, oil can still be understood as a symbol of the activity of the Holy Spirit. People today still use oil on their bodies for comfort and suppleness. Athletes rub themselves with oil for ease of movement. Oil is associated with comfort, healing and preserving. It is used on rusted machines and aching human joints. Oil symbolizes God's own Spirit reaching into our lives, easing and strengthening. In the Old Testament, the psalmist tells us, "You anoint my head with oil, my cup overflows" (Psalm 23:5). Confirmation is a sacrament offering an opportunity to confirm our Baptism and its call to Christian commitment. "Soldiers of Christ" is an image that has lost its luster. Yet Confirmation still offers an opportunity for witnesses to stand up and be counted as Christians, aware of the Spirit in their own lives and the lives of the community.

Eucharist

The sacrament of the Lord's real presence within the believing community has been the subject of thousands of books through the ages. Eucharist (the word means thanksgiving) is the central act of the believing community. The church commemorates the institution of Eucharist each year at the end of Lent on Holy Thursday, as the Paschal event begins to unfold. Each synoptic gospel (Matthew 26:26-28, Mark 14:22-24, and Luke 22:17-20) recounts the story of the Last Supper. In the first letter to the Corinthians, St. Paul summarizes the apostolic church's teaching on the institution and practice of the Sacrament of Eucharist (1 Corinthians 11:23-27). Throughout the story of the early church in the Acts of the Apostles, we can read about communion as a basic part of the worship of early Christians. "On the first day of the week, when we gathered for the breaking of the bread . . ." (Acts 20:7). In St. John, the final gospel, a mystical theological explanation is offered.

> I myself am the bread of life.
> No one who comes to me shall ever be hungry,
> no one who believes in me shall ever thirst (John 8:35).

And in the recounting of Jesus' final meal with his friends, we read about Jesus washing the feet of his disciples. The author of John's gospel carefully chose to associate the presence of Jesus among them as a presence of loving service.

> But if I washed your feet—
> I who am Teacher and Lord—
> then you must wash each other's feet.
> What I just did was to give you an example:
> as I have done, so you must do (John 13:14-15).

Jesus celebrated the Last Supper with his disciples at the time of Passover. The Passover meal was already deeply symbolic. This memorial ritual recalled for the Israelites their liberation, their freedom as God's own people. Jesus gave this meal a new dimension. This meal was now to be celebrated in memory of him. The ancient ritual would become a reminder of his death, the brokenness of his body and the blood shed for all people. The Hebrew mind understood these symbols. Body and Blood have lost some of their ancient significance for the modern, scientific, clinical mind. But Jesus' friends understood bread as body and body as bread. They understood the sign of unity ("One Bread, One Body"), the sustenance, the community participation in the very life of Jesus and of God. They understood the new signifi-cance of their memorial meal. Jesus had entered into total union with them through basic symbols, symbols that actually permeate our flesh and flow in our bloodstream. When Jesus shared the cup of wine, his blood, the Hebrew mind was deeply aware that blood was life, lifeline. Jesus was sharing his life, his blood-line, his ancestry before him. And now all those who followed him would be his descendents, united with him and each other. Into that Passover meal, Jesus drew together the past, the Old Covenant, and became a sign of the future, offering himself as the New Covenant between God and all people. Jesus, God's Incarnate presence, would be forever with us in the eucharistic meal of shared love.

The early church clearly believed that Jesus was among them as they shared bread and wine and their lives with one another. At first, Christians met in private homes, even outdoors, to celebrate Eucharist—their meal of fellowship. They experienced themselves as community, proclaiming the presence of the Risen Lord. As communities grew, larger places of celebration were needed. Eventually, as persecution ceased, churches were built. The early church people brought the gifts of bread and wine for the ritual meal, also sharing other food with those of the commu-nity who were in need. The community, led by the presider, gave thanks and recalled Jesus' words at the Last Supper. The memorial prayers of his death and resurrection (*the anamnesis*) were included, and a prayer asking the Holy Spirit to come upon the bread and wine (*epiclesis*) followed. The people responded to a concluding doxology* with the Great Amen.

Through the centuries, the Eucharist has remained central to our faith life. Shifts of emphasis have occurred. The sacrificial element was stressed before Vatican II, the mass, as the commemoration of the Lord's death on Calvary. In our modern day, with its longing for real intimacy and belonging, the communal dimension has been emphasized; Eucharist is a community celebrative meal. The great cathedrals of the Middle Ages made community gathering difficult. Altars built high above the people with priests intoning the solemn liturgy in Latin, facing the altar, separated the sacrament from the believers. The unworthiness of people to receive the Body and Blood of the Lord was often emphasized. Adoration of the sacred host became more common than regular reception.

Vatican II offered a renewed focus on the faith of the community and the priesthood of all believers. Catholics were encouraged once again to gather, as the early Christians, to celebrate the Lord's Supper. The new liturgical settings, circular space, altar rails gone, table-like altars, and the prayers in the vernacular have all contributed to renewed participation in Eucharist. The ministerial roles of the ordinary people of the parish community, as lectors and eucharistic ministers, also promoted changed attitudes.

The friends of Jesus did not focus their devotion upon the transformation of the symbols of bread and wine. They understood that Jesus lived and died among them to change their lives, to make them his very Body and Blood. The heart of Eucharist is the transformation of the believing community into the Body of Christ. People have stayed away from Eucharist for many reasons, concentrating on their sinfulness or unworthiness, believing Eucharist to be a reward for good behavior. Eucharist is sustenance for life's journey. Christians, left on their own, could not become One Body in Christ. It is this sacramental presence, the real presence of Jesus offered to us that makes this transformation possible. The words "This is my body which shall be given for you" (Luke 22:19). speak a Jesus among us, as one who serves others. They invite our response.

The Eucharist, as the sacrament of sustenance and as a call to service, is a sign of the Kingdom which is to come. Christians cannot share this ritual meal without real awareness of their sisters and brothers who are hungry every day. Eucharist points toward the final banquet, when all humanity will sit together in justice and peace in God's Kingdom. Eucharist, as a sign of unity, is also a sign of hope. It points beyond the divisions of the world to the real, yet mysterious, union of the entire human family. Eating together, sharing a meal is a basic ritual of humankind. It is a sign of human concern for others and of sharing lives. Jesus and his disciples understood the depth and intimacy of sharing a meal. Eucharist reaches beyond self; the word *communion* precludes individual concern. As Jesus feeds us in Eucharist, we are called to feed one another.

Rite of Christian Initiation for Adults

Since 1972, the Church offers people a new approach to conversion. In the past, adults who desired to join the Catholic Church were given private instructions by the local parish priest. Their Baptism and First Communion were quiet events administered by the priest with a few family members or close friends attending. The next time the bishop was confirming at the parish, the converts joined the end of the line. The revised Rite of Christian Initiation for Adults (RCIA) has changed all that. No longer is conversion instruction a private, almost secretive, affair. This new rite brings us back to our roots. The Christian community is again involved. The parish people sponsor the candidates and actually go through the process with them. The original order of the Sacraments of Initiation (Baptism, Confirmation, Eucharist) is restored, and the three sacraments are celebrated with the whole parish at the Easter Vigil. Many have called this new rite the most challenging document of our times. The RCIA demands involvement of the Church members, support and hospitality. More than that, it demands a real faith sharing. Those sponsoring the candidates certainly must reflect on the meaning of their own faith life. The RCIA defines conversion once again as an on-going process, part of the faith journey of every parishioner. Many Catholic parishes throughout the world have enriched the faith life of the entire community by this process of welcoming new converts. It has become far more than a vehicle for conversion-candidates; it has provided an opportunity for all to touch the roots of our tradition and renew their own faith and the faith of the community.

The Sacrament of Reconciliation

For the early Christians, the acceptance of Baptism was a huge step. Initiation into the Christian community was a clear proclamation that one's life had radically changed. Following Christ and the gospel required a totally new lifestyle. In apostolic times, Christians believed that all past sins forgiven at Baptism would never be repeated. The conversion process was such a significant step that it was believed the followers of Jesus would be so faithful to the gospel that they would no longer commit sin. In reality, this was not the case. It soon became obvious that converted people, even while loving Christ and one another, still would occasionally commit serious sin. It was also obvious to the early Christian community that the forgiveness of sin and second chances were high among the priorities of Jesus. They remembered Jesus' parables. Jesus invited Zacchaeus, the cheating tax collector, down from the tree and had dinner at his house. Zacchaeus was forgiven, and his life turned around completely. The repentant Prodigal Son was given a party by his father after his uncaring and self-serving behavior. The early Christians knew Jesus as a person of unending forgiveness.

The Church developed the Sacrament of Penance, now called Reconciliation, as a process of reconversion after Baptsim. A leader of the early Church, the Shepherd of Hermes, called Penance a second plank. Initially, the sacrament was received only once in a lifetime. This system was a rather harsh and public process. The sinner who acknowledged her sinfulness confessed to a community authority, usually a bishop. This leader would lay hands on the sinners, enrolling them in the order of penitents. The penitents were excluded from the Eucharistic assembly. During the long period of penance, the sinners were placed at the church doors, usually wearing sack-cloth. They pleaded for the forgiveness and prayers of the people entering church. As strange as this custom seems to us today, the repentant sinners did receive the encouragement and support of the community, and at the end of the prescribed time they were joyfully reconciled to the assembly. This usually occurred on Holy Thursday, with another imposition of hands by the bishop.

It is no small wonder that this system, called canonical penance, did not last forever. Few people actually used the order of penitents, and those who did were usually near their death-bed. History again intervened. Barbarian invasions brought many new people into our churches. The newcomers were not comfortable at all with the church's method of celebrating God's forgiveness. The answer to the dilemma came from the Irish monks. These men understood spiritual direction and the need to reassure guilty sinners of the love of Christ. A new rite was developed. It was the beginning of private confession. Soon people flocked to the monasteries for forgiveness. The monks began to write penitential guide-books. A listing of sins and appropriate penances was worked out. These penances could be quite severe. Some abuses did creep in. Sometimes forgiven sinners would pay less fortunate people to complete their tariffs. Thus, this form of the sacrament is known as tariff penance. The church struggled with these forms, private and public, trying to follow the directive of Jesus, "Whose sins you shall forgive, they are forgiven." Gradually, the rite which included confession to a priest—an appropriate penance—and immediate reconciliation without long-term waiting or public censure, was used throughout the entire church. The famous Council of Trent, after the Protestant Reformation, put its seal of approval on it. And there it remained for centuries, until the 1960s.

Private confession, a great improvement over sack-cloth and ashes, was not without its pastoral problems. The community was not part of it. The form itself became overly individualistic and mechanical. The joy of the Lord's eager forgiveness was not experienced in the confession format. Many Catholics stopped using the Sacrament of Penance in the late sixties. The long Saturday confessional lines were greatly shortened and then abruptly gone. It is important to note that although the form of the sacrament has changed, what is celebrated remains constant. The forgiveness of God is the heart of the sacrament. It is this forgiveness that is celebrated. It is also important to note that God's forgiveness is not bound to the sacrament. God's forgiveness requires only the sinner's repentance. This repentance may or may not coincide with reception of the sacrament. Sin and alienation will never disappear from the world. Human beings long to be forgiven, healed, made whole. The sacrament provides an opportunity to reflect on and celebrate the forgiveness that God offers us always.

In the New Testament, Jesus spoke often of forgiving one another. "Then Peter came up and asked him, 'Lord, when my brother wrongs me, how often must I forgive him? Seven times?' 'No,' Jesus replied, 'not seven times, I say seventy times seven times'" (Matthew 18:21-22). Forgiveness becomes real within the community. It is among our family and friends that we experience forgiveness. Humans need ritual. Believing that God forgives repentant sinners is not experiencing the Sacrament of Reconciliation. Being human, we need an outward expression, a symbol, to fully know this guaranteed forgiveness of Jesus. The four elements of the sacrament must be included in any rite.

1. Confession: Admitting one's sinfulness;
2. Contrition: Knowing sincere sorrow and a desire to try again;
3. Satisfaction: A willingness to make amends, to balance the scale of justice and love;
4. Absolution: Receiving the forgiveness of God through his people, the Church.

Three New Rites

The Rite of Penance was also revised after Vatican II. Penance was given three new forms. The term *reconciliation* (which means *putting back together that which belongs together and has been apart*) is now used in speaking of this sacrament. The first form of the rite is somewhat similar to the old confessional-type celebration. It is still individual, but the penitent now enters a reconciliation room, a better place to experience the joy of forgiveness. The dark confessional boxes are no longer in use. The penitent has the choice of facing the priest, who represents the Lord and the people against whom he has sinned, or remaining anonymous. Scripture readings for reflection were added to the rite. The priest and penitent pray together in a relaxed manner. Rigid formulas are no longer included. The expression of our sinfulness, our selfish attitudes and our lack of love, has replaced the numerical listing of sins. The priest offers a penance, usually discussed with the penitent, which can be a corrective action for our lives. The forgiveness of God and the community is offered as the priest prays, extending his hand over the penitent.

The second form of the New Rite includes a Communal Penance Service. Many people of the parish community gather together in church to reflect on their sinfulness. Hymns, scripture readings and a homily are followed by an examination of conscience. There is an awareness that people's lives are intertwined, all are sinners, yet attempting to support one another in living out the gospel. In this form, after the communal service, everyone confesses privately to a priest. The third form of the sacrament takes into account the large numbers of people in our parish communities. In consideration of the number of priests, time and space, this communal rite offers general absolution.

God's forgiveness is offered to all by the celebrant and spoken by the people to one another. Large numbers of Catholics have cele-brated this third form of the sacrament in recent years.

Church leadership still has concern about the Sacrament of Reconciliation. Eager to have its members experience the joy of forgiveness, yet the church remains cautious in its development of new rites. Sin is part of Christian life. But Jesus did not want us to remain frozen in our guilt, in our sinfulness. No matter how the sacramental rite changes, it will always afford us an opportunity to encounter the loving forgiveness of the God who walked among us.

The Sacrament of the Sick

Jesus was deeply concerned with sickness. As he healed the brokenness of people from sin and guilt, he cured their bodily ills. When Jesus speaks to his apostles, there is always a con-cern for the whole person, a connection between apostolic preaching, baptizing, forgiving and healing. "Jesus spoke to them of God's reign and healed all who were in need of healing" (Luke 9:11). Care of the sick was an important concern in the early church. Although there is no exact record of a healing rite or anointing of the sick, the epistle of St. James points to what was probably a common experience.

> Is there anyone sick among you? He should ask the presbyters of the Church. They in turn are to pray over him, anointing him with oil in the Name of the Lord. This prayer uttered in faith will reclaim the one who is ill and the Lord will restore him to health (James 5:14-15).

The Sacrament of the Sick, formerly known as Extreme Unc-tion or the Last Rites, is now often celebrated within a parish community. The Vatican II Council restored this sacrament to its earliest roots. The Dark Ages and the Middle Ages had asso-ciated this anointing with a final preparation for death. The plagues of Europe, coupled with the lack of good medical care, contributed to this preoccupation with death. Therefore, the sacrament was looked upon as a final anointing. Far too often the Sacrament of the Sick has been administered to a person much too close to death to be aware of a comforting sacramental experience. Today the thrust of the sacrament concerns itself with healing of mind and body. The new ritual clearly indicates

that Viaticum (Eucharist—food for the journey) is the sacrament
for the dying and Anointing is the sacrament of the sick.

The presence of the community at a parish celebration, or the
surrounding of family and friends at home or in the hospital,
offers the sick person the needed support and faith of others.
Through the concern of the community, God's presence gives
comfort and brings healing to the whole person. Those whose
illness, physical or emotional, causes them suffering and alienation from the normal rhythm of their lives, are invited to experience this sacrament. The anointing of oil, the ancient balm of
healing, symbolizes renewed strength and healing for the sick
person. The ritual assures them that their suffering is not without meaning. The Anointing of the Sick is an experience of hope
and comfort, a graced celebration offered within the Church for
those who are suffering. And it is a sign for all believers of
God's healing presence among us.

The Sacrament of Marriage

The history of the church's theology of marriage is not one of
our brightest accomplishments. Marriage certainly existed long
before the birth of Jesus and the founding of his church. Pagan
and Judaic customs, alike, permitted polygamy.* Since a
woman was considered the property of her husband, the Jewish
law forbade adultery as a violation of property rights. When
Jesus is asked by the Jewish Pharisees if it is "lawful for a man
to put away a wife or not?" (Matthew 29:3), he did not answer
considering property rights. Jesus went back to the beginning
of the Jewish Scripture, the Book of Genesis, appealing to the
divine design that a man and woman in marriage become two in
one flesh. "And what God has joined no man should put asunder" (Matthew 19:6). Jesus did not add anything new to the
concept of marriage, but restored the God-centeredness of the
ancient form. What Jesus did do was teach us new ways for
transforming human relationships. As all of life, marriage is
penetrated with a Christ dimension.

Historically, the Christian Church did not become officially
involved in weddings and marriages until the fifth century. At
that time a liturgical religious ceremony was only absolutely
required at the wedding of a priest. (Obviously, preceding
priestly celibacy by a few centuries.) Through the centuries, the
church has spoken of the goodness of marriage, especially for its

procreation of children. It has offered the words of St. Paul concerning the marriage relationship as imaging Christ's rela- tion- ship to the church (Ephesians 5:22-33). Yet sex, despite its procreative function, has been suspect at best. Celibacy for the sake of the kingdom was often much preferred. The church fa- thers stressed the procreative aspect of the sexual union. St. Augustine even taught that intercourse between married people for the sake of conjugal pleasure rather than procreation, al- though forgivable was venially sinful!

With such a theology, it is no wonder that marriage was not officially designated a sacrament until the eleventh century. The problem of secret marriages was helped by the church's protec- tion. During that time the church acquired almost exclusive con- trol over marriage. Canon law developed teaching on marriage as a sacrament. Yet even then marriage was often looked down upon, considered an inferior state of life. The Council of Trent in the sixteenth century stressed the absolutely permanent character, the indissolubility, of the marriage contract and its primary purpose as the procreation of children.

Only in modern times, with our more accurate understanding of the psychology and physiology of sexuality, did the church's theology of marriage begin to change. There has been a decided return to the scriptural understanding of sexuality as part of God's good creation. In the Old Testament, authors often com- pared God's love for the Israelite nation to the intimate love of a husband and wife. Today we believe that God can be experi- enced in a unique way through the married relationship of love. In marriage alone, among the seven sacraments, the sacramen- tal sign consists wholly in the acts of the recipients. The woman and man marry each other. They are the ministers of marriage. The priest officiates as a representative-witness of the Christian community. The dynamic union of sacramental love is a real sign of God's presence within their married union for their chil- dren and all others.

Vatican II changed the theology and theological language of marriage. Despite serious disagreement among the Vatican II fathers, the primary purpose of marriage was changed from pro- creation to the mutual sharing of life and love. The Council recognized mutual intimacy as life-giving not only in procrea- tion, but in the personal growth of the married partners. Mar- riage is not called a contract, but "a conjugal covenant of irrevo- cable consent." The document does not speak of rights over each other's bodies, but the "mutually bestowing and accepting of one another" as persons. (*Gaudium et Spes*)

The church is presently struggling with questions of divorce and annulment. The present church must consider the large number of broken marriages among Catholic Christian people. Ministries to divorced people are filling some of the need for healing. However the remarriage of divorced Catholics is not celebrated sacramentally within our present tradition. Permanence is certainly the ideal. Marriage is now being studied as a complex human experience. Theologians are looking again at indissolubility, considering whether its roots are in the divine plan or an ecclesiastical decision. Marriage is a most creative sacrament. Through it, a woman and man join their lives and eternal destinies. The church believes God's life is part of that union, and it is, therefore, clearly sacramental. Weddings are wonderful, but marriages are truly events of grace.

Holy Orders

The early Christian communities led by the followers of Jesus did not have a priesthood. Although Jesus did have special followers, his twelve apostles, the people of the early church clearly understood that all who believed in the Lord were called to do his work. Many patterns of leadership developed. No single system was particularly identified as church ministry. It was not until the third century that the office of the priest began to emerge. The term *priest* was first applied to the bishops who led the eucharistic liturgy. The clerical priesthood gradually developed into three orders—deacon, priest, bishop. As communities grew larger and liturgical services more formal, a hierarchy came into place. The Christian ministry, originally the baptismal responsibility of all, gradually became the exclusive domain of the clerical caste. Priests became the sole presiders at the "breaking of the bread." They alone possessed the power to consecrate bread and wine and forgive sins. By the Middle Ages, the clerical hierarchy, now celibate, was cut off from the ordinary believers by lifestyle, spirituality, educational level and even dress. The call to service, originally from within the community, itself, was now understood as a direct call from God.

During the Protestant Reformation, the Reformers challenged the scriptural basis of the priesthood, stressing the power of the Word of God and the priesthood of all believers, against Roman authority and the sacramental powers of priests. In a defensive posture, the church stressed priestly power and de-emphasized the bible and the shared priesthood of all believers. These positions hardened and remained almost completely unchallenged for four hundred years. Vatican II, in its work on church renewal, began to shake the foundations. The council's documents initiated the emergence of a changed priesthood—one combining the old and new. The clerical system, structuring the leadership of our church, is still very much in place. But priests now identify far more fully with the people. Many understand themselves as signs of Christ's presence, enabling the entire Christian community to be ministers in the world. Archbishop Bernardin explains it this way:

> This special identity does not make us better than others, nor does it entitle us to special privileges. But it does signify who we are, whom we represent, what our mission is and what demands are made of us in regard to spiritual growth and commitment to others.

The priesthood is a sign of Jesus' presence. Holy Orders has, at its very core, sacramental ministry. Priests are ordained to enable believers to experience God's presence. The priests' power is not a personal power; it springs from and is at the service of the believing community. In the fourth century at the Council of Chalcedon, the primacy of the community was so strongly stressed that the council issued a canon that a priest could not be ordained unless he was attached to a community. Bishops receive the fullness of the sacrament of Holy Orders. Taken as a body, they are considered successors to the apostles. Already priests, they are ordained as teachers and pastoral rulers. Priests are ordained to preach God's Word, to build up the Christian community, to serve all people and to preside at community worship, especially the Eucharist. The order of deacon (diaconate) is also part of the sacrament of Holy Orders. Vatican II has recommended the restoration of a permanent diaconate for laymen to aid in serving the community. The symbols of anointing with oil and the laying on of hands are central to this sacrament's solemn ritual of ordination.

The future of the Roman Catholic Church may depend upon the future of the priesthood. Theological questions on celibate lifestyles and the ordination of women, along with the emergence of real ministry among lay people, challenge the present structure. By the year 2000 there will be no more than 17,000 diocesan priests in America. The mean age of the American priesthood is already close to sixty. New forms of the priesthood may evolve. Pastoral responsibilities may be shared in new ways. Yet a special answered call to continue the ministry of Jesus will always be a sign of God's presence, an event of grace, a sacrament.

A Sacramental Church

The sacramental system of the Roman Catholic Church is surely one of its richest traditions. It witnesses God's over-whelming presence in all of creation. It assures believers of God's unending desire to be active in our lives. Sacraments are moments of divine/human encounter. They encompass all peo-ple in the Incarnation of Jesus. God's Spirit is acting in us all the time, urging us towards goodness and concern for others, forgiving us, healing us and simply delighting in our lives. The sacraments are special moments of God's communication. In a sense, they focus God's original self-communication in Jesus into special times of our lives. Fr. Richard McBrien sums it up in this way: "The sacraments signify, celebrate, and effect what God is, in a sense, doing everywhere and for all."[3] Yet the work of God's Spirit needs human response. Sacraments happen when a believing, loving community responds.

Endnotes

1. Richard McBrien, *Catholicism* (Minneapolis: Winston Press, 1981), pp. 734-735.

2. Tad Guzie, *The Book of Sacramental Basics* (Ramsey, NJ: Paulist Press, 1981), p. 53.

3. McBrien, op. cit., p. 738.

Glossary

Catechesis: The process of introducing young people or con-verts to the Gospel and the major tenets of the Christian faith.

Catechumenate: The process used by the early church through which people became Christians and were baptized. In the modern church the catechumenate has been restored through the RCIA (Rite of Christian Initiation for Adults).

Covenant: The bond, promise or testament between God and the people of Israel in the Old Testament, and between God and the whole human community in the New Testament established by the life, death and Resurrection of Christ.

Discernment: The process by which we attempt to decide, with the help of the Holy Spirit, what God wills us to do in life's circumstances and in the future.

Doxology: A short hymn or prayer praising the glory of God.

Ecclesial: Understanding the Church as the assembly, the Body of Christ, as distinguished from ecclesiastical which pertains to the Church as institution.

Ex opere operato: A Latin phrase explaining how a sacrament achieves its effects—not through the faith of the recipient or the worthiness of the minister, but through the power of Christ who acts through and within it.

Pelagianism: A heresy of the fifth century, which claimed that human effort alone could gain salvation with God's initiative and continued grace.

Polygamy: The practice of having more wives than one at a time.

Primordial: First in order, original, existing from the beginning.

Discussion Questions

1. Explain the relationship between Jesus and the Church and the sacraments? Why is Jesus called primordial sacrament?

2. What is the sacramental principle? Why is it fundamental to a full understanding of our seven ritual sacraments?

3. In light of the understanding of the sacraments presented in this chapter, what is the significance of ritual and symbol in the Catholic tradition? Use examples from the sacraments to illustrate.

4. What is the RCIA? What is its significance in the modern Church?

5. In Leonardo Boff's book, *Sacraments of Life, Life of Sacraments,* the significance of symbols is explored. Read this short, informative book for a fuller appreciation of human beings as symbol makers. Explain how for Boff, the ordinary stuff of life

becomes sacramental. What are the things or events in your life that have real sacramental significance?

6. Reflect upon your own sacramental experience. Are sacramental rituals moments of divine encounter for you? All life is essentially sacramental. How do you experience God?

Additional Reading

Leonardo Boff, *Sacraments of Life, Life of Sacraments* (Washington, DC: Pastoral Press, 1975).

William J. Bausch, *A New Look At the Sacraments* (Mystic, CT: Twenty-Third Publications, 1983).

Tad Guzie, *The Book of Sacramental Basics* (Ramsey, NJ: Paulist Press, 1981).

George McCauley, *The God of The Group* (Niles, IL: Argus Communications, 1975).

Michael Taylor, ed., *The Sacraments* (Staten Island, NY: Alba House, 1981).

8

Prayer and Liturgy

All through the centuries, people have prayed. Archaeologists have unearthed huge altar-like stone formations dating back to 5000 BC. For thousands of centuries, human beings were offering some type of prayer to some type of deity. Long before the Jewish nation became aware of the presence of the One Creator God, wandering nomads carried statues of their gods before them as they moved about in search of grazing land. Before humankind came to understand the existence of the God of love, worship* was largely sacrificial.* Its goal was appeasement. The ancient gods would protect only those people who offered up the first and finest fruits of the harvest. In pre-Hebrew, pre-Christian days, history includes the sacrificing of one's first child to the gods of fertility to assure the blessing of additional children. Fear was the overwhelming focus of worship in the ancient pagan world. Through the Jewish tradition, God gradually revealed that the Lord wanted the hearts of people, not their sacrifices. In our own Catholic tradition, we learn about prayer through Jesus—Himself a man of prayer. Our modern world greatly values communication. People want to be understood. Skills of open, honest dialogue and deep listening are asked of people in every relationship and occupation. Prayer is communication. Very simply, it is talking to God and listening to God.

To Whom Do We Pray?

To whom do we pray? We pray to God. But how do we humans picture God, the recipient of our prayers? Sympathetic ears? A listening heart? A mighty judge whose attention it is quite difficult to obtain? A busy executive who hopefully has time today for our pleas? A majestic figure, a king, eager for our adoration and praise? A kindly parent who always has time for the children? Or a friend willing to be supportive and caring?

Our image of God certainly influences our prayer-style. Our image of God is basic to our relationship and our communication with God. In Alice Walker's book, *The Color Purple,* two black women discuss their images of God and their difficulties in prayer.

> Ain't no way to read the bible and not think God white, she say. Then she sigh. When I found out I thought God was white and a man, I lost interest. You mad cause he don't seem to listen to your prayers. Humph! Do the mayor listen to anything colored ask?
> . . .
>
> Well, us talk and talk bout God, but I'm still adrift. Trying to chase that old white man out of my head . . .
>
> Whenever you try to pray, and man plop himself on the other end of it, tell him to git lost, say Shug. Conjure up flowers, wind, water, a big rock.

The situation in which we live, our culture, our family environment, our relationship with our parents, our religious background—all these contribute to our image of God and to our prayer. Through the ages, our human images of God have been foundational for our prayer.

Ancient Mythology

Ancient mythology offers a variety of god images. To explain the majestic and sometimes fearful phenomena of nature, primitive humans peopled the sky and the earth with unseen deities. These supernatural beings were essentially human, natural beings, but with great magical powers. The patterns and movements of nature were understood as having human motives. Primitive humans believed that the night spirit grew envious of the sun and convinced the people that the sun was not such a great and powerful being; since it was daily driven across the sky, the people taunted the sun for its lack of power. To remind people forever of their unforgivable insults, the all-powerful sun goes south for part of each year, and the days become short and cold. In this myth, the sun-god acts just as primitive humans would have in the face of insult.

The great creation myths were quite philosophical. The soil of earth received the seed of the sky watered by rain. In union they gave birth to the plant, the earth as the wife and the sky as the husband. The moon, who governed the night when mists fell upon the earth, was connected to the idea of fertility. In Egypt, women prayed to Isis, the moon-goddess, to make them fruitful. Roman women prayed to Juno, queen of heaven, to help them bear children. Greek women prayed to their moon-goddess Hera for fertility. The Aztecs and many American Indians presented offerings to the moon-goddess. Indian women held up their new- born child to the moon-mother for blessing. In Latin America, the Indian culture often associates the ancient moon-goddess with Mary, the Virgin Mother of God. The worship rituals were offered for propitiation* and appeasement. Ceremonial dance and music, charms and incantations, were means of protection and methods of attracting favorable attention. The images of god rooted in unexplained nature determined for primitive people their prayer. The gods were very real to primitive humanity—part of their daily struggle for survival.

Prayer in the Old Testament

Much of the sacrificial, appeasement-style of pagan prayer was carried into the prayer response of the Hebrew nation. The story in Genesis of Cain's murder of his brother Abel is an argument over whose offering is more pleasing to God (Genesis 4:1-10). Until God intervenes, Abraham is willing to offer his young son Isaac as a holocaust* to the Lord (Genesis 22:1-14). In the Book of Leviticus,* long and detailed instructions are written to guide the sacrifices of the Israelites. Prize animals and every type of harvest were offered to God, "sacred oblations to the Lord." In the beginning of Leviticus, specific instructions are recorded for daily holocausts—cereal offerings, peace offerings, sin offerings, community atonement, special cases and guilt offerings. (Leviticus, Chapters 1-6) Sacrificial prayer-life was governed by very rigid Jewish law.

Gradually, it was revealed to the prophets that God did not want the sacrifices and oblations of humankind, but their own willing, loving hearts.

> The people of Judah have done what is evil in my eyes, says the Lord. . . .
>
> In the valley of Benhinnom they have built the high place of Topheth to immolate in fire their sons and their daughters, such a thing as I never commanded or had in mind. (Jeremiah 7:30, 32)

The prophet Jeremiah spoke for God against oblations, beseeching the people to respond to God from their hearts.

> But this is the covenant which I will make with the house of Israel after those days, says the Lord. I will place my law within them and write it upon their hearts; I will be their God, and they shall be my people. (Jeremiah 31:33)

With a new image of a God of love and mercy, the psalmist explains to the Hebrew nation the Lord's desire.

> O Lord, open my lips,
> and my mouth shall proclaim your praise.
> For you are not pleased with sacrifices,
> should I offer a holocaust, you would not
> accept it.
> My sacrifice, O God, is a contrite spirit;
> a heart contrite and humbled,
> O God, you will not spurn. (Psalm 51:17-19)

The prophet Ezekiel speaks clearly of the type of relationship God wants with humanity. God desires the prayer-response of those who love God to emerge freely from loving hearts. "I will give you a new heart and place a new spirit within you, taking from your bodies your stony hearts and giving you hearts of flesh" (Ezekiel 36:26).

The Psalms

The Book of Psalms, or Psalter,* is a collection of religious songs. Traditionally, the psalms number one hundred fifty. This book of the Old Testament offers us rich and varied examples of the prayers of the Israelite nation. They are cries of supplication* to God, pleas for forgiveness, protection, sustenance and courage in battle. Many of the psalms are also hymns of praise and thanksgiving; they speak of undaunted trust in the Lord and total reliance on his help. Traditionally, the authorship of most of the psalms was attributed to King David. Modern scripture scholars, however, doubt that the psalms "which reflect the whole spectrum of Israelite belief and piety over the entire history of Israel could have come from this one author . . ."[1]

Many of the psalms composed for liturgical use were sung or recited by the community. Others are personal, individual prayers concerned with specific life situations. The psalms assure us that the Israelite prayer-experience included music and song for groups of believers and individuals. The psalms spoke spontaneously and openly to God, clearly aware of the needs and the sinfulness of the believers. They spoke joyfully of the love of the Creator, lyrically proclaiming praise with song, dance and musical instruments. Some of the psalms even express great glee in victory over their enemies. Understanding themselves as God's chosen people, the psalmist shows little sympathy for their foes.

> Rise up, O Lord!
> Save me, My God!
> For you strike all my enemies on the cheek;
> the teeth of the wicked you break. (Psalm 3:8)

The Israelites image God as the great King and Judge who protects his own people. This relationship with God does not include all God's people. Those who are unbelieving are considered apart from God's protection, enemies. In battle, the Israelites count always on God's being on their side.

> But I will call upon God,
> and the Lord will save me.
> In the evening, and at dawn, and at noon,
> I will grieve and moan,
> and he will hear my voice.
> He will give me freedom and peace
> from those who war against me,
> for many there are who oppose me.
> God will hear me and will humble them
> from his eternal throne;
> For improvement is not in them,
> nor do they fear God.
> Each one lays hands on his associates,
> and violates his pact.
> Softer than better is his speech,
> but war is in his heart;
> His words are smoother than oil,
> but they are drawn swords.
> Cast your care upon the Lord,
> and he will support you;
> never will he permit the just man to be
> disturbed.
> And you, O God, will bring them down
> into the pit of destruction;

Men of blood and deceit shall not live
out half their days.
But I trust in you, O Lord. (Psalm 55:17-24)

The language of the psalms is poetic, metaphorical. The authors often speak their anguish and longing for God through images of nature.

Save me, O God,
for the waters threaten my life;
I am sunk in the abysmal swamp
where there is no foothold. (Psalm 69:2-3)

Incline your ear to me;
in the day when I call, answer me speedily.
For my days vanish like smoke,
and my bones burn like fire.
Withered and dried up like grass is my
heart. (Psalm 102:3-5)

The image of God in the psalms is sometimes a wrathful, avenging God:

He will do judgment in the nations
heaping up corpses;
he will crush heads over the wide earth. (Psalm 110:6)

. . . at other times a loving, caring God:

Gracious is the Lord and just;
yes, our God is merciful.
The Lord keeps the little ones. (Psalm 116:5, 6)

The psalmists capture the whole range of real emotions that people feel toward God during their lives. The praise and thankfulness of the Israelites are also a major focus of the prayer of the psalms. Many psalms express deep gratitude and admiration for the God of Israel. Theirs was a relationship of constant worship.

I will praise the Lord all my life. (Psalm 146:2)

Sing to the Lord with thanksgiving;
sing praise with the harp to our God. (Psalm 147:7)

The people of Israel cherished their faith in a personal God. Separated from their pagan neighbors by their steadfast trust in one omniscient,* omnipresent* God, they prayed with confidence. This God was with them always.

Lord, you have examined me and you know me.
You know everything I do;
from far away you understand all my thoughts.
You see me, whether I am working or resting;
you know all my actions.
Even before I speak,
you already know what I will say.
You are all around me on every side;
you protect me with your power.
Your knowledge of me is too deep;
it is beyond my understanding.

Where could I go to escape from you?
Where could I get away from your presence?
If I went up to heaven, you would be there;
if I lay down in the world of the dead,
you would be there.
If I flew away beyond the east or lived
in the farthest place in the west,
you would be there to lead me,
you would be there to help me.
I could ask the darkness to hide me
or the light around me to turn into night,
but even darkness is not dark for you,
and the night is as bright as the day.
Darkness and light are the same to you.

You created every part of me;
you put me together in my mother's womb.
I praise you because you are to be feared;
all you do is strange and wonderful.
I know it with all my heart.
When my bones were being formed,
carefully put together in my mother's womb,
when I was growing there in secret,
you knew that I was there—
you saw me before I was born.
The days allotted to me had all been
recorded in your book,
before any of them ever began.
O God, how difficult I find your thoughts;
how many of them there are!
If I counted them they would be more than

the grains of sand.
When I awake, I am still with you. (Psalm 139:1-18)

Prayer in the New Testament

Jesus was part of the Hebrew prayer-tradition. Growing up as a young Jewish man, he was familiar with the Hebrew Scriptures. Several times the Gospel writers portray Jesus as quoting passages from the scriptures. Jesus, however, added a new dimension to prayer, for Jesus' image of God was a new and different image. In the entire Old Testament, the word *father* is used only fourteen times as a title for God. And in most of those instances, the fatherhood which is spoken of points to the father's honored position as ruler of the household, head of the family. In the New Testament, the title *father* is used very frequently. Almost every time the word is used, it is spoken by Jesus. As we have previously noted (Chapter 1) the term *Abba* is an Aramaic word which can be translated *dear Father* or even *Papa* or *Dad.* It is a term of closeness, intimacy. Jesus' use of the term *Abba* clearly defines his image of God. Jesus offers all Christians a model for imaging God and for a prayer relationship. It is important to look carefully into Jesus' understanding ingof God as his Father. The relationship of Jesus to his Father is not a relationship of a dependent child. It is not a relationship of control, status or authority. It is really not possible to love someone with an open heart, if you are in an inferior, dependent position. Dependent relationships do not engender love; they breed fear and, eventually, hostility. Episcopal Bishop Spong explains Jesus' relationship with His Father in his book, *Honest Prayer.*

> But look at the Father revealed through Jesus
> Christ. He is the Father who already has
> given all that he has, hence Jesus is a man
> who no longer expects anything of his Father—
> no presents, no favors . . . Jesus thus could
> recognize in prayer that God was first of all
> the Giver of all things, who asked only that
> this giving not stop with the Son. The one
> who had so freely received had also to freely
> give . . . The Father is one who gives all that
> he has; the Son is he who is heir to all
> things . . . God, understood as Father, gives all

that he is, including his Godhead. He gives
in order to call us into being all that we
can be, persons who reflect the fullness of
life, free people who are capable of giving
to others the gifts of our life and our love.
All this is in Jesus' word for God, "Father."[2]

Our Father

When the friends of Jesus asked him how they were to pray,
he instructed them not "to rattle on like the pagans, who think
they will win a hearing by the sheer multiplication of words. Do
not imitate them" (Matthew 6:7-8). Jesus prayed the Our Father
to teach his disciples how to pray. The *Our Father* or *Lord's
Prayer* is the most familiar of all Christian prayers. Only God
knows for sure, but it is most likely the prayer Christians pray
most frequently. This prayer focuses on God and on oneself and
others. It greets God as *Our Father*, not my father, and prays for
our daily bread, forgiving *our trespasses*, leading *us not into
temptation.* There is certainly a communal sense about the
Lord's Prayer. To truly pray the *Lord's Prayer*, believers have to
be aware of themselves and the others in their lives. The words
are so familiar that perhaps we forget their impact. Actually, we
are asking God to *forgives us* in the very same manner as we
forgive those who trespass against us. The *Our Father* requires
commitment, a willingness to consider what God's will is in our
lives and a willingness to forgive those who have hurt us. The
Lord's Prayer is a prayer of great balance, an expression of both
the needs of humankind and the responsibilities. Often saying
the *Our Father,* or any other familiar prayer, can be simply a
recitation of words, "rattling on like the pagans," just what Jesus warned against. Saying prayers and real praying are quite
different. The former is surely not communication; the latter is,
and it requires honest commitment of the mind and heart.

God Answers Prayer

A passage from St. Luke's gospel directly confronts the issue
of God answering our prayer.

So I say to you, "Ask and you shall receive,
seek and you shall find; knock and it shall
be opened to you." (Luke 11:9)

Yet, most people know from life's experience that many prayers of petition, pleas for health, wealth or success, go unanswered. The child who prays for a new bicycle or a pony is painfully aware of disappointment when the birthday gift is only the needed winter coat. Does God choose to answer some petitions and ignore others? Or does God simply say "No?" Our image of God determines our expectations. The child who pictures God as the kindly Santa Claus type figure in the clouds certainly has different expectations from the adult who understands God as the loving creative source of all the world. An understanding which trusts that the eternal God cares totally about every person on earth enables people of faith to relate to God not as a magician or wonder-worker. If God loves each of us completely, then God wills only good for us. God's Spirit is within us, urging us always towards goodness and fullness of life. Prayer enables us to be aware of God's Spirit within us. Prayer is a time set aside to allow God to write on our hearts. In the famous "ask and you shall receive" passage from St. Luke's gospel, the ending offers a key to the question of answered and unanswered prayers.

> If you, with all your sins, know how to give
> your children good things, how much more
> will the God in heaven give the Holy Spirit
> to those who ask him. (St. Luke 11:13)

The answer to prayer is the gift of the Holy Spirit enabling us to co-create with God, enabling us to live in harmony with our God, other people and with ourselves. Prayer does not change God. Our prayer does not convince the eternal God to change his/her mind. The answer to our prayers is the change of ourselves. Prayer changes us. It is a radical response to God, a willingness to change our attitudes, to look at life with all its problems and mysteries from God's perspective. Prayer demands unselfishness and honesty. We cannot listen to the voice of God's Spirit within us, if our own desires are forever clamoring for attention.

Types of Prayer

Spiritual writers offer us many distinctions in considering prayer and prayer styles. Human beings, incarnational people, need words, symbols and rituals. We sing and even dance in prayer. We pray with the scriptures. We can use our imaginations, picturing ourselves in a gospel story, responding to Jesus. We can listen to music or simply view the oceans or a simple bunch of violets in order to pray to God, the Creator. Prayer can be vocal or mental. In prayer, there is a time to speak and a time to listen. Prayer can be formal or spontaneous. Just as in loving human communication, prayer often is wordless. People who love each other and know each other well are comfortable in silence together. In addition to private, individual prayer, there is communal, group prayer. "Where two or three are gathered in my name I am in their midst" (Matthew 18:20).

In our Catholic tradition, we also identify four basic types of prayer. *Prayer of petition* is asking for our needs and the needs of others. It is not that God is unaware of our needs, yet Jesus told us to speak our needs before God. *Prayer of praise* is offering words or gestures of honor and praise to the goodness and greatness of our God. *Prayer of thanksgiving* is simply the expression of gratitude to God who has given us life and continues to sustain us. *Prayer of contrition* speaks to God of sincere sorrow for our sinfulness and asks forgiveness. These traditional types of prayer require particular attitudes of heart and mind. Thanking God in prayer challenges us to show our gratefulness to the people in our lives through whom God works. Seeking forgiveness demands a forgiving attitude in our relationships with other people. The sincerity of our attitudes, and the honesty of our self-evaluation, are integral parts of prayer. Sincere prayer converts our hearts, propels us into action, changes our lifestyle. Christian prayer is even more. It is the presence of the Holy Spirit within us, urging and enabling us to pray to the Father (*Abba*), as Jesus did, that makes prayer part of the whole Christian mystery.

Monasticism

In the middle of the third century, many Christians became disillusioned with the decadence of the Roman Empire. Men and women from the Roman provinces of North Africa and Egypt felt it was no longer possible to follow Christ living within the Roman culture. They believed the voice of God simply could not be heard in the towns and the cities. Groups of Christians rejected society and began a new life in the desert. These desert-dwellers lived ascetic* lives in prayer, fasting, physical labor and silence. Most of them led solitary existences. The word *monk* comes from the Greek word "alone," *monos*. As the desert spirituality grew, groups of men and women formed monastic communities. These monks and nuns renounced the world and severely disciplined their bodies. Such ideas of bodily discipline were not original to Christianity. Some pagan philosophical systems, most notably neo-platonism,* favored rigorous bodily discipline in service of the mind. There was a certain hatred of the body in both the pagan thought systems and in its Christian counterparts. These religious men and women believed that it was necessary to put rigid restraints on the body in order for the soul to approach God. Strict rules of poverty, chastity and obedience were adopted.

The Jesus Prayer

Sometime during the fifth century, the monks of the Egyptian and Syrian deserts developed a short, repetitive prayer as a powerful, spiritual practice. The Jesus Prayer, "Lord Jesus Christ, Son of God, have mercy on me, a sinner," is repeated over and over inaudibly, serving as a vehicle to attune one to God's presence. This type of repeated formula is a mantra.* To pray the Jesus Prayer is not a simple parroting of words. Its constant reiteration provides a background for contemplative prayer. The Jesus Prayer was often associated with rhythmical breathing which produced a restful state of peace and openness to God's presence. An ancient Greek Bishop of the Eastern rite, St. Diadochus (ca 475-550), promoted the Jesus Prayer for those practicing contemplative spirituality. This prayer has remained part of our spiritual tradition, reminding believers of the constant mercy of Jesus towards all people.

It was not until the fourth and fifth centuries that asceticism* spread to the West. The Benedictine tradition modified Eastern monasticism through the leadership of St. Benedict. In 525, Benedict decided to begin a monastic community. With a few followers, he built a monastery near Naples, Italy. In this monastery, he wrote his famous rule. The Rule of St. Benedict, although not entirely original, brought to Western monasticism a sense of balanced wisdom. Benedict's Rule greatly modified the practices of Eastern asceticism. Nonetheless, Benedict required discipline; a monastic life was to enable a Christian to abandon the world and turn completely to Christ. Benedict's Rule prescribed a sense of balance, adequate sleep and nourishment. The daily routine of monastic life included work, prayer and study. Benedict's Rule also included guidelines for harmonious community living and community prayer at particular times during the day. An important focus of the Benedictine Rule was obedience. The structure of Benedictine monasteries enabled them not only to survive, but to preserve music, art and literature through the Dark Ages.* Benedict had a twin sister, Scholastica, who founded a convent where the nuns followed the rule of her brother, also living productive lives of communal harmony.

The monks and the nuns spent long solitary hours in contemplation,* meditation* and bible reading. Although the work was hard and needed for survival, their prayer-life was considered the core of their existence. The Rule of St. Benedict guided the development of religious communities for centuries. St. Boniface brought this rule to Germany. And during the reign of Charlemagne in the beginning of the ninth century, the Benedictine Rule was imposed on the monks of the Frankish Kingdom. In the Middle Ages, when monasteries had forgotten their original dedication to prayer and the simple life, the Rule of St. Benedict was used for the needed reform. The famous Cluny Monastery (founded 905) used this rule for its rigorous reform. Many levels of Church reform during the eleventh and twelfth centuries sprung from the monastic reform in the spirit of the Rule of St. Benedict. The tradition of monasticism continues to modern times. And the idea of "retreating" from the world remains one model of Christian spirituality.

Meditation and Contemplation

In meditation,* the focus is upon words or events from scripture, Church tradition, the lives of the saints or any of God's creation. In meditation, we place ourselves within the situation. We listen with our hearts for our own lives. If the meditation is on a gospel event, we imagine the whole scene, using our senses of hearing, sight and smell. In becoming part of it, we learn in a deeper, experiential way. Meditation prayer can offer us a new awareness of our present life, a deeper appreciation of God's blessing and resolutions for change.

Contemplation differs from meditation. It is a wordless prayer, an intuitive prayer. Contemplation is a total focus on the mystery of God and all of life. Thomas Merton, contemporary Trappist monk (1915-1968), speaks of contemplation as our discovery of God.

> Our discovery of God is, in a way, God's discovery of
> us. We cannot go to heaven to find Him because we
> have no way of knowing where heaven is or what it is.
> He comes down from heaven and finds us . . . We
> become contemplatives when God discovers Himself
> in us.[3]

William McNamara, a modern Carmelite priest who laments the
fact that American Catholics have not learned to contemplate,
defines contemplation as a "supremely human and intuitive
gaze on truth" and as "the loving awareness of God, the invisible, transcendent, and infinitely abundant source of everything."[4] Although meditative and contemplative prayer forms
require time set aside to pray (Jesus often left his followers to
be by himself to pray), such prayer is not intended to shun the
world. The world is God's creation and it is good. Our bodies
and our physical needs and desires are part of that creation.
Prayer is false if it pretends we are some type of pure spirits
and not human beings. Meditation and contemplation, like all
prayer, challenge us, human beings, to change and to change
the world. An awareness of God is an awareness of the demands of love, truth and justice within our lives. In the *City of
God,* St. Augustine offers the needed balance—"No man must be
so committed to contemplation as, in his contemplation, to give
no thought to his neighbor's needs, nor so absorbed in action as
to dispense with the contemplation of God" (Book XIX,Ch. 19).
The attempt at balance between prayer and action in the Christian life will be with us forever. St. Ignatius of Loyola (1491-
1556), founder of the Jesuit Order and author of the *Spiritual
Exercises,* perhaps best summed up the tension with his famous
admonition, "Work as if everything depended on you, pray as if
everything depended on God."

Mysticism

Christian mysticism* brings to mind images of strange
pheno- mena and experiences way out of the ordinary. Mysticism, though a recognized part of our Christian heritage, is not
only a Christian experience. In Buddhism, the goal of mysticism is experiencing the state of Nirvana.* There are nature
mystics who strive to be at one with the great mystery of nature
itself. Christian mystics seek to be united to God; they strive to
experience real union with the living God. Even for the greatest

mystics, this experience is always partial, imperfect. Christianity has always included a mystical tradition. At times, the Church has been uneasy with its mystics, for mysticism claims a direct access to God without any need for the mediation of the Church. It is quite understandable how an incarnational Church, experiencing God through the people and stuff of God's creation, would be fearful of mystical experience.

Meister Eckhart (1260-1328), whose popularity has recently risen in spiritual/theological circles, was greatly suspect by Church authority in medieval times. He spoke of the "Godhead beyond God," the "eternal God who is eternally young," and the "God who is not found in the soul by adding anything, but by a process of subtraction." Meister Eckhart does not fit our stereotypical image of the mystic alone in a monastery tower in silent contemplation. Eckhart was part of the Order of Dominican friars in Germany. He traveled across Europe, preaching and teaching. He worked as a superior in a monastery and again as a professor of theology at the University of Paris. Eckhart's understanding of God stressed the transcendent otherness, "the God beyond God." He does speak of the God who is known through revelation in history, but his emphasis is on the God who is beyond our words, beyond our knowing. Eckhart's writings used an apophatic* or negative theology, describing God by stating "what God is not." Eckhart stresses the inner silence and detachment which is necessary to know God. This interior quiet, however, is not a withdrawal or a lack of physical activity. Meister Eckhart, himself, was an active person known all across Europe.

> To explain this life of inner silence and outer activity Eckhart uses the image of the stationary center of the axis of a moving wheel, or as T.S. Eliot calls it variously in *Four Quartets,* 'the still point of the turning world' or the 'point of intersection of the timeless with time.'[5]

The life of the mystic, Julian of Norwich (1342-c.1423), offers a totally different lifestyle. Just the opposite of Meister Eckhart, Julian the medieval mystic was a recluse. Although little is known about her life, we do know she spent much of her life in an anchorhold* attached to the parish Church in Norwich, England. She may have received her education from the Benedictine nuns of Carrow and possibly even joined the order. However, her mystical writing, the account of her sixteen visions, *A*

Book of Showings to the Anchoress, indicates that at thirty and a
half years old she was at home in her mother's house. Following these revelations, Julian entered the anchorhold, an enclo-
sure which she never left. To become an anchoress (anchorite is
the masculine), a person had to convince her local bishop that
hers was a call from God to this solitary life. Also, the bishop
had to be assured that adequate support for the lifestyle was
available. Dame Julian of Norwich was mentioned in several
recorded wills. If all requirements were satisfied, the bishop,
following Mass, would officially conduct the person into the anchorage enclosing her until death. The anchorage had a window opening onto the Church so the solitary could hear Mass
and receive Communion. Another window opened into the
street. According to her contemporary, Margery of Kempe, Julian was not unaware of the world around her. From her small
window, she counseled anyone who stopped by. Julian's writings
are a significant contribution to mystical literature. Her description of the visions revealed to her, and her interpretation of
them, offer assurance to all of God's continuing, unending love.
Through her visions, Julian learns much about God and God's
desire for us. Julian shares the insights from her revelations.
The wisdom of her mystical writings is timeless.

> For our natural desire is to have God
> and the good desire of God is to have us.

> The fullness of joy is to behold God in
> everything.

> I am ground of your prayers.

> The fruit and the purpose of prayer is to
> be one with and like God in all things.

> We can never know God
> Until we first clearly know our own soul.

> Just as God is truly our Father,
> so also is God truly our Mother.

The theme that runs through Julian's book is the absolute assurance that our faith will not be in vain. The anchoress struggles with questions of good and evil. She tells us that during
her visions she dared to ask God why evil exists in the world.
She offers us God's answer to her.

> It is necessary that sin should exist. But,
> all will be well, and all will be well and
> every manner of thing will be well.[6]

Julian of Norwich and Meister Eckhart are very different characters. Julian's language is full of imagery, even homey, while Eckhart's language is stark and abstract. Yet similarities exist. Both mystics write about this inner experience of God in prayer. They speak of God's intimacy with us, God's presence in our souls; yet they point to a paradox.* God is within us, yet absolutely beyond any created reality.

The great Spanish mystics of the sixteenth century were Teresa of Avila and John of the Cross. These mystics combined the active and contemplative life. Teresa was a dynamic lady, who founded reformed convents of Carmelite nuns all across Spain. She was the spiritual director of many of these nuns. Teresa's writings emerge from her deep mystical experience and her desire. Teresa wrote the *Interior Castle* as a spiritual instruction for the nuns under her care. Describing the process of a soul toward union with God, Teresa uses the image of a castle.

> I began to think of the soul as if it were a castle made
> of a single diamond or of very clear crystal, in which
> there are many rooms, just as in Heaven there are
> many mansions.[7]

Teresa's emphasis in speaking of prayers is not on human effort, but the gripping presence of God's grace within the soul. She describes the mystical union of the seventh and last mansion as a "Spiritual Marriage" or "we might say that union is as if the ends of two wax candles were joined so that the light they give is one."[8]

St. John of the Cross was also a Carmelite; Teresa encouraged him to begin the reform movement in the Carmelite monasteries for men. Not every Carmelite friar was happy with the reforming style of Teresa and John. Serious dissension arose between the reformers and those who did not wish to be reformed. John of the Cross refused to stop his work of reforming. Ecclesiastical authorities arrested him, imprisoning John in a Carmelite monastery in Toledo, Spain. John escaped after nine months of isolation. Until his death in 1591, he continued to work within the reformed Carmelite order. As Teresa had taken time for contemplative prayer and her books of spiritual guidance and mystical prose, so did John of the Cross leave a record of his mystical prayer. John wrote in poetry, though his books offered long commentary on the poetic stanzas. In his book, *The Living Flame of Love,* John's imagery describes his union with God. The words may seem strange to the modern reader, yet the intensity of his union with God is certainly felt.

Stanzas made by the Soul in the Intimate Union of God

> 1. Oh, living flame of love that tenderly woundest my soul in its deepest centre, Since thou are no longer oppressive, perfect me now if it be thy will, Break the web of this sweet encounter.
>
> 2. O, sweet burn! Oh! delectable wound!
> Oh, soft hand! Oh, delicate touch
> That savours of eternal life and pays every debt!
> In slaying, thou hast changed death into life.[9]

Teresa of Avila and John of the Cross lived during the turbulent years of the Protestant Reformation. A defensive church was suspicious of the work of these reformers. Teresa and John were often suspect and in danger of receiving the paranoid attention of the Spanish Inquisition.* Nonetheless, their centers of Carmelite reform became models for reform for many of the religious orders and the church itself. Teresa of Avila and John of the Cross, the greatest of Spanish mystics, are remembered not only for their contributions to mystical prayer, but as active agents of reform in the Church of the Middle Ages. Prayer had changed John and Teresa, and they changed their world.

Liturgy

The central act of worship in Roman Catholicism is the celebration of the Eucharist. It is the church's public prayer. St. John Vianney, a nineteenth century parish priest, loved community prayer. He explained its strength.

> Private prayer is like straw scattered here and there:
> if you set it on fire it makes a lot of little flames. But
> gather these straws into a bundle and light them and
> you get a mighty fire rising like a column into the
> sky; public prayer is like that.

John Vianney was not known for his learning or scholarship. He is remembered for his deep insights into human nature. He believed deeply in people's need to pray together and proclaim their shared faith. Liturgy is an ancient Greek word. It means *public work* the kind of work that serves the general population. The early church chose this term to name the gathered worship of the Christian community, the central work of the church. Work may seem like a strange and inappropriate way to describe prayer. Yet very often our work is a major way by which we define ourselves. And Roman Catholics define themselves through the communal prayer of the church, through celebrating liturgy. "Work" and "celebration" may seem like strange bed-fellows, yet they are the very stuff of our lives. Liturgy draws together all that we do, all that we are and grounds it in our faith in Jesus. Liturgy actually includes all those rituals* (the actions and the words) used by the church to publicly praise God through Jesus Christ. Sacramental liturgies, like Baptism and weddings, are church liturgy. Other rites,* like those used in the dedication of churches, the blessing of ashes, palms or water, and the vow ceremonies of nuns and brothers, are all part of church liturgy. However, the rite most often understood as liturgy is the Mass, the Eucharistic Liturgy. Its central focus, and the focus of all liturgy, is the major event of human history—the life, death and resurrection of Jesus Christ. When Christians celebrate liturgy, they proclaim their shared faith as a believing people united to Jesus. There is never a moment when the Eucharistic Liturgy is not being celebrated somewhere in the world. The Christian community of the world worships without ceasing, taking time amidst the cares of the world to celebrate God's nearness.

Jewish Passover/Catholic Mass

Jesus celebrated the Last Supper with his apostles. Festive meals were an important part of the life of the people of Israel. When Moses and Aaron were beseeching the Pharaoh for the freedom of their people, they spoke these words. "Thus says the Lord, the God of Israel, 'Let my people go, that they may hold a feast to me in the wilderness' " (Exodus 5:1). Deliverance from slavery is celebrated with feasting before their God. When the rules for the covenant between God and the Israelites are proclaimed, the celebrating rituals conclude with a meal. Moses and the seventy elders of Israel "gazed on God. They ate and they drank" (Exodus 24:116). For the Jewish people, the Exodus event is the central focus of the Old Testament. God intervened, enabling the Israelites to escape from the slavery imposed by their Egyptian oppressors. In the Book of Exodus, we read about the ten plagues afflicting the people of Israel. The tenth and final plague was the visit of the Avenging Angel destroying the firstborn child of every Egyptian family. Moses instructed the Israelites to smear the blood of an unblemished male lamb or goat on the doorposts and lintel of their homes. In this way, the Angel would pass over the households of the Israelites.

> Some of the blood must then be taken and put on the two doorposts and the lintel of the houses where it is eaten. That night, the flesh is to be eaten, roasted over the fire; it must be eaten with unleavened bread and bitter herbs. Do not eat any of it raw or boiled, but roasted over the fire, head, feet and entrails. You must not leave any over till the morning: whatever is left till morning you are to burn. You shall eat it like this: with a girdle around your waist, sandals on your feet, a staff in your hand. You shall eat it hastily: it is a passover in honor of Yahweh. That night, I will go through the land of Egypt and strike down all the first-born in the land of Egypt, man and beast alike, and I shall deal out punishment to all the gods of Egypt. I am Yahweh! The blood shall serve to mark the houses that you live in. When I see the blood I will pass over you and you shall escape the destroying plague when I strike the land of Egypt. This day is to be a day of remembrance for you, and you must celebrate it as a feast in Yahweh's honor. For all generations you are to declare it a day of festival, forever. (Exodus 12:7-14)

The Jewish nation has celebrated this feast for centuries. Every year, around the same time as the Jews celebrate Passover, Christians are celebrating Holy Thursday. Since the time of Christ, these two feasts have been closely linked. Holy Thursday commemorates Jesus' institution of the Eucharist. At this festive meal, with his apostles, Jesus took bread and wine and shared it with his friends. Christians, people of the new covenant, believe that the death and Resurrection of Jesus is the fulfillment of the Jewish Passover. Initially freed by God from the slavery of Egypt all humankind is now freed from the slavery of sin. God's love carries us through suffering, oppression and even death to the new life which we all share in Jesus, the Christ.

Scripture scholars disagree on the actual date of Jesus' Last Supper. The synoptic gospels say that the meal celebrated by Jesus and his friends was actually the Jewish Passover feast (Matthew 26:2, 17-19; Mark 14:12-17; Luke 22:7-14). John's gospel clearly says that the Jews had not eaten the Passover when Jesus died (John 18:28, 19:14). John's timetable indicates that Jesus died on the day before Passover and rose on the day following the Jewish celebration. Scripture scholar, Father Raymond Brown, expert on John's gospel, believes this gospel provides the most accurate dating of the Last Supper. Whatever the actual facts, the Last Supper is the celebration meal of the New Passover, the inauguration of the Christian Eucharist.

Much of the rich symbolism of liberation in the Passover meal celebrated annually in the Jewish tradition is part of our Christian celebration. The unleavened bread, matzoh, of the Jewish celebration was used by Jesus when he replaced the usual blessing words with words that would call together his followers forever. "Take and eat. This is my body." This matzoh, the unleavened bread, was used to remind the Israelites that their escape to freedom was imminent. There was no time for the bread to rise and be properly baked. They were people about to flee Egypt and embark upon a journey to the promised land. The bread of the Eucharistic Liturgy is bread for the journey of life, food for a new beginning, for the freedom and liberation of those on the way to the fullness of God's promised Kingdom. In the Jewish celebration meal after the main course of the Passover lamb is eaten, a third cup of wine, the cup of blessing, is served. The Jewish leader of the celebration raised this cup before drinking and proclaimed the Passover thanksgiving. Again Jesus' words were different. The startled apostles, accustomed to the traditional words of praise and thanksgiving, heard Jesus give thanks as he passed the cup to them, saying, "All of you must drink from it, for this is my blood, the blood of the covenant to be poured out in behalf of many for the forgiveness of sins" (Matthew 26:27, 28).

The Christian Community Remembers

After the death and resurrection of Jesus, his followers remembered this final meal. They remembered the words Jesus had added to the traditional Passover blessing. They remembered his injunction, "Do this in memory of me" (Luke 22:19b).

Celebration is a way of remembering. People really enjoy familiar actions. All families have special rituals that mark family occasions. Meals are usually part of such family celebrations. Birthday cakes and candles, Thanksgiving turkey, Christmas cookies and the barbeques of Independence Day are part of our rituals. These are special occasions when the very best table-cloth is used, Grandmother's candlesticks or the Christmas dishes. Meals and rituals help families to be who they are, to remember their ancestors, to celebrate their blessings, to look toward their future. Such rituals are shared by all. "Happy Birthday" is sung year after year. Ritual traditions fill a deep need for humans. We are not spirits, but people of flesh and blood, who need to celebrate with the gifts of life itself.

Jesus, a man of tradition, understood people. He shared our humanness. He knew that believers would best remember him and his message of liberation from sin by coming together, sharing faith, celebrating with ritual. He took the basic food, bread—the nourishment of the world—and wine—the drink of blessing and celebration—and changed their meaning forever. In the Eucharist, Jesus sealed the New Covenant; his body and blood were to be our food and drink; his very life would unite us with all believers of history and all those to come. The ultimate victory of sin and death was to be overcome forever.

Through the ancient ritual meal, Jesus was proclaiming his approaching death—bread broken, grapes crushed, wine shared, his body broken and his blood shed for all. Through sharing this meal, his followers were entering into his destiny. Gradually, the early Christians would come to understand the experience of the cross and the gift of redemption. They would understand that Jesus was with them, calling them to be part of redemption.

> The eucharistic food is the sharing of a meal by which we enter as a people into the mystery of Christ's sacrifice on the cross which reveals the Father's liberating love . . . So the Mass started out and remains a ritual sacrificial meal, originating in God's deliverance of the Israelites and culminating in Jesus' deliverance of all humankind on the cross.[10]

In Jesus' name, His followers gathered together as liberated people to break bread and share the cup of wine. Throughout the Acts of the Apostles, we read of the believers coming together to celebrate such fellowship meals. In the beginning, the followers of Christ still attended services in the Jewish synagogues on the Sabbath day. It was on Sunday to commemorate the resurrection that Christians gathered to share the bread and wine and their faith in the real presence of Jesus among them. Gradually, the followers of Christ broke with those Jews who did not accept Jesus as Lord. The celebration of Jesus' presence became their central act of worship. The leader of the local community was the leader of the Eucharistic meal. Included in this gathering was an actual meal where believers shared food in common, those who had more sharing with the poor among them. It is within this custom that the offertory collection has its roots. In the very beginning before the gospels were written (70-100 A.D.), the Hebrew Scriptures and the cherished letters from the missionary-apostles were read. This part of the service was separated from the meal. The reading and discussion of the scriptures was usually held on Saturday mornings. The fellowship meal and celebration of the Eucharist occurred on Sunday. The earliest of Christian liturgies of the Word and of the Eucharist were celebrated in the homes of local believers. Wealthy Christians offered their homes for the early church communities. In times of persecution, the celebration of the liturgy went underground.

The Roman Mass

In an account of the second century, we can read about the structure of the liturgy. Justin Martyr (150) tells us that the shared meal was no longer part of the Eucharist. The morning liturgy of the Word was now combined with the ritual meal of bread and wine. By this time, the local bishop was the usual presider of the Eucharist. The eucharistic prayer,* a prayer of thanksgiving, became the central focus. During the eucharistic prayer, formerly called the canon, patterned after the Jewish canons of praise and thanksgiving, the bread and wine are consecrated. Part of Justin's account are the introductory words, "The Lord be with you. And also with you. Lift up your hearts. We lift them up to the Lord. Let us give thanks to the Lord, our God. It is right to give him thanks and praise." These same words are the introductory prayers in our liturgy today. They are also included in the text of Hippolytus, who wrote in 215. As the Church spread through the Roman Empire, various cultures added additional prayers and rituals. Standardization came slowly. Interestingly enough, it was because many people in the empire did not understand the Greek liturgical language that Pope Damassus, in 384, changed the language of the liturgy to Latin to assure participation and understanding. It was not until 1963 that the official Latin was changed once again to the vernacular languages. The word *Mass* itself is derived from a Latin term *missa* which means a dismissal, the concluding blessing of the Church liturgy.

The Latin Mass, as Catholics experienced it before Vatican II, was known as the Roman Canon. The outline of this Mass was almost completely in place by the fourth century. It was with Emperor Constantine and the legalization of Christianity that the special dress of the clergy began. Now participants in the civil power of the emperor, they were given insignia, a *pallium* (outer garb or vestment put over one's shoulders) and special head-gear. When the Roman Empire collapsed, this special dress became part of the spiritual office and liturgical dress. It was Pope Gregory the Great in the sixth century who added more solemnity to the liturgical chants and gestures, along with extended and additional prayers that became part of the Mass in the West. Gradually through the centuries, the Mass became separated more and more from the people. The cathedral structures of the Medieval Ages promoted the clerical Mass. Within the monastic tradition private Masses (no people participating) became a custom. The next step was the votive Mass, a Mass offered for a special intention or person.

> This concept of celebrating Mass for some intention is not entirely foreign to the nature of the Mass, but it became terribly disproportionate and made a noticeable shift in the meaning of Mass. Mass came to be seen in relation to a particular case of need or for specific groups rather than as the worship of the entire Church with God in mind, rather than man.[11]

These changes had a lasting effect on the liturgy. As more and more private Masses were said, communal participation lessened and lessened. The people no longer loudly proclaimed their "Amen" of approval at the end of the canon. Gradually, the priest began to whisper the words, and the people watched in silence. The altar rail separated the celebrant and the community. The chalice of wine was withdrawn from the people's participation. The ritual gestures of elevation of the bread before Communion became a dramatic focus. The priest's genuflection pointed to respect for the sacred host. Devotions like benediction, exposition of the blessed sacrament and perpetual adoration developed feelings of awe. The Eucharistic host was to be worshiped and adored. In the seventeenth century, tabernacles* were prescribed by Rome. "For the liturgy, which was once and always should be the communal act of the priest and people, became now exclusively a priestly duty."[12] People no longer shared communion regularly at Sunday liturgy. The basic symbols of bread and wine, the ritual meal, was difficult to experience under the elaborate embroidery of words, gestures and votive intentions. The priest said Mass, and the people watched.

Vatican II: Constitution on the Sacred Liturgy

A major focus of the Vatican II Council was the self-understanding of the church. The familiar phrases born in Vatican II were basic to the reform of the liturgy. "The Church is the People of God." "We are the Church." "The Christian Community." "A Pilgrim People." The worship of a people's church could no longer be a passive ceremony. Vatican II called the people back from spectators to participants.

> The Church earnestly desired that Christ's faithful, when present at this mystery of faith (the Eucharist), should not be there as strangers or silent spectators. On the contrary, through a good understanding of the rites and prayers they should take part in the sacred action, conscious of what they are doing, with devotion and full collaboration. They should be instructed by God's Word, and be nourished at the table of the Lord's Body. They should give thanks to God. Offering the immaculate victim, not only through the hands of the priest but also together with him, they should learn to offer themselves. Through Christ, the Mediator, they should be drawn day by day into ever more perfect union with God and each other, so that finally God may be all in all. (Constitution on the Sacred Liturgy, 48)

The document on the liturgy put new emphasis on the congregation as a sign of Christ's presence in the world. The liturgy was to be a place of shared experience, of gathering together in anticipation of the establishment of God's Kingdom on earth. "A sign lifted up among the nations . . . under which the scattered children of God may be gathered together until there is one fold and one shepherd" (Constitution on the Sacred Liturgy, 2). The liturgy was structured once again to be an experience of transformation. Believers praying in community, associating themselves with the self-sacrifice of Jesus, committing themselves to the purposes of God in history to the renewing of the face of the earth. Liturgy, our common prayer, must be a celebration that nourishes us, enabling us to actually continue the mission of Jesus. Since Vatican II, Catholics have been struggling to become a more responsive, active worshipping community. Change is not always easy. Many Catholics found vocal communal prayer and shared singing extremely uncomfortable. The mystique of the Latin Mass was much preferred by many sincere believers. Shared gestures, hand shakes and kisses of peace, guitars and innovative music, or even liturgical dance, seemed inappropriate to the generations raised on the Roman missal.* Gradually, Catholics became comfortable with the new Mass, slowly understanding that the "new" emphasis on a communal meal was anything but new. A whole generation has never experienced a priest praying a Latin Mass with his back to the people. Participation of the community as lectors, leaders of song, Eucharistic ministers and, occasionally, even homilists have provided a new spirit of communal worship. Redesigned churches have provided the necessary structural face-lift. The altar is no longer the domain of the priest alone; believers share the sanctuary with the priest-presider. Parish people work as liturgical teams, planning liturgy, coordinating themes, music, readings and decorations. Lay involvement in the planning, as in the participation, is now understood as an essential part of liturgy, for liturgy is the activity of the entire community.

Modern liturgy has many tensions, and rightfully so. The large size of many parish congregations is often part of this tension. A sense of gathering and community sharing is difficult to experience when the hundreds of participants are not even acquainted. Many parishes make creative efforts to overcome this problem of numbers. Liturgy is a human work and at the same time a work of God among us. Liturgy is directed to God, yet human interaction is absolutely essential. Liturgy is a community event, yet each believer needs personally to encounter God. Liturgy is encounter, human encounter with one another, the human offering of worship to God and God's movement to us, making us holy, making us a community, a holy people. The encounter and union with Christ is mediated through our encounter and union with one another. Jesus is present to us in the Word of God, the scripture readings and the breaking open of the Word of God at the homily. Jesus is present to us in the Eucharist, in our communion experience. And Jesus is present in the faith of the assembled community, large or small. "From age to age, I gather a people to myself." Liturgy is part of the human struggle to proclaim our relationship with God and one another. Our liturgical worship is a human need; it affirms our faith, our dependency on God and one another. Through liturgical celebration, we define ourselves as a united, believing community, the Body of Christ.

Liturgy is not always celebrated well. Through the centuries, aberrations and over-emphasis of particular parts of our liturgy have sometimes made liturgy less than it can be. Not perfectly and sometimes quite poorly, but without ceasing, we have followed Christ's words, "Do this in memory of me." The Second Vatican Council offers this challenge concerning liturgy, "the summit toward which the activity of the Church is directed . . . the fount from which all her power flows." The sounds and shapes of the Catholic liturgy will continue to change. Other dimensions will be emphasized as the needs of Catholic people change. The shortage of ordained priests is already raising new questions for liturgical celebrations. We, followers of Jesus, will continue proclaiming God's presence in our lives. Women and men of faith will be gathered, the bread will be broken and the ancient stories of faith, the Word of God, will be shared forever.

Parts of the Liturgy

INTRODUCTORY RITES

ENTRANCE HYMN

GREETING

PENITENTIAL RITE	Preparing for liturgy by recalling our own sinfulness and the Lord's forgiveness.
GLORIA	Prayer of praise used on Sundays and special days.

I. LITURGY OF THE WORD

FIRST READING
(Taken from the Old
Testament.)

Jesus is present in and through the readings from the bible. Just as the believers of the early church retold the stories of Jesus and their Jewish heritage, we listen to the readings, stories from the Old and New Testament.

RESPONSORIAL PSALM
(Taken from the books of
Psalms in the Old Testament or a hymn.)

SECOND READING
(Taken from the letters in
the New Testament.)

GOSPEL
(Taken from one of the
gospels—Matthew, Mark, Luke
or John—in the New Testament.)

HOMILY
(Talk by celebrant based in bible readings.)

PROFESSION OF FAITH
(Nicene Creed)

The believers were strong in their statements of faith.

GENERAL INTERCESSIONS
(Prayer of parish for
needs of universal
church, world,
parish and themselves.)

The early church cared and prayed for one another.

II. LITURGY OF THE EUCHARIST

PRESENTATION OF GIFTS
(Bread and wine, and sometimes other symbolic gifts
are brought to the altar;
people are also asked to give
thanks along with their gifts.)

Jesus is present in faith of people and in bread and wine. Just as early Christians shared food with the needy and offered their support to the Christian

communities, we give of ourselves
and our money at offertory time.

PREPARATION OF GIFTS
(Celebrant asks the Spirit's
blessing on the gifts of bread and wine.)

EUCHARISTIC PRAYER
(A prayer of praise and
thanksgiving to God,
including Jesus' words of
consecration* over the
gifts of bread and wine
and the lifting up of the
bread and cup.)

Just as Jesus took bread and
wine and offered them to God,
so does the priest offer the
gifts in Jesus' name.

GREAT AMEN
(The Eucharistic prayer concludes
with this response, affirming belief.)

OUR FATHER
(The Lord's Prayer is
prayed together.)

Jesus taught His followers to
pray with this prayer.

SIGN OF PEACE
(The people offer Christ's
peace to one another.)

Jesus often spoke to His disciples,
saying, "Peace be with you."

LAMB OF GOD/Fraction rite
(Celebrant prays and
breaks the bread.)

In the Jewish Passover meal,
a lamb was offered to God.
Jesus offers himself. He is the
new lamb of God.

COMMUNION
(The bread and wine are
distributed to all
believers.)

Jesus shared the bread and wine
with his disciples at the
celebration meal.

PRAYER AFTER COMMUNION
(A time of thanking Jesus
for his presence within us.)

CONCLUDING RITES

(Final prayer, blessing and
recessional hymn)

The Liturgical Year

In order that the believing community relive the Christian story, the church celebrates liturgical seasons, reminding us of Christ's life and our journey of faith in Christ.

ADVENT   The four preparation weeks
              before Christmas.

CHRISTMAS   The feast of Jesus' Nativity
              and the following weeks.

LENT   The 40-day season of renewal and
              penance preceding Easter,
              the celebration of the Resurrection.
              Holy Week is the final week
              of the Lenten season.

EASTER   The season celebrating the new
              life of Jesus' resurrection lasts
              50 days.

PENTECOST
              The special feast that celebrates
              the coming of the Holy Spirit,
              the birthday of the church.

ORDINARY TIME
              The rest of the church year.

Traditional Prayers

Roman Catholicism has a broad and rich prayer-tradition. St. Paul has provided the foundation for Christian prayer life. "Rejoice always, never cease praying, render constant thanks; such is God's will for you in Christ Jesus" (1 Thessalonians 5:16-18). Through the centuries, certain prayers have become part of the Catholic heritage. They have served believers through the ages, expressing a relationship with God. There is no one way to pray, or any one prayer that is the best, the most effective. Prayer is a means, a vehicle. It changes our lives, not the mind of God. We do not believe in prayer; we believe in God and in faith, we pray.

The Lord's Prayer

Jesus, himself, taught this prayer to his disciples. Versions of the *Our Father* can be read in St. Matthew's gospel (6:9-13) and in St. Luke's gospel (11:2-4).

THE LORD'S PRAYER

Our Father
who art in heaven,
Hallowed by thy name,
Thy kingdom come;
Thy will be done
On earth as it is in heaven.
Give us this day
Our daily bread;
And forgive us our trespasses
As we forgive those
Who trespass against us;
And lead us not into temptation,
But deliver us from evil.
Amen!

Hail Mary

This prayer is attributed in St. Luke's Gospel to Mary's cousin Elizabeth. It was spoken on the occasion of Mary's visit to Elizabeth who was to become the mother of St. John the Baptizer.

HAIL MARY

Hail, Mary, full of grace,
the Lord is with you!
Blessed are you among women,
and blessed is the fruit of your womb,
Jesus.
Holy Mary, Mother of God,
pray for us sinners,
now and at the hour of our death.
Amen.

Doxology (Glory Be)

This is an ancient Church prayer of honor and praise to the Trinity. This short prayer, or antiphon, was often used in congregational praying or singing of the Old Testament psalms. It gradually became an introduction or conclusion.

GLORY BE

Glory be to the Father
and to the Son
and to the Holy Spirit.
As it was in the beginning,
is now, and ever shall be,
world without end.
Amen.

The Apostles' Creed

Although this ancient faith-prayer was not written by Jesus' apostles, it does go back to the time of the apostles. This creed is a simple statement of the faith of our church. It has been established that the creed's prototype existed in the 2nd century. A more developed version was used in the 4th century as the Roman baptismal creed. The present form was used in France in the 6th century and was officially adopted at Rome for baptism in the 9th century.

THE APOSTLES' CREED

I believe in God,
the Father almighty,
Creator of heaven and earth;
And in Jesus Christ,
his only Son,
our Lord,
who was conceived by the Holy Spirit,
born of the Virgin Mary,
suffered under Pontius Pilate,
was crucified,
died and was buried.
He descended into hell;
the third day he arose again from the
dead;
he ascended into heaven,
sitteth at the right hand of God,

the Father almighty,
from thence he shall come
to judge the living and the dead.
I believe in the Holy Spirit,
the Holy Catholic Church,
the communion of saints,
the forgiveness of sins,
the resurrection of the body,
and life everlasting.
Amen.

The Rosary

The rosary is a meditation prayer. This prayer form, sometimes attributed to St. Dominic (1170-1221), began in early church monasteries. The monks recited the one hundred and fifty psalms. Some monks could read the psalms, others had them memorized, and still others substituted an equivalent number of memorized prayers—usually the *Hail Mary* or *Our Father.* Since keeping count of the prayers was not an easy task, the device of prayer beads came into use. Gradually, the Rosary changed from a single reciting of one hundred fifty rote prayers to a combination of scriptural meditation and prayer recitation. The Rosary includes fifteen scenes from the life of Jesus and Mary. These meditations are divided into three sections: The Joyful Mysteries, The Sorrowful Mysteries, and The Glorious Mysteries. It is customary to pray only five mysteries at a time. While focusing on the scenes from the bible, the *Our Father, Hail Mary,* and *Glory Be* are said silently or out loud.

THE JOYFUL MYSTERIES:

1. Annunciation	Luke 1:26
2. Visitation	Luke 1:39-44
3. Nativity	Luke 2:1-20
4. Presentation	Luke 2:22-24
5. Finding of the Child Jesus in the Temple	Luke 2:41-51

THE SORROWFUL MYSTERIES:

6. Agony in the Garden	Mark 14:32-42
7. Scourging at the Pillar	John 19:1
8. Crowning with Thorns	Matthew 27:27-31
9. Carrying the Cross	John 19:16-18
10. Crucifixion	Luke 23:32-49

THE GLORIOUS MYSTERIES:

11. Resurrection	Mark 16:1-8
12. Ascension	Mark 16:19
13. Descent of Holy Spirit	Acts of the Apostles 2:1-4
14. Assumption	Book of Revelation 12:1, Tradition of Church
15. Coronation of Mary	Tradition of Church

St. Francis Prayer

In this prayer, traditionally attributed to St. Francis of Assisi, the prayer is asking only to be fully in tune with the spirit of Christian service and love. The central focus is the needs of others.

ST. FRANCIS PRAYER
Lord, make me an instrument of your peace
where there is hatred, let me sow love;
where there is injury, pardon;
where there is doubt, faith;
where there is despair, hope;
where there is darkness, light;
and where there is sadness, joy.

Grant that I may not so much seek to be
consoled as to console;
to be understood, as to understand,
to be loved, as to love;
for it is in giving that we receive,
it is in pardoning that we are pardoned,
and it is in dying that we are born to
eternal life.

Come, Holy Spirit

In our tradition, all prayer is in the Holy Spirit. It is the Spirit, present within us, who enables us to pray. Few prayers, however, are actually directed to the Holy Spirit, although many liturgical prayers mention the Spirit in their conclusions. "We ask this through our Lord Jesus Christ, your Son, who lives and reigns with you and the Holy Spirit, one God, forever and ever. Amen."

COME, HOLY SPIRIT

Come Holy Spirit,
fill the hearts of your faithful,
and kindle in them
the fire of your love.
Send forth your Spirit
and they shall be created.
And you shall renew the face of the earth.

Endnotes

1. John McKenzie, S.J., *Dictionary of the Bible* (Milwaukee, WI: Bruce Publishing Company, 1965), p. 704.

2. John Shelby Spong, *Honest Prayer* (New York: Seabury Press, 1973), pp. 36-38.

3. Thomas Merton, *Seeds of Contemplation* (New York: Dell Publishing Co., 1953), p. 26.

4. Robert McNamara, *The Human Adventure* (Garden City, NY: Doubleday and Company, Inc., 1974), pp. 13, 15.

5. Lawrence S. Cunningham, *The Catholic Heritage* (New York: Crossroad Publishing Co., 1983), p. 93.

6. These quotations from Julian's writings are taken from Brendan Doyle's book, *Meditations With Julian of Norwich* (Sante Fe: Bear and Company, 1983). Brendan Doyle has used the critical edition of the Middle English text edited by Edmund Colledge and James Walsh.

7. Teresa of Avila, *Interior Castle* (Garden City, NY: Doubleday and Company, Image Books Edition, 1961), p. 28.

8. Ibid., p. 214.

9. St. John of the Cross, *Living Flame of Love* (Garden City, NY: Doubleday and Company, Image Books, 1962), p. 152.

10. William J. Bausch, *A New Look at Sacraments* (Mystic, CT: Twenty-Third Publications, 1983), p. 133.

11. Ibid., p. 145.

12. Theodore Klauser, *A Short History of The Western Liturgy,* (London: Oxford University Press, 1969), p. 58.

Glossary

Anchorhold: The place of seclusion in which a religious recluse lives.

Apophatic: Pertaining to negative knowledge; that is, we know what God is not.

Ascetic (Asceticism): One who lives a sacrificial life in order to follow the Gospel more faithfully, especially in light of the Cross of Christ.

Consecration: The act of making holy; in liturgy, the priest's prayer over the bread and wine.

Contemplation: A form of prayer giving conscious attention to the presence of God in the world, in others and in the core of one's own being.

Eucharistic Prayer: The central prayer of praise and thanksgiving in the Liturgy. The consecration of the bread and wine is part of this prayer.

Holocaust: A sacrifice to God, consumed by fire.

Leviticus: The third of the five books of the Pentateuch, which begins the Old Testament. The name comes from the Levitical laws of the Hebrew tradition.

Mantra: A repeated prayer-formula, used in centering and contemplative prayer.

Meditation: A prayer style which focuses one's mind on reflection upon the scripture or mysteries of one's faith.

Mysticism: The subjective experience of union or direct communion with ultimate reality, i.e., God.

Neoplatonism: A later modified form of the philosophy of Plato, which devalued the physical, material, bodily world, focusing on the nonmaterial, spiritual world. It stressed the reality of God as Logos.

Nirvana: A stage sought in the Buddhist prayer tradition, which brings one to a state of oblivion to pain, care or external reality.

Omnipresent: The quality attributed to God of being present in all places at all times.

Omniscient: The quality attributed to God of having all awareness, understanding and insight.

Paradox: An idea or statement that seems contradictory or opposed to common sense, yet remains true.

Propitiation: The act of atoning or appeasing to gain or gain back good will.

Psalter: The Old Testament Book of Psalms.

Rite: A ceremonial act or action; liturgy is the worship rite of the church.

Ritual: The established form of a religious ceremony, prescribed words, gestures, actions.

Roman missal: The book which contained all that was said or sung at Mass. In the Roman missal, the text was provided in the official Latin and the vernacular translation.

Sacrifice: An act of offering something precious to (sacrificial) the deity; destruction of something for the sake of a higher value.

Spanish Inquisition: A medieval tribunal existing in Spain for the discovery and punishment of heresy.

Supplication: The act of earnestly and humbly asking God to satisfy one's needs.

Tabernacle: A receptacle on the altar to hold the consecrated elements of Eucharist.

Worship: The act of honoring and reverencing God, a form of religious ritual.

Discussion Questions

1. What is prayer? What is the goal of prayer? How does one's image of God affect prayer?

2. Review the tradition of prayer which is rooted in the Old and New Testament. How did the liturgy develop? Trace its connection to the Jewish Passover.

3. Which prayer styles were used in the monastic tradition? How did the Rule of St. Benedict influence western monasticism.

4. What was the focus of the liturgical reform of Vatican II? What are some specific changes in the "new" Mass? What are the major parts of the liturgy?

5. Prayer is a major part of the Christian Catholic lifestyle. It acknowledges reality and the Creator of reality. Review the

different types of prayer. In which style do you feel comfortable in communicating with God? Spend some time in prayer. Remember, all Christian prayer is united to the prayer of Christ.

Additional Reading

Brendan Doyle, *Meditations With Julian of Norwich* (Santa Fe, NM: Bear and Company, Inc., 1983).

Matthew Fox, *Meditations With Meister Eckhart* (Santa Fe, NM: Bear and Company, Inc., 1983).

Davidson J. Graeme, *Anyone Can Pray* (New York: Paulist Press, 1983).

Robert N. Schaper, *In His Presence* (Nashville/Camden, New York: Thomas Nelson Publishers, 1984).

John Shelby Spong, *Honest Prayer* (New York: Seabury, 1973).

Eugene Walsh, *The Ministry of the Celebrating Community* (Pastoral Arts Associates of North America, 1977).

9

New Perspectives in Theology

It may well be true that there is nothing new under the sun. Yet there seem to be new ways to view the old, new perspectives and insights. The modern age has computerized knowledge. We have new methods of storing our facts and ideas, new processes of making relationships and connections—even new computer languages—to compile and express our knowledge. Our accumulation of knowledge has certainly changed. Are we the same human beings as those who carved their life pictures on cave walls, or those who sacrificed their first-born to unseen deities, in hopes of continued fertility? Do we truly share a collective unconscious with all humanity through all history? Is our God one? Through the ages, humankind has developed, changed its perspective, deepened its understanding of itself and its God. As humankind changes, its self-understanding, its understanding of life's mysteries and life's questions also change. Humanity's relationship with God remains an ultimate question. As we search for new answers, new models of theology emerge. In our time, several of these models have provided new focus for Christian Catholic theology.

What Is Theology?

Theology is defined in many ways. The definition of St. Anselm of Canterbury (d. 1109) is a classic one: *"fides quaerens intellectum"*—faith seeking understanding. Paul Tillich, modern Protestant theologian, believes people theologize when they reflect on ultimate meaning. In his volume, *Catholicism,* Fr. Richard McBrien offers the following:

> . . . theology is that process by which we bring our knowledge and understanding of God to the level of expression. Theology is the articulation, in a more or less systematic manner, of the experience of God within human experience.[1]

The final words of McBrien's definition point to the changes in theology. The experience of human beings changes. Theology changes as people relate to each other and to their environment in different ways. Although faith and theology are not identical, any expression of our faith requires interpretation and articulation and, therefore, theology. Very simply, speaking from our experience about our relationship to God, about our faith, is theology. Theology is an attempt to explain our faith in terms and categories that are appropriate for our time. No one language or one set of categories or analogies is forever suitable for theology.

The experience of Dietrich Bonhoeffer, German Lutheran theologian who was executed by the Nazis in 1945, prompted him to speak of a God who suffers with us. Bonhoeffer also believed the very term *God* itself was so loaded with ideas of mastery, judgment, punishment and reward that it is no longer appropriate for autonomous* human beings. Bonhoeffer's insights born from his life's experience are expressions of faith, interpretations of the relationship between humanity and divinity. As in centuries past, the major events of history influence theological thinking. The horrors of World War II and the holocaust are not put aside when people of faith reflect upon God and their experience of God. After World War II, several new approaches have become part of Christian Catholic theology.

Process Theology

Ewert H. Cousins, process theologian of our times, lists two major cultural forces that had notable impact on theology—war and science. The tragedy of the first and second world wars gave birth to an anxiety and a sense of disillusionment. Humankind's faith in progress and the security of continued moral growth no longer could be seen as a sure and steady thing. Einstein's theory of relativity and Darwin's theory of evolution both pointed to a dynamic reality. A shift from a static world to a world in process was experienced in the culture, in the consciousness of our time and, ultimately, in its theological perspective.[2] Catholic theology spoke about faith and relationship with God in static terms. God was always described as the perfect being, the absolute, the only underived, uncreated, self-sufficient being. Alfred North Whitehead, whose philosophical thought and writings of the 1920s and 1930s are foundational to process philosophy and theology, believed that all too often the divine was defined as "the only genuinely 'real' reality, thus reducing the world of creation to the estate of a minor and relatively unimportant 'Avocation of the Absolute.' "[3] Process theology works from a different definition of divinity. God is not defined as *Being*, but as *Becoming*. For process thinkers, God, the divine reality, although unsurpassable by anything else, can surpass itself. The God of process theologians is not a separate entity, apart from the created world and its creatures. God and the world are in active relationship. There is a definite mutuality between God and creation. Simply put, God is influenced by the world. Creatures make a real difference to God. God experiences delight and pain according to the events of the world, according to the choices of human beings. This image of a caring God, deeply involved in the lives of people, is not a contradiction to the scriptures. In the bible, God's relationship with his/her people is certainly affected by their actions. The Old Testament speaks of God's anger, even of God's jealousy, and of God's faithfulness and love. It must be admitted that the Old Testament also speaks an image of a transcendent God, an untouchable God of power—Elohim. Under the philosophical influence of the Greeks, the early church stressed the Yahweh image over the involved Lord of Love. This emphasis has been part of Christianity ever since. God is seen as over and above the world, watching from timeless eternity. Most Christians would accept the following description.

> God is really not an intrinsic part of history, but one who intervenes from his position in eternity. Time is not real to God, because he knows every event—past, present and future—in a single all knowing act. Furthermore, he is in his essence devoid of emotions and feelings. He permits evil, even though he does not cause it, and he is not personally engaged in the moment by moment struggle against it. He is the complete, self-contained God, fully perfect and without needs. Nothing in the world, or done by the world, can contribute to his intrinsic glory.[4]

The Christian religion, with all its scriptural richness, usually worships the transcendent God of philosophy. Process thinkers cannot accept this Creator God who stands outside of his/her own creation. Alfred North Whitehead envisioned a God in whom all the possibilities of the world are contained. This God is part of reality, an actual entity, related to all other entities. Whitehead developed a theory of divine di-polarity. This means that God is manifest in two ways, two poles. The primordial* nature of God is the abstract side of divinity, the pole that is not influenced by other entities. This primordial nature of God is God as the structure or foundation of all the possibilities of all reality. This side of God has predominated in most of Western philosophical and theological thought. It was from this side of God that the "God is dead" movement of the 1960s arose. A God alone, abstract, simply the foundation of all reality, was not a God who could be part of life, a God who cared, one to whom the world could cry for help. The other side or pole of God, Whitehead called God's consequent* nature. On the consequent side, God is manifest as intrinsically related to the world, to physical reality. Every action of reality is taken in by God through God's consequent nature. Every reality of the world adds to the reality of God. Everything that happens on earth makes a real difference to God. What God's people do affects what God is and how God is to become. The consequent side of God is temporal—God-in-action, God becoming. In God's consequent nature, God knows the actual happening of the moment and, at the same time, sees the ideal. With the total vision of the ideal, along with God's constant love and concern about the world, God acts as a "Lure," always drawing reality to better things, to its fullness. "I have come to give you life, that you might live it to the full" (John 10:10).[5]

Process theologians do not believe that God is the omnipotent arbitrary ruler of all the earth. They understand a God who is limited in power because of the freedom of individuals. At every moment in history, God sees more, knows more and suffers more. God's power is love, not control, luring the world like a magnet of love toward truth, goodness and justice, but never through force. Whitehead expresses the depth of God's love and longing, not through an image of power or divine judgment, but as "the great companion, the fellow-sufferer who understands." The di-polar God of process theologians is easily identified as the transcendent God of eternity, Yahweh, *and* as the Lord of history, God-in-action, God among us. For Christians, the consequent nature of God, the God among us, has been given flesh in Jesus of Nazareth.

Although Whitehead knew nothing of the work of the French Jesuit scientist-theologian, Pierre Teilhard de Chardin, there are many similarities in their perspectives. Teilhard de Chardin speaks of the process of amorization,* which is the development of a relationship in all of creation where all creatures ultimately share in a fulfilling love. It is God's influence forever pouring through the world that shows a constant concern for the increasing growth of this relationship of love. For Whitehead, this amorization is the gradual development of the world toward goodness and fulfillment drawn by God who participates fully in this developing relationship of love. Teilhard de Chardin calls the highest point, where all that has come from God in creation, returns to God in complete fulfillment of perfection. Whitehead's thinking does not include a final or culminative point. He believes there is no beginning point and no ending, but a continual process. For Whitehead, God is never complete, but always increasing.

Teilhard de Chardin's thinking has had considerably more influence after his death in 1955 than in the previous years. The new scientific age, with its emphasis on evolutionary thought, the developing structure of humanity and the universe over the static understanding of the world of the 18th and 19th centuries, has been far more accepting of the dynamic thought of Teilhard de Chardin. In Whitehead's thought, the doctrine of God is the central focus. In Teilhard de Chardin's thought, Christology is central. He is not so much interested in Jesus of Nazareth, but in the cosmic Christ present in all of the universe. At the very heart of Teilhard de Chardin's vision is the idea of evolution. He believes the entire universe is evolving, going through stages which he calls spheres, from the biological sphere ultimately to the spiritual sphere. The high point of this evolution, the Omega, is identified with the Christ of revelation. The presence of Christ, Teilhard de Chardin believes, is in all—even in subatomic particles. It is Christ's presence that provides the energy to draw all to greater consciousness and spiritual awareness. A scientist and a mystic, Teilhard de Chardin was severely criticized for his lack of distinctions between matter and spirit. He understood that "from the beginning stages of its evolution, the living matter which covers the earth manifests the contours of a single gigantic organism." His critics realized that it was not possible to separate his science and his mysticism. His predictions were grounded in a deep faith that the billions of years of evolution would not come to nothing. Teilhard believed, despite the possibility and presence of evil and error, through the freedom of human choices all humankind and all creation would culminate in the Omega point, joined to the Cosmic Christ.[6] The great value of Teilhard's thought was his synthesis of science and religion. This synthesis was a bold step in the understanding of science and religion, not as enemies or even opposites, but as part of the evolving oneness of the universe.

Process theologians who followed Alfred North Whitehead and Pierre Teilhard de Chardin offered Christian theology a new awareness of the God of history, the caring, involved God who is not above the world, but active within it. Process theology enabled the fathers of Vatican II to speak of a pilgrim, journeying Church, incomplete, in process. It points to the need of an ongoing incarnation of Christ within the church, pushing the original message of Jesus forward to the developing horizons of the modern world.

Dualism

The joining of science and religion confronts the issue of dualism.* Dualism divides the world, making clear distinctions of good and evil. It offers an understanding of God's creation that sets forces against one another. Dualism causes hierarchical divisions in our understanding of our relationship with ourselves, with other human beings and with our environment. Dualistic thinking has been a major force in Western philosophical and religious thought. Even in our modern world, with its concern for ecology and holistic living, dualism remains. Officially, the Roman Catholic Church has always taught that dualism is to be rejected. God is the Creator of body and soul, the physical and the spiritual. They are not warring entities, not separate, antagonistic components, one higher, one lower, but part of a unity. The Incarnation stands strongly against any denigration of the physical. God, in Jesus of Nazareth, was fully human, body and soul, flesh and spirit. No part of human or earthly existence was rejected by God. Nonetheless, dualistic thinking took hold in Christian theology.

Where did it begin? Jesus was a Jew thoroughly immersed in the Hebrew culture. For the Israelite nation, God and the world were not at odds. The world and its history were the arena of God's revelation. The goodness of life, the richness of the earth, and the joy of living as humans were clearly understood as God's blessings. God loved the world. "God looked at everything he had made and he found it very good" (Genesis 1:31). Throughout the Old Testament, the goodness of the world is praised. Divisions of persons into body and spirit were not part of Jewish understanding. The good human being was not described as a religious person, but as a whole person, free, fulfilled. In Hebrew, there is no word for *psyche* or soul. God was found through living, within life, and this life was to be celebrated. This holistic thinking sustained great love of the family and family traditions and deep cherishing of the earth and the gifts of nature. Jesus spoke His message upon the foundation of this culture. His parables reflected this understanding. "Look at the lilies of the field, they neither spin nor toil" (Matthew 6:28).

The missionaries who carried the message of the Christ event beyond the Hebrew culture spoke to people of different backgrounds. Gnostic influence with its rejection of the concrete/present and its interest in the sphere of the divine, reached by knowledge and asceticism along with Greek philosophical thought, provided the foundation for dualism. To the Greeks, God was not a creative force in the world. Greek philosophers understood the world as apart from God. Nature and history were thought of as cyclical, having no beginning or no ending and, therefore, not having an ultimate purpose. Physical things were observed as having less value than the spiritual because the physical changed and decayed. The realm of the spirit, of the mind, was the higher realm—the realm of God, timeless and unchanging. The lesser value assigned to the physical world of body and nature gradually took on an evil connotation. To be holy, close to God, a person needed to escape life and the burden of bodily existence. The fathers of the church began to understand the world as hostile and believed Christian spirituality required a retreat from the world. Despite the Hebrew understanding of Jesus and the incarnational focus of Christianity, the church began to look only heavenward for its fulfillment. The earth was just a temporary place; heaven was the reality. The church became associated with the spiritual realm; sacredness existed in the church, apart from the world. An understanding of a changeless church attached itself to this type of thinking.

The practice of celibacy grew out of this dualistic thinking. An understanding of marriage and human sexuality suffered under the grip of dualism. A lack of cherishing the earth and caring for the gifts of nature also were results of dualism. If the body and nature were not to be valued, their needs and their care were of minimal concern. The poor would have their reward in heaven. The earth was a "vale of tears," a temporary test to be conquered in order to get to God. The Middle Ages confirmed dualism with its hierarchical caste system. The hierarchy, priests and nuns were celibate, pure, holy and close to God. Marriage and family life were too close to the physical to be thought of as sacred. This dualistic thinking was not always open to scientific discovery, for science existed in the realm of the physical, non-holy. The church moved against any scientific research which appeared to be in conflict with what was at the time regarded as the true interpretation of scripture. For this reason the church suspected Copernicus, condemned Galileo and protested the findings of Darwin and Freud.

Today much of dualistic thinking is gone. The church no longer takes a position against scientific research. It upholds the holiness of all God's creatures and creation. It supports marriage and family life. Vatican II buried forever any notion that holiness is found apart from the world or, more fully, in those religious living in a celibate state. The fifth chapter of the *Dogmatic Constitution on the Church (Lumen Gentium)* is entitled "The Call of the Whole Church to Holiness." Nonetheless, some dualistic remnants remain. Deep within some lay people is a feeling of unworthiness in religious matters, a feeling that those who are celibate and do not deal with the ordinary workaday routine of making a living or sexual love and family life must be closer to God. Perhaps the church's constant concern with issues of sexuality, homosexuality, birth control and abortion promote these feelings. Struggling Catholics sometimes stay away from the Eucharist because of past or present guilt over sexual failings, yet easily put aside sins of racism, human oppression and social injustice. Dualism fears passion and bodily pleasure. Its understanding of Christian stewardship and "mastery over the earth" has included the exploitation and pollution of the earth. A hierarchical system of spirit over body, cleric over lay person, white over black and man over woman has emerged from dualistic thinking. Sins of oppression and prejudice find their roots in dualism. Linking "the world, the flesh and the devil" has done great harm to the goodness of the world and the flesh. Christian people, believers in the Incarnation of the eternal God, cannot justify a dualistic approach to people and life itself.

A Creation Centered Approach

A creation centered approach to spirituality and theology is a total departure from dualism. It does not divide religion and nature, but sees them as partners. Creation centered thinkers are rooted firmly in the rich soil of the Old Testament and in the tradition of Jesus in the New Testament. Creation centered theologians speak of a relationship with the entire universe. They speak of holiness as being in harmony with the cosmos. Creation centered theologians see God's living energizing presence in the whole universe. They approach creation and all life as blessing. Science and art are understood as contributors to holy life. Matthew Fox, theologian and former priest of the Dominican order, proponent of creation-centered spirituality, quotes Albert Einstein's understanding of the function of art and science: "The most important function of art and science is to awaken the cosmic religious feeling and keep it alive."[7]

Creation theology begins with the idea of original blessing. It rejects the fall/redemption model of theology and original sin as foundational to our relationship with God. Proponents of creation theology believe that the doctrine of original sin is not the basic characteristic of human/divine relationship. Fully aware that human beings do sin, they reject the notion that separation and alienation characterize our initial relationship with our Creator. They see God's abundant blessings and love for all creatures and creation as fundamental to the Judaeo-Christian religious tradition. God calls us to be his/her people. God does not reject us as sinful creatures. The approach of St. Augustine and the Gnostics (see Chapter 7), which associates original sin with the expression of human sexual love within marriage, has fostered a theological understanding which denigrates the celebration of love-making and birth as created by God. Paul Ricoeur, French theologian, whose particular study concerns evil and sin, has expressed this idea concerning the Christian understanding of original sin:

> The harm that has been done to souls, during the centuries of Christianity, first by the literal interpretation of the story of Adam and Eve, and then by the confusion of this myth, treated as history, with later speculations, principally Augustinian, about original sin, will never adequately be told.[8]

Creation centered theology is concerned with the cherishing of all life and all people, as gifts of God. Its sources offer a global ecumenical dimension, believing that people from every religion share creation. It is concerned with ecology and justice. Its saints are prophets, mystics, poets and scientists. It draws upon the spirituality of the American Indian, conscious of the Native American tradition that defines the word *wisdom* as *that the people may live.* Its emphasis is on Jesus the prophet, the story- teller, the Son of God, who calls all people to share in divinity. Creation centered theology claims its place in the Christian tradition. It has not always been a loud voice, but it has never died. In the second century, St. Irenaeus exclaimed, "God's glory is the human person fully alive."

This appreciation of life, with its intense joy and deep suffering, has always existed in the Christian tradition. It has created mystics who found delight in union with God and God's creation. Julian of Norwich, recluse of the Middle Ages (see Chapter 8), speaks of the "glorious union" formed by our soul and body, and of God being not against, but "in our sensuality." Creation spirituality sees all things and all people as interdependent. It strongly promotes compassion as God's outreach to all creation and our Christian response.

> The whole idea of compassion is based on a keen awareness of the interdependence of all these living beings, which are all part of one another and all involved in one another.[9]

A creation centered approach to theology and spirituality is a challenge to our modern world. Wasted human lives and wasted natural resources are a major problem confronting humanity. Cosmic disharmony eventually will affect all people everywhere. If we do not become conscious of the needs of all life on our planet, in the present and in the future, our descendants will not share the blessings of creation. The perspectives of creation theology can awaken in Christians, and all people, the shared human responsibility to cherish life and all of God's creation.

In our American tradition, the famous Indian orator, Chief Seattle, understood the sacred presence of God upon the earth. He gave a great and tragic speech to the assembled Indian tribes who were preparing to sign treaties with white Americans who had taken over their land. Excerpts from this tragic speech of 1884 show the depth of his understanding. Chief Seattle feared the white man's intention for the land he loved. Yet this early creation theologian did become a Christian, accepting the white man's God before he died in 1886. There is no conflict between the Chief's love of the earth and Christian ideas of creation.

> Teach your children . . . that the earth is our mother. Whatever befalls the earth befalls the children of the earth. If we spit upon the ground, we spit upon ourselves. This we know. The earth does not belong to us; we belong to the earth. This we know. All things are connected like the blood which unites one family. All things are connected. Whatever befalls the earth befalls the children of the earth. We did not weave the web of life; we are merely a strand in it. God is the God of all people, and God's compassion is equal for the red and for the white. The earth is precious to God, and to harm the earth is to heap contempt on its creator. So if we sell you our land, love it as we've loved it. Care for it as we've cared for it. Hold in your mind the memory of the land as it is when you take it. And with all your strength, with all your mind, with all your heart, preserve it for your children and love it—as God loves us all.
>
> Chief Seattle, 1884

Mary and the Early Church

In the last decade many new books have been written about Mary, Mother of Jesus, Mother of God. Yet Mariology* has always been part of the Catholic tradition. At the Council of Ephesus (431), Cyril, bishop of Alexandria, and Nestorius, patriarch of Constantinople, led opposing forces on the question of Mary as the true Mother of God. Nestorius and his followers believed Mary could not be called *theotokos* (literally bearer of God), for a true mother had to be of the same essence as her child and older than her child. Nestorius concluded that Mary was Mother of Christ (*Christotokos*), but not Mother of God. In an angry debate, Bishop Cyril insisted that divinity and humanity were totally united in Jesus, the Christ, inside Mary's womb and, therefore, Mary was truly *theotokos*. Tradition tells us that the people of Ephesus rejoiced with great celebration when the

Council finally professed the holy Virgin to be *theotokos,* Mother of God.

Paul Tillich, Protestant theologian, suggested that Protestantism was much too male-oriented. His defining image of God as "ground of being" he characterized as more a mothering-type image than a fathering-symbol. Protestants in recent years have pointed out that Roman Catholicism compensated for the image of a patriarchal God with its strong devotion to Mary. Mary served as the feminine side of divinity. Mary was the tender, compassionate, approachable one who received the prayers and love of Catholic people. Some of the great feasts of the tradition are Mary-centered. The Annunciation,* the Immaculate Conception* and the Assumption* are Catholic doctrines which honor the Mother of God. Through the centuries, the Roman Catholic tradition has stressed the purity and holiness of Mary. Mary's virginity was held up as a model to Christian women. The devotion to the Virgin Mary fostered the identification of virginity and celibacy with holiness and closeness to God. A Virgin Mother was more acceptable to the early church fathers, whose views on sexuality and reproduction were ignorant at best and scandalous at worst. St. Jerome believed a woman's only purpose was bearing virgins who could give themselves totally to God. Remnants of the harsh attitude of St. John Chrysostom, orator of the early church, remain with us. Only virginal women escaped John Chrysostom's censure.

> It is not good to marry! What else is a woman, but a foe to friendship, an inescapable punishment, a necessary evil, a natural temptation, a desirable calamity, a delectable detriment, an evil of nature, painted with fair colors.

Even St. Thomas Aquinas, theologian of the Middle Ages, was misinformed concerning women. Following the biological misinformation of Aristotle, who lived centuries before Christ, Thomas believed that "females are misbegotten males." Brilliant theologian as he was, Thomas shared the lack of scientific knowledge of his era. Although genetic determination is already present the fetus in the womb does not develop male sexual parts for six weeks. But Thomas was totally convinced of female inferiority and misbegottenness. He said, "Women are necessary for only one thing—there is only one area where a man cannot be better helped by another man—procreation." A Church whose leadership was male and celibate developed a mariology that did Mary of Nazareth, along with all those who loved her, an injustice.

Mary of the Scriptures

Mary herself lived in a time and culture where women were the property of men. Women had little authority. They were not even permitted to be witnesses in legal matters. Mary was part of the poor, the oppressed of Israel. From scripture, we know very little about Mary, Jewish woman, daughter of Anna and Joachim. Her name, Mary, in Hebrew is *Miryam,* which means rebellion. This image is very different from the sweet and sometimes passive picture of the "lovely lady dressed in blue" of Roman Catholic tradition. The Annunciation event of St. Luke's gospel provides the first glimpse of the young Jewish girl (Luke 1:26-38). To the Angel Gabriel's fearful yet marvelous announcement, Mary, a young woman of faith and courage, responds simply, "I am the servant of the Lord. Let it be done to me as you say." Mary's "Yes" is the beginning of her part in the redemption of humanity. She will bear the "holy offspring who will be called Son of God." As Mary arrives at the home of her cousin, Elizabeth—who is pregnant with St. John the Baptizer, St. Luke has her proclaim the ancient prayer of the prophet Isaiah (Isaiah 61). In this Magnificat,* Mary speaks up for Israel's oppressed people, the *Anawim.* Mary's concern, here, is for justice for all God's people.

> Mary said,
> "My heart praises the Lord;
> my soul is glad because of God my Savior,
> for he has remembered me, his lowly servant!
> From now on all people will call me happy,
> because of the great things the
> Mighty God has done for me.
> His name is holy;
> from one generation to another
> he shows mercy to those who honor him.
> He has stretched out his mighty arm
> and scattered the proud with all their plans.
> He has brought down mighty kings
> from their thrones, and lifted up the lowly.
> He has filled the hungry with good things,
> and sent the rich away with empty hands.

He has kept the promise he made
to our ancestors, and has come
to the help of his servant Israel.
He has remembered to show mercy to Abraham
and to all his descendants forever!"

The infancy narrative of St. Luke's gospel follows. It is the well-remembered story of the first Christmas (Luke 2:1-19).

In the synoptic gospels, Mary is actually mentioned very little. The Jesus of St. Mark's gospel seems to be rather harsh to his mother who wants to speak to him from outside the crowd. Jesus begins to establish the relationship of people in the Christian community of his followers by exclaiming, "Whoever does the will of God is brother and sister and mother to me" (Mark 3:35). Yet according to the gospel of St. John, Mary is there in the beginning of his public life at the wedding of Cana (John 2:1-11) and at the end of his life at his death on the cross (John 19:26-28). She is also present in the Upper Room with the apostles at Pentecost. "There were some women in their company, and Mary the mother of Jesus and his brothers" (Acts of the Apostles 1:14). Church tradition through the centuries has given Mary a far more central place than afforded her in the scriptures. The virginity of Mary, part of Catholic tradition from its very first creeds, is not totally evident in scripture. The conception of Jesus is "through the power of the Holy Spirit" (Matthew 1:25, Luke 1:35). Matthew also connects the birth of Jesus with the ancient prophecy from Isaiah: "The virgin shall be with child and give birth to a son, and they shall call him Emmanuel" (Matthew 1:22-23).

The gospels say nothing of Mary's virginity during the birth of Jesus or following the birth of Jesus. Actually, the New Testament speaks of the sisters and brothers of Jesus, yet the words *brother* and *sister* were the same as words used for *cousin* and *relative*. Although these terms do not preclude Mary's continued virginity, they do not argue for it.

Father Richard McBrien points out that the virginal conception is a statement primarily about Jesus and only secondarily about Mary.

> Through this belief, the Church clearly taught that Jesus is from God, that he is unique, that in Christ the human race truly has a new beginning, that the salvation he brings transcends this world.[10]

The original focus of the virginal conception was somewhat lost in the emphasis on Mary's pure virginity before, during and after the birth of Jesus. This modeling became part of a spirituality that downgraded the dignity of ordinary women believers. Marriage theology suffered under the spiritual elevation of Mary's virginity. The Church is in the process of leaving behind this narrow focus, Mary—as woman of courage, as first believer in Christ, as voice for justice for the oppressed and as the feminine side of divinity—is once again being upheld as a model for Catholic Christian women and men.

Feminist Theology

Feminist theologians in our modern world are concerned with many issues. Their voices are no longer being overlooked. In discussions concerning the American Bishops' Pastoral Letter on Women, women across the country have been consulted. This seems like a normal, common sense approach. Yet only a very few years ago, the church's bishops would not have even considered asking women to share their views on their own needs and experiences. Men in the Catholic Church were accustomed to speaking for women. Feminist theologians look forward to the day when women themselves will be asked to write such a paper and a day when women's voices in the Catholic Church will be given equal weight. The entire process included several revisions. None proved acceptable to Rome and the American Bishops. In the end, no pastoral letter on women was published.

Women in the Catholic Church have concerns about inclusive* language. They are concerned about sexual and reproductive issues. Their demands include justice, non-discrimination and fair wages for women employed by the church. They seek a real, permanent voice in the hierarchical structure of the church. And ultimately women look forward to a church free of sexism,* a church where men and women equal as created by God, will share ordained ministry.

The most basic dualism that exists in humanity is the male/female dualism. It undergirds much of human relationships. This dualism still governs most theological models. In the last decades the patriarchal* approach to theology has been strongly challenged by women all over the world. The women's liberation movement which emerged in the 1960s, questioning the role of women in all of society, became a new springboard for a feminist

approach to theology. Undergirding the many questions of
women's role in the church is the theological perspective. Essentially women have stated that women are equal before God and,
therefore, should be equal in God's church. In 1963, Pope John
XXIII, in his encyclical *Pacem in Terris,* particularly noted the
women's movement: "women are becoming ever more conscious
of their human dignity" and are now demanding all rights "befit-
ting a human person both in domestic and public life" (Part 1,
41). Women in the world and women in the church are burdened with centuries of patriarchal history and tradition. Male
supremacy has been accepted as God's intention, as simply the
way it is. Theology written by men is not called masculine theology. It is assumed to be normative, while theology written by
women is called feminist theology. Despite the words of St. Paul
"In Christ there is neither Jew nor Greek, slave nor free, male
nor female" (Galatians 3:28), the male/female dualism is not
easily overturned.

Unlike its ancestors in Catholic theology, feminist theology
uses women's experience. All theology uses experience. The
scriptures are the recorded faith experience of the Israelite nation and the early Christian communities. Tradition is the experience of the church through the centuries. The problem upon
which feminist theologians focus is the nearly total lack of attention to women's experience in a patriarchal church offering
only patriarchal theology.

Women in Scripture

In Jesus' time, men had all the power. Although there were
many women of strength in the Old Testament, Sarah, Rebekah,
Ruth, Naomi, Miriam, Judith, Esther, the custom in Jesus' time
forbade women to study the scriptures. Eliezer, a first century
rabbi, said, "Rather should the words of the Torah* be burned
than entrusted to a woman." Jewish women were under many
restrictions. A rabbi would not speak to a woman in public, not
even his own wife. Women were separated in the synagogues,
not considered part of the needed number to make a quorum for
communal worship. In the daily prayers of the Jews, one of the
three prayers of thanksgiving offered this petition: "Praised be
God that he has not created me a woman." Despite the anti-
woman Jewish culture of His times, Jesus never treated women
as inferiors. Women were always a part of Jesus' ministry. The
first witnesses to the resurrection were women. No male bibli-

cal author would have stated this, knowing women, like children, could not even testify in court, unless it were true. Jesus rejected all of the blood taboos of ancient Judaism. He did not concern Himself with the supposed ritual impurity or uncleanness of women. In the question of divorce, only a right of men for the Jews, Jesus insisted on the same rights and responsibilities for men and for women.

Jesus' teaching on divorce honored the equal dignity of women, reminding His audience that the Creator made male and female in God's image (Genesis 1:27, Matthew 19:3-9; Mark 10:2-12). Jesus, a Jewish male of His times, was completely counter-cultural in His treatment of women. "Jesus was a feminist."[11]

Despite the egalitarian attitude of Jesus, the early church gradually compromised his teaching and succumbed to the patriarchal culture in which Christianity was attempting to survive. The shared leadership, deaconesses and deacons together serving the Christian communities, devolved into a male dominated, hierarchical system, where women's equality and basic dignity were once more put in jeopardy. Elisabeth Schüssler Fiorenza, German scripture scholar now living and teaching in the United States, has made a major contribution to feminist theology. In her book, *In Memory of Her: A Feminist Theological Reconstruction of Christian Origins,* Fiorenza has reconstructed the first three centuries of the church's life from the perspective of women of the time. Fiorenza believes that women were very much a part of the early church. The title of her book refers to the gospel story of the women who publicly anointed Jesus against the objections of some of his followers. Jesus' words at the end of the anointing—"I assure you, wherever the good news is proclaimed throughout the world, what she has done will be told in her memory" (Mark 14:9)—have been rarely given emphasis when the events of Jesus' ministry are told. It was male leadership taking all the authority that determined the Scriptures—what was included, what was emphasized and what was de-emphasized. The male bias gradually becomes the norm of tradition. Fiorenza, a most respected Roman Catholic scholar, compares her work to that of a detective:

> It is crucial, therefore, that we challenge the blueprints of androcentric* design, assuming instead a feminist pattern for the historical mosaic, one that allows us to place women as well as men into the center

of early Christian history. Such a feminist critical method could be likened to the work of a detective insofar as it does not rely solely on historical 'facts' nor invents its evidence, but is engaged in an imaginative reconstruction of historical reality.[12]

Fiorenza's work has been praised by men and women in all circles of biblical scholarship. It has contributed much in raising the awareness of men and women alike to their equality and full membership in the church and the world.

Feminist Theological Perspectives

Rosemary Radford Ruether is the most prolific feminist theologian of our day. She has spoken out through her many books against the suppression of human potential in our Christian tradition. Ruether has exposed the sin of dualism in theology. Her vision insists on an inclusive language that does not denigrate women or their experience. Ruether is a strong advocate of a Christology that stresses the union of the divine with the human in Jesus and not the union of God and man.

A Christology that identified the maleness of the historical Jesus with normative humanity and with the maleness of the divine *Logos,** must move in an increasingly misogynist* direction that not only excludes woman as representative of Christ in ministry, but makes her a secondclass citizen in both creation and redemption.[13]

Ruether speaks strongly against hierarchicalism which sets up a rigid structure of power based on a patriarchal imaging of God and society. Religion has used the masculine authority image of God to suppress women. A hierarchical change of command exists in the minds of many Christians: God—man—woman—children—the earth. In the redemptive community envisioned by Ruether, power is shared. It is not power over, but empowering everyone that is understood as the work of the Holy Spirit. All associations of women with the lower part of human nature, as the temptress, the source of sin, are part of sinful dualism that divides mind and body, the spiritual and physical, and reinforces man's domination over woman. Although Ruether believes that the full humanity of women is yet to be fully known in history, anything less cannot reflect the divine.

Ruether is not seeking simply a reversal of sexism; she speaks clearly for an inclusive definition of humanity where no dualism exists; white people are not privileged above black, rich above poor, educated above uneducated. She urges women to claim the fullness of their humanity. Ruether challenges the church to return to its roots and recognize and promote the image of God in women and men alike. "Theologically speaking, whatever diminishes or denies the full humanity of women must be presumed not to reflect the divine or authentic reflection to the divine, or to reflect the authentic nature of things."[14] Feminist theology is no longer viewed as a passing theological fad. It has become part of the Catholic theological landscape. Feminist theology challenges theology in general to rise to its full potential, to include all humanity, men and women. The imaging of God, and humanity's relationship with divinity, is not a male phenomenon. If the human family is to be redeemed, to stand before God in a free relationship of love, one half of the community must not be excluded—"In the image and likeness of God, male and female, God created them" (Genesis 1:27).

Liberation Theology

Liberation theology is most often associated with Latin America. Yet any theology which focuses on the liberation of people is part of this general theological movement. Feminist theology promotes the freedom of women. It rejects the image of God as authoritative man, as patriarch modeling a community where men have power over women. Black theology promotes the freedom of people of color. It rejects the image of God as powerful and exalted—a superior white God who models a society where white people are privileged and black people are oppressed. Black theologians point directly to the sin of racism. At times in the development of black theology, the Christian Church was charged with racism. Since the time of Martin Luther King, Jr., the black theology movement has been intertwined with the civil rights movement. The black churches were the only structure of organized black power previous to the civil rights movement. James Cone, a black Protestant theologian, became a leader in the black theology movement in the 1970s. His book, *For My People,* traces the black theology movement, and his own thinking, in the last decades. James Cone is now a strong advocate for a Christian theology that frees not only black people, but all those who are oppressed. Although black Catholics are a very small part of the Catholic population, nonetheless black Catholic theologians, clergy and lay people are determined to purge Catholicism of its racist attitudes.

Latin American liberation theologians took up the challenge of Vatican II, seeking the new Pentecost about which Pope John XXIII had spoken. Liberation theology is a political theology—that is, it is committed to the transformation of history. It is interested in the present world as the place of God's Kingdom. Liberation theology rejects a religion interested only in the reward of the after life. Liberation theologians, and the millions of poor Latin American people who share their faith, believe that the extreme poverty and oppression of Latin America is contrary to the will of God. In their book, *Introducing Liberation Theology*, the Boff brothers—Leonardo, a Franciscan priest to whom I have referred many times, and Clodovis, a Servite priest—offer statistics from the undeveloped countries of Latin America and the rest of the third world. The starting point of liberation theology is its perception and depth of compassion for the scandal of these statistics:

- five hundred million persons starving
- one billion, six hundred million persons whose life expectancy is less than sixty years
- one billion persons living in absolute poverty
- one billion five hundred million persons with no access to the most basic medical care
- five hundred million with no work or only occasional work and a *per capita* income of less than $150 a year
- eight-hundred-fourteen million who are illiterate
- two billion with no regular, dependable water supply[15]

Most of the people suffering the poverty and oppression in Latin America are Catholic Christians. Many of those causing the suffering are also Catholic Christians. How does theology respond to such suffering? What do the scriptures tell us?

Liberation theology compares the situation of the poor and oppressed to the situation of the Israelites enslaved by the Egyptians. The Israelites were liberated from their slavery through God's intervention. The Exodus, the liberating event which shows God's deep compassion for the down-trodden, is most significant for the Latin American believers. As God led his people out of the land of Egypt, they believe that through their faith in the same God, they will be freed from their oppressors. The Latin American Bishops' Conference, CELAM, met at Medellin, Columbia in 1968. This conference, building on the spirit of the Vatican II Council, gave birth to a theology of liberation, a theology concerned with the present, with the events of history. Life experience is the starting point of liberation theology. It is in daily living that faith becomes real. Liberation theologians believe that our faith, our commitment to the gospel of Jesus Christ, cannot be real unless it has real impact on human history. The Pastoral Constitution on the Church in the Modern World, *Gaudium et Spes,* states it in this way:

> This split between the faith which many profess and their daily lives deserves to be counted among the more serious errors of our age. Long since, the prophets of the Old Testament fought vehemently against this scandal, and even more so did Jesus Christ Himself in the New Testament threaten it with grave punishments. (#43)

The theologians of Latin America are determined to unite the theory and practice of the faith. The liberation theology movement has given birth to a new church in Latin America, a church of the poor. The poor can no longer be faithful to a patronizing church which offers occasional charity and comfort, but does nothing to transform the oppressive structures. During past centuries, the Catholic Church in Latin America allied itself with the rich and powerful who oppressed the poor of Latin America for their own profit. For centuries, the church rarely spoke out against the privileged, the ruling classes. The authority of the church was an authority of power, not of service.

Gustavo Gutierrez, a priest-theologian from Peru, is considered the father of liberation theology in Latin America. Gutierrez, born in 1928, had originally enrolled in the National University in Lima, Peru, to study medicine. During his time in Lima, he became actively involved in political groups at the university. At this point, Gustavo Gutierrez's life took a new direction. He ended his medical studies and began theological and philosophical studies to prepare for the priesthood. During these years, he went to Europe to study at the University of Louvain in Belgium. In 1952, Gutierrez became friends with Camille Torres, a Columbian priest from a well-to-do family. Torres had come to Louvain to study sociology. Camille Torres and Gustavo Gutierrez were deeply concerned with the problems of poverty and oppression in Latin America. As a sociologist,* Torres learned how to measure the effect of the Catholic faith upon the predicament of the people of his country. Torres was greatly disturbed to learn what little effect Christian commitment had had. Church life and church practice offered little help to the hungry of his country.

Penny Lernoux, American journalist living in Latin America since 1962, describes what happened in her book, *Cry of the People.*

> Unlike his classmate, Gutierrez, Torres was a doer, not a thinker, and when all his attempts at peaceful persuasion failed, he shed his cassock to take up arms with the Columbian guerrillas. He died in his first encounter with the Army, on February 15, 1966, in the central Columbian Andes.

> Camille Torres' death sent tremors through the Latin American Church, which was unprepared for the phenomenon of the guerrilla-priest . . . . The thirty-seven year old priest instantly became a martyr for the Latin American Left, particularly high school and university students, and bishops everywhere worried about his influence on their own young clergy.[16]

Gustavo Gutierrez, ordained a priest in Lima (1959) after eight years of study in Europe, took a different road from his friend, Camille Torres. Gutierrez was not satisfied with the approach to theology generally accepted throughout the Western world. Like Torres, Gutierrez could not separate the suffering of his people from his understanding of his faith, of the gospel of Christ. The new political awareness, coupled with the concrete situation of active fighting in Latin America, encouraged Gutierrez to find new perspectives in theology and toward the poor. In 1967, Gutierrez presented a course on poverty in Montreal, Canada. Here he looked at the poor from a new standpoint. He saw the poor as a distinct social class and as authentic bearers of God's word. Gutierrez offered his church and all people a new way of doing theology. This praxis* method has been adopted by all liberation theologians and is now part of the thinking of large segments of the church in Latin America and the world. The classical work, now translated into languages all over the world, is Gustavo Gutierrez's *A Theology of Liberation,* published in Lima, Peru, in 1971, and in English translation by Orbis Books, Maryknoll in 1973. Juan Luis Segundo, a Jesuit priest born in Montevideo, Uruguay, offered another book which presents a comprehensive critique of the accepted method of academic theology and a presentation of the praxis method in theology, *The Liberation of Theology* (Orbis Books, Maryknoll, 1976).

Liberation theology rejects a theological method that begins in the head. Gutierrez and Segundo believe that God is known in the events of history. Reflection about these events is the best starting point for theology. Liberation theologians do not reject study or the need for expertise, but they strongly believe that theologians need to be in touch with human experience. They also believe that real commitment is necessary. Liberation theologians are not involved in an intellectual, academic endeavor. They are committed to the poor and choose to be identified with them. Gustavo Gutierrez speaks of the utter insignificance of the poor. The father of liberation theology, now known throughout the world, is painfully aware that he no longer shares this insignificance. His fame as a theologian has "elevated" his social status. However, his heart remains with his people, though his work in their behalf brings him all around the world.

Liberation theology is a theology far more concerned with orthopraxis* than orthodoxy.* Liberationists believe that truth is found in concrete historical events. It is the people living these events, whose experience and insights provide the basis for theology. It is not possible simply to speak of Christian love of one's neighbor, while the large numbers of people have not experienced such love from other Christians who profess to be people of faith. Liberation theologians speak of a saving God who desires to free all people and wills a just society. The new awareness of the people of Latin America has recognized the need for justice in the present life and rejects a pie-in-the-sky, bye-and-bye answer to all their problems. They have come to believe that Christianity must liberate and serve the people of the world within history in order to prepare the fertile environment for God's Kingdom on earth.

Liberation theology has changed the face of the Catholic Church in Latin America. This change is ongoing. It has been and is a journey of pain and suffering. Oscar Romero, Archbishop of San Salvador, understood the suffering that would be part of the struggle for liberation. He became the "voice of the voiceless" despite the threats from the oppressive government. Before he was martyred himself, Romero traveled to Rome to complain to the Pope about the murders and torture of his people. His words, "If they kill me, I will rise again in the people of El Salvador," have not been forgotten. Dom Helder Camara, elderly archbishop in Brazil, has spoken out against some practices of his own church and against the government. He has supported the development of small Christian communities where people could share faith and bring strength to one another in their efforts to live the gospel. "Where two or three are gathered in my name, I am with them" (Matthew 18:20). Dom Helder calls such groups "Abrahamic minorities," people who are willing to support one another while risking their own security. These communities, like groups of the poor nomads who followed Abraham, Father of Israel, are seeking the "promised land" of freedom. Latin American governments are threatened by the huge numbers of small Christian communities. They fear their new found power. Dom Helder cautions the members of such committed groups, comparing them again to the Israelites in the desert.

> We must have no illusions . . . We shall not walk on roses, people will not throng to hear us and applaud, and we shall not always be aware of divine protection. If we are to be pilgrims for justice and peace, we must expect the desert.[17]

As the poor of Latin America, encouraged by its theologians and by a good portion of the Latin American church leadership, began to see themselves as agents of their own liberation, the "others" of Latin America took notice. Conservative leadership in the church, for centuries allied with the power structure, feared the new spirit. Cries of Marxism and communism were heard from church and from government leaders. Dom Helder objected, "When I feed the hungry in my country, my Church calls me a saint; when I ask *why* there are always so many hungry, my Church calls me a communist." The basic ecclesial communities, known now as BECs, continued to grow through Central and South America. In Brazil alone, one hundred thousand of these grass roots communities exist. These communities, rich in the Catholic tradition and still very much nourished by their popular piety, now meet to discuss God's word in Scripture and, through a praxis method, apply it to their present life situations. The consciousness-raising technique of Paulo Freire,

Brazilian educator, has helped the poor, uneducated of Latin America, to see themselves and their problems in a new light. Freire's famous book, *Pedagogy of the Oppressed,* has made a tremendous impact on the problem of illiteracy. His method, proven through much experimentation with the poor, illiterate peasants of Brazil, has enabled adults to learn to read and write in six weeks. His method is based on an awareness that all people have something to learn from all others. His method requires dialogue and trust. It builds self-awareness and self-image and enables people to see themselves as creators of their own culture. The church now encourages the people of the small communities to use the Bible in that way, reading the stories together and discussing present application to their own lives. In this way, the poor have come to understand themselves, their faith and God's Word as ongoing revelation, a living word.

Liberation theology is not without its problems. Its use of the Marxist theory to study and analyze the economic conditions of Latin America has brought major criticism upon Latin American theologians. Liberationists make clear distinctions between using the method of Marx, a respected sociologist,* and supporting Marxism or communism. Liberation theologians and the people of faith, the church of the poor in Latin America, reject communism as a system totally in conflict with their Christianity. They have accepted Marx's idea of relationship between experience and theory and believe that scientific knowledge is necessary to understand their reality. And understanding is basic to changing that reality. The governments that wish to keep the poor in their place have used the threat of communism to alarm people from the grass roots communities and the liberation theology movement in general. The church, sympathetic to the poor and their need for liberation, is also cautious concerning Marxist connections. Leonardo Boff, Franciscan priest whose liberation theology is founded on a St. Francis love of the poor, has written many books explaining liberation theology. He speaks often of the reinvention of the church, of a new grass-roots church based on the shared faith of the people of God. His challenge to the central authority of the Roman Catholic Church is part of an ongoing dialogue between Rome and the Latin American Church. Boff's book, *Church: Charism And Power,* received the censure of the Congregation for the Doctrine of the Faith, and he was forbidden to write or publish for nearly one year. Boff's work offers a type of uncentering of church authority, a willingness for continued renewal and a genuine openness to the Word of God, alive in all people of faith. His vision, and that of the theologians and believing people of Latin America, is now part of the mainstream of Roman Catholic theology. An option for the poor is alive. The voice of the oppressed of the world is now being heard.

Liberation theology continues to nourish the church of Latin America and provide a new foundation for all theological endeavor. Process theology, feminist theology, black theology and liberation theology are all part of the new spirit of our modern age. This spirit is alive in Christians of committed faith. Catholic believers in the 1980s all over the world view themselves in a new perspective. Tensions with hierarchical authority will no doubt continue, but the church has never been free of tension. The need for continued dialogue is a sign of life and growth. The importance of one's life experience, and one's own story of faith, has been afforded a place in the development of theology. God is building the Kingdom within history, within our present reality. And people of faith throughout the world are part of this process. "You too are living stones, built as an edifice of Spirit . . ." (1 Peter 2:5).

Endnotes

1. Richard McBrien, *Catholicism* (Minneapolis, MN: Winston Press, 1981), p. 26.

2. Ewert H. Cousins, *Process Theology* (New York: Newman Press, 1971), pp. 3-7.

3. Norman Pittenger, *Catholic Faith in a Process Perspective* (Maryknoll, NY: Orbis Books, 1981), p. 5.

4. Robert B. Mellert, *What Is Process Theology?* (New York: Paulist Press, 1975), p. 41.

5. John B. Cobb Jr. and David Ray Giffin, *Process Theology* (Philadelphia PA: Westminster Press, 1976), pp. 59-67. This text offers in summary much of the thought of Alfred North Whitehead's *Process and Reality,* Macmillan Company, 1929.

6. Teilhard de Chardin's *The Phenomenon of Man* (New York and Evanston: Harper and Row, 1959) is his most important work. This book was originally published in France as *Le Phénomene Human* in 1955.

7. Matthew Fox, *Original Blessing* (Sante Fe, NM: Bear and Company, 1983), p. 66.

8. Paul Ricoeur, *The Symbolism of Evil* (Boston: Beacon Press, 1967), p. 239.

9. Thomas Merton, "Marxism and Monastic Perspectives," John Moffett, ed., *A New Charter for Monasticism* (Indiana: Notre Dame University Press, 1970), p. 8.

10. McBrien, op. cit., p. 518.

11. Leonard Swidler, "Jesus Was a Feminist," *Catholic World,* January, 1971.

12. Elisabeth Schüssler Fiorenza, *In Memory of Her* (New York: Crossroad, 1984), p. 41.

13. Rosemary Radford Ruether, *Sexism And God-Talk* (Boston: Beacon Press, 1983), pp. 134-135.

14. Ibid., p. 19.

15. Leonardo Boff, Clodovis Boff, *Introducing Liberation Theology* (Maryknoll, New York: Orbis Books, 1986), pp. 2-3.

16. Penny Lernoux, *Cry of the People* (New York: Doubleday and Company, 1980), p. 29.

17. Dom Helder Camara, *The Desert Is Fertile* (New York: Orbis Books, 1974), p. 24.

Glossary

Amorization: The process through which all creatures and all creation are drawn by God into a relationship of love and fulfillment. In Teilhard de Chardin's thought, the Omega Point is the highest point of this process.

Androcentric (Androcentrism): Characterized by an understanding of males as the norm for humanity.

Annunciation: This tradition celebrated on March 25th commemorates the announcement to Mary and her acceptance that she was to be the Mother of God.

Assumption: This dogma, celebrated on August 15th, was defined by Pope Pius XII in 1950. It states that the body of the Blessed Virgin Mary was taken directly into heaven after her death.

Autonomous: Governed by self, guided by an intrinsic law, dependent upon self.

Consequent: In process theology, the temporal side of God intrinsically related to physical reality; in God's consequent nature, God is constantly changing.

Dualism: The theological perspective that believes all reality is divided into two distinct, independent principles—good/evil, spirit/matter, man/woman.

Encyclical: A letter written by the pope for circulation throughout the whole Church and even beyond the Church to the whole world.

Immaculate Conception: This dogma, celebrated on December 8th, was defined by Pope Pius IX in 1854. It states that Mary was free from sin from the very moment of her conception. Note: Often Catholics confuse the Immaculate Conception with the Virgin Birth. The Virgin Birth is a belief about Jesus, that is, Jesus was conceived without the contribution of a human father.

Inclusive: Language that includes the feminine and the masculine. Religious language is often exclusive. For example: "Pray Brothers," "For us men and our salvation," "Good will toward men."

Logos: The Word of God as Son, the Second Person of the Trinity, who became flesh through the Incarnation in Jesus of Nazareth.

Magnificat: The prayer of Mary in St. Luke's Gospel. (Luke 1:46-55) This prayer is based on Isaiah's prophecy in the Old Testament. (Isaiah 61)

Mariology: The theological study of Mary in terms of her role in the Church and in our redemption.

Misogynist: Characterized by a hatred of things feminine.

Orthopraxis: That which is consistent with sound religious practice or commitment.

Orthodoxy: That which is consistent with sound religious doctrine.

Patriarchal (Patriarchy): A system in which male domination is understood as natural and normative.

Praxis: A method of reflective action. Praxis begins with a reflection that comes from one's concrete situation and experience. Action springs from reflection.

Primordial: In process theology, the abstract, conceptual side of divinity, "alone with himself," God as the foundation of all possibilities of reality.

Sexism: Attitudes, practices, language, etc., that discriminate according to sex; that is, man over woman, or woman over man.

Sociologist (sociology): The science which treats the structures of society and the laws which regulate them.

Discussion Questions

1. Theologians begin from various perspectives. What is the perspective of process theologians? Which image of God does this perspective include? Which modern-day events influenced process thinkers?

2. Mariology has always been an important focus in Roman Catholic tradition. What major shifts have occurred in Catholic understanding and devotion to Mary in the last decades?

3. Relate dualism to creation theology and feminist theology. How are the perspectives, or starting points, of creation and feminist theologians similar?

4. What are the basic perspectives of liberation theology? How are these perspectives being lived in Latin America today?

5. Paulo Freire's method of combatting illiteracy is explained in his famous book, *Pedagogy of the Oppressed.* Read this book, and write a paper on Freire's method and its successful use.

6. The account of the silencing of Leonardo Boff is fully detailed in a recent book by the famous Protestant theologian Harvey Cox. Read *The Silencing of Leonardo Boff,* (Bloomington, IN: Meyer Stone Books, 1988). What are Cox's insights into the problem? Do you agree?

7. The new approaches to theology challenge theologians and all believers to connect faith and lifestyle, God's living Word and one's life experience. The new approaches challenge believers to reject dualism and accept all God's people and creation, itself, as equally precious before God. Reflect upon your own faith. Does it govern your lifestyle? Does your thinking and value-system include dualisms? Are you comfortable with a theology that demands faith commitment?

Additional Reading

Leonardo Boff, Clodovis Boff, *Introducing Liberation Theology* (Maryknoll, New York: Orbis Books, 1986).

Matthew Fox, *Original Blessing* (Sante Fe, NM: Bear and Company, Inc., 1983).

Raymond Gunzel, *Renewing the Gift, Releasing the Power* (Kansas City: Sheed and Ward, 1988).

Rosemary Radford Ruether, *Sexism and God-Talk: Toward A Feminist Theology* (Boston: Beacon Press, 1983).

Majorie Hewitt Suchocki, *God Christ Church: A Practical Guide to Process Theology,* (New York: Crossroad Publishing Company, 1982).

10

Catholic Social Teaching: A History of Commitment to Social Responsibility

People who are religious have established a faith relationship with God. There is no question that being religious involves "religious" practices: prayer, worship, anticipation of an afterlife, etc. Believers correctly cite their devotions and the creeds they profess as indicators that they are religious. They point to the existence of a vertical dimension in their lives; in a sense, they reach up beyond themselves, to God, whom they know as ally and sovereign Lord.

For those who stand within the Judaeo-Christian tradition,* religious faith is incomplete if it consists solely in a vertical dimension. In the first book of the bible a conversation is recorded in which Cain asks the Lord a rhetorical question*: "Am I my brother's keeper?" (Gen. 4:9). For Jews and Christians the answer to that question has always been clear: Yes, brothers and sisters are bound in love and responsibility to one another.

Accordingly, there is a horizontal aspect of faith according to which believers reach out to secure human rights* for those who are oppressed and to meet the needs of those who suffer. This horizontal dimension is a vital element of *the faith** which Catholics hold. In a broad sense Catholic social teaching consists in the witness of the Church to action on behalf of justice for all people. In a narrower sense, Catholic social teaching is the one hundred year old body of teaching[1] in which the Church speaks to theological and philosophical principles supportive of just social, political, military and economic structures, sometimes recommending strategies to establish such structures.

268

The Prophets* as Advocates of Social Justice

The Church has learned from many teachers the lesson that it ought to witness to justice. In the Old Testament, prophets instructed the Hebrew people to be just and merciful, especially in their dealings with those who could most easily be exploited. The prophets frequently extolled personal moral responsibility, reminding their listeners that the living God is a God of action who demands active involvement on behalf of justice.

A point made by the prophet Isaiah was similar to that made by several other prophets: God is not satisfied with the sacrifices offered by self-centered, self-indulgent people. Writing to such people, Isaiah advised: "Learn to do good. Make justice your aim; redress the wronged, hear the orphan's plea, defend the widow" (Is. 1:17). Malachi warned Israel of God's harsh judgment against "those who defraud the hired man of his wage" (Mal. 3:5). And Jeremiah said that he was sent by God to the palace of the King of Judah to deliver the message that those who sit upon the throne of David* ought to "Rescue the victim from the hand of his oppressor" (Jer. 22:3).

Individual prophets spoke against specific social injustices to particular audiences; concern for the powerless was a recurrent theme in prophetic teaching. It is important for people today to understand how fidelity to the covenant* along with a commitment to social justice are part of the legacy of the prophets. It is imperative that contemporary believers identify social injustices, work to correct them, and acknowledge that God requires such action of them.

The New Testament and Catholic Social Teaching

Jesus did not teach social ethics as such. And, although he confounded his contemporaries by his warmth toward social outcasts (e.g., the blind, lepers, tax collectors, an adulteress and a Samaritan woman), Jesus was not a social reformer. There is no record that Jesus condemned slavery or argued for its abolition. Neither did Jesus challenge the patriarchal biases* of his time which resulted in the unjust subordination of women.

In the New Testament social teaching is not separate from the integral religious vision which sees individuals and communities as responding to God's invitation. It would be a serious error if, in trying to determine the principles in the gospel which are instructive for social ethics, we began to think of the New

Testament as an abstract book of theory. On the contrary, it is a dynamic account of faith in action. We can discover principles in the gospels which provide the foundation for Catholic social teaching, but we need to realize that in this search we are engaging in a deductive and inferential task.* It is a worthwhile endeavor to the extent that comprehending these principles leads to an awareness of the virtues* and attitude which should characterize the individual Christian and Christians in community, the Church.

In the gospel Jesus told his followers who they were. "You are the salt of the earth" (Mt. 5:13). "You are the light of the world" (Mt. 5:14). Committed Christians are entrusted with the tasks of working against all forms of injustice and disclosing God's will to people everywhere. The identity of disciple* is attained by people who are willing to repent, i.e., turn away from their sins, and obey the voice of the Spirit who speaks in their hearts. Both self-righteous attitudes and superficial protestations of allegiance were rejected by Jesus as unworthy of his followers. Jesus exposed the hypocrisy of the pharisee* who considered himself good because he could tally points. "I give you thanks O God, that I am not like the rest of men, grasping, crooked, adulterous . . . . I fast twice a week. I pay tithes* on all I possess" (Lk. 18:11-12). Jesus, speaking of the little regard he had for people who pay him only lip service, said: "None of those who cry out, 'Lord, Lord' will enter the kingdom of God, but only the one who does the will of my Father in heaven" (Mt.7:21). Being right with God, then, and being humble in one's discipleship, are the requirements for doing good works in Jesus' name.

The second injunction of the Great Commandment stipulates "You shall love your neighbor as yourself" (Mt. 22:39). In the parable* of the Good Samaritan Jesus taught the lesson that his followers should be neighbor to each and every person who is in need. (Lk. 10:30-37) Just as the priest and the Levite who passed the man who was beaten by robbers did not recognize the requirements of love in those circumstances, so also Christians today will not recognize the concrete demands of love unless they are open to the Spirit.

Two unique elements in Jesus' teaching are his injunctions to reject violence and to love one's enemies. (Mt. 5:38-48) The implications of living up to such standards individually and communally demand prayer, dialogue and a penetrating examination of contrary cultural biases.

Much of the motivation for good deeds of generosity and compassion and for Church-sponsored programs of social outreach comes from the instruction contained in the description of the last judgment in Matthew 25:31-46. In this account Jesus established meeting the needs of one's neighbor as the basis upon which eternal salvation would be granted. He also revealed that he would count generosity to the least of the brothers or sisters as an act of kindness done on his behalf. In contrast, indifference or hard-heartedness toward those who are hungry, thirsty, lonely or homeless are to be cause for eternal punishment.

There is evidence that in the early Church Christian believers cared for one another because this was what was expected of Jesus' followers. In the Acts of the Apostles* we read:

> The community of believers were of one heart and one mind. None of them ever claimed anything as his own; rather, everything was held in common. . . . nor was there anyone needy among them, for all who owned property or houses sold them and donated the proceeds. They used to lay them at the feet of the apostles to be distributed to everyone according to their need. (Acts 4:32-35)

A passage from the Epistle of James* makes clear the fact that faith which lacks a horizontal dimension is only a sham.

> What good is it to profess faith without practicing it? Such faith has no power to save one, has it? If a brother or sister has nothing to wear and no food for the day, and you say to them, "Good-bye and good luck! Keep warm and well fed," but do not meet their bodily needs, what good is that? (James 2:14-16)

It would be an error to conclude on the basis of the citation from the Acts of the Apostles that the first Christians lived in an earthly utopia.* The problems in their society were different from the ones we face today, but they had their share of religious, social and political conflicts.* However, their love for one another, together with their commitment to solving their problems, remains an inspiration to people today.

The exhortation contained in the Epistle of James should be seen as a challenge to sinful people to live up to their faith. Lazyness, greed and self-absorption were sins which James probably observed among the early Christians; these sins caused some fortunate Christians to ignore the needs of the less fortunate.

While there was obvious attention paid to the physical needs of the disadvantaged, the first generations of Christians gave little thought to one aspect of social ethics, i.e., the way in which Christian values should impact upon and effect change in the institutions of society. In a sense, the early Christians distanced themselves from the secular order. Jesus had taught them "Render to Caesar the things that are Caesar's" (Mt. 22:21). And the writers of the epistles repeated the message that Christians be loyal and obedient to secular authorities. However, concern about the secular world seemed to be at the back of the minds of the early Christians, and the institutions of the world were dismissed as having little or no enduring value. The main item on the early Christian agenda was the preaching of the *kerygma*.* Their eschatological* conviction was that the end of the world would come soon, and Christ's second coming* would precede the end of time. Accordingly, Saint Paul expressed his very real belief when he wrote: "The form of this world is passing away" (1 Cor. 7:31).

The Relationship between Christianity and Culture

It has been more than nineteen hundred years since Paul's first letter to the Corinthians, and the world has yet to pass away. In view of this fact, significant questions demand a response: What should be the relationship between Christianity and culture? Does it still make sense to dismiss most aspects of culture as irrelevant to Christians? A Protestant theologian, H. Richard Niebuhr, in the book *Christ and Culture,* brought stimulating analysis to bear on these questions. Let us first consider Niebuhr's understandings of what a Christian is and in what culture consists, and then review the five possible ways for the two to interact.

> A Christian is "one who counts himself as belonging to that community of men for whom Jesus Christ—his life, words, deeds, and destiny—is of supreme importance as the key to understanding themselves and their world, the major source of their knowledge of God and man, good and evil, the constant companion of conscience, and the expected deliverer from evil."[2]

Culture or civilization (in the New Testament referred
to as "the world") is the "'artificial, secondary environment' which man superimposes on the natural. It
comprises language, habits, ideas, beliefs, customs,
social organization, inherited artifacts, technical processes, and values." ". . . it is inextricably bound up
with man's life in society, it is always social."[3]

H. Richard Niebuhr described five ways in which religions
typically respond to the world. According to the first model,
"Christ against Culture," Christian faith should keep believers
from involving themselves in the secular order. Christians cannot avoid being "in the world," but they should not be "of the
world." The institutions of society are rejected and there is an
explicit decision to withdraw from them. The sole loyalty of the
Christian is to Christ; secular society makes no claims upon
believers. In this radical approach, there is a desire to separate
Christian communities from the dominion of sin which is "the
world."

The second model, "The Christ of Culture," recognizes little
opposition between Christian faith and "the world." Christianity and culture coexist in harmony, and the teachings of Jesus
are seen as having a positive influence on much of secular society. Persons who adopt this model do not experience tension in
professing loyalty to both Christ and the culture in which they
live. And they tend to deny the power and pervasiveness of
personal and social sin.

"Christ above Culture" is Niebuhr's third model. In this way
of understanding the relationship of the Christian to culture, it
is believed that God is the creator of all, and that the person is,
in a sense, a co-creator. Free and intelligent persons are meant
to create culture. In so doing they must contend with individual
and social sin, but they can achieve their goal as a result of
strength which comes from above, i.e., the grace of Christ.

This way of identifying the relationship of Christians to culture, generally known as the "synthesist" model, is distinguished by the fact that it assesses human nature and human
institutions in a very positive way. The human ability to reason
and to choose worthy goals makes possible the creation of just
political and social structures. In the synthesist model politics
and culture take on an autonomy of their own, and there is an

inclination to expect that these institutions will serve the common good.

The fourth model is called "Christ and Culture in Paradox." The theory behind this model is different from the three preceding ones in that it does not seek so much to work out a relationship between Christians and secular society as to disclose the relationship between the all-holy God of grace and people who need to be delivered from sin by the grace of God. This model stresses the transcendence of God and presupposes a disassociation from society. Law, the state and social institutions serve only to prevent anarchy. They are not agencies through which people accomplish social union, respect each others' rights and meet the needs of the disadvantaged. Consequently, a negative attitude toward culture, a sober appraisal of the pervasiveness of sin, and a reliance on God to rescue the believer, characterize this approach.

The final model described by Niebuhr is "Christ the Transformer of Culture." Those who follow this approach see culture as under God's dominion and believe that Christians must carry on cultural work in obedience to the Lord. The goodness of creation and its renewal through Christ's incarnation* are emphasized by proponents of this model. Bringing about the conversion of culture in the present is regarded as a real possibility because of the on-going action of Jesus in history.

This model, known as the "transformationist" or "conversionist," sees a great deal of tension between secular culture and the Christian ideal. The misuse of human freedom has caused culture to be distorted by sin, and sin has become so deeply imbedded as to be ingrained in the institutions of society. However, the presence of sin simply underscores the need for cultural transformation through the grace of Christ which makes possible loving actions toward God and neighbor.

From our brief review of Niebuhr's models it becomes apparent that resolving the issue of how Christians should relate to culture is much more complex than deciding what should be done for a homeless orphan. Still, while Niebuhr's theory does nothing to minimize complexity, it does provide clear conceptual categories within which to determine how it is possible for church and society to interrelate.

Catholic Christians understand all that is created as the work of God's hands, and as good. Nature is God's creation and is good. So, too, is the human person who uses God's gifts of intellect and will to create structures of order and justice. Sin, as a subjective reality, leads to selfishness and a lack of commitment to the common good. And sin, when experienced as an objective social reality, impedes efforts to effect social justice. But even though sin is powerful and discouraging, followers of Jesus share in the fruits of his incarnation and redemption. By taking on human flesh at his incarnation Jesus renewed and transformed all things human. By redeeming humankind through his death on the cross, Jesus triumphed over sin and death. As a result, Catholic Christians are optimistic people who believe that justice can be attained. They identify themselves as devoted to the establishment of just social institutions. However, Catholic optimism does not extend to the belief that God's kingdom of perfect justice and peace will ever be established in this world. Their faith is that only in the next life will they live in the fullness of the kingdom.

In terms of Niebuhr's categories, the Catholic approach to culture is closest to the third model. In choosing the third category as the one which is probably the most Catholic, insights offered by advocates of models one, four and five are not rejected. We should take due note of the way they understand the radical nature of the faith commitment, God's transcendence, the prevalence of sin, and God's immanence. These are profound religious truths which Catholic social ethics seeks to incorporate into its teaching without affording them the same emphasis as their proponents. The second model, "Christ of Culture," is assessed as deficient because it recognizes little difference between culture as it exists and culture as it ought to be. Were there in fact little difference, there would not be a need for the development and promulgation of Catholic social teaching.

Catholic Social Teaching—Papal Encyclicals, Papal Addresses, and Conciliar Statements*

During the past century Catholic social teaching has been formulated by popes, Vatican Council II,* and bishops, both individually and collectively. When Catholic social teaching comes from a pope, it is presented in a document called an encyclical. An encyclical is a *literae encyclicae*, i.e., an open circular letter addressed to Church hierarchy, all Catholics, or, more recently, all people of good will. Encyclicals are written in

Latin; the title of an encyclical is determined by the first few Latin words which appear in the text. The reason a pope writes an encyclical is to instruct Catholics on an important subject. Some encyclicals address issues of sexual morality or Catholic doctrine. Others deal with matters of social justice. In this chapter the latter group will be of concern to us.

In the years following the issuance of the *Communist Manifesto** by Karl Marx in 1848, there was considerable dissatisfaction with the institutions of the existing social order in Europe. Several questions surfaced. How were the state, capital and labor meant to interact? What was the purpose or function of each? Could there ever be a situation in which the workingman* would be in a just relationship with capital and the state, or were these institutions inherently exploitative? Pope Leo XIII reasoned that what the Church knew about justice and charity could provide insight to government leaders, employers and employees. On May 15, 1891 he issued the encyclical *Rerum Novarum*, "On the Condition of Labor." In it Leo XIII sought to explain the components of a balanced relationship. Workingmen had a right to organize into labor unions and a responsibility to give their employers a fair day's work. Employers have the responsibility to pay workers a fair wage. Private ownership of the means of production, i.e., capitalism, is a just social arrangement. Concerning socialism and private ownership, Leo XIII wrote:

> . . . the fundamental principle of Socialism which would make all possessions public property is to be utterly rejected because it injures the very ones whom it seeks to help, contravenes the natural rights of individual persons, and throws the functions of the state and public peace into confusion. Let it be regarded, therefore, as established that in seeking help for the masses this principle before all is to be considered as basic, namely, that private ownership must be preserved inviolate.[4]

Quadragesimo Anno was issued by Pope Pius XI on May 15, 1931. *Quadragesimo Anno* means "forty years afterwards." In this encyclical Pius XI reaffirmed the principles contained in *Rerum Novarum*. *Quadragesimo Anno* went beyond *Rerum Novarum* by suggesting that ways be explored for including workers in industrial ownership and by providing ways for workers to share in profits. The encyclical made the point that the way to a just situation was through adherence to the principle of subsidiarity.* In the context of the interrelationship among government, capital and labor the principle of subsidiarity requires that individuals or small groups take action to bring about just structures because those who experience needs or have problems should be given the responsibility to work toward their solution. Government intervention should be a last resort and only undertaken if individuals and/or labor unions are unable to achieve reasonable goals.

Quadragesimo Anno, responding to proponents of socialist ideology,* reaffirmed the right of persons to own property and the responsibility of the state to safeguard this right.

> First, then, let it be considered as certain and established that neither Leo nor those theologians who have taught under the guidance and authority of the Church have ever denied or questioned the twofold character of ownership, called usually individual or social according as it regards either separate persons or the common good. For they have always unanimously maintained that nature, rather the Creator himself, has given man the right of private ownership not only that individuals may be able to provide for themselves and their families but also that the goods which the Creator destined for the entire family of mankind may through this institution truly serve this purpose. All this can be achieved in no wise except through the maintenance of a certain and definite order.[5]

In *Quadragesimo Anno* Pope Pius XI sketched the features of an ideal society which avoided the extremes of individualistic capitalism and collective socialism. There is no question that the principles presented in the encyclical are cogent. However, the abstract and theoretical way in which the pontiff described society as it ought to be offered little practical guidance to people who struggled with the political, economic and military structures of the 1930s. Pius XI's plan for reconstruction of society was not advocated by his successors because the way to implement it was too vague.

The issues addressed in *Rerum Novarum* and *Quadragesimo Anno* include the role of government in society and the economy, the right of laborers to organize, the essence of a just wage, and the faults of both capitalism and socialism. Papal analysis since World War II has been more ambitious in its scope because it has considered political, economic and strategic issues* within an international framework.

Pope Pius XII occupied the papacy from 1939 until 1958. Although he did not issue a major social encyclical, Pius XII did speak to social-ethical issues on many occasions, usually in papal addresses. During the years in which Pius XII served the Church as its administrative and spiritual leader, people suffered enormously from the horrors of World War II and the dislocation and instability which came with the postwar years. In addition, the dawning of the nuclear age brought with it a long list of social, political, economic and military issues. In response to denials of fundamental rights experienced by people all over the world, Pius XII tried to explain the principles which had to be honored before social justice could be achieved.

Pius XII stressed that each and every human person is the bearer of dignity who has the right to the goods and opportunities essential for living a decent human life and participating in culture. The purpose of the state is to protect human rights and enable people to perform their duties. Thus, the state should be supportive of parents, employers, workers, students and all other groups as they seek to carry out their responsibilities. Pius XII insisted that might did not make right but that there is a higher order in which human rights come before the right/responsibility of officials to govern. The state was described as a community of morally responsible citizens, and democracy as a form of government was endorsed.

In 1961, Pope John XXIII, a beloved pope of modern times, issued the encyclical *Mater et Magistra*. Translated literally, this means "Mother and Teacher;" the encyclical is also called "Christianity and Social Progress." In *Mater et Magistra* Pope John acknowledged the need to balance the principle of subsidiarity which had been advocated in *Quadragesimo Anno* with the principle of "socialization." By "socialization" was meant the proliferation of organizations, voluntary and otherwise, (including the state) which connect the members of society with each other, and which hold the promise of meeting the needs of people in this technological age. Thus, if the breadwinner in a family is unemployed, he/she cannot provide food for the family. The Red Cross' food bank or state welfare office should supply for the family's needs.

The welfare state model was suggested as acceptable because, in the welfare state, the needs of the poor are met. Pope John XXIII echoed Pope Pius XII when he affirmed the dignity of each human person and explicitly stated that government and other social institutions exist to serve persons. The aspirations of people to participate in the political process were noted, and there was an endorsement of democratic participation in government. The enormous gap between rich and poor nations was addressed, with Pope John XXIII urging the rich to come to the aid of the poor.

Pacem in Terris (Peace on Earth) was the second major social encyclical issued by Pope John XXIII. Written in 1963, this encyclical set forth the steps which should be taken to establish peace among nations along with justice, truth, charity and liberty.

While recognizing the complexity of national and international social organization, Pope John explained that similar attitudes and commitments should characterize good relationships between and among nations as characterize good relationships between and among persons. In addition, John XXIII criticized the arms race and the balance of terror it created, and challenged world leaders to establish structures to deal with the problems of the nuclear age. John XXIII built on the work of his predecessors by uniting the quest for peace with the responsibility of the state to protect human rights. *Pacem in Terris* developed, for the first time, a comprehensive treatment of human rights within the context of the Catholic social-ethical tradition.

Pacem in Terris contained a hopeful, challenging message, but it was not a naive document. Pope John stressed that because of the sin and selfishness which exist in the world there has to be humble reliance on divine assistance to achieve the goals of justice and peace.

In 1967 Pope Paul VI issued the encyclical *Populorum Progressio,* "The Development of Peoples." It contained a bold restatement of the social doctrine of the Vatican II document *Gaudium et Spes,* a discussion of which follows. As with prior papal encyclicals, *Populorum Progressio* insisted that individuals and social institutions respect the dignity and rights of persons, especially the disadvantaged. The encyclical also called for urgent reforms to correct international injustice.

Paul VI was a person of global vision who used his encyclical to teach the lesson that the fruits of God's creation should be available to all people. The affluent have no right to claim or hoard a disproportionate share of the earth's resources. *Populorum Progressio* urged that the economic expansion of industrial nations not be accomplished at the expense of under-developed countries. Paul VI alluded to the unique perspective and empathy of the Church in its role as a teacher of social ethics when he wrote:

> Sharing the noble aspirations of men, and suffering when she sees them not satisfied, she wishes to help them attain their full flowering, and that is why she offers men what she possesses as her characteristic attribute: a global vision of man and of the human race.[6]

Gaudium et Spes,* known as "The Pastoral Constitution on the Church in the Modern World," is a pivotal document in Catholic social teaching. Composed by a committee at Vatican Council II, and approved by Pope Paul VI together with the bishops in attendance at the Council, *Gaudium et Spes* restated the essence of previous papal teaching. In addition, the Pastoral Constitution broke new ground by addressing the specific issues which faced the world a generation ago. In so doing, it set the tone for the social analysis and articulation of principles which we have since come to expect from the Church.

Gaudium et Spes begins with a discussion of the nature of the human person. Such discussion is described as "theological anthropology," i.e., a speaking to the identity of the person in light of the human and transcendent qualities which characterize each individual. The authors of the Pastoral Constitution remind us of the great dignity humans possess. Made in the image of God, imbued with the ability to know and love God, and entrusted with dominion over the created order, people are called to live out their lives in freedom and responsibility. Worry is expressed about the trends in the world of that time: atheism, agnosticism, and "sorrow, evil and death amidst so much progress." Convinced "that the world stands in peril unless wiser men are forthcoming," the authors reassert the truths that God's help is available to those who trust and believe, moral action will lead to justice and peace, and people should obey the voice of conscience.

According to *Gaudium et Spes,* the mission of the Church in the world should be understood in primarily religious terms.

The Church offers people a religious heritage which they are free to accept. In many ways the Church is a countercultural institution. In contrast to the anxiety of the world, she offers a hopeful message. The Pastoral Constitution was humble in acknowledging that the Church does not always have at hand solutions to particular problems. The document envisioned the Church casting the light of Christ over the earth and awaiting the coming of God's kingdom. *Gaudium et Spes* contains a negative assessment of the world only when "the world" is understood as "that spirit of vanity and malice which transforms into an instrument of sin those human energies intended for the service of God and man."[7] Otherwise, the Church's self-understanding fits Niebuhr's third model, Christ above culture. The Church can instruct people in how to work creatively to establish just structures and can point the way beyond selfishness to creative engagement.

In regard to the vocation to marriage, *Gaudium et Spes* asserts that people have the right to choose a state of life freely and to found a family. The family is the basic unit upon which all of society is built. Wife and husband have equal dignity and are enjoined to be faithful to each other. The unity, or bonding of spouses one to another, their mutual support and affection, are encouraged. So are the procreation and education of offspring. The authors of *Gaudium et Spes* called for responsible parenthood but did not endorse artificial contraception. While the personalist tone* of the Pastoral Constitution is a welcome improvement over the abstractions and legalisms which characterized prior treatments of marriage and family, no significant revision occurs. The conservative notion that "woman's place is in the home," for example, is echoed in the statement, "The children, especially the younger among them, need the care of their mother at home."[8] Today, one instinctively asks, "Couldn't Dad do a good job with the little ones, too?"

The authors of *Gaudium et Spes* saw their world as one in which "luxury and misery rub shoulders." They spoke to leaders of government and industry asking that technology be put at the service of people. A bias in favor of cooperation is reflected in the statement: "It is proper that at every level the largest possible number of people have an active share in directing (economic) development."[9] Undoing economic inequities was seen as the crucial precondition for securing world peace. The dignity of poor people and underdeveloped nations should be respected by extending to them the means to climb out of poverty through self-help. *Gaudium et Spes* reiterated previous Catholic social teaching by proclaiming the right of workers to unionize, the right of unions to strike, and the concomitant responsibility of workers to be conscientious and productive. In addressing the difficult question of how much people are entitled to, the Pastoral Constitution says that "the right to have a share of earthly goods sufficient for oneself and one's family belongs to everyone."[10] Because of the reasonableness of owning what one needs and is entitled to, ownership of private property is once again deemed appropriate.

The point that political authority exists to serve the common good is made in *Gaudium et Spes*. Persons possess rights. It is the responsibility of the state to recognize, honor and foster those rights. And it is the correlative responsibility of the citizen to obey the law, acknowledging the rightful authority of government. Citizen participation in democratic forms of government is consistent with the nature of politics and the dignity of persons; totalitarian forms of government, on the contrary, are difficult to justify. *Gaudium et Spes* set the Church apart from the world: "The role and competence of the Church being what it is, she must in no way be confused with the political community, nor bound to any political system."[11] The Church wisely admitted that her competence is limited to matters religious, but in so doing, the Church did not relinquish the responsibility to comment on the moral and religious aspects of modern life.

The authors of the Pastoral Constitution took a sober look at the horrors a major war would bring to humankind. In the mid 1960s the nuclear arsenals of the superpowers contained enough destructive capacity to obliterate civilization, and the amount of money spent on armaments constituted a theft from the poor. (Sadly, these facts are even more true today.) In addition, terrorism, a new form of warfare, had the potential to cause enormous harm. In light of these realities, government leaders were asked to observe right conduct in war and do all in their power to restrict the horrors of war. The right of individuals to declare themselves conscientious objectors* was upheld. And targeting of civilian areas was absolutely condemned:.

> Any act of war aimed indiscriminately at the destruction of entire cities or of extensive areas along with their populations is a crime against God and man

himself. It merits unequivocal and unhesitating condemnation.[12]

Looking at the situation which they experienced in their
time—the denial of human rights, a great disparity between rich
and poor nations, and the ominous threat of war—the authors of
Gaudium et Spes endorsed the idea of a universal public authority to work on behalf of justice and peace. "If an economic order
is to be created which is genuine and universal, there must be
an abolition of excessive desire for profit, nationalistic preten-
sions, the lust for political domination, militaristic thinking, and
intrigues designed to spread and impose ideologies."[13] Vatican
Council II did not think there would be easy solutions for the
problems of the world. However, in calling for a world authority
capable of directing interdependent nations toward a peaceful
resolution of conflicts and a more equitable distribution of the
goods of creation, it challenged humanity to work toward what
can be accomplished through the grace of Christ.

In 1971 Pope Paul VI issued *Octagesima Adveniens*, "A Call to
Action," which commemorated the eightieth anniversary of *Rerum Novarum* and the fortieth anniversary of *Quadragesimo
Anno*. In this encyclical Paul VI examined the role of politics in
securing justice. The state rightly exercises political power and
should use this power to intervene in order to obtain economic
justice for those in need. While Paul VI expressed a tentative
tolerance of Marxist economic theory as a tool of social analysis,
he rejected the possibility of a Catholic-Marxist alliance. The
type of political system endorsed by Paul VI was democratic
government which rests on a foundation of shared responsibility
and is sincerely committed to the common good of people everywhere.

In contrast to the reconstructionism evident in *Quadragesimo
Anno*, *Octagesima Adveniens* seemed much more aware of the
differences and complexities among societies and was, therefore,
much more tentative in its suggestions and proposals. Pope
Paul VI expressly rejected the temptation to put forward a solution which claimed to have "universal validity." He wisely counseled individual communities to engage in dialogue to discern
the options which they had and the commitments which they
should make in order to bring about necessary social, political
and economic changes.

Bishops from around the world gathered for a synod (meeting) in Rome in 1971. The document issued by the synod, *Justice in the World,* is a forward-looking example of Catholic social teaching. *Justice in the World* reflected the spirit of the social teaching of Vatican II and it reaffirmed the vision of Medellin. [Medellin is the name of the city in Colombia at which the Latin American bishops gathered in 1968 to set forth the contours of what has come to be known as "liberation theology." (See Chapter 9.) The document issued by the Latin American bishops was entitled, "The Church in the Present-Day Transformation of Latin America in the Light of the Council."]

Justice in the World cautioned against an attitude of fatalism. By fatalism is meant the assumption that there will always be poor people and that there are no totally effective measures for eradicating poverty. Fatalists tend to give up rather than engage in actions to overcome injustice. They fall into two socioeconomic groups: people with money and political power who are indifferent toward the plight of the poor, and people mired in poverty who believe that there is no way out of their hopeless situation. The synod of bishops spoke to both kinds of fatalists. They admonished the rich and privileged to stop offering as an excuse the notion that "the poor you will always have with you," and argued that they should become actively involved in eliminating the causes of poverty and discrimination. They advocated education for poor and deprived peoples so that they would be able to reconstruct their lives and determine their own destiny.

In respect to the mission of the Church, the bishops, speaking in the prophetic tradition, called for justice for the marginalized, i.e., migrants, refugees, political prisoners, the elderly, sick and orphaned and all who are denied human rights. The bishops also acknowledged the unique contributions the Catholic Church is capable of making. They said that the liturgy of the Word, catechesis and the celebration of the sacraments have the power to both commemorate the Church's tradition of justice and call the contemporary Church to action on behalf of justice. The bishops envisioned the practice of the sacrament of penance as having an educative dimension to the extent that it emphasizes the social dimension of sin.

The first encyclical letter of Pope John Paul II, *Redemptor Hominis,* was issued on March 9, 1979, *Redemptor Hominis* is Latin for "Redeemer of Humankind"; it was to Jesus Christ as redeemer and as the center of the universe and of history that John Paul looked for the religious and social wisdom people seek as the second millennium* draws to a close. The pontiff offered a sober appraisal of the contemporary world. He acknowledged the accomplishments of our time, "the space flights, the world of previously unattained conquests of science and technology," but he also lamented the immorality which endangers civilization: "the threat of the pollution of the natural environment in areas of rapid industrialization, the armed conflicts continually breaking out over and over again . . . the prospectives of self-destruction through the use of atomic, hydrogen, neutron and similar weapons, . . . the lack of respect for the life of the unborn."[14]

How can people today harness technology and human creativity so that our progress has a social conscience and the cause of justice is served? John Paul II built upon the tradition of his predecessors in suggesting the process by which peace with justice might be realized.

Pope John Paul II asked religious people to be open to the Holy Spirit in order to understand in what truly human conduct consists. Non-religious people can also know what is appropriately human by reflecting on the requirements of their rational nature. (This insight is entirely consistent with the natural law tradition.*) The need for people to comprehend how materialism, chauvinism, imperialism and neocolonialism result in the unjust denial of human rights is obvious. It is altogether immoral to permit the exploitation of persons in order to achieve material gain, or to place the lives of people in distant lands in jeopardy in order to pursue political or military superiority. The freedom to which persons are entitled is not a crass individualism; rather, it is precisely the ability to serve one another with love. And the function of government is not to deny the rights of citizens or to stoke the embers of international distrust; it is to serve the common good of its citizens and to work toward mutual cooperation in a world which grows daily more interdependent.

Pope John Paul II broke new ground in *Redemptor Hominis* by citing the principle of solidarity as the rationale for reorganizing economic systems so that greater justice is achieved:

> The principle of solidarity, in a wide sense, must inspire the effective search for appropriate institutions and mechanisms, whether in the sector of trade, where the laws of healthy competition must be al-

lowed to lead the way, or on the level of a wider and more immediate redistribution of riches and of control over them, in order that the economically developing peoples may be able not only to satisfy their essential needs but also to advance gradually and effectively.[15]

Pope John Paul II commemorated the ninetieth anniversary of *Rerum Novarum* by issuing the encyclical *Laborem Exercens* on September 14, 1981. *Laborem Exercens* means "On Human Work." John Paul's treatise on the subject of work amounts to a sophisticated discussion of the profound meaning work holds for human persons. In his encyclical the pope addressed such concrete issues as capitalism, socialism, workers' rights, unions, wages, technology, and a whole range of national and international factors which impact on the economies of both industrialized and developing countries.

John Paul II answered the question, "Why does man work?" by saying:

> Man must work both because the Creator has commanded it and because of his own humanity, which requires work in order to be maintained and developed. Man must work out of regard for others, especially his own family, but also for the society he belongs to, the country of which he is a child and the whole human family of which he is a member, since he is the heir to the work of generations and at the same time a sharer in building the future of those who will come after him in the succession of history.[16]

Because the 1980s are vastly different from the 1890s, John Paul II sought to focus the light of reason on contemporary reality. A century ago in the industrialized nations long hours and poor working conditions jeopardized the health and safety of workers. Today this is much less frequently the case. However, technology is causing many new problems: In some cases workers are being replaced by machines, while in others people are being robbed of satisfaction because their work is mechanical and boring. Technology in the workplace is good and acceptable as long as it does not diminish the humanity of workers. To the extent that technology is harmful to persons its utility and value should be reassessed.

Leo XIII's analysis of the economic situation of his time centered on the rights of workers and the dynamics of the class

struggle between capital and labor. Pope John Paul II went beyond a consideration of power struggles. He envisioned contemporary issues within an international context and recommended
that ethical examination and proposals for moral solutions take
the international aspects of situations into consideration. For
example, industrialized nations tend to "fix the highest possible
prices for raw materials or semi-manufactured goods," thus increasing the disparity which already exists between rich and
poor nations. Should this inequity continue, and the standard of
living of poor people in underdeveloped nations keep deteriorating, the stability and peace which all peoples desire could be
undermined.

In regard to capital and labor, John Paul II cautioned against
conceptualizing them as two forces existing in opposition to one
another. Instead, the pope described how capital and labor are
inseparably linked, and urged that both those who own the
means of production and those who labor recognize their responsibility to serve the common good.

John Paul II looked to the Judaeo-Christian religious heritage
to discern a spirituality of work. The scriptural account of creation* is quite informative in that it discloses the human duty to
subdue the earth, encourages people to imitate God by working
and resting, and discloses the human task as being one of co-
creation with God. In addition, the pontiff spoke of the toil
which is inextricably connected to human work: "toil connected
with work marks the way of human life on earth and constitutes
an announcement of death."

There is an ambivalence in *Laborem Exercens* concerning
women and work. On the one hand, discrimination against
women and exploitation of women are condemned. ". . . It is
fitting that they (women) should be able to fulfill their tasks in
accordance with their own nature, without being discriminated
against . . . ." But, on the other hand, a strong case is made
that married women who are mothers should be in the home
caring for their children.

> It will redound to the credit of society to make it pos-
> sible for a mother—without inhibiting her freedom,
> without psychological or practical discrimination, and
> without penalizing her as compared with other
> women—to devote herself to taking care of her chil-
> dren and educating them in accordance with their
> needs, which vary with age. Having to abandon these

> tasks in order to take up paid work outside the home
> is wrong from the point of view of the good of society
> and of the family when it contradicts or hinders these
> primary goals of the mission of a mother.[17]

The economic need of mothers in the United States and many other parts of the world who find that they as well as their husbands must be breadwinners, and the situation of mothers who have skills or professional training and who *want* to work outside the home are not taken into account. Neither are alternative approaches to child care. *Laborem Exercens'* failure to dialogue with the feminist agenda* constitutes a defect which needs to be admitted and rectified in future papal teachings.

On February 19, 1988, Pope John Paul II issued the encyclical *Sollicitudo Rei Socialis,* "The Social Concerns of the Church." *Sollicitudo Rei Socialis* commemorated *Populorum Progressio* and spoke to the social context of the world twenty years after Pope Paul's memorable encyclical.

In his encyclical John Paul II theorized about the reasons for economic injustice in the world. The pope indicated that suspicion and rivalry between East and West, the Soviet Union and the capitalist nations, has resulted in the "retardation or stagnation" of nations in the southern hemisphere. The third world suffers because of an "exaggerated concern for security" on the part of East and West. This concern is actualized in unbelievable expenditures for armaments; it deadens the desire to cooperate in working to attain the "common good of the human race."

The refusal of totalitarian governments to safeguard the human rights of their citizens was faulted by the pope. So too was the greed and indifference of capitalist countries who fail to share their wealth with poor nations. The pope challenged the idea that the superdevelopment of capitalist countries leads to true happiness. He said that the availability of all kinds of consumer goods might make people slaves of material things and cause them to become obsessed with multiplying possessions.

John Paul II made clear that the Church was not in a position to propose a third approach to economic, political and social organization as an alternative to Marxism and capitalism. Instead, the pope defined the Church's task as that of presenting "a careful reflection on the complex realities of human existence, in society and in the international order, in the light of faith and of the Church's tradition." The work of changing suspicion to trust, inequity to fairness, and polarization to common concern is ultimately that of all people of good will. What the Church has consistently pointed out is that a commitment to human rights and an openness to being inspired by the message of Jesus lead to a dissatisfaction with the *status quo* and a willingness to engage in action on behalf of justice.

Social Teaching of U. S. Catholic Bishops

Since the Second Vatican Council the Catholic bishops of each nation have organized themselves into conferences. In the United States the organization of bishops is called the National Conference of Catholic Bishops. All the bishops of the United States belong to the conference and get together once a year for an annual meeting. In addition, individual committees of bishops and their advisers meet to carry out particular tasks. The work of the NCCB and its various committees includes administration, arrangement for provision of services, resolution of doctrinal issues,* and the articulation of ethical positions. The moral stances advocated by the NCCB are relevant to the subject matter of this chapter. Accordingly, we will consider the thrust of statements of the U. S. Catholic bishops on racism, the challenge of peace, economic justice, the AIDS epidemic, and sexism in the Church.

On November 14, 1979 the National Conference of Catholic Bishops approved the distribution of a pastoral letter* on racism. Entitled "Brothers and Sisters to Us," the pastoral took an uncompromising stand against racism. The bishops said that racism is a radical evil that divides the human family and denies the creation of a redeemed world. In spite of legal and social sanctions against racism, the authors of the pastoral saw racism flourishing because of the self-centeredness so much in evidence in the United States. They challenged people to consider how "the triumph of private concern over public responsibility, individual success over social commitment, and personal fulfillment over authentic compassion" result in a situation of indifference to racial injustice.

The bishops condemned the prejudice, stereotyping and ridicule which are frequently directed at black, Hispanic, Native American and Asian people. They called instead for restitution to minorities of the human rights which are denied to them, restoration of their dignity in circumstances in which it is subtly or blatantly denied, and redistribution of employment and educational opportunities in order to overcome circumstances of deprivation in which the marginalized often live.

Racism is a sin for which most people do not take personal responsibility. If individuals do not see themselves as influenced by racial stereotypes, are not given to ethnic slurs and racial jokes, would willingly sell their homes to minority families, and would be as likely to hire a marginalized person as a member of the social mainstream, they would probably deny responsibility for the existence of racial injustice. Responding to such a contention, the bishops write:

> The absence of personal fault for an evil does not absolve one of all responsibility. We must seek to resist and undo injustices we have not caused, lest we become bystanders who tacitly endorse evil and so share in guilt for it.[18]

Active participation in the democratic political process, an openness to on-going education about the historical and contemporary realities of racism, and a commitment to equal opportunity and affirmative action were suggested as ways to move from indifference to involved commitment.

The bishops acknowledged that "too often the Church in our country has been for many a 'white church,' a racist institution," but they pledged themselves to work untiringly for justice in the Church. They promised to begin by adhering to the gospel of Jesus which affirms the innate dignity of each and every person. They pledged themselves to continue to educate minority young people in inner city Catholic schools, to pay fair wages to members of minorities who work in Catholic institutions, to eliminate racial barriers in the clergy and episcopacy, and to join in ecumenical efforts for racial equality. The bishops rejected the temptation to think that there are simple solutions to the deeply entrenched evil of racism; they admitted the need for humility and courage in the struggle to uproot racism from both the Church and society.

On May 3, 1983 the Catholic bishops of the United States voted by an overwhelming majority to issue the pastoral letter "The Challenge of Peace: God's Promise and Our Response." This document, divided into four parts, set forth a complex and comprehensive analysis of the essence of peace and the horrors of war in the nuclear age. The bishops' purpose in writing the letter was not only to bring the insight and wisdom of Catholic tradition to bear upon an extremely urgent issue; they also sought to bring about a fearless and open discussion of the most frightening subject of our time: human engagement in nuclear warfare.

The first part of "The Challenge of Peace" examined the religious perspective within which Catholics understand God, themselves and the nature of peace, and the moral principles upon which they base their ethical decision making. Catholics worship God, simultaneously recognizing God's divine sovereignty and God's caring love for the Church, a pilgrim people who value peace as God's great gift. Because of the dignity of human persons, the Church acknowledges its obligation to speak untiringly in behalf of the protection of human rights. Peace, which God intends that his people enjoy, can only be attained through human effort. By working for justice, by humbly speaking the truth, by respecting the freedom of each individual, and by loving one's neighbor as one's self, Catholics and all people of good will can bring peace to the world. One of the biggest challenges confronting the present generation is to overcome apathy and make a commitment to participate in working on behalf of peace and justice.

The moral principle which the Church upholds in response to the question, "What is a nation to do when the lives of its citizens are threatened by aggressive enemy forces?", is the principle of legitimate self-defense. According to this principle, a nation's leaders have the right and responsibility to defend innocent civilians by recourse to war. However, restraint should be exercised in the conduct of war so that the least amount of hardship and suffering are inflicted on aggressive forces and the lives of civilians are not endangered. The so-called "just war criteria" present specific directives regarding the decision to go to war and the manner of conducting war so as to minimize the amount of suffering and hardship which are an inevitable outcome.[19]

The second section of "The Challenge of Peace" assessed the dreadful possibilities of the nuclear age. Nuclear arsenals contain enough destructive power to wipe out all of creation many times over. Young children today are verbalizing the fear that they may not grow up because bombs could kill them. The elderly, the disabled and the poor are complaining that military expenditures are robbing them of the necessities of life. Concerned people everywhere are waking up to the dangers of nuclear weapons, fearful of the outcome should they ever be used. Against this background the bishops of the United States raised their voices to alert people everywhere to the dangers of nuclear war. They stated emphatically that three possible uses of nuclear weapons are immoral: "First, counter-cultural population warfare. Under no circumstances can there be a justification for targeting areas populated by civilians for nuclear annihilation. Second, the initiation of nuclear war. The probable effect of using nuclear weapons would be escalation into a major nuclear war and the inevitable destruction of the planet earth. Third, limited nuclear war. The concept of a 'limited nuclear war' is inherently flawed. It assumes that some rational restraints will prevail after a nuclear strike(s) occurs. It is folly to think in this way."[20]

The bishops also took the position that stockpiling *some* nuclear weapons might result in deterring an enemy from mounting either a conventional or a nuclear attack against the United States. They said that it may be morally tolerable to have a minimum number of weapons for deterrence, but urged that meaningful steps be taken to eliminate nuclear weapons altogether. Because of the provisional nature of the moral acceptability of nuclear weapons as a deterrent the bishops committed themselves to regularly reexamine the issue. Their 1988 reexamination yielded the same conclusion, along with a call to pursue all possible avenues to bring about disarmament.

The third part of "The Challenge of Peace" suggested specific steps to reduce the dangers of war. These include accelerated work for arms control, arms reduction and disarmament, efforts to reduce political tensions between nations, and openness to negotiation as a means of settling disputes between countries. The bishops also warned against thinking of conventional war as an appropriate alternative to nuclear war. They wrote "The history of recent wars (even so-called 'minor' or 'limited' wars) has shown that conventional war can also become indiscriminate in conduct and disproportionate to any valid purpose."[21] They suggested that the wisest way to answer aggression might be with nonviolence, which may actually require more courage and virtue than fighting for what one believes in.

Echoing *Gaudium et Spes,* the bishops reaffirmed the right of an individual to declare himself/herself a conscientious objector.

They counseled military personnel to refuse orders if they are ever ordered to launch a nuclear attack against a civilian population center. Such a refusal of orders would constitute an act of selective conscientious objection.

While admitting the reality of the problems that exist between the U.S. and the U.S.S.R., the bishops advocated that the United States initiate efforts to lessen the rivalry and promote dialogue and collaboration. They also suggested that converting defense industries to other purposes could lead to funding for worthwhile human assistance programs throughout the world.

The final part of the episcopal statement on war and peace addressed several audiences. Educators were asked to teach the ways of peace and young people were encouraged to choose work which would build up the human family. All American citizens were asked to accept responsibility to work toward nuclear disarmament so that our nation's nuclear arsenal would no longer imperil civilization.

On November 13, 1986, the Catholic bishops of the United States issued a pastoral letter entitled "Economic Justice for All: Catholic Social Teaching and the U.S. Economy." The bishops, as pastors,* addressed the complicated and controversial issue of economic justice because they recognized their obligation to point out how economic injustice causes human suffering. In addition, they thought it important to indicate the attitudes and policies which might lead to a better situation for poor people and poor nations. "Catholic Social Teaching and the U. S. Economy" seeks to be faithful to the vision of the gospel and responsive to the material needs of disadvantaged people in the United States as well as underdeveloped countries throughout the world. While economic issues are complex and the way to their resolution is often elusive, the bishops argue that closing one's mind to economic suffering is morally inexcusable: "No one may claim the name Christian and be comfortable in the face of the hunger, homelessness, insecurity and injustice found in this country and the world."[22]

The bishops maintain that people who claim to follow Christ should be converted and become active on behalf of justice, serving the least of their brothers and sisters with joy and gratitude. When Catholics gather as a community of faith to celebrate the Eucharist they are a sign of what God wills for all humanity: A fellowship of equals who listen together to God's word and are nourished from the same loaf, and who also take specific concrete measures to meet each other's spiritual and temporal needs.

The bishops assert that two principles which recur in Catholic social teaching should be applied to contemporary economic situations. Commutative justice, i.e., fairness in dealing with others, should be the foundation upon which all economic transactions are built. And distributive justice, according to which there should be a reallocation of income, wealth and power in society so that the needs of all are met, is advocated. The theory of a preferential option for the poor is articulated because of a conviction that "the deprivation and powerlessness of the poor wounds the whole community. The extent of their suffering is a measure of how far we are from being a true community of persons."[23] A call is sounded to bring justice to the poor by fulfilling their basic needs, increasing their participation in the life of the community, and investing wealth, talent and energy on their behalf.

New forms of cooperation among labor, management, government and others is encouraged, as the bishops prod all economic agents to move beyond token gestures in making a sincere commitment to work for justice. They point out the suffering caused by being out of work, and state that employment is a basic right. They also affirm the work of small and medium sized farmers who stay in agriculture even though they find it difficult to make a decent living. And the bishops address international economic issues, including the disparity between rich and poor nations, urging that inequities be corrected and exploitation be stopped. As far as the Church's own economic dealings are concerned, the Catholic bishops of the United States pledged themselves to examine their policies and practices, and put their house in order.

On December 11, 1987 the administrative board of the United States National Conference of Catholic Bishops issued a statement entitled "The Many Faces of AIDS: A Gospel Response." In this statement the bishops attempted to set the tone for a morally sound and scripturally inspired response to AIDS. AIDS, acquired immune deficiency syndrome, is a fatal affliction. There is no cure for AIDS. There is no vaccine to prevent infection by HIV, the AIDS virus. And, as yet, there are no effective treatments to eliminate, reduce or forestall the various illnesses suffered by persons with AIDS. Statisticians predict that by 1996 one million people in the U. S. will be diagnosed as having AIDS. AIDS is a crisis of great magnitude and the wisdom of the Catholic moral tradition represents an especially valuable resource for persons struggling with the social-ethical issues raised by AIDS.

In "The Many Faces of AIDS" the bishops rejected the hysteria with which society tends to respond to AIDS. Based on the evidence presented by the medical community, the bishops concluded that AIDS is not spread in situations of casual contact. Consequently, there is no defensible reason to avoid association with persons with AIDS. Ostracizing persons with AIDS, as well as stigmatizing them and rejecting them based on fear were assessed as immoral. The members of the administrative board called instead for compassion toward persons with AIDS, and practical outreach to meet their needs.

AIDS is spread primarily by heterosexual or homosexual intercourse with a carrier of HIV (human immunodeficiency virus) or by sharing intravenous needles and syringes which contain traces of HIV. Much less frequently AIDS is contracted through transfusions of infected blood or accidental puncture with a contaminated needle. Fetuses conceived by women who are infected with HIV are also at risk of contracting AIDS.

Aware of the manner in which AIDS is transmitted, the bishops exhorted people to practice self-discipline and restraint so as to avoid infection with HIV. The Church's constant teachings that sex is proper only for married persons and that drug use is self-destructive behavior and, therefore, immoral, was restated. People who carry the HIV virus were reminded of the human obligation not to harm others and were directed not to engage in acts which would put others in danger of getting AIDS.*

For their part the bishops pledged to commit the efforts of the Church to meeting the spiritual, emotional and physical needs of persons suffering from AIDS, their families and friends. They also urged the development of educational programs[24] to instruct young people in Catholic schools, colleges and religious education programs about transmission, prevention and compassion. The members of the administrative board emphasized their belief that a willingness to accept the binding force of moral principles combined with an openness to dialogue about the requirements of individual and collective moral responsibility would bring about a reasonable and mature response to AIDS.

On April 12, 1988 a committee of six U. S. bishops, who were assisted by five women scholars, released a 164-page draft of a pastoral letter on sexism in the Church. Entitled "Partners in the Mystery of Redemption," the letter recognized the harm caused to the Church by the sin of sexism. The draft recommends that the Church consider allowing women to minister as deacons, altar servers, and lectors (readers of scripture during mass). The bishops did not endorse the ordination of women to the priesthood, but they did suggest that further study of the question might be in order.

"Partners in the Mystery of Redemption" is unique among Catholic social teachings in that it did not come to be through a process of theoretical analysis directed toward a social problem. Instead, the draft took shape in a dialogical process. Seventy-five thousand women in dioceses and at colleges and military bases spoke about their experiences within the Church, as well as their hopes, and expectations for the Church. "Partners in the Mystery of Redemption" records women's concerns, and seeks to respond to them. The bishops' plan was to seek comments on their draft letter before issuing a final version late in 1989. As it turned out, the bishops could not reach consensus on this subject and they wound up abandoning their project in 1992.

Developing a Social Conscience

Cain was his brother's keeper. People are interrelated. We are bound to some by blood, to others by friendship, to still others by circumstances of nationality, profession, school attended, or other affiliational factors. We are bound to all by a shared humanity, a common Father-Mother God, and a shared destiny, "heaven," where there are many different mansions. For some, admission of human interrelatedness goes against the grain: they are more comfortable with individualism and autonomy. The indifference, hedonism and greed so prevalent in society complement the motto "me first." These sentiments do not fit an understanding that people should be actively engaged in pursuing justice for all.

As you have learned from your reading of this chapter, Catholic social teaching embodies a moral vision in which the challenge to social responsibility is recurrent and unambiguous. If you have decided to identify yourself as a Christian, or if you make such a decision at some time in the future, you will recognize that you should be involved in efforts to bring about social justice. In determining how much time you are going to spend on such endeavors, or what concrete actions you are going to take, you should be guided by your conscience. Conscience is an ability possessed by sane mature people which enables them to evaluate various actions and courses of action and make judgments about which are ethically appropriate and which are morally wrong. On November 11, 1976, the Catholic bishops of the United States approved the pastoral letter "To Live in Christ Jesus" in which they commented on the process in which people engage before making decisions of conscience.

> We live in good faith if we act in accord with conscience. Nevertheless our moral decisions still require much effort. We must make decisions of conscience based upon prayer, study, consultation and an understanding of the teachings of the Church. We must have a rightly formed conscience and follow it.[25]

Not to inform our consciences and act on behalf of social justice is to sin by omission. The body language of social sin includes shaking one's finger at suffering people, blaming them for their problems, shrugging one's shoulders rather than admitting an obligation to get involved so as to better a bad situation, and turning one's back on the beggars in one's path in order not to be troubled by their misery. When we let ourselves become close-minded and hard-hearted we create a sinful attitude which is at odds with the spirit of the Judaeo-Christian tradition.

It is fairly easy to recognize the many ways in which individuals commit social sin, but a bit more difficult to comprehend how structural sin manifests itself in policies, institutions and relationships. When a policy such as racism, an institution such as a ruthless totalitarian government, or a relationship based on blackmail, greed or lust is evaluated, the reality of structural sin cannot be disputed. And, even in complex arrangements which are founded upon noble principles and sentiments, such as the democratic form of government of the United States, defects and injustice can become an unmistakable part of the system. Sin is ingrained in any social arrangements which result in human degredation and the denial of human rights, especially arrangements which lead to the entrenchment of poverty.

Pope John Paul II, in his encyclical *Sollicitudo Rei Socialis,* emphasized that Christians are conscience-bound to act against structural sin and to help to bring about social reform. As unfashionable as the notion of "sin" is in contemporary society, and as novel as the concept "structures of sin" may seem, Pope John Paul II maintains that men and women cannot comprehend the social problems of the present time unless they are able to recognize the objective reality of sin and admit personal moral responsibility to overcome this sin:

> "Structures of sin" are only conquered . . . by a diametrically opposed attitude: a commitment to the good of one's neighbor with the readiness, in the Gospel sense, "to lose oneself " for the sake of the other instead of exploiting him, and to "serve him" instead of oppressing him for one's own advantage.[26]

Endnotes

1. In 1891, Pope Leo XIII issued the encyclical *Rerum Novarum,* the first papal statement on a social issue, i.e., on labor, justice and the international order.

2. H. Richard Niebuhr, *Christ and Culture* (New York: Harper & Row, 1975), p.11.

3. Ibid., p. 32.

4. *Rerum Novarum,* 23 (Paragraphs in encyclicals are numbered. The number 23 in this in this citation refers to paragraph #23 in the encyclical.)

5. *Quadragesimo Anno,* 45.

6. *Populorum Progressio,* 13.

7. *Gaudium et Spes,* 37.

8. Ibid., 52.

9. Ibid., 66.

10. Ibid., 69.

11. Ibid., 76.

12. Ibid., 80.

13. Ibid., 85.

14. *Redemptor Hominis,* 8.

15. Ibid., 16.

16. *Laborem Exercens,* 16.

17. Ibid., 19.

18. *Brothers and Sisters to Us* (Washington, DC: USCC, 1979), p. 4.

19. For a complete discussion of the just war criteria, cf., Eileen P. Flynn, *My Country Right or Wrong? Selective Conscientious Objection in the Nuclear Age* (Chicago: Loyola University Press, 1985), pp.57-60.

20. *The Challenge of Peace,* 147, 150, 157, 158.

21. Ibid., 217.

22. *Economic Justice for All,* 27.

23. Ibid., 88.

24. To learn more about AIDS and AIDS education, cf. Eileen P. Flynn, *AIDS A Catholic Call for Compassion,* (Kansas City: Sheed & Ward, 1985), and Eileen P. Flynn, *Teaching About AIDS* (Kansas City: Sheed & Ward, 1988).

25. *To Live in Christ Jesus* (Washington, DC: USCC, 1976), p.10.

26. *Sollicitudo Rei Socialis,* 38.

Glossary

Acts of the Apostles: A book of the New Testament of the bible written by the evangelist (gospel writer) Luke. In Acts, Luke provided a broad summary of the Church's development from the resurrection of Jesus to Paul's first Roman imprisonment.

Acts which would put people in danger of getting AIDS: Heterosexual and homosexual genital or oral sex by a person who tests antibody positive for HIV with a partner not infected by HIV, and sharing an IV needle with a person who is not antibody positive. Donating infected blood or becoming pregnant if a carrier of HIV would also put innocent persons at risk.

Christ's Incarnation: The act of the Word of God taking on human flesh within the womb of Mary through the power of the Holy Spirit.

Christ's second coming: Also known as the Parousia, is the event foretold in the scriptures (Mt. 24: 29-31) according to which Christ will come again at the end of history.

The Communist Manifesto: Co-authored by Karl Marx and Friedrich Engels, presented the economic theory which came to be known as Marxism.

Conciliar statements: Position papers which are written and approved by bishops in attendance at church councils, such as Vatican Council II.

Conscientious objectors: . . . or pacifists, refuse to participate in combat because of a belief that all killing is morally wrong.

A deductive and inferential task: The undertaking of a process of rational analysis of a given premise or premises with the stating of logical conclusions based upon those premises.

Disciple: A pupil or follower. The contemporaries of Jesus who listened to his teachings and followed his instructions were called disciples.

Earthly utopia: The attainment here in this world of a state devoid of conflict and replete with personal satisfaction and enjoyment.

The Epistle of James: A book of the New Testament which addresses Jews who believe in Jesus and who live outside Jerusalem (the twelve tribes of Israel in the dispersion). The entire focus of James' letter is on Christian moral conduct.

Eschatological: A theological way of understanding reality which measures events and conditions against what reality will be in the coming kingdom of God.

The feminist agenda: . . .consists in the elimination of sexism and calls for the equality of the sexes in the churches and all other aspects of life.

Fidelity to the covenant: The covenant is a bond which God established with the Hebrew people and which is recorded in the Old Testament. Jesus broadened the covenant so that since his death this bond exists between God and the whole human community. God's fidelity cannot be doubted; God will always be faithful to his people, sustaining, loving and guiding them. For God's people, however, fidelity is always imperfect, requiring constant efforts at conversion and renewed commitments to generous service.

Gaudium et Spes: Literally, joy and hope.

The Judaeo-Christian tradition: The legacy of faith, principles and wisdom which Christians value. This tradition begins with the role played by Abraham approximately ten thousand years before the birth of Christ and continues to the present time. The faith and witness of the contemporary Church both build upon and enrich this tradition.

Human rights: Those things to which persons are entitled simply because they are human. Persons reasonably claim the rights to food, clothing, shelter, medical care, education and freedom of association in order to live in accordance with their dignity.

Kerygma: The proclamation of the message of the gospel.

The natural law tradition: . . .holds that persons can use their ability to reason to determine morally correct actions and courses of action.

Parable: A story which teaches a theological lesson through use of metaphors which a particular audience can understand.

Pastoral letter: A letter addressed by a bishop or group of bishops to Catholic people and all people of good will. Pastoral letters serve to instruct, educate, challenge and motivate people on matters of religious or moral import.

Pastors: Priests whose concern is for the spiritual, psychological, physical and economic well being of the people they serve.

Patriarchal biases: Ingrained prejudices which point to an innate superiority and competence of males who are believed to rightly hold positions of authority or responsibility, together with a corresponding notion that females are incapable of understanding or acting as males are able to understand and/or act.

Personalist tone: Taking into account the spiritual aspirations and emotional dimensions of people. The inclusion of a personalist tone in theology corrects a tendency to be mostly abstract and analytical when considering issues which are of concern to people.

Pharisee: A member of a Jewish sect which emphasized strict observance of all ritual laws. Some Pharisees came to see the perfection of ritual observance as equivalent to being a good religious person. Jesus taught that true human goodness consists in loving God, neighbor and self.

The principle of subsidiarity: Nothing should be done by a higher authority or agency which can be done as well, or better, by a lower agency.

Prophets: Persons who spoke to the Hebrew people on behalf of God. The Old Testament contains the messages of sixteen prophets, each of whom delivered a specific message from God to a particular group of people.

Religious, social and political conflicts: . . .were experienced by the first generation of Christians. For example, Peter, the leader among the apostles, and Paul, the "apostle to the Gentiles" (non-Jews), came together with other leaders of the Church to decide whether or not non-Jewish men who wanted to become Christians should have to go through the Jewish rite of circumcision. Jews thought that they should and Gentiles thought that they should not. The dispute was resolved with the decision that circumcision was not necessary. At the so-called "Council of Jerusalem" an issue was discussed at a forum and was resolved through the grace of the Holy Spirit and the good will of those who participated.

Resolution of doctrinal issues: A work shared by bishops and theologians with the ultimate authority resting in members of the hierarchy. A doctrinal issue arises when there is controversy about what the Church teaches (or should teach) about a disputed matter. Questions are resolved by consistent application of principles which have long been honored or by determining what the constant faith of the community has been.

Rhetorical question: A question to which no answer is expected.

The scriptural account of creation: An account contained in the first two chapters of the book of Genesis. In Chapter 1, the first story of creation, the work of creation was accomplished by God in six days, and God rested on the seventh day. In Chapter 2, the description of God's creating man from the earth, thereafter all other life, and finally, woman, is found.

The second millennium: The period of time from 1001-2000, that is, the second thousand years since the birth of Christ.

Socialist ideology: The doctrine that the ownership of the means of production should be by the society and all members should share in work, receiving goods according to their needs.

Strategic issues: This represents a new category in Roman Catholic social-ethical analysis and includes all the moral questions pertinent to modern conventional and nuclear warfare.

***The* faith:** The composite of beliefs held by Catholics. These "beliefs" are generally expressed as "doctrines," that is, teachings about what is believed. Two doctrines in which Catholics believe are the virginity of Mary and the resurrection of Jesus. The social ethical doctrine that all people have a right to share in the goods of creation is another element of *the* faith.

Tithes: Portions (one-tenth) of one's crops or income which are donated to cover the administrative costs and social outreach programs of one's religious community.

The Throne of David: David was a great king of the Jewish people who was promised an eternal dynasty by the oracle (revelation) of Nathan the prophet: "Your house and your kingdom shall endure forever; your throne shall stand firm forever" (2 Samuel 7:16). The prophecy to David is the basis for the Jewish expectation of a messiah, which Jesus fulfilled. The purpose of the genealogy (family tree) of Jesus which begins the gospel of Matthew is to trace Jesus' roots back to David via Jesus' foster father Joseph, and to present Jesus as the heir to the throne of David.

Vatican Council II: An assembly of Roman Catholic bishops and theologians who met in Rome from 1962-1965. The spirit of openness and dialogue which were evident resulted in a development in the way the Church understood herself and her mission.

Virtues: Good actions in which people habitually engage because of the help of God's grace with which they freely comply. Honesty, generosity and chastity are examples of virtues.

"Workingman": An example of the noninclusive language in which papal encyclicals are written. Unfortunately, the encyclical *Sollicitudo Rei Socialis* (1988) continues sexist usage. Cf., its opening words, "The social concern of the church, directed toward an authentic development of *man* and society. . . ." It is much easier to understand why the hierarchy employed sexist language in the past than to comprehend the reasons for its continuing contemporary usage.

Discussion Questions

1. Read Matt. 25:31-46. Then state specific ways in which Christians can respond to the needs of others. Speculate on why there are hungry and homeless people, and suggest steps for assisting them,

2. Read H. Richard Niebuhr's definition of a Christian and then propose one of your own. Compare your definition with definitions of your classmates and discuss similarities and differences.

3. How should Christianity influence secular culture in the United States today? In answering this question determine how each of Niebuhr's five models would assess a technological society which places a great value on leisure and pleasure.

4. State four principles you have learned from the survey of papal encyclicals and discuss how the implementation of these principles would change the political, social and economic orders.

5. Describe the racism of which you are aware. What strategies would you suggest to counter racism?

6. Should Christians earn their livelihood by building nuclear weapons? Why or why not?

7. Make a list of the economic injustices of which you are aware and a corresponding list of measures which could be taken to correct them. Try to include international instances as well as examples close to home.

8. What is sexism? Why should Christians reject sexism as sinful?

Additional Reading

Justice in the Marketplace: Collected Statements of the Vatican and the U.S. Catholic Bishops on Economic Policy, 1891-1984, (Washington, DC: USCC, 1985).

Eileen P. Flynn, *My Country Right or Wrong? Selective Conscientious Objection in the Nuclear Age* (Chicago: Loyola University Press, 1985).

H. Richard Niebuhr, *Christ and Culture* (New York: Harper & Row, 1975).

Gerhard von Rad, *The Message of the Prophets* (New York: Harper & Row, 1965).

The following statements of the U.S. Catholic Bishops are available from the United States Catholic Conference, 1312 Massachusetts Avenue, N.W., Washington, DC, 20005-4105:

- "To Live in Christ Jesus," 1976.
- "Brothers and Sisters to Us," 1979.
- "The Challenge of Peace: God's Promise and Our Response," 1983.
- "Economic Justice for All: Catholic Social Teaching and the U.S. Economy," 1986.
- "The Many Faces of AIDS," 1987.
- "Partners in the Mystery of Redemption," 1988 (first draft).

The encyclical *Sollicitudo Rei Socialis* of Pope John Paul II is also available from the USCC.

11

Catholic Sexual Ethics: Recognizing the Values in Human Intimacy

What Is Sexuality?

Sexuality is a profound aspect of the human personality. Persons are sexual: They are masculine or feminine, men or women. It seems as if people are more familiar with thinking in terms of "sex," that is, of genital sexual actions, than of "sexuality," that is, of the composite of physical, emotional and psychological factors which make up sexual identity. James B. Nelson, author of *Embodiment: An Approach to Sexuality and Christian Theology*, tells us that it is crucially important to comprehend the distinction between sex and sexuality:

> . . . sexuality involves more than what we do with our genitals. More fundamentally, it is who we *are* as body-selves who experience the emotional, cognitive, physical, and spiritual need for intimate communion—human and divine.[1]

Our bodies, with their distinctively masculine or feminine biological characteristics, are ourselves. We can truly say that we are our bodies. We are also more than our bodies because we can transcend ourselves, that is, we can objectively reflect upon our subjective reality. Without in any way denying the spiritual dimension of our being, we know for certain that here and now we would have no existence apart from our bodies. Our bodies are not extraneous to ourselves. They are not an impediment keeping us on earth and preventing us from making the trip to heaven. Neither are they somehow soiled and dirty, standing in the way of our becoming holy. On the contrary, our bodies are the good and wholesome concrete centers of our personal consciousness. The Christian who professes belief in the resurrection of the body is proclaiming the hope that embodied existence is destined to be eternal.

Almost every individual possesses either male or female sexual organs. (The exceptions are hermaphrodites, persons in whom the physiological sexual characteristics of both male and female are found.) Biology, however, does not determine identity. There is no one predetermined way of being male or female, that is, of giving expression to one's sexuality. The "soft" parts of a man's personality and the assertive aspects of a woman's personality need not be repressed or denied. Neither are they reasons for shame or discomfort.

There is a tendency to think that males and females should act in particular ways; in other words, we assign roles in accordance with gender. Individuals learn gender roles from their cultures and from role models who influence them. Unexamined role expectations, for example, that it is always a male task to take the garbage out and always a female task to raise children, are being challenged as society attempts to understand how unfair it can be to force roles on individuals based solely on gender, and to deny roles on the same basis.

In addition to gender roles there are also gender traits. There is a tendency to associate certain gender traits with one or the other sex: For example, a trait such as responding to upsetting news by breaking down and crying is considered feminine. A young man who is raised by women, has only sisters and has no strong male role models may know no other way to react to bad news than by weeping. It is not difficult to determine how this young man acquired a so-called "feminine" gender trait and it would be incorrect to question his masculinity based on a particular trait. Just as it is wrong to assign roles on the basis of gender, it is illogical to conclude that a person is a "real man" or a "real woman" on the basis of gender traits.

Although stereotypical ways of thinking about men and women abound, most people agree that stereotypes are not true to life. When we prejudge what is masculine and what is feminine, and seek to impose these judgments as standards, we deny to individuals the right to be themselves. Thinking that men should never cry or that women are capable of fulfilling only nurturing roles prevents both men and women from developing all aspects of their individuality. It would be more consistent with reality to encourage people to androgynous development, that is, to accept both the masculine and feminine qualities which they discover within themselves. Only after people reconcile the masculine and feminine aspects of themselves will they be able to establish satisfactory interpersonal relationships of mutuality and equality.

Ultimately, we need to grasp the fact that our sexuality, including the drive to genital sexual intercourse, is God's good gift. We can love because we are embodied, sexual. Christians learn from the scriptures that they are expected to love themselves. Honest reflection discloses that only people who are capable of loving themselves are able to love God with their whole hearts and their neighbors in comparable measure to themselves.

James B. Nelson identifies the various ways of expressing Christian love:

> It is commonplace and useful in Christian ethics to utilize the classic distinctions in speaking of love. *Epithymia* (or libido) is the desire for sexual fulfillment. *Eros* is aspiration and desire for the beloved. *Philia* is mutuality and friendship. And *agape* is freely offered self-giving.[2]

Love is a unity which is expressed in different ways according to circumstances. Libidinal satisfaction and erotic love are appropriate for persons who are lovers and married. Friendship and self-giving love are expressions of the deep care and concern that sexual persons have for others, both those with whom they share a relationship of sexual intimacy and others to whom they are related in a nonintimate way.

Confusions Regarding Sexuality

The importance of accepting one's sexual nature cannot be overstated. This acceptance is a prerequisite for healthy self-development as well as mature relationships. In spite of this, there seems to be a great deal of confusion regarding the objective nature of the human body and, particularly, its sexual aspects.

Hellenistic dualism,* sometimes called "angelism,"* is an anti-corporeal way of thinking which results in a devaluing of sexuality. According to Hellenistic dualism, the body is understood to be an undesirable addition to the soul. Dualists think that it would be better if humans were angels because angels do not have to endure the fatigue, distractions, weakness and sexual temptations which are associated with the body. Dualists miss the points that the body is God's good creation and that it is in and through the body that persons communicate love, care and compassion to others. Only when people are bearers of such attitudes and gestures to one another do they carry out the mandate of the Gospel.* When persons love one another they are sacraments, that is, signs or illustrations of how God relates to beloved friends.

Jansenism is another movement which devalues sexuality. Cornelius Jansen, a Roman Catholic bishop in France who died in 1638, wrote a book entitled *Augustinus* which contained a very negative appraisal of human nature in general and sexuality in particular. *Augustinus* was condemned by Pope Urban VIII in 1644, but the condemnation did not put Jansenism to rest. On the contrary, three aspects of Jansenism played a significant part in Catholic thinking up until the Second Vatican Council. These aspects were an obsession with sexual morality, a rigorism* in dealing with sexual sins, and the belief that people are sinful because embodied. To the extent that Jansenism prevented a positive appreciation of bodiliness and tended to equate sex with sin, it exercised a negative influence on Catholic thinking about sexuality.

Confusion Regarding Sex

Dualists and Jansenists fail to grasp the values in human sexuality; as a result, they are uncomfortable with sexuality and sex. There are many people in contemporary society who seem comfortable with sex (genital sexual activity) but who devalue sex because they understand its purpose in solely recreational terms. They do not comprehend the fact that the erotic and libidinal satisfactions which are experienced in sexual intercourse are meant to enhance the bonds which unite lovers to one another. They see these satisfactions as ends to be pursued whether or not there is a context of love and commitment. They refuse to admit that engaging in sexual activity solely for self-gratification, with little or no attention given to the personal or social ramifications of what is done, is immoral. And they receive constant reinforcement for this attitude from the media; each year the average viewer sees nine thousand scenes on television which hint at or portray sexual intercourse *sans* commitment. Four specific confusions about the meaning of sex are causing a devaluing of sex and are creating an atmosphere of unhealthy permissiveness and relativism.*

The first confusion is the trivialization of sex. To take human experiences which are meant to have a significant meaning—sexual desire, sexual arousal and genital sex—and to promote these realities as casual and/or bereft of any particular significance, is to trivialize sex. To justify casual sex by saying that everybody is doing it, or by suggesting that everybody ought to be doing it, is to reach a conclusion without engaging in a process of honest examination. Accordingly, insufficient account is given to the nature of intimacy and the relational bond which should exist between persons who are sexually intimate. A handshake is casual; sexual intercourse is not. And if a contracepted act of recreational intercourse backfires, the pregnancy which results will force sexual partners to acknowledge that sex frequently has far-reaching consequences.

To the extent that people deny that acts of physical sexual intimacy have a meaning and purpose beyond passing pleasure at a given moment of time they trivialize sex. If they should engage in casual sex, they run the risk of experiencing psychological and physical harm. The depression which accompanies the experience of rejection by a "lover," and the development of a sexually transmitted disease are examples of harm which may be suffered by people who act on the conviction that sex is meant to be casual. And harming oneself or another is immoral.

A second confusion is the depersonalization of sex. Those who depersonalize sex engage in intercourse for the sole purpose of attaining physical pleasure. Partners are not valued as persons and their physical, emotional and spiritual needs have little or no bearing on the attitudes or actions of the person who initiates the sex. Rape is the most extreme example of depersonalized sex. (Psychologists suggest that physical pleasure is only infrequently a motive for rape; much more often rape is motivated by aggressive rage.) Sex with prostitutes, one night stands, and anonymous homosexual encounters are also examples of depersonalized sex.

The privatization of sex similarly leads to confusion. According to this way of thinking, all sexual activity is totally private, and no moral judgments should be made concerning what is done between consenting adults. It is true that sexual acts usually occur behind closed doors because people's sense of modesty and desire for a degree of intimacy dictate the need for a private setting. (The exception to this is group sex, that is, genital sexual activity in an orgy-like setting, or sex with more than one partner.) However, the fact of a subjective desire for privacy does not in any way negate the binding force of objective moral standards governing sexual conduct. At the least, these objective standards include the facts that sex should be characterized by sentiments of love and respect for the partner, and persons engaging in sex should make and honor commitments to fidelity. In addition, since sexual intercourse is the means for the continuation of the human species, the Judaeo-Christian tradition has consistently held that it has a social meaning. Attempts to deny this meaning are frequently rationalizations made in order to evade taking responsibility for all the ramifications of genital intimacy. Like it or not, humans are not always able to make deals with "no strings attached."

Sexual innuendo and sexual seduction are used to sell everything from toothpaste to luxury cars. The advertising industry has learned to profit from people's ambivalence about sex. The common inclination to feel insecure about sexual attractiveness is used to promote products which will yield the desired comeliness. And consumers are frequently misled by subtle messages that they will achieve sexual prowess if they possess extravagant items. The commercialization of sex illustrates a profound confusion about the nature of sexual intimacy. It is a logical outcome of the trivialization and depersonalization of sex. Contemporary society will probably continue to use sex to sell products until such time as people begin to understand and articulate three truths. First, sex is not an achievement; it is a moment of physical, emotional and spiritual sharing. Second, sex is not something to have and possess; it is a human experience characterized by intangible qualities and ought to generate delightful memories. And, third, sex is not just something for two persons in a given place at a specific time; it is a bond which strengthens each of them, which grows as they grow, and which unites them to generations yet unborn.

Pornography

Exposure to pornography is the worst possible form of sex education. Pornography is a multi-million dollar industry which insults the human spirit and degrades sex. It is available from such restricted sources as film and the print media, and it invades the home through VCR rentals, cable TV, and "dial-aporn" telephone messages. While there are legitimate differences of opinion concerning which questionable material is protected by the freedom of speech guarantee of the U.S. Constitution and which definitely constitutes pornography, a consensus has developed regarding material which is undoubtedly pornographic. This category includes sexually explicit material involving children, sado-masochistic material, explicit portrayals of bestiality, material showing extreme sexual degradation of women, and sexually violent material.

Pornography creates an unhealthy moral climate in which the sacred meaning of sex is lost and the dignity of sexual beings is denied. The harm it causes to the subjects who are photographed or filmed is extraordinary. So are the confusion it breeds, the demeaning of women to which it leads, and the total exploitation of children and teenagers whose bodies are used for the illicit gratification of people willing to pay a few dollars. People who habitually turn to pornography for stimulation and diversion become desensitized to the values of sex and sexuality. Their growth toward sexual maturity is retarded and they keep themselves from developing a capacity to enjoy committed sexual love.

Psychological and Spiritual Problems Resulting from Sexual Confusion

As we have seen, there is a great deal of confusion in contemporary society about sexuality in general and sexual intercourse in particular. Young people are likely to have only a superficial grasp of the meaning of sexual intercourse. They know that sexual intercourse is a physically pleasurable experience and that if it is engaged in without contraception it may result in pregnancy. But they seem ignorant of the fact that sexual intercourse bears other meanings and values as well. Confusion about sex is compounded by the reluctance of people to discuss the subject, often because of fear, self-consciousness or embarrassment. And, ironically, in circumstances in which sex is the topic, it is an impoverished notion of sexual intercourse that people speak to, sing of, joke about, or graphically portray.

One of the tragic facts of life is that young men and women can and do engage in sexual intercourse before they come even remotely close to comprehending the meaning of what they are doing. Writing in 1987, William J. Bennett, U.S. Secretary of Education, reported the following data:

> Statistics show that sexual activity increases dramatically during the teenage years. By age 15, 16 percent of boys and 5 percent of girls in the United States have had heterosexual intercourse at least once. By age 17, these rates almost triple for boys and increase 5 times for girls. By age 19, three-quarters of all boys and almost two-thirds of all girls have been sexually active.[3]

The irresponsible sexual behavior of so many teenagers is prompting society to seek to determine the cause and find a way to rectify the situation. Considering both the developmental and attitudinal aspects of precocious sexual activity may provide necessary insight for understanding why teenagers are having sex and reveal what they need to learn in order to act with real maturity.

The road to personal maturity stretches from infancy and the young childhood years to latency in middle childhood, thence to puberty, adolescence, and hopefully to adulthood. Unfortunately, a lack of understanding and self-restraint, combined with strong drives for libidinal satisfaction, often lead teenagers to experiment sexually. A typical form of experimentation entails auto-erotic acts, that is, acts of masturbation. Driven by curiosity and a craving for pleasure, people discover that self-stimulation provides a way to release pent-up sexual tension and experience physical satisfaction. Much more frequent among boys than girls, masturbation is considered morally deficient behavior because it does not involve opening oneself to another (an intrinsic aspect of sexuality), it is not expressive of love for another and, if it becomes a deeply entrenched habit, it stands in the way of mature sexual development. Fortunately, however, the incidents of masturbation which result from curiosity and gradual awareness of one's sexual potency at puberty do not significantly impede most people's moral and sexual development.

In addition to the practice of masturbation, teenagers may experiment sexually by engaging in heterosexual intercourse. It is interesting to note that the same factors which motivate young people to engage in masturbation may motivate them to have sex with a partner. They may simply want to satisfy curiosity, and experience pleasure and self-gratification. To the extent that this is the reason for participating in sexual intercourse, the needs and feelings of the partner are of virtually no concern and the partner is merely used in order to provide the experience of pleasure.

Why is somewhat impersonal and experimental sexual intercourse a reality which the majority of teenagers in the United States experience by the time they are nineteen years old? Does casual sexual experimentation have the same psychological and spiritual effects on young men as on young women? And, since the advent of the birth control pill, is there really all that much harm in premarital sex?

One reason for premarital sex is to conform one's lifestyle to that of one's neighbors, friends and schoolmates. Many young people have sex because they want to be like everyone else and because they think that everyone *expects* that they will be sexually active. Young people may also have difficulty practicing self-control. And they do not seem to comprehend that it would be better for them not to gratify their impulses and to wait to have sex until they are in permanent, committed relationships, are ready to honor the meaning intrinsic to sex, and are prepared to stand by the children they might bring to life.

Another reason why adolescents engage in sexual intercourse is because the atmosphere in which they live is not supportive of self-restraint. Laziness, self-indulgence and greed are very common sins. In a sense, the fundamental values of our society are being jeopardized by our self-seeking ways. When committed Christians analyze the causes of sexual permissiveness and point out the harms it brings, their analysis is frequently dismissed as out of touch with reality. In spite of this, however, some assertions concerning the moral aspects of premarital sex are hard to ignore:

> • Such activity contributes little of a positive nature to the human development of those engaging in it.

> • It is not inevitable that there must be widespread premarital sex with all the attendant personal and social harms which follow therefrom.

> • It is possible (and laudable) to say no to those internal and external forces which taunt, tease and urge premarital sexual coition.

Casual sexual experimentation does not seem to hold the same meaning for both sexes. I do not think that I am employing a stereotype when I say that a woman tends to feel one with her body and to understand the act of sexual intercourse as the loving gift of herself to another. The giving of herself in love is not a casual thing; the woman truly desires that her sexual partner comprehend all that sexual intercourse means to her and that he value the gift which she imparts. Women who have sex before they are married usually justify what they are doing by a process of rationalization. They convince themselves that their partners really love them. They also believe that by giving in and having sex they will not lose their boyfriends, but instead will hold onto relationships which will eventually become permanent. If things do not work out as women want, they are left feeling used, stupid and guilty. After all, they gave themselves in the belief that they were beloved but they were exploited so that their partners could feel passing pleasure. They thought that by having sex they would strengthen a relationship they really valued; instead, they discover that the strength of the relationship was only a figment of their imaginations. And they feel guilty—angry with themselves—because they know that they are to blame for the loss and unhappiness which they feel. An intimate relationship is so important to a woman that she tends to identify herself primarily in terms of that relationship. In the absence of an intimate relationship she may feel that she is nobody because somebody does not lover her. The complex psychological and social factors which result in this conclusion are described in the seminal work of Carol Gilligan, *In A Different Voice* (Cambridge, Mass: Harvard University Press, 1982).

Men do not seem to feel the same oneness with their bodies which women experience. In many ways they tend to be alienated from their bodies. Father David Knight describes an extreme stereotype of male alienation which seems to be endorsed by our culture:

> A boy acquires the impression quite early that his body is simply an instrument for him to use. His body is his weapon, his tool. His task is to strengthen it, harden it, train it, and then go out and do something with it. His value is in what he can do, not in what he is in himself.[4]

Because men think of their bodies as separate from themselves, sexual intercourse can be a very impersonal act for them.

Men "score" by getting women to have sex with them; their sexual "conquests" may be reasons for boasting. Penetration and coupling may represent little more than the way to excitement and release. If men feel guilt following casual sex, it will likely be because they realize that they hurt their partners and let them down. It will probably not be because they grasp the fact that sex is meant to be expressive of love and that it is a language only appropriately spoken by lovers. However, while men usually have difficulty understanding sex as expressing love for and union with another they seem to have a clear grasp of the meaning of commitment. Commitment means that they are required to work for, protect and care for the beloved. Men are tempted to rationalize by arguing that sex has nothing to do with loving commitment. And, as statistics illustrate, many succumb to this temptation. In so doing, however, they hinder their development into mature and sensitive persons; instead, they experience a sense of bitterness because of the feelings of emptiness and disillusionment which follow upon their uncommitted sexual encounters.

The solution to the problems resulting from sexual confusion is to face the fact that sexual intercourse has a dual meaning, that is, it is meant to express the bond of marital unity which exists between two persons, and it is the means by which human life is propagated. The proper context for sexual intercourse is marriage, and a good relationship between married partners depends upon a willingness to commit themselves to loving fidelity until they are separated by death.

Teenage Pregnancy

In the United States close to one million unmarried teenage girls become pregnant each year. Girls bear the obvious consequences of pregnancies which result from premarital sex. If they become aware of the pregnancies, male partners may also be affected by them. The severe distress experienced by the girls, however, is not as frequently the lot of the boys. Within two years of the first pregnancy, thirty percent become pregnant a second time. There is no question that the consequences of teen pregnancy are dreadful. Only one-half of teenage mothers graduate from high school. Over the course of their lifetimes, teenage mothers earn fifty percent of what other women in the workforce earn. Teen pregnancy is frequently a recurrent family pattern: the mothers of eighty-two percent of teens who get pregnant were themselves unwed mothers when they conceived their daughters.[5] Teen pregnancy affects all socio-economic groups, but it most often occurs in poor communities. A sense of hopelessness and desperation, combined with the desire to have a doll-like baby to love, make pregnancy appear attractive to many young girls. The fact that babies are not dolls, but rather dependent human beings who make many demands upon their parents, can bring resentment and disillusionment to immature young women who are cast too soon into the role of mother. Tragically, abuse and neglect of children sometimes accompany unwed motherhood because little children give so little and ask so much.

What is the solution to the epidemic of pregnancies among unmarried adolescents in the United States? Many people reason that society should simply accept the fact that teenagers are sexually active; they think that comprehensive programs of sex education and the ready availability of birth control will remedy the situation. In other words, eliminate the generation of new life through sexual intercourse, and then give up on efforts to keep unmarried teens from sexual intimacy. Unfortunately, the articulation of an attitude such as this reveals a belief that unmarried young people lack the ability to be chaste.* It assumes that they cannot wait until they are married to have sexual intercourse. It considers pregnancy the only problem which results from casual sex. And it ignores the pain, guilt and emptiness which are felt by young men and women who engage in casual premarital sex.

The way to deal with teen pregnancy is through programs of sex education which include moral and spiritual components, and through addressing situations of poverty which give rise to immense demoralization. Young men and women who understand that they bear responsibility for their actions and who realize that through sexual intercourse they become co-creators with God appreciate the seriousness and significance of coitus. By grasping the full scope of the meaning of sex they are enabled to decide that casual sex is very harmful. By respecting adolescence as a season of life in which growth toward maturity is accomplished, they prepare themselves for young adulthood. When they have finished their educations and become economically self-sufficient they will be ready to consider committing themselves to the love and fidelity which characterize Christian marriage.

Abortion

Direct abortion is the intentional expulsion of a developing embryo or fetus from the womb of a pregnant woman. (In Catholic moral teaching a distinction is usually made between *direct* abortion and *indirect* abortion.*) During the first trimester of pregnancy abortion is usually accomplished by one of two methods: Suction or dilation and curettage. In the first procedure, the contents of the uterus are sucked out by a vacuum-like apparatus. In the second procedure, the cervix (the mouth of the uterus) is expanded and the developing fetus is scraped from the womb. Later in pregnancy abortion is effected by injecting saline into the uterus. The injection kills the developing fetus and causes the pregnant woman to go into labor; she eventually delivers a dead fetus. A new drug, which is not yet available in the United States, (as of 1994), RU486, causes self-induced abortions in women who are in the early stages of pregnancy.

On January 22, 1973 the United States Supreme Court struck down restrictive abortion laws and made it possible for women to procure abortion on demand at any time during the first six months of pregnancy. The number of abortions currently performed each year in the United States is approximately one and one-half million. Unwed pregnant teenagers account for more than four hundred thousand abortions per year. Women use many reasons to justify procuring abortions. They choose abortion because circumstances make a pregnancy a hardship or because they learn through testing* that the fetuses they are carrying bear mental or physical defects. There is no question that retarded and deformed children require care and training beyond that needed by normal offspring. And it is easy to sympathize with women who think themselves unable to cope with pregnancy because they are alone, or in dire emotional or economic straits. Such women need encouragement and support services, including counseling, in order to deal with the crises they face.

Even though most people empathize with pregnant women who find themselves in desperate straits, it does not follow that resorting to abortion to solve problems is a morally defensible choice. On the contrary, to deny to a person-in-becoming his/her most basic right, the right to continued existence, is morally wrong. Pregnant women need to be assisted to solve their problems; a reasonable solution to an unplanned or unwanted pregnancy is not to kill the fetus.

The harm that is done to a fetus by abortion is totally devastating; in some cases the fetus is ripped from the uterus; in others, it dies a slow, painful death because a saline solution burns away its flesh. The fetus is an innocent being whose presence in a woman's uterus may be a great inconvenience to her. Pregnant women who are confronted with a choice between coping with the problems a pregnancy presents and killing a fetus should choose not to harm another. In other words, they should suffer harm to their reputations, economic deprivation, or the other hardships which accompany pregnancy instead of destroying the fetus. In time, a woman can rebuild her reputation, resume her education or career, and recover the other things she loses because of her pregnancy. When aborted, a fetus is deprived of its life and all the possibilities and potential which constitute its life. The Roman Catholic Church, along with many other religious and moral commentators, argues that there are no convincing reasons to deprive the unborn of life. That is, the fetus' claim to life surpasses the pregnant woman's desire not to be inconvenienced, even when the inconvenience causes great physical and emotional suffering. The Church proclaims the cogency of this truth in spite of the fact that many people support abortion on demand.

It may seem difficult to believe, but the psychological harm suffered by women who undergo abortions is usually much worse than the pain they would have experienced had they allowed their babies to grow to term. Michael T. Mannion, author of *Abortion & Healing: A Cry to Be Whole,* relates the anguished story of a young woman who aborted her child. Her grief at her loss and her guilt over her wrongdoing caused her enormous pain.

> They never knew! My parents never knew. I mean, how could I tell my parents that their "little girl" had lost her virginity at 15 years old. After all, I was the one they expected to go to college, to make "something" of my life.
>
> Besides it was the first time I ever made love. Now I had missed my third period and my mother was starting to ask questions. I had to do something!
>
> My boyfriend didn't know what to do either, so we talked to one of his teachers. She gave me the num-

ber of Planned Parenthood and told me to call right
away.

They gave me an appointment right away. After going through the necessary exams, tests, etc. they sent
me upstairs to a nice grey-haired lady. She said,
"Your tests show you are probably 14 weeks. What do
you want to do?"

"I don't know. I'm only 15 years old and my parents
would kill me if they found out that I was pregnant!"

She gave me the number of the abortion clinic. She
even let me call on her phone! They made the appointment for the following week.

She warned me it might be a little more expensive
because I was already 14 weeks and they could do up
to 12 weeks with no problems.

My boyfriend cried. "Couldn't we just get married
and have the baby?"

"Please don't cry! I just can't ! They'd hate me."

So he took me anyway. My sister came to support me.
We were very close. We walked up to the front door. I
remember thinking that abortion was dirty, but this
office was really nice. "It must be okay," I reasoned.

One girl sat next to me and asked if it was my first
time, "Yes," I said, "And you?" "Oh," she exclaimed,
"this is my third time."

Then a nicely dressed woman took me in a room and
explained the procedure. Of course there was no
mention of baby, only "tissue." With gentle gestures
she demonstrated how the doctor would remove "the
tissue" with the suction tube.

The time came. I signed my release and paid my
$275.00 cash and was led downstairs. I was in-
structed to undress and put on a hospital gown. I got
on the table and put my feet in the stirrups. They
asked me if I wanted sodium pentothal or ether. I
chose the sodium pentothal. "Count back from 100,"
she said and smiled.

I remember thinking what are they going to do with it? There was a stainless steel bowl with stuff in it but I thought it must be iodine or something. Oh well, 98, 97 . . . I was out.

I woke up, back in my stall, where I was told to get up, it was time to leave. They gave me some Darvon for the pain and I left.

I cried all the way home. I don't know why, I just couldn't control my tears. (To this day I can't even listen to the same music he played on the tape deck as it brings back all the details.)

Within two years we had broken off our relationship. This really put a strain between us.

My sister asked me if I felt guilt. "No," I said, "What for?" But years later the guilt came, and the pain and the remorse, but I kept denying it as I drank another drink. Drugs and alcohol really numbed the pain. I never consciously thought of why, just that it made the hurt go away.

I met a man and dated him for four years. Then I found out I was pregnant. I was ready to break off the relationship before I found out I was pregnant. This time I knew I couldn't go through an abortion again. So we got married.

I almost died the first time I read a detailed description of a 16-week-old "Baby." That's when I first broke down and cried. That's when I realized that "it" was a baby. I don't think I've stopped crying since.

Even harder to accept is that the man I married has a son from his previous marriage who was born the same week as mine would have been.

I learned of Jesus' love and forgiveness two years ago. It was the first time in over eight years that I've had any peace. I still lapse into feeling guilty at times but I search during those times for a closer walk with God, and He is faithful as He gives me peace.[6]

What has happened to the moral fabric of the United States in the years since the Supreme Court made abortion legal? Un-

fortunately, permissive abortion has resulted in dreadful consequences. Most obvious, of course, are the tens of millions of
persons-in-becoming whose fragile young lives have been
snuffed out. But there have also been other subtler changes as
well. The bishops of the United States have frequently pointed
to evidence of a desensitized attitude* toward all human life so
that the dignity and sacredness of each individual are not necessarily understood as self-evident. There is a widespread tendency to deny that persons have responsibility for the choices
they make and, instead, to justify the choice to abort based on
trauma experienced in connection with problematic circumstances. And there is real confusion about the nature of sex as
procreational: Many people want sex to be solely recreational
and want to wish away its procreational dimension.

Sexual Transmission of AIDS

AIDS (acquired immune deficiency syndrome) is rightly
placed within the category "sexually transmitted diseases." The
AIDS virus, HIV (human immunodeficiency virus), is transmitted from person to person in two sexual body fluids, semen and
vaginal secretions. It is possible to contract AIDS through heterosexual intercourse. Infection is much more likely to proceed
from man to woman than vice versa; however, both routes of
transmission are possible.[7]

AIDS is relatively new to the human community. It is a
dreadfully debilitating affliction which is always fatal. The first
cases of AIDS appeared in the early 1980s. The unfortunate
tendency during the early years of the epidemic was to think in
terms of AIDS as a "gay disease" because homosexual men who
engaged in anal intercourse were afflicted with AIDS in significant numbers. The possibility of heterosexual transmission of
AIDS is now widely recognized and serious attempts to educate
people to the risks which accompany heterosexual intercourse
are being undertaken.

(The AIDS virus is transmitted in blood as well as semen and
vaginal secretions. A large percentage of intravenous drug users
have been infected with HIV through the sharing of needles and
syringes. Their sexual partners and any children conceived
from their sexual intercourse are at risk of developing AIDS.
So, too, are the female partners and offspring of bisexual men.
To a much lesser extent, people who receive blood transfusions*

run a risk of HIV infection. AIDS could then be passed on to their sexual partners via their sexual body fluids.)

There are a lot of people in contemporary society who believe that sexual experimentation, even to the extent of rampant promiscuity, is a fact of life. They deal with the threat of AIDS by advocating the use of condoms in all instances of sexual intercourse except those involving partners who are absolutely certain that neither has been infected with HIV.

Advocating condoms as protection against AIDS reveals a twofold confusion. First, from a technological point of view, it is misleading because condoms are not foolproof. They can tear, or they may have tiny undetectable defects and thus not prevent an exchange of body fluids. People are likely to be aware of media messages advising the use of condoms but they are at a disadvantage because it is impossible to include in sixty second commercials all the cautions which should be observed in the use of condoms. The more startling misconception is that those who advise using condoms implicitly suggest that abstinence until marriage is an unreasonable expectation. They assume that they are being realistic by educating young people to use condoms for casual sex. They miss the point that they should be trying to communicate with unmarried young people about the deep, powerful and intimate nature of sex. They should be counseling young people to await the pleasures experienced by lovers who enjoy sex within the context of committed marital relationships.

Sex, Sexuality and the Teaching of the Roman Catholic Church

The Catholic Church teaches that genital sexual acts are proper only for married people. There was a time when the Church taught that the sole purpose for sexual intercourse was procreation. According to Saint Augustine,* married spouses committed a venial sin* if they did not intend their intercourse to result in pregnancy. Augustine's opinion influenced past Catholic teaching on sex in marriage, but it is not part of official teaching* today. During the last century the Church has become quite positive in its assessment of physical intimacy and has incorporated insight regarding the value of sex into its teaching. The testimony of persons who are married and the deliberations of personalist philosophers* have led to an appreciation of the unitive meaning of intercourse. The Church, at Vatican Council II, expressed its understanding of the unitive dimension of marriage:

> Marriage to be sure is not instituted solely for procreation. Rather, its very nature as an unbreakable compact between persons, and the welfare of the children, both demand that the mutual love of the spouses, too, be embodied in a rightly ordered manner, that it grow and ripen.[8]

Sexual intercourse is an activity in which married spouses have a right to engage. They do so because of the physical pleasure which accompanies the act, sometimes because of a desire to beget children and, ideally, because they want to express the deep reality of their love through physical union. To say the least, a loving union requires much of lovers. To be willing to enter into physical union with another person, one needs to esteem oneself, to trust the other, admire the other, forgive the faults of the other, and acknowledge the existence of a significant bond with the other. In sexual intercourse spouses express these sentiments, strengthen the bonds of their relationship, and celebrate the love they have for each other.

The Church maintains that sexual intercourse is a sacred and special form of interpersonal sharing. It is so special, and its ramifications so serious, that sex should be shared only by persons who are married to each other. This basic assumption leads the Church to conclude that sex between persons who are not married, adulterous sexual affairs,* and all homosexual acts are morally wrong. Among moral theologians* there are some who hold less absolute positions than the magisterium.* However, there is a general consensus that the full meaning of genital sexuality is attained only by heterosexual spouses who have publicly pledged their love and entered into the covenant* of marriage.

One result of sexual intimacy is the deepening and strengthening of the love spouses have for each other. For married persons of child-bearing age who are not troubled by infertility, a second result is the conceiving of new life. Life conceived through sexual intercourse is the incarnating of the love of two married persons. Children are a source of blessing and joy to spouses who should readily embrace their responsibility to nurture and educate their offspring.

Even when life is conceived by persons who are not married, or is "accidently" conceived by married spouses, an embryo or fetus deserves reverent regard. As we have seen, the Catholic Church teaches that, regardless of the reason, abortion* is always wrong because it is a flagrant denial of the fetus' right to life.

The Church, in its official teaching, also argues against the practice of artificial contraception and the creating of life by asexual means* (other than through the act of intercourse). The reason for the prohibition of both practices is that the Church reasons that God designed the physical act of intercourse as the means through which human life is to be transmitted. In the encyclical *Humanae Vitae** Pope Paul VI said that those who seek to enjoy intercourse while frustrating its procreative potential refuse to honor the full meaning and design which God intends the act of intercourse to convey. To attempt to bring life into being by technological means is likewise regarded as unethical. In the "Instruction on Respect for Human Life in Its Origin and on the Dignity of Procreation," issued March 10, 1987, Joseph Cardinal Ratzinger, Prefect of the Sacred Congregation for the Doctrine of the Faith* explained the reasoning behind the prohibition of technological reproduction:

> Conception *in vitro* is the result of the technical act which presides over fertilization. Such fertilization is neither in fact achieved nor positively willed as the expression and fruit of a specific act of the conjugal union. In homologous IVF and ET,* therefore, even if it is considered in the context of 'de facto' existing sexual relations,* the generation of the human person is objectively deprived of its perfection, namely, that of being the result and fruit of a conjugal act in which the spouses can become "cooperators with God for giving life to a new person."[9]

Within the Church there is a significant body of dissent* from official teaching on artificial contraception and asexual reproduction. There are two reasons for the dissent. The first is the dissenters' understanding of the person as moral subject who has been entrusted with dominion over all aspects of life, including procreation. Based on the biblical concepts of dominion and stewardship* dissenters suggest that spouses have the rightful authority to decide to practice artificial contraception or to use technology to try to become parents. The second reason for dissent is disagreement over what constitutes the perfection or completeness of the act of intercourse. Dissenters consider the loving attitude of the spouses toward each other the most important moral aspect of intercourse. Their love and responsibility in coupling are seen as more morally relevant than the biological structure of the act and the possible subsequent penetration of ovum by sperm. Accordingly, an act of intercourse which is loving and contracepted for a serious reason, is not considered morally wrong. Likewise, they propose that the choice to try to conceive a child through technological means because of a condition of infertility should not be understood as necessarily undermining the biological and human bonds between parents and child.

Catholic Teaching about Homosexual Acts

Heterosexual acts are performed by heterosexual persons, that is by men who are sexually attracted to women and by women who are sexually attracted to men. (At times homosexuals may engage in heterosexual acts; bisexuals engage in both heterosexual and homosexual acts.) The Catholic Church teaches that it is obvious that heterosexual intercourse should occur in marriage and is a right claimed by persons who love one another. Since humans experience passion and feel a drive to intimacy, those who are heterosexual have a socially-sanctioned and Church-endorsed structure (marriage) within which to satisfy their sexual needs. But what are homosexual persons to do? Homosexual men and women also experience passionate drives and may want to achieve sexual gratification by genital intimacy with persons of the same sex. In view of Catholic teaching on sexual acts, do homosexual persons have any options in regard to engaging in homosexual behavior?

The official teaching of the Church is very clear on the matter of homosexual acts. The document, "On the Pastoral Care of Homosexual Persons," issued by the Sacred Congregation for the Doctrine of the Faith on October 31, 1986 evaluated the homosexual condition as an objective disorder and maintained that no person has a right to engage in acts which are objectively immoral. Accordingly, persons who feel themselves sexually attracted to members of their own sex have no ethical option other than total lifelong abstinence. If a person were to give into temptation and engage in homosexual acts, that person would be acting immorally. The Church's magisterium is perfectly clear in its teaching on homosexual acts: These genital, sexual acts are always wrong regardless of the intentions of the participants, the circumstances in which they are performed, or any good feelings which might be experienced as a result.

As with some other Catholic sexual-ethical teachings, there is reservation among revisionist* moral theologians in regard to the *absoluteness* of the prohibition of all homosexual genital acts. The reasons for the reservation are theoretical, experiential and religious. At the theoretical level, two points are raised for consideration. One is that the human person is the subject of moral theology and that the discipline should provide guidance and instruction which is realistic and reasonable; the injunction to be celibate for an entire lifetime is seen as not taking due account of the reality of human emotions and drives. The second point is that the abstract and idealistic framework which sanctions genital sex only for married spouses may be inadequate because it fails to take account of the meaning and value of genital sex for partners who bear the same gender.

At the experiential level, there are two areas of disagreement with official teaching. The first involves the rationale behind the Church's distinction between homosexual orientation and homosexual behavior. (Orientation refers to the condition of being sexually attracted to those of the same sex; behavior means acting on this orientation by having sex with a same sex partner.) In regard to the Church's acceptance of a homosexual orientation in the face of a condemnation of all homosexual acts, the Task Force on Gay/Lesbian Issues of the Archdiocese of San Francisco concluded:

> As for all embodied persons . . . embodied sexual orientation finds its natural expected expression in embodied sexual behavior. What makes it moral or immoral is not some abstract "thingness" about it, but how it supports and sustains what is best in one's humanity, hence, moral, or destroys that humanity, hence, immoral. The orientation/behavior distinction ignores the dynamic interplay between the two to the point of being practically meaningless and pastorally useless. The easy presumption that the lifelong charism of celibacy is automatically given with the discovery of one's embodied homosexuality flies in the face of the centuries' long tradition that celibacy is a

rare and beautiful charism, given to the few, and given by God alone.[10]

A second point of disagreement which is rooted in human experience is articulated by the behavioral sciences. This point is that persons need to have the opportunity to integrate meaningful expressions of intimacy into significant interpersonal relationships in order to develop into psychologically healthy individuals. Moral theologians join psychologists in negatively evaluating genital sex which is compulsive and/or promiscuous. Revisionists think compulsive, promiscuous sexual encounters are likely for homosexual people who try to live by the Church's "no sex" teaching, but occasionally give in to temptation. Recognizing how harmful are the guilt and self-hatred which follow anonymous homosexual acts, and considering official teaching too demanding to be successfully followed for an entire lifetime, some moralists suggest a compromise. They think that the way for many homosexual men and women to achieve personal maturity and a desired level of intimacy may be for them to form committed same sex unions, promising fidelity and love to each other. This is obviously a radical departure from official teaching; understanding the reasons for the departure should facilitate an evaluation of its merits and drawbacks.

Religious insight may also provide reasons for assessing committed homosexual unions in positive terms. One insight is derived from the doctrine of creation. God, an all-good Mother and Father, created everything that is, blessing humans with the gift of sexuality. Why did God create approximately ten percent of humankind homosexual, a condition the Sacred Congregation for the Doctrine of the Faith called "inherently disordered"? Might it not be that the search to discover in what truly moral human conduct consists has not yet been completed, especially in respect to the complex undertaking of determining in what genital ways it is proper to express one's sexual nature? A second powerful religious insight points to the love, compassion and reverence Jesus instructed his followers to have for one another. These affections stand in sharp contrast to the homophobia and tendency to condemn which, unfortunately, have become ingrained in patriarchal religions.* Removal of this bias might lead to a rethinking of the moral prohibitions which have traditionally been attached to all homosexual acts.

Individual Conscience and Sexual Decisions

Conscience is a faculty* of sane, mature, free persons which enables them to determine in particular situations which course of action is right and which is wrong. In reaching decisions of conscience people employ their intellects to analyze the implications of the possible courses of action they might follow, and they try to make their choices conform to the values and principles which they hold. It is their willpower which enables them to do something or refrain from taking action. Knowing that one has a conscience goes hand-in-hand with the recognition that people are responsible for what they do and what they fail to do.

Taking the position that people should be governed by conscience is somewhat out of fashion. In contemporary American society there is a tendency to think that people are products of their environment and that their decisions are caused by external and/or unconscious forces. Catholic moral tradition rejects such an analysis. While it acknowledges that people experience pressure from forces within and without, Catholic teaching steadfastly holds that people are free to do what is right and that they are obligated to follow their consciences.

Forming One's Conscience

There are occasions in all our lives when we have to wrestle with decisions of conscience. Questions such as, "Should I have an abortion?" "Should I move in with my boyfriend/girlfriend?" "Should I comply with draft registration?" "Should I blow the whistle on my coworker who is stealing from our employer?" "Should I plagiarize on my term paper?" "What should I do to help the homeless?" need to be answered. In coming to decisions on issues such as these, we realize that conscience does not work in the same way as a vending machine. It is not a matter of inserting a question into an imaginary slot in one's forehead and waiting for detailed instructions to emerge from a second slot. Neither is it a matter of being quiet and awaiting instructions from a mysterious inward voice. Conscience is not a "thing"; it is a power of the intellect. Conscience needs to be formed and informed, and the process in which one must engage in order to carry out this task requires maturity and good will. The answer to the subjective confusion caused by a doubtful conscience is not to ignore the whole business of reaching a decision of conscience. Rather, we have a serious responsibility to work through our doubtful consciences so that we come to understand and to admit to ourselves in what a morally right course of action consists. The steps to be taken in the formation of conscience include:

1. Prayer to God, our Mother and Father, for wisdom to know what choice is the right choice, and for strength to be able to act in an upright manner. Our prayer should also include a recognition of God's sovereignty over us and an explicit willingness to live out the vocation* to Christian discipleship.

2. Reflection on who one is and what one desires to become. When faced with a decision of conscience, a person is aware that at least two courses of action are possible. The introspective task consists in resolving the issue of how to grow in humanity, and determining how not to retard that growth. Obviously, keeping a boyfriend by sleeping with him brings a desirable result. However, compromising one's principles in order to insure the continuance of a relationship diminishes the character and integrity of a person who capitulates to pressure. Honest reflection and soul-searching frequently force us to admit that the easy thing to do is not the same as the right thing to do.

3. Consultation with the wisdom contained in scripture and with the stories of people who followed their consciences in dilemmas similar to those we face. In regard to the woman who must contend with an unplanned and unwanted pregnancy, the biblical insight that life is sacred because it is created by God may prompt her to respect the other who is growing within her. And the counsel of women who confide in her that they achieved peace of mind by enduring the embarrassment and inconvenience of pregnancy rather than compromise their principles may support her in the choice to respect the life she is carrying.

Inviolability of Conscience

Once one has engaged in the prayer, reflection and consultation necessary to form conscience, that person has the authority to follow what is known to be the morally right course. In fact, the person is *required* to follow a *certain* conscience. Catholic moral theology teaches that a certain conscience is inviolable, that is, the person has an absolute responsibility to follow a well-formed conscience. The justification for this teaching is that a person cannot do better than follow the light of reason. Even if a person is objectively wrong regarding a specific judgment of conscience, the nature of conscience requires that the judgment be followed. People need to do what they subjectively know is morally right. For example, consider the case of the girlfriend of a soldier stationed overseas who discovers that she is losing her affection for him and developing a strong attachment to a young man in her home town. She feels herself caught in a bind and seeks to resolve her dilemma. She asks God for guidance, earnestly tries to figure out the proper thing to do, and asks a few close friends for advice. She decides that the proper thing to do is to continue to correspond with the soldier and to pretend that she is still his girlfired. In this way she will not disappoint him while he is far away from home. The young woman in this case is *objectively* wrong in her judgment. It would be much kinder to tell the truth immediately and not take part in deception. Since she is convinced *subjectively* that she is right, however, she must follow the light of conscience and act in accordance with its dictates.

People must be true to themselves and uphold their integrity. In so concluding, there is no suggestion that people are free to do whatever they feel inclined to do, or that people need not be required to justify their actions. Instead, there is a conviction that once a person has undertaken the process of forming conscience the person must be guided by the decision of conscience in order to maintain integrity.

Being a person of integrity means that one is whole, that one does not cheat or diminish oneself by compromising principles, and that one acts in accordance with principles. In regard to sexual choices, people should be able to justify these choices both to themselves and to the community. The principles which they hold, and the esteem they have for these principles should be clearly evident. Men and women who comprehend what sex means know that, as a shared activity, the interests, pleasure and needs of the other are just as important as one's own interests, pleasure and needs. Thus, any kinds of sexual actions which are degrading, exploitative, selfish or impersonal are immoral. Listening to one's conscience in regard to sexual conduct is very different from merely drifting along and succumbing to the countless temptations to engage in irresponsible conduct.

Marriage

Christian marriage is the union of husband and wife which is approved by their faith community and by the universal Church. The characteristics of marriage are four-fold: it is sacramental, relational, corporeal and visceral.

Marriage is the joining of two persons who pledge fidelity to one another. Fidelity means being true to each other in good times and in bad, in sickness and in health, loving and honoring each other until death. Wife stands by husband, and husband stands by wife. The spouses are allies and friends; in spite of arguments and differences of opinion, they have each other's best interests at heart. To the extent that spouses fulfill their vow to be faithful, their marriage is a sacramental one. A sacrament is a sign of God's personal love for, presence to, and involvement with those who believe. God addressed Abraham and promised to be faithful to him and to the Hebrew people: "I will maintain my covenant with you and your descendants after you throughout the ages as an everlasting pact, to be your God and the God of your descendants after you" (Gen. 17:7).

Although the Hebrew people were often unfaithful to God, God was always true to the commitment. Jesus also promised fidelity to his people, the Church: "I will be with you all days, even to the end of time" (Matt. 28:20). And Jesus has followed through perfectly on his promise. Married persons are imperfect and their fidelity is imperfect. When they take seriously their commitments to sexual fidelity and to acting in each others' best interests, however, they are a sign or reminder of God's being with those who believe, and Jesus' continual love for the Church. One way of understanding the sacramentality of marriage is to see it as the living out of vowed fidelity.

Persons are multifaceted, and to think of them as merely biological is to distort the reality of who they are. Likewise, to overemphasize the importance of the biological act of intercourse, thinking that it alone constitutes marriage, is obviously inaccurate. In some past Catholic teaching there was a tendency to consider persons married if they had exchanged vows before a priest and two witnesses and subsequently consummated the marriage through an act of sexual intercourse. Exchanging the so-called "right of marriage" through coitus resulted in the conclusion that a couple was married because there was a tendency to incompletely understand marriage in terms of a biological act. In fact, the reality of marriage is far more than simply the biological. Psychological, emotional, moral and spiritual aspects must also be present before the mating of a woman and a man can be termed a marriage. However, this fact notwithstanding, corporeality is one essential aspect of marriage.

Christians celebrate the holiness of their bodies. St. Paul instructed the early Christians that they were temples of the Holy Spirit and that God's spirit dwelled in them (1 Cor. 3:16). One of the most significant requirements of marital fidelity is the absolute prohibition of extra-marital sex. Neither spouse is permitted in desire or action to pursue physical intimacy outside the marital relationship. Jesus considered two persons becoming one flesh so profound and sacred that he expected the community to support and affirm the couple in their marriage. At the same time, he forbade divorce. "At the beginning of creation God made them male and female; for this reason a man shall leave his father and mother and the two shall become as one. They are no longer two, but one flesh. Therefore, let no man separate what God has joined" (Mark 10:6-9).

Through intercourse a couple celebrate their love and bring forth new life. Marriage is corporeal. To understand marriage in solely physical or biological terms is to miss much of the richness of marriage. To undervalue the corporeal dimension is likewise to misconstrue what marriage is.

Christian marriage must contain a visceral ingredient. By visceral is meant a gut level commitment to make what is promised come to fruition. The familiar terms "for better or worse, for richer or poorer, in sickness or health, until death do us part" need to be taken literally, without hedging or half-heartedness. Given the alarming divorce rate* of contemporary American society and the sloth and self-seeking which characterize flawed and broken people, this may seem like a very tall order. It is. But since the essence of marriage is fidelity and commitment without reservation, those who enter Christian marriages need to honestly mean what they say. And when problems are experienced in making the marriage work, the spouses need to summon their will to be with and for each other. In this way people who love each other will manage to work through the difficulties which will inevitably confront them.

Kathleen and Thomas Hart write that people can only give the gift of self to the other if they are willing to open their hearts to each other, that is, to relate to each other on a deep personal level.

"One can do many external deeds of love and still hold back the really precious gift, the inner self. This gift can be given only through communication."[11] For this reason marriage is said to be relational. Wife and husband are equal partners who need to know each other and agree to the roles they are willing to assume. Spouses should realize that neither comes close to being perfect and that good communication requires effort, patience and humor. Through communication spouses come to appreciate each other's beauty, needs, pains and hopes and they manage to strike the compromises necessitated by the complex difficulties they will undoubtedly face.

Marriage as Lifestyle

Christian marriage should reflect the love and commitment of spouses and their openness to the nurturance of new life. Their love, fidelity and fecundity become a demonstration or sign of God's relationship to humanity. These notions are ideal and beautiful, but to what extent are they lived out in contemporary culture in the United States? Two present day lifestyles vary remarkably from the concept of Christian marriage derived from scripture and the tradition of the Church. One is the Yuppie phenomenon, and the other is known as the DINK movement.

Yuppies are young, upwardly mobile professionals who put primary emphasis on cashing in on their good looks, abundance of energy and college degrees. Yuppie married couples want to drive upscale cars, live at fashionable addresses, and enjoy the good life. Career-advancement and personal gratification are their goals. Their values were formulated by the advertising industry, and their philosophy of life can be condensed into two words: "Me first." When yuppies have children they initiate their offspring into their value system and do all in their power to make certain that the little ones do not detract from the pleasures and pursuits of their parents.

D.I.N.K. stands for "dual income, no kids." Dinks are married couples who are so swayed by the yuppie mentality that they can discern no reason to have children. Neither wife nor husband wants to pay the financial, physical and emotional costs of rearing children. A decline in income, babies crying during the night, the responsibilities and heartaches attendant to parenthood—dinks fear the cost of becoming parents, and they simply refuse to pay the price. (Of course, there are altruistic dinks who are the exception to the rule. They do not manifest the selfishness I describe.)

Yuppies and dinks are not motivated to pursue a vocation to social involvement with a stress on giving of oneself to better the marital relationship and the human community. In a sense, they marry for better and better, focusing attention on the satisfaction of self-interest. When conflict and suffering mar the peace and happiness of their unions, they are not apt to walk the extra mile and often wind up abandoning their marriages.

However, yuppies and dinks *do marry*. They seek societal approval of their relationship and they embrace an institution, even if they understand it very imperfectly. In contrast, more and more people are not marrying, and are merely cohabiting. By living together they share friendship, sex, domestic expenses and each other's time. And they are free of commitments, not "tied down." If they find that their compatibility withstands the test of time, they may choose to marry. If they grow weary with each other, they are free to walk away from their living arrangement without the hassle of legal proceedings or the emotional trauma associated with divorce. The skyrocketing divorce rate, difficulties encountered in delineating spousal roles, and the general reluctance of people to work courageously to craft good marriages have resulted in the present decline of marriage. If cause and effect are linked together, it is not hard to figure out why people simply settle for living together. However, an unavoidable question remains: Are half-hearted* attempts at marriage the best we can do, or is it possible for spouses to enter into the richness of Christian sacramental marriage?

In St. Paul's first epistle to the Corinthians (1 Cor. 13:4-8) the Apostle to the Gentiles* presents a rich reflection on the nature of love. To the extent that spouses try to live up to the ideal which Paul proposes they will progress in their living out of Christian marriage. Let us examine Paul's words, considering how they might translate into a marital agenda.

Love is patient. Patient with one's own moral, intellectual, physical and emotional limitations, as well as with the faults of spouse and children. Humans are in process, trying to become all that they are meant to be. At each step along the way patience is required with both self and others, because the process of development is painful, erratic and never complete.

Love is kind. What types of kindness does love manifest? A backrub, a bouquet of flowers, a compliment, an unanswered insult. The greatness of heart which is evident when a child's shortcomings are forgiven or a spouse's indiscretion is buried, never to be resurrected. The sensitivity to respond in gentleness and encouragement to the weariness or defeat of the other.

Love is not jealous. Persons who love one another trust one another. They do not attempt to isolate the other or prevent the other's full use of God-given talents. The accomplishments of spouse and children are reasons for rejoicing because their well-being is truly a priority.

Love does not put on airs; it is not snobbish. Many human relationships entail wearing masks and playing games. The family is a setting in which people should feel confident and secure. Spouses and their children need to be loved unconditionally, simply because they are precious to one another. They should not have to pretend to be different from what they are in order to merit another's love.

Love is never rude. It is gentle and respectful to all, especially significant others. The one you love deserves your best. This best should be characterized by cheerfulness and consideration. It should not jar the other by harsh words, intolerant put downs, or any kind of psychological or verbal abuse.

Love is not self-seeking. This does not mean that a loving person does not truly love and care for herself or himself. Rather, it suggests that the happiness and welfare of spouse and children count at least as much as one's own. The pride according to which one craves recognition, the covetousness which leads to unrestrained consumerism, the lust which attempts to gratify urges through using the other, and the gluttony which flourishes in hedonism are foreign to the notion of unselfish love proposed by Saint Paul.

Love is not prone to anger. To be sure, lovers get angry about many things—from the way the spouse squeezes the toothpaste to the spouse's speeding ticket, with its resultant increase in auto insurance. Anger is one of the most common human emotions, and the way married people handle their anger says a lot about their commitment. Guarding against getting angry about petty things which really do not amount to anything is one way to learn from Paul's instructions. And working out major issues which trigger angry, hostile feelings is another. Literally heeding Paul's advice in Ephesians is also important: "The sun must not go down on your wrath" (Eph. 4:26). People who love each other should sincerely endeavor to begin and end each day at peace.

Love does not brood over injuries. Jesus taught his followers to forgive one another. The act of forgiving may be easier than the task of forgetting, but Christians are obliged to engage in the process of letting go of past hurts. The hurt may be something as small as a birthday not remembered, or as great as an act of infidelity which shatters one's self-confidence. In both instances, brooding does not help the situation. Healing only happens when loving people resolve to work through their pain, forgive and forget.

Love does not rejoice in what is wrong, but rejoices with the truth. To be amused at the error or suffering of another is unworthy of human beings. When the other is the spouse, such amusement is cruel. Likewise, immoral choices or patterns of behavior rightly give rise to heart-felt sorrow. Spouses should sincerely attempt to discern in what good conduct consists so that they can rejoice in knowing that their behavior is morally appropriate.

There is no limit to love's forbearance, to its trust, its hope, its power to endure. Love is an unconditioned will to build a viable marriage. NO MATTER WHAT. When the faults of the spouse and the children wear one down, when one is depressed, anxious and insecure, when there is a temptation to throw in the towel, an inner resilience is discovered. The will to go on building the relationship becomes manifest. Humility, wisdom and courage are accepted as God's gifts which enable spouses to honor their commitments to each other and their children.

Marriage Preparation

It goes without saying that people should be adequately prepared for marriage. They should receive thorough instruction so that they understand the nature of Christian marriage as a demanding and ennobling vocation. They should go into marriage with their eyes open, having already discussed the practical aspects of setting up a household, including how they will divide chores, budget and pay bills. They need to agree on the amount of time they will reserve for each other, and how much time they will spend with their respective families and friends. When children come, which parent will be the primary care-giver? There are certainly many things to be resolved. While it is unrealistic to imagine that an engaged couple can design a blueprint which will need little or no future revision, there is no question that it is important for them to discuss issues which will impact on both of them. It is also crucial that they examine their feelings for one another and that they come to the honest conclusion that they trust and love each other enough to make the commitment to marriage.

Preparation for marriage should last at least twelve months. As they seek to reach one of the most important decisions they will ever make, engaged couples should be assisted by pastoral ministers and married couples. Programs such as Pre Cana and Engaged Encounter may also provide engaged couples with opportunities to consider the ramifications of the serious step which they contemplate taking.

Divorce and Annulment

The Catholic Church teaches that marriage is monogamous (one husband and one wife) and indissoluble, that is, permanent. The Church recognizes that many spouses are unable to build happy marriages, and it allows them to go through the procedure of civil divorce, but it does not allow remarriage. This is because the bond established by the two can only be broken by death. As long as both divorced spouses are living, neither is free to remarry in the Catholic Church.

Given the large numbers of contemporary American Catholics who divorce, there is an understandable interest in the possibility of the Church's allowing remarriage after divorce. Several arguments are presented in favor of a change of policy. One is that Jesus' words "What God has joined together let no one put asunder" (Matt. 19:6) should be taken as a norm for guidance, not an absolute law. A second is respect for the conscientious discernment of individuals who repent of whatever sins they might have committed in not making their Church-sanctioned marriages work, and who sincerely believe that entering or remaining in a second marriage is morally appropriate. Another argument cites contemporary phenomena such as increased life expectancy and the dissolution of the extended family and reasons that a long life lived in relative isolation is more of a burden than most people are capable of bearing. While it is possible that the official teaching office of the Church may at some future time allow for remarriage after divorce, at present there is no indication of movement in this direction.

An annulment is different from a divorce. It is a declaration by a tribunal (Church court) to the Church that a marriage never legally existed as a sacramental union according to canon law.* If the marriage was not what it appeared to be, that is, a binding commitment of two persons, then it follows that the woman and man are free to enter into true sacramental marriages with other spouses in the Church. The most common psychological reasons for granting annulments are a lack of due discretion and a lack of due competence. The former means that one of the two parties was unable to exercise proper judgment at the time of the marriage (maybe she was pregnant and afraid; maybe he was intoxicated). The latter implies that one party was unable to carry out as promised his/her responsibilities to the marriage. In addition to these relatively new and fairly open-ended grounds for annulment, there are many other technical and procedural indices for declaring that a valid marriage did not take place.[12]

Conclusion

Sexuality is a gift of God. Sex is a pleasurable and meaningful human experience. As saturated as society is with sexual innuendo, it is uncommon to find a correct and balanced appraisal of the meaning of sex. Within the Catholic Church there is a centuries old tradition of respect for the sexual dimension of the human person, but there is also disagreement about such sexual issues as artificial contraception and homosexual genital acts between gay people in committed relationships. This disagreement does not in any way invalidate the wisdom of the tradition, but it does challenge us to continued dialogue and reflection.

Endnotes

1. James B. Nelson, *Embodiment: An Approach to Sexuality and Christian Theology* (Minneapolis: Augsburg, 1978), p. 18.

2. Ibid., p. 110.

3. William J. Bennett, *AIDS and the Education of Our Children* (Washington, DC: U.S. Department of Education, 1987), p. 5.

4. David Knight, *The Good News about Sex* (Cincinnati, OH: St. Anthony Messenger Press, 1979), p. 271.

5. These statistics were taken from Claudia Wallis, "Children Having Children," *Time,* December 9, 1985, pp. 78-90.

6. Michael T. Mannion, *Abortion & Healing, A Cry to Be Whole* (Kansas City: Sheed & Ward, 1986), pp. 61-65. See also Mannion's *Post-Abortion Aftermath,* essays on personal, psychological, pastoral and social effects of abortion. Also, *Catholic Women and Abortion: Stories of Healing,* edited by Pat King, six first-person accounts by post-abortive women. Both published by Sheed & Ward, 1994.

7. For a thorough education about AIDS, cf. Eileen P. Flynn, *AIDS A Catholic Call for Compassion* (Kansas City: Sheed & Ward, 1985) and Eileen P. Flynn, *Teaching About AIDS* (Kansas City: Sheed & Ward, 1988), especially, "What Teachers Need to Know" and Lessons two, three and four, grades 9-12.

8. "Pastoral Constitution on the Church in the Modern World," 50.

9. Joseph Cardinal Ratzinger, "Instruction on Respect for Human Life in Its Origin and on the Dignity of Procreation: Replies to Certain Questions of the Day," March 10, 1987, Part II, Section 5.

10. Report of the Task Force on Gay/Lesbian Issues of the Archdiocese of San Francisco, *Homosexuality and Social Justice,* July 1982, pp. 47-48.

11. Kathleen Fischer Hart and Thomas N. Hart, *The First Two Years of Marriage* (New York: Paulist Press, 1983), p. 19.

12. For a comprehensive guide to annulments, cf., Joseph P. Zwack, *Annulment* (Cambridge MA: Harper & Row, 1983).

Glossary

Abortion: . . . is prohibited even in instances of rape and incest because the fetus thus conceived is innocent and presents no threat to the pregnant woman. Hence, the trauma which surrounds such pregnancies notwithstanding, there is no proportionate reason to consider the fetus an aggressor and to strike out against it. The solution to such unpleasant situations is to support and assist pregnant women, not to destroy their offspring.

Adulterous sexual affairs: . . . are carried on with a person other than one's spouse; these relationships include sexual intercourse.

Angelism: A theory which holds that the state of being an angel is superior to the state of being a human person simply because angels are not troubled by the demands or temptations of the flesh. Angelism fails to give due regard to human nature which God created and Jesus ennobled at the incarnation.

Apostle to the Gentiles: A title given to St. Paul, a Christian convert from Judaism, who carried the message of Jesus to non-Jews living in such places as Cyprus, Antioch, Lystra, Phrygia, Galatia, Philippi, Thesalonica and Athens. (For an account of Paul's dramatic conversion, cf., Acts 9:1-21.)

Asexual means of creating life: Processes such as artificial insemination and human fertilization *in vitro* in which conception does not follow from the act of intercourse but rather occurs as the result of a technological intervention.

Biblical concepts of dominion and stewardship: Concepts inferred from texts such as Genesis 1:28: ". . . fill the earth and subdue it. Have dominion over the fish of the sea, the birds of the air, and all the living things that move on the earth." To have dominion means to have the right to order and use the fruits of the earth. To have stewardship implies the exercise of responsibility in such ordering and use so as to conserve the goods of creation for future generations.

Blood donations: . . . have been screened by U.S. health authoriies since 1984. As a result of the screening, public health officials offer the assurance that today it is almost impossible to become infected with HIV as a result of a blood transfusion.

Canon law: The law which governs the Roman Catholic Church. It is contained in a volume known as the *Code of Canon Law*. A revised and updated Code was issued in 1982. Church law addresses such matters as the principles under which the Code is applied, the roles of ordained, vowed religious and lay Catholics, the means used by the Church to achieve its purpose, procedures and rules governing annulments, and the Church's penal code.

Chaste: An adjective which is used to describe persons who not only avoid unlawful sexual acts, but who also endeavor to be pure in thought and action, modest, and uncontaminated by such things as pornography or an irreverent attitude towards sex.

The covenant of marriage: The solemn promise which spouses make to give of themselves to each other, to be faithful, and not to count the cost of loving. In viewing marriage as a covenant, spouses acknowledge that they are entering into a relationship which entails much more than the fulfilling of a contract. A contract specifies a particular payment for detailed goods or services, and it is only valid if its terms are honored. The self-gift which is marriage is based upon shared love and is meant to be unconditional.

'De facto' existing sexual relations: . . . means that a married couple regularly has sexual intercourse. Since, for infertile married people, conception does not follow sex, the theory has been proposed that they be allowed to seek extra-corporeal technological intervention to achieve pregnancy while turning to intercourse for physical and spiritual intimacy. This theory has been rejected by the Sacred Congregation for the Doctrine of the Faith because it holds that God designed the act of intercourse, and *only* the act of intercourse, as the means for transmitting life.

A desensitized attitude toward all human life: . . . is evident in the lack of concern for the homeless and the military buildup which threatens all of humanity.

Dissent from official procreative teachings: Disagreement with the reasoning behind and/or the conclusions reached by the magisterium on such matters as the absolute prohibition of artificial contraception and extracorporeal conception. Despite widespread dissent by a majority of priests and lay Catholics in the United States, magisterial teaching has remained unchanged.

The divorce rate in the United States: is at an all-time high. In 1985 there were 2,425,000 marriages and 1,187,000 divorces. Currently, one out of two marriages ends in divorce.

The encyclical *Humanae Vitae*: was issued by Pope Paul VI on July 29, 1968. The Latin title means "Of Human Life." This encyclical reaffirmed the teaching of Pius XI (*Casti Connubii*, 1930) and Pius XII (*Humani Generis*, 1950) and stated that the use of artificial contraception is morally wrong.

A faculty: An innate power or ability to perform certain tasks. Conscience is the faculty of the intellect employed by people in the making of moral decisions.

Half-hearted attempts at marriage: refer to entering marriage with the idea that if the relationship is not as beneficial or enjoyable as desired the spouses will simply divorce andthere will be little or no social disapproval of their decision.

Hellenistic dualism: The way of understanding reality of many Greek philosophers, devalues matter and time while stressing the intrinsic worth of the spiritual and unchanging. It is difficult to appreciate the value and dignity of human sexuality within a perspective influenced by Hellenistic dualism.

Homologous IVF and ET: is *in vitro* fertilization using the husband's sperm and wife's ovum (ova) with any resulting embryos transfered into the uterus of the wife-ovum donor.

An indirect abortion: is one result of a hysterectomy performed on a pregnant woman, or the removal of a fallopian tube due to an ectopic pregnancy. The reason a hysterectomy might be performed on a pregnant woman is because of a necessity to remove a cancerous uterus. The direct intent of both patient and surgeon is the removal of the life-threatening pathology. The undesired secondary effect is the death of the fetus which is termed an indirect abortion and is morally tolerable. The same rationale supports removal of an ectopic pregnancy, because, if the fetus were to continue to grow within the tube, the tube would rupture and the patient's life would be in jeopardy.

The magisterium: is the official teaching office of the Roman Catholic Church. The moral teaching of the magisterium is contained in encyclicals, instructions, and pastoral letters.

A mandate: of the Gospel is a charge or commission handed to Jesus' followers to act as Jesus taught his disciples to act.

Moral theologians: are women and men who are trained in the morality of the bible, moral philosophy, and Catholic tradition. They serve the Church by applying this wisdom and theory to contemporary moral questions.

Official teaching: is doctrine which is formulated by an official, hierarchical teacher or teaching body, e.g., a pope, a pope in union with the bishops throughout the world, a Vatican congregation such as the Sacred Congregation for the Doctrine of the Faith, or an episcopal conference, i.e., the bishops of a particular region, state, or country.

Patriarchal religions: are those which stress the superiority of the masculine, claiming that the male sex governs because such is the divine plan. Since the concept of masculinity includes the assumption that the male is normatively heterosexual and dominant over the female, patriarchal religions have an ingrained bias against homosexual men who do not enter relationships of dominance over women.

Personalist philosophers: were twentieth century scholars such as Dietrich von Hildebrand and Heribert Doms who influenced the Church to understand marriage as the loving union of husband and wife rather than primarily as an institution ordained for the procreation of offspring.

Relativism: is an approach to ethical judgment according to which objective moral principles do not hold significant force. Instead, an individual's inclination to follow one or another course, based on feelings or hunches, is accepted as the norm. The result is a permissive moral climate in which people "do their own thing," and manifest little concern about objective standards governing conduct.

Revisionist moral theologians: disagree with some of the magisterium's absolute prohibitions of sexual and procreative practices. Such people as the Rev. Charles Curran, Philip S. Keane, S.S., and the authors of Human Sexuality (Paulist Press, 1977) have been characterized as revisionists.

Rigorism: An approach to morality which holds that the most stringent letter of the law must always be applied.

The Sacred Congregation for the Doctrine of the Faith: is an office of the Vatican which presents the official teaching of the Church and which examines the writings and teachings of Catholic theologians.

St. Augustine: (354-430), a bishop in North Africa, was a great theologian whose writings had a significant influence on the development of Christian doctrine.

Testing done during pregnancy: can be either by amniocentesis or chorionic villi sampling. In both cases analysis of uterine fluid discloses whether or not a fetus is afflicted with a genetic disease.

Venial sin: An offense against God which diminishes a person in his/her humanity but does not seriously undermine the person's relationship with God.

Vocation: The choice to lead one's life in one of three ways: as a married spouse, a committed single person, or a vowed celibate (priest, religious brother or sister). In the Christian tradition people tend to assume that God calls them (*vocare* is Latin for "to call") to the life for which they find themselves best suited. All Christians also recognize a common call to follow Jesus, i.e., to be disciples.

Discussion Questions

1. Discuss three reasons for coming to a very positive assessment of human sexuality.

2. In your opinion, what harms are caused by thinking of sexual intercourse in solely recreational terms? In answering this question, be specific, and include instances of both personal and social harm.

3. What concrete steps can society take to reverse the sexual promiscuity of adolescents?

4. Discuss the ways in which it is possible to exploit people sexually, and suggest what feelings are experienced by people who are sexually exploited.

5. Teen pregnancy is a tragedy. Why does the Catholic Church teach that abortion is not a moral solution?

6. How do you think a young Christian should approach the unitive and procreative dimensions of sex? What is the instruction of the Church in this regard?

7. What does the Catholic Church teach about homosexual acts? What do dissenting moral theologians contend?

8. If your friends told you that they were thinking about living together, but were not sure that it was the right thing to do, in what kind of a process would you suggest that they engage?

9. Describe the kinds of personal attributes which people need to have in order to build successful marriages.

10. What changes do yuppies and dinks need to make in order to make their marriages "Christian" marriages?

Additional Reading

Eileen P. Flynn, *AIDS A Catholic Call for Compassion* (Kansas City: Sheed & Ward, 1985).

Eileen P. Flynn, *Human Fertilization in Vitro: A Catholic Moral Perspective* (Lanham, MD: University Press of America, 1984).

John F. Harvey, O.S.F.S., *The Homosexual Person* (San Francisco: Ignatius Press, 1987).

Philip S. Keane, S.S., *Sexual Morality* (New York: Paulist Press, 1977).

Odile M. Liebard, ed; *Official Catholic Teachings: Love and Sexuality* (Wilmington, NC: McGrath, 1978).

Michael T. Mannion, *Abortion & Healing, A Cry to Be Whole* (Kansas City: Sheed & Ward, 1986).

John J. McNeill, *The Church and the Homosexual* (Kansas City: Sheed, Andrews and McMeel, 1976); 3rd edition, (Boston: Beacon Press, 1988).

James B. Nelson, *Embodiment: An Approach to Sexuality and Christian Theology* (Minneapolis: Augsburg, 1978).

12

Facing Death and Finding Freedom

The Hard Truth

Contemporary culture glamorizes the young, the fit, the energetic—those bursting with life. Life *is* a good and youth *is* a season to be celebrated. However, we have a problem if we are unable to value the other stages of life, and, especially, if we lack the wisdom and courage to seek out the meaning of death. Is it accurate to think of ourselves as people who are fearful of confronting death? In spite of the pioneering work of Dr. Elisabeth Kubler-Ross, the offering of courses on death in high schools and colleges, and the availability of counseling and self-help groups for people with terminal illnesses and the bereaved, in general, the way in which we handle death seems to suggest as much. We tend to keep dying people in antiseptic hospital rooms, out of sight, so as not to have to be too close to them. We feel awkward when faced with terminal diseases, pain management, lapsing consciousness, and the spiritual and emotional struggles of dying people. Once death comes we quickly arrange for the embalming of the deceased, hoping that the undertaker will do a good job, muting the harsh reality of death with state of the art cosmetics. We take care to shield children from death, frequently excluding them from the dying process, wakes and funerals, in order to spare them sad experiences. And, because we feel it necessary to deny that death affects children, we do not encourage them to ask questions about death, express bewilderment, or engage in a grieving process. Thus, adults tend to pass their discomfort with death on to the next generation.

When we talk about death we choose our words carefully, trying to disguise the harsh and distasteful nature of what has occurred. People "pack their bags," "pass on," "pass away," "move on," "fall asleep," "go on a long journey," "enter the pearly gates," and so on. The reality that a healthy vibrant person developed an incurable form of cancer, lost fifty or sixty pounds, endured operations, chemotherapy and radiation without much benefit, suffered from pain which was difficult to control, went through a traumatic spiritual and emotional process before accepting his/her disease and dying, and did, in fact, die, is sometimes glossed over. Death is a hard truth to accept. And it is much, much harder to accept the truth of one's own death than to accept the fact of another's demise.

In spite of all our attempts to put death out of sight and out of mind, each of us is aware, at least occasionally, of the facticity of our own death. Often this awareness is experienced when we get news of the death of a friend or family member, or when we attend a wake or funeral. We know that "It could have been me," and we feel relief because it was someone else. When we lose a close friend or loved one to death, we have no choice but to accept the fact that the dead person is separated from us. As people mature, many grow in the ability to deal with their own mortality. Responsible adults do such things as make wills, buy burial plots and prearrange funerals. They learn from their own illnesses and loss of energy that life is a fragile commodity which eventually ebbs away. But young people have a much harder time accepting the fact that they will die. They leave their friends' funerals clinging to the myth of their own immortality: they count on at least another sixty or seventy years of life. And, while they *know* that they are kidding themselves, they choose to believe that they have more than enough time left in which to do everything they want; they refuse to become preoccupied with morbid thoughts or activities.

Trying to evade the fact of our own eventual demise does nothing to alleviate the pain which we experience as a result of the deaths of people who are close to us. People who grieve feel sad, lonely, hurt, angry and diminished because a person whom they love is no longer present to them. Most people know what grief is like—how it is after a loved one dies—but no one knows what it is like to be dead. The recounting of life after life experiences* notwithstanding, no one has ever come back from the dead to tell us what awaits us. And there is no denying that the unknown aspects of death can be terrifying.

Many people, perhaps most, are afflicted by a conspiracy of silence surrounding death, the perennially frightening nature of death, and the inclination to assume that issues of death can be postponed indefinitely. At the same time, each of us must contend with the possibility that universal death could occur over a period of hours or days, that it could be death for every person and for all of creation, and that it could be accomplished by the ferociously destructive power of nuclear weapons. Should this happen, there will be no more appointed times for men and women to die, and no more lives to be lived. The bleak possibility of a nuclear holocaust triggers a number of defensive responses: "Why worry about forces over which I have no power?" "We are probably going to have a nuclear war, and nothing can be done to change things." "Things are getting better all the time. A nuclear holocaust is impossible. No one would ever be foolish enough to push the button." Indifference, hopelessness and naievete have a way of combining to erode the conviction that the human community has the responsibility to prevent a nuclear holocaust which would lead to the death of all life. Having the capacity willfully to destroy creation also situates the issue of death within a radically new context.

Death causes suffering to those who die and those who grieve. It is the kind of evil from which we spontaneously recoil. There is a mystery in suffering and evil, one which serious students should examine. The appendix to this chapter, "The Mystery of Suffering and Evil," by Thomas L. Sheridan, S.J., considers the nature of mystery, suffering and evil, seeking to press the limits of intelligibility as far as is possible. By reflecting upon this article you will come to appreciate the philosophical and theological context in which death is correctly situated.

Some Hard Questions

Temporary or permanent breaks in the wall of denial give rise to some hard questions. Why must I die? Why does death have to be so frightening? Why are there so many tragic deaths: teenagers killed in accidents, athletes dying from drug overdoses, young men and women—even babies—enduring slow, painful deaths from AIDS, despairing, gifted people committing suicide? Life is fairer to people who live a long time, experience a weariness toward the end, and die peacefully, surrounded by attentive friends and loved ones. In the scriptures, a long, full life is considered a blessing bestowed on good people. In Deuteronomy we read: "Honor your father and your mother as the Lord, your God, has commanded you that you may have a long life and prosperity in the land which the Lord, your God, is giving you" (Deut. 5:16). And Proverbs declares: "The good man leaves an inheritance to his children's children" (Proverbs 13:22).

What, then, are we to think when a young child dies of leukemia? That the child was cursed along with the grieving family? That there was some fault which resulted in a heartbreaking death out of season? While it is undoubtedly true that men and women are blessed if they enjoy a measure of prosperity and have satisfying relationships with their children and grandchildren, it does not follow that people who are not so fortunate are cursed. It is very difficult to offer sensitive advice to people who feel devastated as a result of sudden, tragic death. But there are some Christian insights which may be helpful:

• People become much more sensitive to the needs of others as a result of their own personal suffering; they also tend to develop a deep understanding of what is truly valuable.

• Not attaining one's full potential should not be considered a fault or deficiency. Each person, no matter what his/her age, is incomplete at the moment of death. It is only through union with God that persons experience completion.

• There are not two categories of people, the fortunate and the unfortunate, with the former immune to the pain and suffering of the latter. In contrast, there is one human family, and all are somehow diminished by the pain of those who suffer.

• People who live long lives and seem to have everything going for them have not been totally spared from suffering. Although the duration and extent of their problems is not apparent, they, too, have experienced difficulties.

• A tombstone reads, "Weep for the mourners, not for the dead." The lesson it teaches the living is how foolish it is to rail against death or pity the dead. There is every reason to empathize with the sadness and loneliness of the grieving, but no justification for feeling sorry for the person who is at peace with God.

Incidents of suicide present us with a different set of questions. A person who commits suicide chooses death. Death is considered preferable to life. Suicide is the strategy which is adopted to cope with unmanageable problems. Family members and friends are shocked in the aftermath of a suicide. They feel angry, guilty, confused and very desolate. In coming to grips with what happened, they do not seem to know where to begin. They know that God gives life and believe that it is God alone who should take life away. They know that problems can seem overwhelming, but are bewildered by the desperation of a person who turns to death instead of asking them for help. They are unsure about how to phrase their question: How could life, which is the basic good enjoyed by every living person, be so completely impossible? Or, most people want to deny death, keep death at least at arms length distance. Why did the person we love seek death out and embrace it?

There are no easy answers to why people commit suicide, but there are some clues. Each year in the United States more than five thousand young people kill themselves. Another five hundred thousand attempt suicide. The suicide rate among people aged fifteen to twenty-four has more than doubled in the past twenty years, and suicide is the second leading cause of death among college students. Two reasons are generally given for the large incidence of suicide: the confusion which results from widespread social upheaval, combined with severe psychological problems.

There is no question that U.S. society has endured radical and far-reaching changes since the end of World War II. Traditional gender roles have been challenged, people are unsure of the purpose of life, because of the prevalence of divorce the nuclear family is in crisis, the extended family, with its built-in support system, is a thing of the past, religions no longer exercise significant influence, there is widespread use of illegal drugs and abuse of alcohol, and there is pervasive anxiety about environmental pollution, terrorism and nuclear weapons. Young people are affected by the instability and malaise which surround them. In addition, they are apt to be subject to a considerable amount of pressure to get good grades, qualify for a prestigious position, and "amount to something." Trying to cope with more pressure than they can handle while being confused about who they are and what life means, can lead to grave personal problems, and, tragically, sometimes ends in suicide.

Why is it that most young people manage to survive pressure and confusion, while others do not? What psychological factors predispose a person to take his/her life? There is no completely satisfactory answer to these questions, but it is apparent that people who choose to kill themselves tend to see their deaths differently from those who do not commit suicide. They may suffer from a deep protracted depression and, as a result, be bereft of any positive feelings. In such a state, suicide may appear very appealing. According to Francine Klagsbrun, many young people choose suicide because of a romantic attitude toward death or because of their fantasies:

> (Romantic attitude:) When young people contemplate suicide they often think of it as a long, peaceful sleep or interlude that will somehow make things better. Or they picture death as a way to punish others or to make others show love for them. And, always, somewhere in their minds, is the belief that they will be present to benefit from the punishment their death has inflicted or the love it has aroused.

> Lonely and unhappy young people, too, may build fantasies about death that give them deep satisfaction. Suicidal teenage girls sometimes picture death as a lover who will seduce them and carry them away. Young people who have lost a parent may dream of death as a way to be reunited with their loved one. Young lovers may make suicide pacts to immortalize their love through joint deaths.[1]

We will live fuller, happier lives if we accept the fact of our own deaths, while recognizing that we do not have the right to cause our death. In order to accept death a person needs to ameliorate the denial and morbidity which make death a fearsome subject. We would be much less likely to deny death if we talked openly about it and did not attempt to hide it from our sight. Allowing dying relatives to spend their final days at home, and keeping company with them as they die, would lead to the recognition that death is a natural part of life. As far as morbidity is concerned, it seems as if no one wants to stand accused of excessive preoccupation with gloomy matters. But to use the determination not to be morbid as an excuse for never reflecting on the nature of death is unproductive self-deception. By being so dishonest one prevents oneself from knowing the truth and from achieving the freedom to walk in the light of the truth.

Dying: A Hard Process

A generation or two ago people were apt to pray: From a sudden and unprovided death, deliver me, O Lord. They wanted to be prepared for death. Preparation included taking care of pressing concerns, such as paying debts and arranging to provide for family members; reconciling with those from whom one was alienated; and making peace with God by confessing one's sins* and receiving God's pardon. After one's spiritual and temporal affairs were in order, one considered oneself ready to meet God. The final days or weeks of life were seen as a blessing because they provided an opportunity for attending to serious, somber, unfinished business.

Medical technology has had an enormous impact upon the contemporary experience of dying. Respirators and various methods of artificial feeding have resulted in lengthening the time it takes to die. Dying people who have put their affairs in order frequently experience profound weariness and discomfort because modern technological advances make it so difficult to die. Although people today do not wish for unprovided deaths, many have come to think of dying quickly, in a warm and caring nonhospital setting, as a very real blessing.

Dying entails being engaged in a difficult physical, spiritual and emotional process. There are no data available concerning how stressful dying is for men and women who are surrounded by the machines and other apparatus found in modern hospitals. We are indebted, however, to Elisabeth Kubler-Ross, a physician, writer and thanatologist,* who has given us an inciteful analysis of the emotional tasks faced by dying persons. The process people engage in after they hear a terminal diagnosis consists in five predictable stages. Each successive stage needs to be worked through so that death can be faced with a measure of serenity.

The first stage is denial and isolation. The news that one has an illness which is going to end in death will most likely trigger the response, "No, not me, it cannot be true." Denial is a psychological defense which is employed until such time as a person can mobilize less radical defenses (e.g., general acceptance of the diagnosis combined with occasional lapses into denial). For the overwhelming majority of people it is hard to face the truth that death is imminent because of a belief in the myth of immortality. The problems of dealing with the shocking news of a terminal diagnosis are compounded by the isolation many patients experience. Family members, friends, and hospital personnel may be uneasy about death and uncomfortable with the dying. For this reason, they may leave the dying patient alone, or avoid discussions with the patient which focus on feelings about death and dying.

The second stage is characterized by strong feelings of anger. The patient may not be in complete denial, but may consider impending death very unfair. Anger, rage, envy and resentment fester in the dying person, and are projected almost at random onto caretakers and visitors. While it is hard to deal with the anger of a dying person, knowing what the dying are going through can make it easier. For some, death means that their life's work will never be finished; for others, it means that they will not have time for the retirement which they anticipated. All dying persons experience a loss of power and control, and this is hard to accept. The dying need to be allowed to express their feelings of anger and helped to understand the causes of this emotion. Repressing angry feelings is psychologically detrimental; people are enabled to move beyond anger only if they learn to acknowledge and deal with this feeling.

The third stage which people experience on the road to acceptance of death is known as bargaining. This stage is characterized by futile attempts to exercise control. People want to postpone death, so they try to strike bargains with God. "Please don't take me until after my daughter's wedding, my son's college graduation, or the completion of my project." Part of the bargain is the patient's promise to be content if this one request is granted. However, few patients can be counted on to keep their promises. The finality of death is so hard to accept that dying persons tend to keep trying to extend their deadlines through more bargaining.

The fourth stage described by Kubler-Ross is that of deep and pervasive depression. A sense of great loss is experienced by the person for whom death is close at hand. The loss of health is accompanied by other losses: the terminally ill are unable to work, they are frequently forced to exhaust their savings to pay medical bills and they are no longer able to carry out their roles in the family. It is helpful to dying patients to allow them their sadness; they are in the process of losing everything and everyone they love. They need affirmation and support as they work through their anguish and anxieties. Sometimes this support takes the form of reassurance that the family is adjusting to new circumstances; at other times it consists in the gentle presence of care takers and loved ones who are not uncomfortable with the grief and sadness with which the dying are burdened.

The final stage which dying patients come to is that of acceptance of death. Those who accept their fate have given up their numbed disbelief, angry rage, bargaining for more time, and the debilitating sadness which accompanies depression. They are ready to die. Their readiness is not characterized by eagerness or happy expectancy. "It is almost void of feelings. It is as if the pain had gone, the struggle is over, and there comes a time for 'the final rest before the long journey.'"[2] The dying appreciate the quiet company of people who are willing simply to be present to them. Those who take time to sit at the bedsides of the dying learn through their experiences that death is not something to be feared; it is the inevitable final stage of life.

Christian Beliefs about Death

While it is possible to reduce the amount of denial and terror which surround death, it is not possible to completely neutralize death so that it loses its sting. If given the choice, many people would prefer not to die. Still others would choose to refashion death, eliminating the suffering and pain which accompany illness and the dreaded separations caused by death. Why are mortals ultimately powerless before death, and why is death so harsh? The Christian faith teaches that death as we know it is a consequence of sin. Sin is part and parcel of the human condition. Each and every human person commits sins, and, even before the commission of specific, concrete, personal sins, men and women are aware of a brokenness or division within themselves. The weakened condition which is actualized in sinful deeds is called original sin. The theological notion of original sin is very complex, but one of the simplest ways of explaining it is to say that it is the shared human tendency to pride, disobedience, and rebelliousness toward God. The pain and anguish which are experienced in connection with death are a consequence of the original sin which affects all humans. If men and women did not consider themselves wiser than God, if they did not seek their own satisfaction at the expense of their neighbors, and if they were not so lazy and self-centered, theologians speculate that death would not be a traumatic experience.

Christians believe that after death there is judgment. Strictly speaking, it is incorrect to refer to the moment after death, because death brings entry into eternity, and eternity is a timeless present which is without end. In spite of this fact, we are accustomed to cite a time immediately after death at which each person is required to render an account of how talents and abilities were used. This event is called the particular judgment. By acknowledging that we will have to account for how we used our time and talents, one admits the crucial importance of using this one decisive lifetime well. Because the Christian anticipates a face-to-face meeting with God for the purpose of accounting for his/her stewardship, there is ample motivation for conscientiously approaching one's responsibilities. However, it would be an error to fear meeting a God who is disdainful toward human imperfection and who is impossibly demanding. Like the psalmist we should feel confident that a humbled, contrite heart will not be spurned by God (Ps. 51:19), and find courage in knowing that our Father-Mother God has compassion for us in our weakness.

Moses veiled his face when he saw the burning bush because he was afraid to look at God. (Ex. 3:6) Peter, James and John were with Jesus on Mount Tabor when he was transfigured, i.e., manifested divine characteristics, and they were so moved that they fell on their faces. (Matt. 17:1-6) The scriptures disclose how awesome and frightening it is for humans to come into proximity to the divine. One reason is because God is all-good and all-holy, and humans are tarnished by sin. Most people die still bearing the marks of sin. We live our entire lifetimes without completely overcoming the sinfulness within ourselves: the pride, covetousness, lust, anger, gluttony, envy and sloth. (This compilation is known as the seven deadly sins.) As a result, we believe that it is necessary to be purified before we come into God's presence. We hold that the process of being purified is accomplished in a state called purgatory. Belief in the existence of purgatory is really trust in the justice and mercy of God. People who die sudden deaths or people who struggle unsuccessfully to the end to conquer their sins, are given a chance to set things right. We need to repent of the sins we still have at death so that we will become holy enough to look upon the face of God. Although no one knows what the process of purgation will entail, it is incorrect to think of purgatory as some kind of temporary torture chamber. Instead, we should consider it yet another gift which the all-loving God holds out to us.

Just as God will render judgment on each individual, so Christians expect that all humankind will be judged by Jesus, the Son of God, at the end of time. This event is referred to as the last judgment or the general judgment. In the presence of all the persons who have ever lived, the general judgment will affirm the fundamental truths which Christians believe:

> . . . that history is the work of God, that its center is Jesus Christ, and that its moving force is the Holy Spirit. This is at the same time, the consummation of all things,* (and) the disclosure of God's acceptance of the world in the incarnation.*[3]

We do not know when time will cease, or what it will be like to be at the general judgment. However, the gospel reveals through the metaphor of wheat and weeds (Matt. 13:30) that at the last judgment we will see clearly how people who cooperated with God's grace (saving help) contributed to the establishment of God's kingdom, and how those who turned from God's way caused misery and suffering to themselves and others. At the general judgment the kingdom of God will finally be realized in its totality. Those who have loved and cared for themselves and their neighbors will experience an eternity of unimaginable delight.

Christians believe the promise which Jesus made to them:

> I am the resurrection and the life: whoever believes in me, though he/she should die, will come to life; and whoever is alive and believes in me will never die. (John 11:25-26)

Christians understand death as an experience of transition, and profess faith that in death life is changed, not taken away. The human mind is very limited in respect to its ability to comprehend what heaven will be like. The scriptures provide us with some hints of what is to come. Mark says that in heaven people will interrelate in a new way: "When people rise from the dead, they neither marry nor are given in marriage, but live like angels in heaven" (Mark 12:25). A much less uniform picture is suggested by Jesus who declared: "In my Father's house there are many mansions" (John 14:2). It is not easy to imagine on what basis individual persons will be assigned to particular mansions, but this only underscores how little we actually know of what lies beyond death.

Heaven is reputed to be a delightful place. St. Paul wrote: "Eye has not seen, ear has not heard, nor has it so much as dawned on humankind what God has prepared for those who love him" (1 Cor. 2:9). And Paul told us that only in heaven can we know what it is that we will be given: "Now we see as through a veil darkly, but then we shall see face to face" (1 Cor. 13:12).

Theologians teach that the beatific vision, i.e., the direct, immediate contemplation of God, constitutes the essence of heaven. The sight of God, being united to God, and being in communion with God are understood as the realities which will provide persons with unmeasurable satisfaction.

Going to heaven, being in heaven, enjoying the ultimate degree of happiness, seems to encapsulate the human expectation of heaven. The words we speak in connection with heaven—peace, rest, joy—and the ethereal images we have of heaven—fluffy clouds and choirs of angels, strike us as pleasing—and unnerving. Contemporary men and women are unlikely to exhibit a strong desire to be in heaven. To the extent that listening to angels and looking at God sound like an eternal church service, they are afraid that heaven will be boring. They anticipate a place with a perfect climate but not many interesting activities.

It is not necessary for the churches to hire marketing consultants to devise ways to make heaven seem attractive. Instead, what needs to be done is to help people understand how limited is their ability to comprehend what they will experience within the categories which they have at hand. In addition, the spiritual dimension of the person needs to be discovered and revered so that the deep, persistent longings of the human heart can be identified. St. Augustine* put this longing into words: "Our hearts are restless and they will not rest until they rest in Thee, O! Lord." In heaven we will receive the fulfillment of all our human desires. According to the Book of Revelation:

> Never again shall they know hunger or thirst, nor shall the sun or its heat beat down on them, for the lamb on the throne will shepherd them. He will lead them to springs of lifegiving water and God will wipe away every tear from their eyes. (Rev. 7:16-17)

Christians believe that the creative intention of God is for them to find a generous measure of happiness during their lifetimes on earth and the fullness of happiness in the hereafter. They further believe that each and every person is given the opportunity to earn eternal life with God. Faith in God is the precondition for the attainment of eternal life. In the Gospel of Mark we read, "The person who believes in the good news and accepts baptism* will be saved; the person who refuses to believe in it will be condemned" (Mk. 16:16).

Believers who trust in God, lead good lives, and who are committed to action on behalf of justice have received the promise of eternal life. While the fate of faithful believers is undisputed, there remains much concern about what ultimately happens to persons who through no fault of their own die without faith. If there are people who never once close their eyes and pray with their hearts, "Dear God, I believe in you, I love you, and I want to conform my choices to your will," what happens to them? According to theologian Monika K. Hellwig, there is no warrant for doubting God's engagement with people who appear to be nonbelievers, or for underestimating the value of their responses to God:

> There was through the ages a rather persistent sense that persons who grow to adulthood could not help but be confronted with the fundamental exigence* of God on their lives, no matter what the religious or nonreligious language used to express this exigence. Though the explanations varied, the predominant sense of the tradition seems to be that all adults are sooner or later, perhaps even at the moment of death itself, confronted with the call to, and opportunity for, faith, hope and charity in response to the saving God.[4]

If there is a final option, a last chance to decide whom one loves and what one's life means, this opportunity is surely a manifestation of God's loving relationship to each person. For believers who cross over into eternal life without having sincerely and completely repented of all their sins (which is probably the vast majority of us), as well as for people who have never been able to understand why they should believe in God, or how they could, there will finally be an encounter with an all-loving Parent. At this encounter the pieces will fall into place and each of us will realize what dynamics properly fit the human relationship to God. We will then understand how appropriate it is for us to worship and love God, to rest in God's peace, and this will represent our last irrevocable choice.

The most terrifying aspect of eschatology (the study of the last things) is hell. The questions we most frequently ask say more about our fear and confusion than they do about God's graciousness and human freedom. How hot does it get in hell? Is it crowded? Does hell really exist? The fire and torments of hell should be understood as metaphorical because these symbols are used to point to the dreadful suffering which would be endured by anyone who totally rejected God's claim to love and allegiance. The Catholic Church has never taught that hell is populated by specific individuals who have been damned. What the Church teaches is that free people can choose to damn themselves to an eternity of deprivation. The reason people can opt not to find deep satisfaction in God's presence is because God is too gracious to force a friendship upon an unwilling person. God is too respectful of human freedom to force people to believe or to surrender in love. Because people are free to say yes to God, they are also free to say no to God, and this freedom even extends to the choice of hell. The fact that our eternal destiny depends on how we live this one life should prompt a thoughtful respect for our autonomy. The decisions which determine the moral and religious directions of our lives, as well as the fundamental option which we make, (cf., Chapter 2) are of the utmost importance.

The Dogmatic Constitution on the Church (*Lumen Gentium**), one of the documents of Vatican Council II, presents a restatement of the long-established belief of the Church in the communion of saints. The so-called "communion of saints" is the name given to a conviction that there is a union among all who share in the life of Christ: the church triumphant in heaven, the church suffering in purgatory, and the church militant on earth. The council fathers wrote:

> . . . in various ways and degrees we all partake in the same love for God and neighbor, and all sing the same hymn of glory to our God. For all who belong to Christ, having his Spirit, form one Church and cleave together in Him. Therefore the union of the wayfarers with the brethren who have gone to sleep in the peace of Christ is not in the least interrupted. On the contrary, according to the perennial faith of the

church, it is strengthened through the exchange of spiritual goods.[5]

By "exchange of spiritual goods" is meant that the living offer efficacious prayers for persons who are being purified, and that the just in heaven intercede on behalf of those on earth and in purgatory. The limits of our language become apparent when we try to describe in precise terms what we who belong to Christ can effect on each other's behalf. We introduce a pragmatic element into a mystery which defies concretization and quantification. The doctrine of the communion of saints is only intelligible within the context of the reality which it proclaims: All faithful Christians living and dead are united in Christ. This connectedness provides inspiration and encouragement.

Christians believe in the resurrection of the body. At the end of human history, when time and space no longer exist as we know them, we believe that we will be alive as full human beings, and not just as our spiritual selves. We may be accustomed to think of the time which elapses between the individual's death and the general judgment as an interval when the soul is in purgatory or heaven and the body is in the process of decomposing (or decomposed). Then, when the trumpet sounds, an invigorated body and a fully cleansed soul will come together to enjoy a new form of life in God's eternal kingdom. While this kind of explanation makes use of familiar categories, it would be wrong to think of it as a blueprint for what is going to transpire. It would be more realistic to learn to live with the firm hope of the resurrection while admitting our ignorance of how it will actually happen. And it might make more sense to think of our resurrection destiny in terms of psychic wholeness and loving union with one another and God rather than in dualistic terms of reassembling the higher and lower parts of the person.

Facing Death

Life is a series of dyings and risings. The person who struggles to break a bad habit and replace it with a good one endures a kind of death and resurrection. If we quit smoking, stop nagging, or overcome a disorganized approach to school work, we witness the death of a form of self-indulgence. And we emerge as better people; in a sense we are new women and men who are more pleased about ourselves.

There are many contemporary movements whose aim is to make society more just and humane. These movements unfold along similar lines. Situations of injustice are exposed and confronted. Ways of correcting the injustices are delineated. Consciousness raising, education and political action are undertaken in order to effect change. And, finally, after an extensive effort, more equitable arrangements become the norm. Society dies to its old way of being and is reconstituted in a new form.

It is also possible to witness the death of destructive patterns of relationship. The ordering of human relationships according to models of domination and submission is ingrained and difficult to alter. Nevertheless, recognizing how inherently unreasonable these ways of relating are, and resolving to muster the humility and determination necessary to bring about change, will lead to the establishment of liberated relational contexts. If we come to appreciate personal and social instances of dying as positive events because they usher in new ways of living, we may come to a more positive assessment of the death we will surely die. To the extent that we separate death from resurrection, we distort the dynamic nature of the transition which death effects and significantly increase the fearsomeness of our inevitable fate.

People who are caught up in hectic, unreflective lives are not apt to look within themselves to comprehend why they must die. However, those who dare to enter the deepest centers of themselves unfailingly discover a longing for the satisfaction of their desires. They recognize a need to become integrated, to have all the parts of themselves fit together in a harmonious way. They want to be sated. They want things to be right within themselves and in the milieu in which they exist, they want to be one with their sisters and brothers, because they are sincerely interested in the well-being of others. While they seek to satisfy their desires during their lifetimes, the limits of the human condition inevitably force them to acknowledge that the deepest longings of their hearts will only be met by the communion with God and neighbor which they anticipate in the final phase of life.

In spite of all that faith and reason have to tell us, it would be wrong to say that we have no fear, confusion and ambivalence about death. Instead, we should be honest about our feelings and seek to work through them so that they no longer exert unseemly power over us. The need to end the conspiracy of silence surrounding death is apparent; it would be much more wholesome to allow people to talk freely about dying, death and the afterlife. Seeking psychological counseling about the particular anxieties we experience in relation to our own deaths and the trauma connected to the deaths of loved ones would also be of benefit.

When we admit that death is a fact of life we begin to develop a sounder and more balanced approach to living. The purpose of life becomes apparent: For a limited period of time it falls to each of us to use our talents, and to love God, our neighbors and ourselves. Our moral choices are significant because they ennoble us or destroy us, and they have either positive or negative effects on the human community. Life is not meant to be about accumulating wealth or attaining positions of power; rather, it is a season during which wise people reject the folly of idolatry.* After attending a wake, a funeral, or a burial service, most of us are keenly aware that life is a precious gift. Life should be profoundly respected, and we should value only that which is worthwhile. When we are able to incorporate this insight into our consciousness we are freed to enjoy our lives and attain our human potential.

A Hard Sadness: The Grieving Process

Whether the death of a friend or loved one is sudden or long in coming, it leaves survivors sad, lonely, and, frequently shocked. The issues the grieving face range from "How can I go on?" to "Will I ever feel okay again?" Granger E. Westberg, in a very helpful book entitled *Good Grief*,[6] describes a ten-stage process of grieving, and contends that grieving well contributes to growth and the establishing of new patterns of interaction. As with most stage theories, Westberg maintains that there are variations and overlapping in the way people actually work through their individual losses.

Stage One: A temporary state of shock keeps a person from fully realizing that a loved one is dead and will no longer be part of the family. Being in shock enables mourners to buy some time before facing the tragic finality of death.

Stage Two: After the shock begins to wear off, emotions well up within us. It is at this stage that we break down and cry our hearts out. It is beneficial to express our sorrow with tears; bottling up our emotions causes us additional unnecessary pain.

Stage Three: We find ourselves in the depths of despair and feel certain that no one ever grieved as we grieve. There is no brightness or warmth in our lives. There is a gnawing conviction that things will never get better. But depressions pass, and those who see us through our time of desperation are a source of consolation.

Stage Four: Psychosomatic illnesses may be experienced because physical and emotional health are intertwined. When we try to deny or repress our grief the energy we use in repressing it can cause such physical symptoms as headaches, digestive distress, nervous disorders, etc.

Stage Five: We are unable to do our work, and find that we cannot concentrate. As a result, we become panicked and distressed, sometimes wondering if we are losing our minds. It is helpful for grieving people to know that panic is normal.

Stage Six: We feel guilty about some of the things we did (or did not do) to (for) the deceased. Some feelings of guilt are appropriate; others are neurotic. Since it is hard for a grieving person to make distinctions about the kind of guilt which is being experienced, it is important to talk things over with someone who understands what is going on. We need to know that God graciously forgives us for the deliberate wrongs we have done, and that we will find peace of mind only after we stop holding ourselves to unreasonable standards of behavior, which cause neurotic guilt.

Stage Seven: Normal feelings of anger and resentment surface, and need to be dealt with. We should not be ashamed that we have these feelings, but should admit them, seeking to move beyond them. It is normal to be angry with God, with the doctors, even with our loved one who abandoned us by dying.

Stage Eight: We resist getting back to normal, preferring to be alone in our grief. We fear going back into the world and tackling new situations. And we feel uncomfortable because we think that no one wants to know how preoccupied we still are with the loss of our loved one.

Stage Nine: We begin to feel hope. For some people, this happens after a short time; for others, it takes much longer. We find new friends, new mates, or new reasons to walk the road of life once again.

Stage Ten: We emerge from our loss and our struggle as new people. Now we can empathize with others who suffer as we did, and we greet each day of life with gratitude for our conviction that God is with us is firmer than it ever was before.

Hard Decisions Associated with Death and Dying

Medical technology is constantly growing in sophistication. As a result, those of us who do not die sudden deaths will probably have to make complex decisions regarding the manner in which we want to die. Human decisions are not made in a vacuum; they reflect our judgments and values. It is not easy to describe in a comprehensive way the attitude people should have toward their dying, but it is possible to identify some basic Christian convictions.

Christians hold that life is a great good. Embodied existence is the only form of life which we actually know and it is the precondition for entering into relationship with self, others and God. Death, on the other hand, is seen as an evil event because it means the termination of the only kind of existence we know as well as separation from everyone and everything we love. Christians believe, however, that life is not an absolute to which we must cling no matter what, and death is not to be absolutely resisted. For the Christian, God alone is absolute and it is proper to direct the totality of our being only to God. In view of these convictions Christians reject both vitalism and euthanasia. Vitalism is a commitment to preserve biological life at all costs, with the employment of every available treatment until it becomes completely impossible to stall death any longer. The vitalist is far more concerned with living as long as is humanly possible than with letting go of life when it is apparent that death is imminent. An approach to dying which is the complete opposite of vitalism is the advocacy of euthanasia. Some people see no benefit in the suffering that goes with dying, and so they argue that dying patients have the right to kill themselves in order to avoid pain. They are also apt to argue that it is morally permissible for health care workers, family members or friends to kill patients who request a quick end to their misery.

Both vitalism and euthanasia are at odds with the way Roman Catholics traditionally approach the morality of dying. According to Catholic medical ethics, patients have a responsibility to take reasonable care of their health throughout their lives and during their dying. Patients have the right to choose among the options available to them those treatments which offer a reasonable hope of benefit. They are not obligated to submit to medical procedures, medications, etc., which are excessively burdensome, which offer little potential benefit, or which are essentially useless. For example, people with very advanced kidney disease are justified in discontinuing dialysis. Likewise, people who are in the final stages of their battles with cancer are not morally required to submit to experimental therapies or to undergo additional chemotherapy. Furthermore, the next of kin of comatose patients for whom there is no possibility of recovery to a state of cognitive awareness have the right to request that such equipment as respirators be turned off so that the patient can die.

It is a good idea for people to take the time to determine their own approach to death. At times of crisis we are at a distinct disadvantage because we discover that we cannot think clearly. There is much wisdom to be gleaned from prayer, reflection, dialogue and study. Since dying is the final stage of our human growth, deciding how we can conform this process to our values is a very worthwhile undertaking.[7]

Conclusion

The hard truth is that each of us will have to deal with the deaths of those we love and will one day experience our own dying. This hard truth is softened to the extent that we summon the courage to come close to death. Death is transformed for Christians who believe that the counterpart of death is resurrection to a new life. Such Christians are free to live life with confidence and serenity because their ultimate hope is grounded in the promise of union with God.

Endnotes

1. Francine Klagsbrun, *Too Young to Die: Youth and Suicide* (New York: Pocket Books, 1985), p. 127.

2. Elisabeth Kubler-Ross, *On Death and Dying* (New York: Collier Books, 1970), p. 113.

3. Richard P. Mc Brien, *Catholicism* (Minneapolis, MN: Winston Press, 1981), p. 1103.

4. Monika K. Hellwig, *What Are They Saying About Death and Christian Hope?* (New York: Paulist Press, 1978), p. 29.

5. Dogmatic Constitution on the Church, 49.

6. Granger E. Westberg, *Good Grief* (Philadelphia PA: Fortress Press, 1962).

7. Cf. Eileen P. Flynn, *Hard Decisions: Forgoing and Withdrawing Artificial Nutrition and Hydration* (Kansas City: Sheed & Ward, 1990) and Eileen P. Flynn, *Your Living Will* (New York: Citadel, 1992) for a thorough review of the medical and moral issues which arise in conjunction with dying.

Glossary

Baptism is a precondition for eternal life: The Catholic Church teaches that women and men must be baptized in water and the Holy Spirit in order to enter the kingdom of heaven. It also teaches that baptism can be of desire or of blood. Baptism of desire is achieved by persons who have not heard the preaching of the gospel but have tried to the best of their ability to live good and caring lives. Baptism of blood is achieved by martyrs who are put to death because of their religious or moral beliefs.

Confessing one's sins: The Catholic practice of confession of all serious sins is an integral aspect of the individual reception of the Sacrament of Penance or Reconciliation.

The consummation of all things: refers to a time of completion at the end of the world after good has triumphed over evil and at which all men and women of good will are united to Christ, the center of reality.

Exigence of God on one's life: The urgent presence of a personal Lord who requires immediate attention to his presence and invitation.

God's acceptance of the world in the Incarnation: When Jesus took on human nature he elevated it, restored and sanctified it, so that God was pleased to look with renewed beneficence on all things human.

Idolatry: The worship of idols such as pagan gods, money, prestige, power, oneself, or another person. The folly of idolatry consists in its misdirectedness. There is only one God, a person both immanent and transcendent, who is worthy of worship.

Life after life experiences: Recounted in Raymond A. Moody's *Life After Life,* (New York: Bantam Books, 1975). Dr. Moody reports that people who were near death and who had experienced such phenomena as traveling through dark tunnels, meeting departed relatives, seeing a bright light, feeling a sense of peace, being apart/outside their bodies, and wanting their experiences to continue, developed a serene and accepting attitude toward death. The study was based on 150 interviews.

Lumen Gentium: The "Dogmatic Constitution on the Church in the Modern World" of Vatican II begins with the words *Lumen Gentium* which are translated as Light of the Nations. They refer to Jesus Christ, the light of all nations.

St. Augustine: A great Christian theologian who was a bishop in North Africa and died in 430.

Thanatologist: One who studies death, especially the medical, psychological, and social aspects of dying.

Discussion Questions

1. What have you experienced in regard to the deaths of friends or relatives? Do you think that efforts have been made to shield you from death? If so, what is your reaction to these efforts?

2. What kinds of actions could you take to lessen the possibility of the annihilation of all life by the use of nuclear weapons?

3. What can be done to make young people value their lives? What practical strategies can you suggest as measures to prevent suicide?

4. Describe the physical, emotional and spiritual aspects of dying. How can the living help the dying to achieve a good death?

5. What do Catholic Christians believe about the final option, the particular judgment, purgatory, the communion of saints, the general judgement, and condemnation to hell? What do you believe about death?

6. What would you do to help a person who was grieving? How can people become comfortable about sharing another's pain?

Additional Reading

Eileen P. Flynn, *Hard Decisions: Forgoing and Withdrawing Artificial Nutrition and Hydration* (Kansas City: Sheed & Ward, 1990).

Eileen P. Flynn, *Your Living Will* (New York: Citadel, 1992).

Monika K. Hellwig, *What Are They Saying About Death and Christian Hope?* (New York: Paulist Press, 1978).

Karl Rahner, *On the Theology of Death* (New York: Herder & Herder, 1961).

Appendix

The Mystery of Suffering and Evil

---

by Thomas L. Sheridan, S.J.

Tune in to the news any evening on television, and you can be sure that most of the coverage will be devoted to accounts of human suffering and wickedness. We have become so used to the pain and the evil around us that now we react to only the more sensational cases. But when evil and suffering strike home, as in the untimely death of a loved one, the birth of a deformed child, the cold-blooded murder of someone who lives on my street, then we begin to question.

Why Do Bad Things Happen?

To borrow a phrase from Rabbi Harold S. Kushner, "when bad things happen to good people," they instinctively ask, "Why?" or "Why me?" or even "Why me, Lord?"[1]

The fact that we ask these questions means that we expect that there *is* some meaning to our world, that things *do* add up, and that somehow there must be a way of fitting suffering and evil into this total context of meaning. To have this expectation that our lives and our world do have some meaning is to believe that there is some Meaning Giver besides ourselves. Otherwise, the simplest answer to the question "Why?" or "Why me?" is "Why not?" Why should there be any meaning to anything at all? This is, of course, the nihilist* answer which seems to be gaining ground in our western society, as reflected in the works of certain contemporary playwrights, novelists and poets.[2]

But those who still believe in meaning and a Meaning Giver also sometimes ask, "Why, *Lord*?" And we of the Judaeo-Christian tradition ask the question this way because of our fundamental belief in the oneness and goodness of God.

370

After atheism the simplest solution to the problem of evil is what is called theological dualism.* In theological dualism the problem is solved by attributing all that is good to a good Principle, or god(s), and all that is bad to a bad Principle, or god(s).

Actually neither atheism nor theological dualism really solves the problem. Atheism is left with what might be called "the problem of the good," viz., how one explains all the goodness and beauty in our world and in human life. Theological dualism ends up with two gods—but what kind of a god would either of them be? If Ultimate Reality, the Ground of Being, the Mind behind it all, is really the Divine, then there can be only one.

We of the Judaeo-Christian tradition believe that God is one and that he is good, all good, all loving in fact. And so when something bad happens we say "Why, Lord?" And sometimes we say, "Lord, I know you are all loving; then why didn't you *do* something to stop the bad thing from happening?" Implicit in this, of course, is the belief that not only is God all-loving, but he is also all-mighty. So many of our prayers are addressed to "Almighty God" that we presume that he can simply do anything, and therefore he could stop suffering and evil if he really wanted to. Hence the traditional formulation of "the problem of evil."[3]

> If God is all loving, then he would want to eliminate all suffering and evil.
>
> If he is all powerful, then he could do so.
>
> The fact that suffering and evil do exist means, therefore, that *either*:
>> (a) there is no such God;
>> *or* (b) God is not all loving;
>> *or* (c) God is not all powerful.
>
> One of these has to go. Which one will it be?

Does God Cause Suffering and Evil?

Oddly enough, we Jews and Christians seem to have been more willing to sacrifice God's goodness than his power. Oh, to be sure, we continue to talk about the goodness and love of God. But the way in which we safeguard his all-powerfulness leaves us with a picture of God which is something less good and less loving than we would like to maintain.

One classic answer to the question why bad things happen to good people was dealt with centuries before Christ in the Book of Job. The author of the Book of Job took an old folk tale about a very good man named Job. One day God was talking with some of his counselors (this was a *very* old folk tale), and one of them, "the Adversary," says, in effect, "You're always saying what a great guy this fellow Job is, but why wouldn't he be when he's always had it so good? Let's see how good he is when something bad happens to him." So God—in the story—says, "OK, do what you want with him, short of killing him." And the things the Adversary does to poor old Job! He loses everything, but everything, and ends up on a dung heap cursing the day he was born. And now comes our author's own contribution. He has three friends come to visit Job, and they try to console him by showing him the meaning of his sufferings. It is quite simple: Job must have done something wrong, and he is being punished for it.

Job steadfastly rejects this solution. The bad things that are happening to him are not punishments from God, for the simple reason that he really is a just man and has not done any wrong. At the end of the book Job meets God face to face. The problem is not solved, but he is able to cope with the mystery.

The author of the Book of Job rejected the simple solution to the problem of evil, which says that it is a punishment by God. And yet many still feel this way even in our own day. How often we hear people say, "He must have been doing something wrong, and now God has punished him for it." But what kind of a God would that be who would be so intent on punishment? Does he have to punish? Why can't he just forgive? And how then are we to explain the suffering of countless innocents? How can we square this with the picture of the God of love which we have come to learn from Jesus? This punishing god sounds more like a mean old man waiting to get even than the gracious Father of the Prodigal.[4]

Some have thought that this problem could be avoided if we were to keep two points in mind. The first is the distinction made by St. Augustine and St. Thomas[5] that evil is not a being in itself, but a negation or, to be precise, a privation of being, i.e., the absence of some perfection which should be there. In this way we can say that everything that is owes its being to God; since evil is not a being, however, but a privation of being, God can in no way be said to *cause* evil. The second point, which also goes back to some of the classical theologians, is that God does not inflict suffering and evil; he merely permits them. This line of reasoning then continues to maintain that God permits evil since he will not interfere with our freedom, and he permits suffering so that through our sufferings we may grow and develop. Suffering is a kind of divine discipline. Athletic trainers tell us, "No pain, no gain." And that's the way it is with all human suffering.

The first point is so theoretical that I doubt if it has ever helped anyone cope with the mystery of suffering and evil. Suffering is all too real, and evil seems all too powerful a force in our world for us to categorize it as simply the privation of being.

The second point has helped a lot of people who have accepted their trials and sufferings as coming from the hands of a loving God who sends, or better, permits them for some greater spiritual profit. But is this really a solution? What of the many people who aren't able to cope with suffering and are destroyed by it? How could an all-wise and all-loving God permit this kind of suffering? Or even in the case of those who do grow through their sufferings, could God not choose some less drastic means for their spiritual discipline? But the real question is: Is it really true that God permits suffering for our greater good? Is this the only way we can deal with the problem?

Why don't we have another look at that other attribute of God, his almighty power? *Is* it really true that God could prevent suffering and evil if he really wanted to? Could he really?

When I was a very small child, my granduncle Louis once asked me, "Tommy, can God do anything he wants to do?" Proudly I answered with the words I had learned from my *Baltimore Catechism,* "Yes, God can do all things, and nothing is hard or impossible for him." "Well then," Uncle Louis asked me, "Could God make a stone so big he couldn't lift it?" That really stumped me. It wasn't until years later when I was in high school that I remembered this incident. The teacher asked the question: "Could God square a circle?" This time it didn't take long to figure out the answer. Of course not, since a squared circle is a contradiction in terms, like Uncle Louis' stone.

Theology has always recognized this principle and, with few exceptions, Christian theologians have always maintained that God could do anything as long as this did not involve some contradiction, like "squaring a circle." John Macquarrie explains that "when we talk of the omnipotence of God, we do not mean an irrational force that might break out in any direction, but a power that is ordered and which cannot therefore do some things without disrupting itself."[6] Why then do we not extend this principle and apply it to the problem of evil?

What I would like to maintain is that God is *unable* to eliminate all suffering and evil, for to do so would be a contradiction in terms. For God to be able to eliminate all suffering and evil he would have to create an entirely different world from this one. If God were to act to prevent all evil and suffering, this would mean that he would "simultaneously," so to speak, be *creating* this world and *negating* it. Or, to use the theology of creation which we find in the first chapter of Genesis, God would at one and the same time be reducing to chaos that which he was bringing out of chaos.

Suffering and Evil in an Evolving Universe

What kind of a world is this? It is, first of all, a world in which, after billions of years of evolution, there came into existence a planet on which life eventually appeared and then finally human beings with the power of stepping outside of the stream of evolution, looking around at themselves and their world, seeing what the possibilities were for further development, and then freely choosing to do something about it. In a word, it is a world in which there are beings who can choose to act wisely and well—but who can also choose to act foolishly and do evil. By choosing to create a world in which there would one day be free human beings, God *limits* his own power. Had he chosen to people the earth with robots, there would have been no possibility for human goodness—or for human evil. But once he chose—and I speak anthropomorphically*—to create *this* world, moral evil was a distinct possibility, and all too soon, alas!, an actuality.

But what about all the suffering that comes from events in our world which happen outside the control of human beings? What about natural disasters like earthquakes, volcanos, droughts, floods, hurricanes, tornados, etc.? What about birth defects? What about pain? What about death?

Let me tackle the easiest one first, pain. Is pain a bad thing or a good? Don't ask me that question when I am suffering from a toothache. But what if we lived in a world without any pain at all? Have you ever been to the dentist and had a novocaine injection which benumbed one whole side of your mouth? Do you remember how careful you had to be afterwards when you chewed? Have you ever picked up a hot pot from a stove thinking it was cool—and immediately dropped it? Why? Because the pain caused your autonomic nervous system to react instantaneously, quicker than you could decide to do, and you were spared a serious burn. Pain is one of the greatest defenses the body has. It warns us of disease, of danger, of broken or strained organs. Without it the higher forms of life on this planet would be impossible.

We'll say more about death later on. But what about natural disasters and birth defects? This is where Charles Darwin's evolutionary theory can be a great help to us.[7] For evolutionary theory—especially if we extend it beyond Darwin to include non-life as well—shows us a world constantly in a process of change and in which random events play a very important part. Once again we realize that once God chooses to create this particular world, he limits his own freedom in this respect also. For to create this particular world and not some other world means that random events and genetic mutations are not only a distinct possibility but a necessity. Could God have created a different kind of world, made of a different kind of matter? Einstein asked this question.[8] I wouldn't presume to try to answer it. But it would seem to be true that if it *were* a different kind of world, made of a different kind of matter, *we* would not be a part of it. For it is of the stuff of *this* world that we are made.

In other words, to speak anthropomorphically again, if you were God you may have had only two choices: to create or not to create. Why did he—or better, does he—choose to create, and to create this particular world? That is the mystery. But as Christians we believe that it must have had something to do with his love.

Finally, human freedom does have an influence on all of these natural causes of suffering, and that both before and after the event. How many birth defects are the result of carelessness, greed, selfishness, culpable ignorance on the part of people—not all, to be sure, but far too many. As far as natural disasters are concerned, the distinction is now being made between the physical event itself (referred to as the "disaster trigger") and this event plus the human suffering that follows upon it (the "disaster," without further qualification). A recent study has shown that "though triggered by natural events such as floods and earthquakes, disasters are increasingly man-made," and it documents the extent to which the human-suffering component is directly related and inversely proportional to the financial and social status of the victims (in other words, the poorer and less influential you are, the more likely you are to suffer from "natural disasters").[9]

And how much of the human suffering that is the result of such natural causes is compounded after the event by the way in which the victims are treated by their fellow human beings? Or better still, let's put that positively. To what extent cannot such suffering be mitigated and at times transformed into the occasion of great human achievements? Helen Keller was the innocent victim of an event—natural or unnatural it does not matter—which rendered her blind and deaf. But the courage and tenacity and love of other people, notably of her teacher Annie Sullivan and of Helen herself, enabled her to lead a much fuller life than many of her contemporaries.[10]

The human sufferings that we have been considering, therefore, are not simply the result of an "act of God." We free human beings contribute to them, and we can also ease them.

Having taken another look at God's power and discovered that it is not as literally "almighty" as we may have thought, let us now have another look at his goodness. Have we really given him credit for being as all loving as we should?

Can God Suffer?

Ask anyone the question, "What happens when someone you love suffers?" and you will almost inevitably receive the answer, "You suffer too." But when you ask, "Can God suffer?" you almost as inevitably get the answer, "No." The reason for this is that our thinking about God, here in the West at least, has been in great part shaped by Greek philosophy.[11] As a result we tend to think of God as (the) Perfect Being. But a Perfect Being cannot change, since that would imply either the loss or the gain of some perfection and it would, therefore, either no longer be perfect, or it would not have been perfect to start with. For God to be affected by what happens to his creatures, however, would mean some kind of change in him. Suffering was also ruled out for other reasons, for example, the Aristotelian notion that God is substantial act, no potency—but suffering, *"passio"* in Latin, is in the category of potency, not act.

In this way we ended up with a notion of God as totally re-mote from his creation, loving it, to be sure, but not in any way affected by what happens to it. Now what kind of love is that? It is certainly not the kind of love, or the kind of God, that the bible speaks of. Here we have a very "passionate" God indeed, a far cry from the remote God of Greek philosophy, a God who suffers along with his creation, who grieves at evil and suffer-ing, and gets angry at it too.

God Helps Us When We Suffer

He is also a God who *does* something about it, but not like a fairy-tale god. He usually acts through us.

A friend of mine recently told me a story which fits in very well here. There was a man who lived in a two-story house who found himself stranded in the course of a tremendous flood. The water had reached the first floor when a boat came by and the pilot of the boat urged him to get quickly on board. "No," the man replied, "I believe in Jesus, and I know that he loves me and will save me." "Well, I have no time to argue with you," said the man in the boat, and off he went. An hour later the boat came by again. This time the man had been forced by the rising waters to the second floor of his house, but he made the same protestation of faith and refused once again to be saved. Still a third time the boat came by, and this time the man was sitting on the roof of the house, but he still refused to get into the boat, professing his belief that Jesus would save him. When the boat came by again, there was no sign of either house or man. But up in heaven the man accosted Jesus and said: "I thought you loved me, and I trusted in you. Why didn't you save me?" Jesus replied, "What did you expect me to do, pilot that boat myself?"

What does God do about evil and suffering? First of all, he does bring good out of both, and this is what the idea of suffer-ing as a discipline sent or permitted by God seems to be getting at. "All things work together unto good for those who love God," said Saint Paul (Rom 8:28). He is the Lord of History, and in his own transcendent* fashion, not by manipulating his creation, but by working through it in a truly divine, transcendent man-ner he brings about the accomplishment of his designs.

He also reveals himself as a God of love and evokes our com-passion for our fellow men and women. The Old Testament prophets insisted again and again that God was far more inter-

ested in how we treated one another, particularly the more help-
less ones among us like widows and orphans and aliens, than he
was in "burnt offerings and sacrifices."[12] We see this in other
great religions as well. In Gandhi's non-violent principle of
ahimsa we can see that the ultimate solution to evil is not punishment but the overcoming of evil by goodness.[13] This is surely
a divine solution.

Jesus: God's Definitive Response to Suffering and Evil

But it is especially in the person of Jesus that we see how
God deals with the mystery of suffering and evil. In Jesus we
see that God is Emmanuel, he is God-with-us.[14] God is not
remote from our world. His immanence is the measure of his
transcendence.* From its very beginning he has been at work in
it, fashioning it according to its own laws. But as Christians we
believe that at a certain moment in history, "in the fullness of
time" the Bible says, at just the right moment he entered our
history in a unique, though not entirely different fashion in the
person of one man, Jesus of Nazareth. And how does Jesus deal
with suffering and evil?

First of all, when he encounters human suffering, Jesus does
something to relieve it. About one-fifth of the gospel accounts
are about his acting to relieve human misery. He is com-pas-
sionate—he suffers—with anyone who suffers, and he heals.
How does he do this? By eliciting the person's faith. Notice how
often in the gospels Jesus says, "Your *faith* has saved you." Up
until very recently theology had become very preoccupied with
the business of proving that Jesus really was divine, and it
came to look at Jesus' healings and the rest of his miracles almost exclusively for their value as proofs of his divinity. The
problem with a lot of this was that we came to look upon Jesus
as a wonder worker, a kind of magician out to prove his divine
origin by means of these acts of power. But in the gospels Jesus
plays down the miraculous aspect of his healing actions and
calls attention to the faith of the ones who had requested his
aid.

Secondly, when he encounters sinners, Jesus does not punish!
Instead he reveals God's own love and compassion for sinners.
And what happens? A lot of people who were sinners are completely transformed by this experience of being loved. There are
many instances of this in the gospels. My favorite is the one

about a very wicked man by the name of Zacchaeus (Luke 19:1-10). He was a publican, a tax collector for the Roman occupying forces, and publicans were a really bad bunch. Zacchaeus was very short, and he was curious to see Jesus but unable to do so because of the crowds, so he climbed a tree. Imagine his embarrassment—horror, more likely—when Jesus spotted him and called the crowd's attention to him. What looks of contempt and hatred he saw in their eyes, and how he must have feared for his life! But the look in Jesus' eyes changed everything. I like to try to imagine what love and compassion that look of Jesus conveyed. When I recall this story I stop at this point and try to bask in the warmth of that love, for I am a sinner too and I know I can be changed by it. Zacchaeus was totally transformed. Immediately he started to plan how to dispose of his ill-gotten wealth for the benefit of the poor.

But, unfortunately, this approach did not work with a lot of people. Their hearts remained closed even to the power of this love. Some of them had too much to give up, their wealth, their positions of power. Jesus could not make them believe; they were free to refuse his love, and they did. In the end it cost him his life. And in this we see God's supreme tactic for dealing with suffering and evil, the death and resurrection of Jesus.

We sometimes speak of Jesus as "coming to die for us," and we isolate his death from the rest of his life and make it an end in itself. But this is a serious misunderstanding, I think.

Did Jesus *have* to die such a horrible death as the death upon the cross, or could he have lived to a ripe old age and then have died peacefully having accomplished what he set out to do, that is to say, to elicit such a change of heart (*metanoia*) in his contemporaries that God's love working through them could gradually spread throughout the world and eliminate selfishness and egoism, greed and exploitation, hatred and envy, and all the evils that make the human lot a vale of tears, and in this way make "God's reign" a reality on earth? Theoretically, maybe. But it didn't work out that way, and given the extent to which collective sin had already taken hold in our world, probably couldn't have. But he did try. In fact, he seems to have begun by thinking it really was possible. Perhaps only gradually did it dawn upon him that God's reign was going to come about through his rejection, and his death, though I dare say that at the time he didn't see clearly how.

It was, therefore, with anguish and dread that he approached his death. "His sweat became as drops of blood," so horrible was his agony in the Garden of Gethsemane that night before he died (Luke 22:44). But it was with complete fidelity to the mission entrusted to him by God and with utter trust in God his Father that he went to his death, even to a most horrible death on a Roman cross.

And it was in response to this loving fidelity to the Father's will that God raised Jesus from the dead. In the resurrection of Jesus God set his seal of approval on all that Jesus said and did, transforming his mangled body into a new mode of existence in which he is seen to be truly the Son of God in power (Rom 1:4). In the resurrection of Jesus lies our great basis for hope that evil and suffering and death will not have the last word. Like him, and in him, and with him, we too can triumph over all the ills that do beset us.

But that means that we must be disciples of the Crucified and Risen Lord. This does not mean that we go out of our way to seek suffering. That would be masochism, albeit for the best of motives. It means that, allowing ourselves to be transformed by God's love revealed to us in Jesus, we accept the sufferings that being his disciple is necessarily going to entail.

"And the last enemy to be destroyed is death" (1 Cor 15:26). Death is at one and the same time the most natural and the most unnatural event in the world. It is natural for any multi-celled organism to die (only amoebas don't die a natural death; they split!). But *my* death, that's different (as Tolstoy's Ivan Ilych discovered to his horror).[15] My death is horrible to the extent that I cling to my selfhood in a self-protective way that has no room for God or any other person at the center of my being. But if I am able to let go, to "uncenter," as Monika Helwig puts it,[16] death can be transformed into a newness of life, a sharing in divinity. The death and resurrection of Jesus makes that possible.

Endnotes

1. *When Bad Things Happen to Good People* (New York: Schocken, 1981). This excellent book is also available in paperback from Avon Books. The principle catalyst for my own thinking on the problem of evil was a chapter in S. Paul Schilling's *God in an Age of Atheism* (Nashville, TN: Abingdon, 1969), espe-

cially pp. 179-90. In 1977 Schilling further developed the ideas therein in a book from the same publishers, *God and Human Anguish*.

2. This is found most particularly in the "literature of the absurd," which had its roots in Europe between the first and second World Wars in the writings of people as different as James Joyce (an Irishman living mostly in France) and Franz Kafka and Kurt Weil in Germany. After the war the French writers Jean Paul Sartre (author of such works as the novel *Nausea* and the play *No Exit*) and Albert Camus (author of *The Stranger* and *The Myth of Sisyphus*) stressed the absurdity of human existence. Human beings are not created by a good God for any sensible purpose, they maintained; we are simply thrown into a meaningless existence. We come from nothing and are heading for nothing. *Waiting for Godot*, written in 1955 by Samuel Becket (another Irishman living in France) is probably the best known example of this type of literature. Other contemporary authors who can be classified under this heading are Jean Genet in France, Harold Pinter in England, and Edward Albee in the United States.

3. This is the traditional term for speaking about what I prefer to call "the mystery of suffering and evil." For, to use Gabriel Marcel's distinction, suffering and evil are more than just abstract problems. French Catholic philosopher and playwright, Gabriel Marcel (1889-1973), was deeply affected by his experiences during World War I, which convinced him of the inability of abstract thought to come to grips with the realities of human existence. He claimed that people who try to reflect on the meaning of human life too often detach themselves from it and view it simply as an *object* to be studied like other objects. The only way to understand life's mysteries, he believed, was to be open in fidelity, hope and love to the entire world of the Interpersonal Other. If we treat evil as a problem, therefore, we will not arrive at any entirely satisfying solution. But as a Christian I believe that we can successfully come to terms with the mystery.

4. See the so-called "Parable of the Prodigal Son" in Luke 15: 11-32. As a number of authors have pointed out, the parable is wrongly named. It is mainly about the father of two sons, and he is the one who is "prodigal," i.e. "wasteful" with his love and forgiveness.

5. St. Augustine of Hippo in North Africa (354-430) and St. Thomas Aquinas (1225-1274) are considered by many to be the two greatest theologians in the history of the Church.

6. *Principles of Christian Theology*, 2nd edition (New York: Scribners, 1977), p. 206. Scottish theologian John Macquarrie was Professor of Systematic Theology at Union Theological Seminary in New York City for eight years before returning to England to take up the Lady Margaret Chair of Divinity at Oxford University.

7. Charles R. Darwin (1809-1882) is best known for his book, *The Origin of Species*, which he published in 1859. Some years earlier he had made a trip around the world as a naturalist on a British naval ship, the Beagle. By the end of the trip he was convinced that the different life forms which he had seen on his trip had evolved from earlier forms, but he wondered how this could be. He knew that when a cattle breeder wants to produce a new species of cattle, he selects the right parents to get the offspring he wants. But how does nature select? He finally came to see that the key to the answer lay in how well a particular species was adapted to its environment. He theorized that in the course of evolution minute changes took place in individuals. As a result of these changes—which Darwin supposed took place completely by chance—some individuals were better adapted for survival than others, and they were able to pass these "genetic mutations" on to their offspring. Darwin called this process "natural selection." It is sometimes referred to as "the survival of the fittest," but "fittest" means "best adapted for survival." Most biologists today use some version of Darwin's natural selection as at least one "mechanism" to explain evolution.

8. Albert Einstein (1898-1948) was an American physicist born in Germany and best known for his theory of relativity.

9. Anders Wijkman and Lloyd Timberlake, *Natural Disasters: Acts of God or Acts of Man?* (Washington, DC: Earthscan, 1984).

10. Helen Keller (1880-1968) was born blind, deaf and mute. But thanks to the patience and skill of a teacher, Anne Mansfield Sullivan, she learned to communicate through hand signals and eventually graduated *cum laude* from Radcliffe College in Cambridge, Mass. She recounted this in *The Story of My Life* (1902) and *Helen Keller's Journal* (1938). But her story is best known from the award-winning play, *The Miracle Worker*, which was later made into a motion picture film.

11. I am referring principally to the way of thinking developed by the Greek philosopher Aristotle (384-322 B.C.), who in turn was the disciple of Plato (427?-347? B.C.). There was a revival of Aristotle's system of thought in Europe during the 12th century, and it was considered one of the great achievements of St. Thomas Aquinas (see note #5) to have rethought all of Christian teaching and given new expression to it using Aristotelian categories of thought. This gave rise to what came to be known as "scholastic" philosophy and theology, which dominated Catholic thinking in these fields up until very recently.

12. The first chapter of the book of Isaiah in the Old Testament is particularly strong (especially verses 10-17). It pictures God as rejecting the Jewish people's temple sacrifices in the starkest terms ("I have had enough of burnt offerings of rams and the fat of fed beasts . . . who requires of you this trampling of my courts? Bring no more vain offerings; incense is an abomination to me.") Instead God asks that they "seek justice, correct oppression, defend the fatherless, plead for the widow."

13. Mohandas K. Gandhi (1869-1948), also known as *Mahatma*, "Great Soul," was a leader in the movement for Indian independence and social reform. For a recent interpretation of his life, see the movie *Gandhi*.

14. See the Gospel according to Matthew 1:23.

15. In this short novel, the leading character, Ivan Ilych learns that he has a fatal illness. He muses:

> The syllogism he had learned from Kiezewetter's Logic: "Caius is a man, men are mortal, therefore Caius is mortal," had always seemed to him correct as applied to Caius, but certainly not as applied to himself. That Caius—man in the abstract—was mortal, was perfectly correct, but he was not Caius, not an abstract man, but a creature, quite separate from all others. He had been little Vanya, with a mamma and a papa, with Mitya and Volodya, with the toys, a coachman and a nurse, afterwards with Katgenka and with all the joys, griefs, and delights of childhood, boyhood, and youth. What did Caius know of the smell of that striped leather ball Vanya had been so fond of? Had Caius kissed his mother's hand like that, and did the silk of her dress rustle so for Caius? . . . "Caius really was mortal, and it was right for him to die; but for me, little Vanya, Ivan Ilych, with all my

thoughts and emotions, it's altogether a different matter. It cannot be that I ought to die. That would be
too terrible." From Leon Tolstoy, *The Death of Ivan
Ilych and other stories,* (New York: New American Li-
brary, Signet edition, 1960), pp. 131-132.

16. In a short but very rich book, *What Are They Saying
About Death and Christian Hope?,* American Catholic theologian
Monika Hellwig sees death as "not only a point at the end of
life, but a dimension of our whole experience of living." We
need, to be sure, to become independent and take responsible
control of our lives; this is what marks the passage from childhood to true adulthood. But, she says, besides this "centering"
task, there is another, less well recognized need, which she calls
"uncentering," the process of learning to accept dependence, to
relinquish control, to trust without understanding, to adapt oneself to the managing and organizing of others . . ." Without this,
she says, "there can be no genuine service or community, no art
or contemplation, no family or friendship, no peace or security."
To learn to do this, she maintains, "is to be about the business of
dying now" (New York: Paulist, 1978, pp. 14-16).

Glossary

Anthropomorphic: From the Greek *anthropos,* "human being," and *morphe,* "shape, form." To speak of "the hand of
God," or "the face of God," is to speak anthropomorphically, for God has neither hands nor face. It is to give a
human form to God so as to be able to think more realisti-
cally about Him (even that "Him" is anthropomorphic,
since God has no gender).

Dualism: From the Latin *duo,* "two." There are various forms
of dualism. Theological ("pertaining to God") dualism
maintains that there are two gods (or two classes of gods),
the good god(s) responsible for what is good in the world,
the bad god(s) responsible for what is bad in the world.

Immanence: Said of God, it refers to His presence in all of
creation.

Nihilist: From the Latin *nihil,* "nothing." Nihilism takes
atheism to its logical conclusion. We come from nothing,
and we are heading for nothing. If there is no Creator
who is responsible for the existence of this world, then it

is the product of the blind forces of matter and there is no meaning or purpose in life, except for the meaning and purpose that we give to it.

Transcendent: To transcend means literally "to rise above or beyond the limits or powers of someone or something." Thus human knowledge and freedom transcend the powers of knowing and acting of the lower orders of animals. God is viewed as absolutely or completely transcendent, since he is beyond all the limitations of created being.

Index